AFRICAN ETHNOGRAPHIC STUDIES OF THE 20TH CENTURY

Volume 62

THE BAVENDA

THE BAVENDA

HUGH A. STAYT

LONDON AND NEW YORK

First published in 1931 by Oxford University Press for the International African Institute.

This edition first published in 2018
by Routledge
2 Park Square, Milton Park, Abingdon, Oxon OX14 4RN

and by Routledge
711 Third Avenue, New York, NY 10017

Routledge is an imprint of the Taylor & Francis Group, an informa business

© 1931 International African Institute

All rights reserved. No part of this book may be reprinted or reproduced or utilised in any form or by any electronic, mechanical, or other means, now known or hereafter invented, including photocopying and recording, or in any information storage or retrieval system, without permission in writing from the publishers.

Trademark notice: Product or corporate names may be trademarks or registered trademarks, and are used only for identification and explanation without intent to infringe.

British Library Cataloguing in Publication Data
A catalogue record for this book is available from the British Library

ISBN: 978-0-8153-8713-8 (Set)
ISBN: 978-0-429-48813-9 (Set) (ebk)
ISBN: 978-1-138-59835-5 (Volume 62) (hbk)
ISBN: 978-0-429-48637-1 (Volume 62) (ebk)

Publisher's Note
The publisher has gone to great lengths to ensure the quality of this reprint but points out that some imperfections in the original copies may be apparent.

Disclaimer
The publisher has made every effort to trace copyright holders and would welcome correspondence from those they have been unable to trace.

Due to modern production methods, it has not been possible to reproduce the fold-out maps within the book. Please visit www.routledge.com to view them.

THE
BAVENDA

By HUGH A. STAYT
M.A. (CANTAB.), PH.D. (CAPETOWN)

With an Introduction by
MRS. A.W. HOERNLÉ
(M.A. CANTAB.)
LECTURER IN SOCIAL ANTHROPOLOGY AT
THE UNIVERSITY OF THE
WITWATERSRAND

Published for the
INTERNATIONAL INSTITUTE OF
AFRICAN LANGUAGES & CULTURES
by OXFORD UNIVERSITY PRESS
LONDON : HUMPHREY MILFORD
1931

OXFORD UNIVERSITY PRESS
AMEN HOUSE, E.C. 4
LONDON EDINBURGH GLASGOW
LEIPZIG NEW YORK TORONTO
MELBOURNE CAPETOWN BOMBAY
CALCUTTA MADRAS SHANGHAI
HUMPHREY MILFORD
PUBLISHER TO THE
UNIVERSITY

PRINTED IN GREAT BRITAIN

TO
MY WIFE

INTRODUCTION

IT has always been a matter of great regret that no adequate monograph on any of the South African tribes has been written during all the years in which the White and the Black races have been in contact in the sub-continent. It is true that in the course of the 300 years since white people settled permanently in Southern Africa a great deal of information concerning the organization, the beliefs, and practices of the various Bantu tribes has gradually been accumulated. In particular, from the records of travellers, of settlers, and later of missionaries and administrators, it is possible to gain a connected idea of the history of these Bantu peoples during these years and to check native tradition by independent written accounts in a way that is not possible for most African people in other areas during the same period. It is true, further, that various Government Commissions have made careful inquiries into certain aspects of Bantu custom and belief for administrative purposes. Above all, missionaries and disinterested travellers have tried to gain an adequate idea of the culture of the peoples with whom they came into contact. Nevertheless, no one has found it possible to give us a full picture of the life of any of these tribes nor the whole background of belief on which their culture rests. The Union of South Africa has no monograph which can at all compare with Henri Junod's *Life of a South African Tribe* which portrays the whole cultural background of the BaThonga of Portuguese East Africa, and which to this day ranks as one of the most complete accounts of the culture of any African people.

Since the Great War, however, a decided impetus has been given to the study of African peoples. The whole continent has been opened up. The increasing importance of Africa, both as the source for many of the raw products and also of many of the metals needed in modern industry, has made it essential that those nations which are at work in Africa should know better the African peoples upon whom they will have, in the main, to rely for the production of the things they want. The increased need for the co-operation of these Africans comes at a time when the very causes which make them valuable to the Europeans are threatening to destroy their own indigenous societies and to lay them open to all the dangers of cultural disintegration.

viii INTRODUCTION

More disinterested students, alarmed for the well being of the Africans themselves who are exposed increasingly to contact with an economic and social system totally new to them, are anxious to understand all the institutions in African cultures which may be supported and strengthened, with a view to helping the Bantu in the transition period. Finally, purely theoretical students of Culture are coming more and more to realize that Africa, with all its variety of societies subjected to intense influence by an alien culture of very different order, offers an unrivalled field for the study of the processes of diffusion of culture, and of all the forces which are at work in its maintenance and gradual remoulding.

Both in Europe and in Africa itself the universities have set to work to train students especially in the methods of field observation, so that now, year by year, students are going out to Africa for the single purpose of immersing themselves in the whole life of some one particular African community. Their aim is to come gradually to understand it and to describe its institutions and their functions.

The Monograph which Mr. Stayt has written on the BaVenda of the Northern Transvaal is one of the first-fruits of this new type of research that is being carried on among Africans. Mr. Stayt is himself South African born; he grew up among the people to whom he was later to return as a student of their culture. Blinded in the Great War, he decided to devote himself to the study of Anthropology. When the opportunity came he returned to what we may call his own people, who received him with all the greater kindliness and solicitude because of his handicap. They vied with one another to help him, as he and his wife worked together during all the months they spent in various part of the Zoutpansberg with different communities of the BaVenda.

The results of these labours are of the utmost value to all students of culture. Of all the tribes living in The Union of South Africa the BaVenda are the latest arrivals from the North. In their social organization and beliefs, as revealed by Mr. Stayt's study, they differ in many respects from the rest of the tribes in the Union.

Both in their legends and in some of their customs they seem to be linked more closely with the culture that has been revealed in connexion with the ruins of Southern Rhodesia than any of the other Union tribes. In general their affinities are not so close with the tribes in the Union as with those of Southern Rhodesia. Their language, their older type of building, links them with these latter, while they

INTRODUCTION

alone of Bantu peoples in the Union used formerly to weave a cloth from wild cotton and they alone (and those influenced by them) plant the eleusine grain whose proper home is far to the north.

Mr. Stayt further furnishes evidence that these BaVenda worked the copper mines around Messina in the Northern Transvaal, whether they were the first in the field or not, and he further proves them to have been skilled workers and traders in iron.

The whole social organization of the BaVenda shows that they had a very advanced type of culture for an African people. The well-knit political organization is excellently described, and the whole account of the various officials who assisted a chief in his administration gives one a clear idea of the actual working of a Bantu society The chief is revealed as the representative of a ruling family controlled by properly appointed and hereditary officials, and the whole people is drawn into the circle of government by the system of three councils through which the administration works. Unique for South Africa is the high position given to women in this society both in administration and in religious ritual. No account of the function and the capacity of women in Bantu societies will henceforth be complete which does not take account of the responsible and efficient work which is being done by women among the BaVenda.

Another feature of BaVenda organization which is extremely interesting and important is the double system of kinship groups. A man belongs not only to a patrilineal lineage but also to a matrilineal one. By a very careful analysis of the physiological beliefs of these people Mr. Stayt shows us why it is that it is the mother's maternal kin and the father's paternal kin who are of the most importance to him all through life. The great care that has been taken to show the interconnexion of all aspects of the custom and belief of these people is specially to be commended. Thus Mr. Stayt shows us that it is because certain parts of a child's body are thought to be built up by the male, and other parts by the female alone, that we get these double controls right through the life of a MuVenda; further it is because of these twofold influences that it is necessary in the religious life of the people to keep in touch both with the patrilineal ancestors on the father's side and the matrilineal ancestors on the mother's side. The sacred bull representing the paternal ancestors, and the female goat representing the maternal ancestors, are very important in BaVenda religion, the ceremonies in which they play an essential part have been admirably described in this monograph. Especial

INTRODUCTION

care has been taken to study the native beliefs connected with the stars and with the phenomena of nature in general. A full account is also given of the method of divination used by these people. Indeed, every effort has been made to give as complete a picture as possible of the life of the BaVenda, though owing to the rapid changes that have been brought about by the intensive settlement of white people in their country, many of the customs are now falling into decay.

It is impossible to deal with all the features of culture in which the BaVenda differ from most other Bantu around them. Attention must, however, be called to their complex system of initiation schools. Mr. Stayt has given us fuller and more connected accounts of these various schools than have been given before, and has also been able in many cases to get at the function of ceremonies which on the surface seem entirely purposeless.

No one can read this book without gaining a deeper understanding of the ways of thought of a Bantu people, and every one will, I think, be amazed at the wealth of detail Mr. Stayt has been able to bring together. I know that Mt. Stayt has spared himself no pains to gather all the information that was available. In spite of his blindness he has climbed rugged mountains, pushed into remote valleys, climbed almost inaccessible crannies in his search for the right informant to fill in a gap in his information. I think that those who read the result of his labours will be grateful to him for his efforts and filled with profound respect for the courage and perseverance with which he has accomplished his task.

A. W. HOERNLE

UNIVERSITY OF WITWATERSRAND
JOHANNESBURG.

PREFACE

THIS monograph is the outcome of three successive seasons' work among the BaVenda in the Northern Transvaal and Southern Rhodesia. Research was made possible by a Frank Smart Studentship from Gonville and Caius College, Cambridge (renewed for three years), and by grants from Capetown University. Through the kind interest of Professor Westermann the publication of the book was undertaken by the International Institute of African Languages and Cultures, helped by generous contributions from the Bantu Research Grant Fund of Capetown, from the Capetown University, and from the Rivers Memorial Fund.

The photographs in the book (except plates xxvii, xxxvii, xlvi, and xlviii, which were given to me by the Rev. G. Westphal of the Berlin Missionary Society) were taken by my wife, who was my companion throughout my wanderings, and to whose enthusiastic help, both in the field-work and in the preparation of the monograph, I am deeply indebted.

Most of the information recorded here was collected as we travelled in the country of the BaVenda, camping beside their villages, and visiting all the important chiefs in their own kraals. The extent of the country, the mixed origin of the BaVenda, and their increasing contact with European culture, all add to the difficulty of the ethnographer and make it almost impossible to recapture indigenous beliefs. Customs and rites differ, or may be differently interpreted, according to the locality. However, when my informants disagreed about the data they gave me, I always sought an opportunity of laying the disputed matter before the district chief. When he and his councillors had thrashed out the subject, often with much heat, I was generally able at least to arrive at the opinion of the majority.

Two successive non-Christian interpreters, Mafunisa Masia Senthumule and Mashinya Mbizaan, made themselves invaluable to me. These boys, who were fully initiated members of the tribe, were familiar with the whole country and understood the different Venda dialects in addition to knowing Zulu, English, and Dutch. They helped us to make contact with their people and created a friendly atmosphere between us and them.

Being neither a linguist nor a trained musician I should like to apologize here for any inadequacies in my rendering of Tshivenda

PREFACE

words, phrases, and songs. Some of the secret formulae are so difficult to obtain that I have ventured to include them for the benefit of other investigators, even when I am not prepared to vouch for their exact linguistic accuracy. The songs, some of which were given to me by Stephanus Dzivani, a Venda teacher and evangelist at Sibasa, also fall short of accuracy, in so far as the Western notation is inadequate to represent the intervals of the African scale.

We received help and kindness from numbers of other BaVenda and were treated most courteously by their chiefs. I should like to thank particularly Chief Senthumule and Chief Tshivhase's brother Takalani for the valuable information they gave me, for their willing assistance, and for their courteous hospitality.

It is only possible to make a general acknowledgement here of the friendly co-operation and hospitality shown to us by government officials, missionaries, farmers, and traders. Colonel Lyle of the Native Affairs Department at Louis Trichardt helped me in finding interpreters and in many other ways. The Rev. G. and Mrs. Westphal of Makonde, the Rev. D. and Mrs. McDonald of the Gooldville Presbyterian Mission, the Rev. F. and Mrs. Burke of the American Mission at Nzhelele and Mr. S. A. Cilliers of Happy Rest Farm gave us wonderful hospitality.

In the actual preparation of the monograph, I owe much to the Rev. G. Westphal who, having made a special study of Tshivenda, translated many songs and phrases for me; he also helped my wife to prepare the map. Mrs. Stanford, who has made a study of Bantu music, was kind enough to transcribe some of the songs which appear in this book.

I also take this opportunity of thanking Dr. A. C. Haddon, Professor T. Barnard of the Capetown University and Mrs. A. W. Hoernlé of the Witwatersrand University for their encouragement and help.

The few passages which treat of the Venda connexions with Zimbabwe, together with five photographs which illustrate them, appear as a short appendix to Miss Caton-Thompson's book, *The Zimbabwe Culture: Ruins and Reactions*, as well as in the text of this volume.

H. A. S.

LONDON,
March 1931.

CONTENTS

I. GEOGRAPHY	1
Position	1
Topography	2
Flora	4
Fauna	4
Climate	5
Archaeology	5
II. HISTORY	9
III. PHYSICAL AND PSYCHICAL CHARACTERISTICS, CLOTHING AND DECORATION	20
Physical Characteristics	20
Psychical Characteristics	21
Clothing	22
Ornaments	25
Beads	26
Personal Decoration	27
Scarification	28
IV. THE VILLAGE, AGRICULTURE, AND DOMESTIC ANIMALS	29
Village	29
Huts	31
Agriculture	34
Cattle	37
Dipping	42
Other Domestic Animals	44
V. FOOD AND NARCOTICS	46
Food	46
Beer	48
Snuff	50
Smoking	50
VI. INDUSTRIES	52
Pottery	52
Calabashes	53
Woodwork	54
Basketry	56
Wirework	58
String	58

xiv   CONTENTS

VI. INDUSTRIES (*cont.*)—
    Weaving 58
    Skin-dressing 59
    Ivory 59
    Iron 59
    Copper 62

VII. WAR, TRADING, TRAVELLING, AND HUNT-
    ING 69
    Weapons 69
    Warfare 70
    Travelling 74
    Trading 75
    Hunting 76
    Fishing 80
    The Crocodile 81

VIII. BIRTH AND INFANCY 83
    Pregnancy 84
    Normal Births 85
    Abnormal Births 90
    Twins 91
    First Teeth and Weaning 93

IX. CHILD LIFE 95
    Boys 95
    Girls 97
    Mixed Games 97
    Mahundwani 99

X. PUBERTY AND INITIATION 101
    Boys' School (*thondo*) 101
    Girls' School (*vhusha*) 106
    Pre-marital Unions 110
    Joint Initiation (*domba*) 111
    Boys' Circumcision (*murundu*) . . . 125
    Girls' 'Circumcision' (*musevheto*) . . . 138

XI. MARRIAGE 142
    Lobola 143
    Marriage Arrangements 144
    Marriage Ceremonies 147
    Elopement 150
    Avoidances 151
    Marriage Irregularities 152

CONTENTS xv

XII. FAMILY LIFE AND ETIQUETTE . . . 153

XIII. MORTUARY RITES 161
Death 161
Burial 162
Unusual Deaths. 163
Purification 164
Mourning. 165

XIV. PROPERTY, SUCCESSION, AND INHERITANCE
Property 166
The Heir 167
Inheritance of Widows 169
Heir to Female Fathers 170

XV. RELATIONSHIP TERMINOLOGY AND KIN-
SHIP SYSTEM 172

XVI. SOCIAL GROUPINGS 185
Patrilineal Lineage 185
Matrilineal Lineage 185
Sibs 185
Dialectic Divisions 192
Age-sets 193

XVII. THE CHIEF 195
Nature of Chieftainship 195
Officials 198
The Chief's Wives 201
The Chief. 201
Death of the Chief 205
Installation of New Chief 208
Variations in Burial and Installation Procedure . 210

XVIII. TERRITORIAL DIVISIONS, GOVERNMENT,
REVENUE AND TAXATION, LAW AND JUSTICE 214
Territorial Divisions 214
Government 215
Revenue and Taxation 217
Law and Justice. 218

XIX. CONCEPTIONS OF THE UNIVERSE . . 225
Meteorology 225
Astronomy 226
Time and the Seasons. 228
Numbers 229

xvi CONTENTS

XX. RELIGION 230
    The Supreme Deity 230
    The Spirit World 236
    Dissociated Spirits 238
    Ancestor Cult 240
    Sowing and Harvest Rites 252
    Review of Ancestor Cult 259

XXI. MEDICINE AND MAGIC 262
    The Medico-Magician and his Work . . . 263
    Diseases and their Treatment . . . 267
    Witchcraft 273
    Black Magic 276
    Divination 279
    The Effect of the Medico-Magician on Society . 300
    Possession 302

XXII. RAIN-MAKING AND FERTILITY OF CROPS . 309
    Rain-making 309
    Fertility of Crops 313

XXIII. MUSIC, DANCING, AND SONG 316
    Musical Instruments 316
    Tribal Dances 320
    Other Dances 323
    Songs 325

XXIV. FOLKLORE 330

XXV. MISCELLANEOUS BELIEFS AND SUPERSTI-
TIONS 362

APPENDIXES

I. *MEFUVHA* AND *NDODE* 364

II. TABLE OF HEAD AND HEIGHT MEASURE-
MENT 368

III. PLANTS AND THEIR IDENTIFICATION . . 374

ARCHAEOLOGICAL NOTE 376

BIBLIOGRAPHY 377

LIST OF CERTAIN TSHIVENDA WORDS . . 380

INDEX 383

LIST OF ILLUSTRATIONS

I.	Phiphidi Falls	*facing p.* 2
II.	Lake Fundudzi	,, 3
III.	Ruins on the Farm Verdun	,, 4
IV.	Dzata	,, 5
V.	Part of the Wall of Milaboni's Kraal	,, 6
VI. {	Stone on the Wall of Milaboni's Kraal	,, 7
	Stone near Mukombani	,, 7
VII.	Old Stone in the Yard of Petty Chief Ratomba	,, 8
VIII.	MuVenda Man	,, 22
IX.	MuVenda Woman	,, 23
X.	NeThengwe's Village	,, 30
XI.	Huts in Course of Construction	,, 31
XII. {	Look-out from which the Crops are Watched	,, 34
	Granaries	,, 34
XIII. {	Stamping the Corn	,, 46
	Winnowing	,, 46
XIV. {	Pots	,, 52
	Calabashes	,, 52
XV.	Wooden Utensils	,, 54
XVI.	Wooden Door from Tshikobakoba's Kraal	,, 55
XVII. {	Baskets and Sleeping-mat	,, 56
	Drums	,, 56
XVIII.	Basket-making	,, 57
XIX.	Wire Bracelet-making	,, 58
XX. {	Bellows	,, 59
	Axe, Adze, and Hoe-head	,, 59
XXI.	A MuLemba	,, 62
XXII. {	Iron Tools	,, 66
	Musuku (belonging to Chief Mphephu)	,, 66
XXIII.	Old Warrior, showing *Tshiala*	,, 71
XXIV. {	Part of Old Hunting-net	,, 80
	Trap	,, 80
XXV. {	Boy	,, 96
	Girl	,, 96
XXVI.	Girls Practising the Drums	,, 97
XXVII.	Girl Initiate in the River	,, 108
XXVIII.	Girl after the *Vhusha* in the Humble Attitude Wearing the *Thahu*	,, 110
XXIX.	The Python Dance	,, 114
XXX.	The *Sali*	,, 116
XXXI.	Wooden Models	,, 120
XXXII.	Girls Saluting, soon after the *Vhusha*	,, 158
XXXIII.	Chief Tshivhase	,, 202
XXXIV.	Chief Senthumule, with Two Wives and Some of his Councillors	,, 203

LIST OF ILLUSTRATIONS

XXXV.
- Chief Mbulahene Mphephu . . . . . *facing p.* 204
- Chief Phaphuli . . . . ,, 204

XXXVI. Chief Lwamondo. . . . . . . ,, 212

XXXVII.
- The Rite of the Hoe Handle . . . . . ,, 242
- Ranwasha's Sacred Stones . . . . . . ,, 242

XXXVIII.
- Tshikobakoba's Sacred Stones . . . . . ,, 243
- An Offering to the Spirits. The Sacred Spears and Axe on the Stones . . . . ,, 243

XXXIX. Woman Wearing *Malembe* and Small Wooden Charm . ,, 248

XL. Mushapa Throwing the Bones, with his Horn, Switch, and Medicines behind him . . . . . . ,, 266

XLI. Mushapa's Dice and Supplementary Objects . . . ,, 267

XLII. Divining Dice . . . . ,, 286

XLIII. Tshiobi's Divining Bowl . . . . . . ,, 292

XLIV. Mukharu's Divining Bowl . . . . . . ,, 296

XLV. Decorations on Backs of Divining Bowls . . . . ,, 300

XLVI.
- *Tshijolo* with Bow . . . . . . ,, 318
- *Mbila* . . . . ,, 318

XLVII. The *Tshikona* Dance . . . . ,, 320

XLVIII.
- *Mefuvha* . . . . ,, 364
- *Ndode* . . . . ,, 364

MAP. Vendaland in the Zoutpansberg District of the Northern Transvaal . . . . at end

I

GEOGRAPHY

Position—Topography—Flora—Fauna—Climate—Archaeology.

Position.

THE BaVenda occupy approximately a third of the inhabited territory of the Zoutpansberg district in the Northern Transvaal. Owing to the mingling of the tribes on all the boundaries, and the fact that the tax pass receipts are framed on a territorial and not a tribal basis, it is very difficult to obtain adequate information as to the numerical strength of the BaVenda proper. According to the figures supplied to me at the office of the Sub-Native Commissioners in Louis Trichardt and Sibasa, the population may be roughly estimated at about 150,000.

The territory is bounded on the north by the Limpopo river, on the west by the Sand river, and on the south and east by the Levuvhu river, which rises east of Louis Trichardt and flows east for some distance forming roughly part of the southern boundary; the remainder of the southern boundary is formed by the farms adjoining the south of Senthumule's location. Owing to the incursion of the Europeans and their annexation of lands for farms, the bulk of the people are to-day concentrated in locations and crown lands, approximately from longitude 29° 40′ E. to 30° 50′ E. and latitude 22° 20′ S. to 23° 10′ S. (*see Map*).

Scattered groups have filtered back across the Limpopo into Southern Rhodesia and are to be found around Nuanetsi and Bubye and west as far as Gwanda and the Shabani river. Other small groups have wandered south and west, where, although in some cases they have left a cultural mark, they have been absorbed by the tribes among whom they settled and have completely lost their identity.

The Mashona, whom the BaVenda call collectively BaKaranga, are their neighbours on the north; these people call the BaVenda BaVeya. The BaThonga live on the east and south-east and are known as BaThonga to the BaVenda, whom they call BaVesha. On the west and south west are the Sutho groups, Maguvhu to the BaVenda; to them the BaVenda are BaDzweda. Near Mara, on the extreme west, there is a small group of half-castes, called the Buis, after the founder

GEOGRAPHY

of the group. He was a European named Buis, who in the early days settled among the natives of that part, took their women as wives and made himself their head.

Topography.

The Zoutpansberg district is mountainous and rugged with a varied climate and rainfall, and a rich sub-tropical vegetation. The Zoutpansberg mountains stretch roughly east and west for approximately eighty miles, with several branches and only one large break. The range is bounded on the east by the Rooi Rand, where it runs down into small kopjes and finally terminates in Tshikundu Kop. The western boundary is the Harlequin river, which the early Voortrekkers mistook for the Nile. Just opposite Louis Trichardt there are three distinct branches of the mountains. The whole width of the range varies between eleven and twenty miles, with large table-lands. The range received its name from the early settlers, who called it Zout Pan, after the large salt-pan at the west of the range. Excellent salt is obtained from this vicinity.

The BaVenda are scattered over the greater part of this range. Its kopjes and spurs, precipitous slopes and general unapproachable character, have played an important part in protecting them from their enemies, and account for their being the last tribe in the Transvaal to submit to white domination.

The Zoutpansberg range cuts the country into two distinct areas. To the north of the mountains it is dry and arid, with small rainfall and few rivers. Except in the extreme east, the Nzhelele is the only river of importance in that part; it provides a plentiful supply of water throughout the dry season, and flowing as it does through the parched bushveldt, is extremely beautiful; it rises near Khalavha in the heart of the mountains and runs down through Mphephu's mountains where it is joined by four small tributaries; it continues in a north-easterly direction, joined in its course by the Mufumgodi and Matamba spruits, until it reaches the Limpopo, into which it empties itself about four miles east of the Sand river; it is a swift stream of good water, teeming with crocodile and fish, and flowing through tracts of easily irrigable land. Most of the other rivers are of little use to the people, as, except in flood times, they are quite dry apart from occasional water holes which provide little more than drinking water. In contrast with this hard, dry, cruel country are the well-watered southern and eastern areas, with the Levuvhu and Mutali rivers and

PLATE I

PHIPHIDI FALLS

PLATE II

LAKE FUNDUDZI

GEOGRAPHY

their various tributaries always full of water, making the whole country fertile and providing for abundant vegetation, in spite of several intractable marshes. The Levuvhu rises just east of Louis Trichardt, running due east and then turning north at Mphaphuli's location, from which point it is often called the Mphaphuli river; it is joined in its course by various tributaries, the largest being the Dzindi, the Mutshindudi and the Mutali, before reaching the Limpopo in the extreme north-east corner of Vendaland. The Phiphidi Falls (Plate I) are on the Mutshindudi river, a few miles from Sibasa; though small, they are in an extremely beautiful setting, and are the centre of numerous mythological beliefs. Perhaps from a purely artistic viewpoint the river Mutali is the most picturesque of any in the Zoutpansberg; it rises in the mountains above Lake Fundudzi and trickles gently down through dense, almost impenetrable bush into the lake below, where it apparently ends; but some distance below the lake it bubbles up again from beneath the rocks and then flows on uninterruptedly in a north-easterly direction until it joins the Levuvhu, fed on its way by several smaller tributaries.

Lake Fundudzi (Plate II) situated in the heart of the mountains, cannot be reached readily except on foot, or on horseback, and then only by small footpaths, crossing the mountains from Tshivhase's kraal, Khalavha, or Tshikombani. The lake is about three miles long and two miles broad when it is full, but in the winter months it is very much smaller. Although it is fed continually by the Mutali river and two or three smaller streams it has no apparent outlet; it was formed originally by a large landslide, which completely blocked the river, so that the whole valley, shut in as it is on all sides by mountains, soon became a lake; gradually the water trickled through and found an outlet among the rocks, a long distance beyond the rocky boundary formed by the landslide. It is full of crocodiles and the centre of dreadful interest to the BaVenda. The isolated position and rather forbidding appearance of the lake, combined with the fact that water is continually running into it and apparently never out, have given it an unfavourable notoriety and have resulted in its being connected with all manner of strange and sinister occurrences. Apart from its ethological connexions, it is a site of unusual interest to the traveller. From the far end, where the river eventually bubbles out from underground, there is a view of unparalleled breadth. The Drakensberg mountains and Portuguese East Africa can be seen across the low-lying country, and Southern Rhodesia beyond the Limpopo

GEOGRAPHY

river; also the Sabi river and Sabi mountains, the Waterberg range and Bechuanaland.

The mountains and valleys, beautiful well-watered lowlands, dense forests and wide plateaux make all this district one of peculiar beauty and variety. The network of rivers formed by the tributaries feeding the Mutali and Levuvhu rivers form very fertile valleys, rich pastureland, and in some parts dense vegetation. This district is the most populated part of Vendaland, in marked contrast to the practically unoccupied area to the north.

Flora.

Until some thirty years ago the whole mountain range was clothed in valuable timber, including yellow-wood, stink-wood, sneeze-wood, red almond, African iron-wood, bitter almond, and many others. Mimosa trees flourish all over the country, in at least fifteen varieties. In certain localities the mupani tree is found in profusion, although it does not occur beyond a certain point on the southern slopes. The baobab tree is found in the mountain gullies on the northern side of the mountain, especially near Messina, but not south until one reaches the low country and the far east. The veldt is very variable. On the virgin mountain soil the tombeitje and dekgras (used for thatching) grow, but as soon as the ground has been disturbed sweet grass takes its place. Good sweet buffalo grass grows all over the country.

The fertile red loam which covers a large proportion of the land is excellent for crop raising, and the favourable conditions make it possible to raise two crops a year, one in December and the second in April, without any fertilizing or special treatment of the soil. The traveller in Vendaland finds ample variety on his journey. There is the dry, stubborn bushveldt on the south-west, growing on hard, rocky, unpromising ground, turning into green pasture land on the plateaux and by the rivers, and stretching out on the east into beautiful wide parklands with large stately trees and a profusion of wonderful flowers.

Fauna.

Until fifty years ago big game of every description roamed all over the BaVenda country. Elephant were plentiful, as were herds of koodoo, sable, buffalo, giraffe, zebra, eland and wildebeest. Rhinoceros were sometimes encountered, while the lion, leopard, hyena, wild dog, and jackal played havoc with the natives' herds. Innumerable smaller buck and other game such as waterbok, impala, duiker,

PLATE III

RUINS ON THE FARM VERDUN

PLATE IV

DZATA

GEOGRAPHY

stembok, warthog, and bush-pig were a constant source of trouble and danger in the land. Hippopotamus, the *muvuvhu*, after which the Levuvhu river was named, were to be found near most of the rivers, all of which were infested with crocodile.

To-day elephant, rhinoceros, hippopotamus, and buffalo have completely disappeared. Giraffe and zebra are rare, and there is a yearly decrease in all the other animals, owing to the steady encroachment of civilization and the large toll taken by hunters both black and white. There is now the Shingwedzi game reserve, bounding Vendaland on the east, where it is to be hoped that many of these one-time owners of the bushveldt will find sanctuary.

Climate.

The year is divided into two seasons, the wet and the dry. The dry season is in the winter between May and September, when the weather is very pleasant, with fresh bracing days and cool nights. On the southern slopes of the mountains it is often intensely cold with heavy frosts at night, but there is seldom frost to the north, except near the rivers. In normal seasons the rains start in October or November, and from that time onwards the weather becomes moist and hot, the shade temperature generally ranging between 80° and 90°, and north of the mountains often being 110° or more. South-east of the mountains the rainfall is very good, but it is not always regular so that local droughts are fairly common. At Louis Trichardt the annual rainfall is over 30 inches and at Sibasa the records for the last ten years show an average of 45 inches. December, January, and February are generally the wettest months, and at this time practically all the rivers are in flood. North of the mountains it is very different, the annual average rainfall being about 10 inches and often much less; droughts are frequent and often prolonged, the people being obliged to buy food from their more fortunate southerly neighbours. During the wet season the whole country is malarial.

Archaeology.

In the north-west of Vendaland there are traces of some very ancient occupation. Colonel Piet Moller, who was an early settler in the Zoutpansberg, has found what he considers to be indisputable evidence of ancient irrigation works. Most of the old furrows are near Chepisse and it appears that the water was diverted from a small stream there in a series of furrows to a distance of about four and a

GEOGRAPHY

half miles south. Traces of furrows are also discernible at Sulphur Springs, and at several places by the Nzhelele river, where some of them have been reopened and are utilized by the BaVenda to-day. Colonel Moller says that when he first came across these some forty years ago, there was no doubt of their antiquity; to-day they are very difficult to trace, as roads, modern agriculture, and furrows have altered the face of the country considerably and have practically hidden the ancient workings.

In the extreme north, near the Limpopo river, ancient workings for copper ores, extending from the Limpopo southwards for a distance of twenty-five miles, were traced by Mr. J. M. Calderwood, M.I.M.M., when the Messina area was first surveyed for copper. Further reference will be made to these workings in connexion with native copper work.

There are also stone ruins, similar to the smaller and rougher outcrops of the Zimbabwe Ruins in Southern Rhodesia. One of these is situated on the farm Verdun, four miles west of Mopani, (Plate III) on the summit of a small kopje. It shows the remains of a rounded passage, leading into what must have been the main structure. The two sides of the wall are constructed of smooth, regular, brick-shaped stones, the intervening space being packed with rubble; there are only fragments of two or three walls standing. On the farms Rembander, south of the Lwamondo location, and Diamond on the Sand river, and at Pont's Drift on the Limpopo similar ruins are to be found.

No history of the origins of these ruins has survived. All definite traditions are associated with the ruins of Dzata (Plate IV), situated about two miles from Chief Mphephu's village. Dzata is well known to every MuVenda as the remains of the first permanent home of the MaKhwinde sib, after they crossed the Limpopo to settle in Venda-land. It is reputed to have been built by Thoho-ya-Ndou, from stones carried from Vembe, just the other side of the Limpopo. One tradition says that Thoho-ya-Ndou was afraid to use the stones of the newly conquered country for his capital; another that he forced the BaKaranga under his domination to bring the stones as tribute, making them carry them the long distance from across the Limpopo, to demonstrate his power. The ruins of Dzata are situated on a slight elevation, with a stream of water running near, except in times of severe drought. The whole site covers two or three acres and consists of very fragmentary remains of a series of walls, most of which appear to be made from the ordinary stones of the locality packed up with

PLATE V

PART OF THE WALL OF MILABONI'S KRAAL

PLATE VI

STONE ON THE WALL OF
MILABONI'S KRAAL

STONE NEAR MUKOMBANI

GEOGRAPHY

earth. Towards the middle of the site there is an inner structure of ruined walls which are different. The stones on the two surfaces of each wall, which is about 6 feet thick, are fitted one on top of the other, to make a strong, regular face, and then the space in between is packed up with rubble. These walls, which are very much broken down, measure about 6 feet in the highest part, and no consecutive piece of wall is more than from 10 to 15 feet long. The stones are large, flat, and fairly regular, much larger than those in the ruins at Verdun; they could, however, all be handled easily by a single man. The largest, an odd stone not actually part of the wall, measures 54 inches by 15 inches by 6 inches.

There is reputed to be another ruin at Tshiendeulu. NeTshiendeulu was chief of the Vhatavhatsinde people when Thoho-ya-Ndou's father first led the MaKhwinde into Vendaland and conquered him. The traditions of these two ruins are definitely Bantu and show that the early BaVenda settlers had a considerable knowledge of the method of stonework employed by the builders in Southern Rhodesia. Indeed, in some of the mountain villages to-day, villages actually built by the veterans still living in them, a similar building plan and technique has been employed. At the kraal of NeMenanga at Milaboni, in the Tononndwa location, (Plate V) the walls and passages are built in this way, and if the huts were to be removed this village would give a very similar appearance to that presented by the ruins of Dzata.

There is other evidence that the BaVenda were accomplished stone-masons in the days when they were bound to take refuge in their mountain fastnesses to escape from their enemies. Near Makonde, on the face of the mountain there stand some interesting ruins, formerly inhabited by the forbears of the headman still living in the district. The small creeks and recesses in the sheer precipice have been bridged and fortified with stone-masonry, making an impregnable hiding-place from which the defenders could do yeoman service with the bow and arrow, unseen by the enemy; the little balconies and recesses appear like so many swallows' nests, most of which were reached by the defenders by scrambling to their perches, with the help of monkey ropes, up the sheer face of the cliff.

Another feature of some interest is the occurrence, in different places, of odd stones (Plate VI) put up for some undiscovered reason. The shape of these stones suggests that they were of phallic origin, and possibly that the people who erected them were influenced by their contact with Zimbabwe, where so many phallic symbols have

GEOGRAPHY

been identified. Frequently one or more such monoliths are placed on the wall at a village entrance or in the main yard (Plate VII) apparently for no specific reason, but merely in imitation of their ancestors.

Impressions resembling human footprints have been found in rock near Mphephu's village, and others near Mutali resembling footprints of human beings, buck and dogs.[1] These discoveries have not been properly investigated but would seem to be similar to those in Bechuanaland.

There are Bushman paintings at Waterberg.

The archaeological wealth of Vendaland has not yet been explored. Most of the ruins referred to here are in the north-west of the country; it is highly probable that in the future many other ruins, and other evidence of the past occupants of the country will be brought to light.

The whole country has undergone considerable changes since the advent of the European. Louis Trichardt is a fair-sized farming town, and Messina one of the richest copper mines in the Union of South Africa. The railway was brought through Louis Trichardt and on to Messina in 1914, and is now being extended across the Limpopo into Southern Rhodesia. A road, which is fast becoming the main arterial road from Johannesburg to Rhodesia, passes right through western Vendaland. From Louis Trichardt it traverses the mountains and passes through Wylie's Poort, one of the most remarkable gorges in South Africa, and continues through Messina to Rhodesia.

The mineral potentialities of Vendaland are considerable. Besides the rich copper that is found in such abundance at Messina, there are deposits at Matamba and Mutali. There are evidences of vast coal deposits, and there is little doubt that in the course of time great mineralogical wealth will be discovered in this country where, up to the present time, only the surface has been scratched.

The fertility of the soil and, in parts, the good rainfall are favourable to the farmer, who finds that conditions are excellent for citrus, bananas, rubber, cotton and other tropical growths as well as for mealies and staple crops. The administrative centre of Vendaland is Louis Trichardt, and at Sibasa there is also a Sub-Native Commissioner and a police camp. For over fifty years now the natives have been subject to missionary influence, and for about the same number of years there have been growing up ever-increasing numbers of European trading stores.

[1] See note on p. 376.

PLATE VII

OLD STONE IN THE YARD OF PETTY CHIEF
RATOMBA

II

HISTORY

THE BaVenda are a composite people who have been gradually welded into a compact whole in the locality which they now occupy. The tribe is composed of sibs and groups of unrelated peoples who have, in varying circumstances and localities, come in contact with a small homogeneous nucleus and become identified with it. The ethnological origin of this nucleus, in which many diverse races have become incorporated, is uncertain. In spite of cultural differences among the various sibs the Venda tribe to-day considers itself as a single unit which, with slight dialectic differences, speaks a common language. Lestrade[1] says, in discussing the language of the Venda group:

The phonesis and phonology of TshiVenda finds its nearest equivalent in the Karanga group, and it is quite sharply distinguished from the Sotho and Thonga groups in this regard, though from the former far more than the latter. This is of interest, since the ethnic influence of the Thonga upon the Venda tribes seems to be the least of all the influences brought to bear on them, except in very recent times. With regard to grammatical structure, TshiVenda is sharply marked off from the Sotho and Thonga groups, and as sharply reminiscent of the Karanga group and of the groups to the north-east of the latter, namely the whole of the East African group of Bantu languages, of which Swahili, in its grammatical structure at least, and in such of its vocabulary as is not Arabicised, may be cited as an example.'

There can be little doubt that linguistically and culturally the BaVenda have a place in the congeries of people that form the wedge which starts north of the Zambesi and passes through Mashonaland, tapering away amongst the BaPedi south of Vendaland.

All current oral traditions show that the important migrations came from north of the Limpopo river. Many of these migrations were composed of small sibs or sections of sibs, and there are many sibs among the BaKaranga to-day whose names have their counterpart in Vendaland. Two migrations stand out among the smaller infiltrations, that of the Vhatavhatsinde group, composed chiefly of the VhaKwebo and Ndou sibs, followed later by the MaKhwinde group, who became masters of the whole country. The traditions of these two groups make

[1] Lestrade, G. P., 'Some Notes on the Ethnic History of the BaVenda and their Rhodesia Affinities', *South African Journal of Science*, vol. xxiv, p. 487.

HISTORY

a reasonable reconstruction of the history of the BaVenda in their present country possible.

The word *mutavhatsinde* has been variously interpreted. The Rev. G. Westphal of the Berlin Missionary Society, living at Luvhimbi, has obtained what appears to me to be the most reasonable interpretation and one that has been confirmed by many informants. It is, according to him, composed of the words *muta* (the small yard surrounding the women's huts) and *tsinde* (the stem or trunk of a tree). At one time members of this group used to erect a pole in the yard of their kraals, and so were dubbed *muta vha tsinde* (yard of the stem) by their neighbours. The plural, *vhatavhatsinde*, doubtless followed when the appellation became general. The exact significance of this obsolete custom has been forgotten, but it probably had a religious motive and was associated with the fact that many families in this group were great medicine men, and that a powerful antidote for evil was supplied by them from the *mutavhatsinde* tree, which grows in their part of the country; it is possible that this was the same tree that was erected in their yards. Nethengwe and his family used to have a great reputation among the Vhatavhatsinde, and indeed through the whole country, as powerful medicine men.

When the Vhatavhatsinde crossed the Limpopo and settled along the Zoutpansberg range they found another tribe, the BaNgona, in occupation there. The BaNgona were a non-warlike rather disorganized people, who allowed the invaders to settle peacefully among them, soon recognizing them as their superiors. The chief of the Vhatavhatsinde group was Netshiendeulu, whose descendants still live on their original mountain, in what is now Mphephu's location. Other important petty chiefs were Matidza of Luonde; Nemaungani of Maungani; Rapuli, whose village was at Tshirululuni near Louis Trichardt, but whose line is now extinct; Netshiavho, who first settled at Khalavha and then went to Lake Fundudzi; Manenzhe at Manenzhe; and Nethengwe, whose old village was at Shakhadzi, but who fought his way two generations ago to his present stronghold where his descendant is the only Mutavhatsinde chief who has maintained his independence.

One of the great cultural differences between the Vhatavhatsinde and other Venda groups is their method of disposing of the dead. The Vhatavhatsinde practise a form of cremation; the bones of the dead are exhumed some months after burial and burnt ceremonially at certain specified rivers, in which the ashes are finally scattered. Other groups generally bury their dead.

HISTORY

Very little is known of the BaNgona. It is probable that they were concentrated in the eastern portion of the country. Many places that were associated with the BaNgona in the past are feared and avoided by the BaVenda. There is a superstition that they should not build where the BaNgona have built, as it is feared that the BaNgona ancestral spirits may still have a sinister influence over their old territories. This dread has been the sole agent in retarding their complete absorption into the tribe of their conquerors. It seemed impossible to find a self-avowed MuNgona to question as to their early history, until a discussion on an irrelevant subject revealed the interesting fact that a certain religious ceremony could not take place without the co-operation of a MuNgona hereditary priest. This priest, Netshitumbe, until three years ago lived at Tshaula the home of his ancestors; he was turned out to give place to one of the chief's relatives, and now lives at Luvhimbi. He was very willing to talk, but unfortunately had only a limited knowledge of the history of his people; he did, however, volunteer the following facts and also gave me the names of his paternal ancestors for the last sixteen generations. According to Netshitumbe the original inhabitants of the eastern part of the Zoutpansberg were BaNgona, a race of short, slight, dark, flat-nosed people. The chief at the time of their subjugation was called Diwase. He lived at Tshaula, where he was powerful and influential, receiving tribute in ivory, skins, &c., from many neighbouring peoples; he was subjugated by Bohwane, of the MaKhwinde sib, but was obliged to remain at Tshaula as high priest to forestall the vengeance of the BaNgona ancestors. Certain other petty chiefs still have BaNgona priests, and encourage them to live in the district to act as mediums between them and the BaNgona ancestral spirits. Netshitshivhe, Nedzinghe, Tshisinavhutu and Nephindula are all BaNgona priests living at Thengwe, Thenzheni, Mianzwi and Mukula respectively. There are probably others, scattered about the country, and a short time ago quite a large group are reputed to have been living in Majaji's country near Pietersburg. The BaNgona have adopted Venda sib names in place of their own and their women have been married by the BaVenda, so that except in connexion with their religious rites, they have completely lost their identity and race-consciousness and become absorbed into the body of the Venda tribe.

It is impossible to determine the relative position and numbers of the BaNgona and Vhatavhatsinde peoples or to what stock either originally belonged. When the MaKhwinde entered the Zoutpansberg

HISTORY

they were living side by side, the former to the east and the latter, apparently the rulers of the country, mostly concentrated to the north and centre of the mountain range. It is probable that the Ma-Khwinde sib, often called *vha-ila-mbudzi* (those who tabu the goat) were led across the Limpopo under a certain Vele Lambeho or Dimbanyika. Mr. G. Wessman, of the Native Affairs Department at Sibasa, found some evidence that this man was descended from Mambo, who was reputed to be the ruler of both BaKaranga and BaVenda in Southern Rhodesia at this time, before the migration. The term *mambo* signifies chief, and it is quite possible that in view of the numerous names these chiefs possess, that particular Mambo and Vele Lambeho are one and the same person. It is uncertain when the name Venda was first used among them; there is a tradition that Vele Lambeho called the country Venda after his settlement in the Zoutpansberg. The German missionary Beuster[1] says that *BaVenda* means 'people of the world' derived from *Venda* ('land' or 'world').

This migration probably took place towards the end of the seventeenth or the beginning of the eighteenth century, and must have consisted of a strong body of people, who found no difficulty in making themselves masters of the country, completely subjugating the Vhatavhatsinde and BaNgona. Vele Lambeho, or Dimbanyika, as he is more popularly called, placed his various sons as petty chiefs throughout the country and himself settled at the stronghold of Tshiendeulu.

The death of Dimbanyika is a favourite and much disputed myth. Some traditions say that his eldest son, Popi, was guilty of parricide and having killed his father, declared himself chief, boasting that although the elephant was dead, he, the head, still remained and was called Thoho-ya-Ndou (Head of the Elephant). The present Netshiendeulu tells another story. He says that Dimbanyika was hunting rock rabbits with his dog and followed the dog into a deep cave; a rock fell across the entrance of the cave entombing him alive inside; his son looked everywhere for him and after a long search found the cave with the dog keeping guard outside; he called out to his father, 'Are you there?' and Dimbanyika answered, 'Yes, take care of the dog and leave me here. I shall not return. I am quite content.' Popi returned to his father's village and said, 'My father is imprisoned in a cave here so that I cannot remain'. He then set off across the mountain with his followers and built a new capital at Dzata, which is to-day regarded as the ancestral home of the BaVenda in the Zoutpansberg.

[1] Beuster, C. L., 'Das Volk der Vawenda', *Berlin. Zeits. Ges. Erdk.*, 14, 1879, p. 236.

HISTORY

He never saw Netshiendeulu again, and from that day it has been tabu for any chief of the MaKhwinde sib to look on the face of the descendants of Netshiendeulu or any of the other Vhatavhatsinde chiefs. This tabu has lapsed in the case of the Thengwe chiefs, probably on account of their great power as medicine men. But even to-day, if Chief Mphephu wishes to speak to Netshiendeulu, he must do so with an intervening wall between them. The MaKhwinde also fear to visit other places occupied by the Vhatavhatsinde. Another result of the incarceration of Dimbanyika is that *tshiendeulu* has become the traditional name for ancestral graveyards.

Thoho-ya-Ndou is the great legendary hero of the BaVenda. Many and various are the stories told about him. He is said to have ruled over a large country, some traditions include parts of the Karanga country and also ascribe to him domination over certain Sutho groups in the Transvaal. He was undoubtedly enormously rich and powerful, and even the sound of his drum was reputed to bring instant death to any of his subjects who heard it. His great power provoked the jealousy of his brothers. He set out one day with a small following, possibly on a hunting trip, but more probably on an expedition to solicit support against his hostile brothers. He crossed the Nzhelele river and was never seen again. It is still believed that one day he will return to his people to restore the BaVenda to their former greatness.

The MaKhwinde and Vhatavhatsinde form the nucleus of the BaVenda as they are to-day. At frequent intervals infiltrations of unrelated peoples have penetrated into the country and been absorbed. The VhaMbedzi, living in the extreme east, probably entered the country at an early date. The VhaDau, living around Messina, came later in their history, and other small Sutho groups have also settled in different parts, each retaining vestiges of their own culture, while becoming absorbed in the wider culture complex of the Ba-Venda as a whole.

Traditions concerning the early history of the original BaVenda, prior to their entry into Rhodesia, are vague and fragmentary. Beuster, one of the earliest missionaries among them, came to the conclusion, on the slenderest evidence, that they originated in the Lower Congo. He based this supposition on a supposed similarity of name and language to a tribe in that region. Lestrade,[1] however, demonstrated the improbability of this theory and supports an alternative possibility,

[1] Lestrade, G. P., 'Some Notes on the Ethnic History of the BaVenda and their Rhodesia Affinities', *South African Journal of Science*, vol. xxiv, p. 490.

HISTORY

namely, that their place of origin was on the east coast in the neighbourhood of the great lakes. Linguistic and cultural evidence both support this theory which was first propounded by the missionary Gottschling[1] and enlarged upon in a paper by Stubbs[2] containing oral traditions collected by himself. It appears that the BaVenda lived originally in a very warm climate where many rivers emptied themselves into large 'silent stretches of water', the description of this country all leading to the assumption that it must have been in the great lake region of East Africa. Most of my own informants who have any opinion to offer as to the original home of their ancestors, confirm this view. Chief Senthumule is vehement in his assertions that the ancestral home was in the region of Nyasaland, and says that he can readily understand the language spoken there. So many changes have affected the original group, around which the BaVenda tribe has grown up, that it is impossible to speak with any degree of certainty on this subject. From this region, wherever it may have been, a tribe, which formed the nucleus of the BaVenda, journeyed south into Rhodesia, absorbing on the way a certain tribe called the Mashamba and other unknown peoples. After a long march, possibly occupying centuries, they eventually settled at a place in Rhodesia of which the locality is unknown. This place of settlement was called Dzata, and when they resettled on the Nzhelele after a second migration they not unnaturally called their new home Dzata as well. All the stories and traditions concerning these migrations are associated with the MaKhwinde sib. The Vhatavhatsinde and other sections of the BaVenda group have no traditions of their early history prior to their entry into the Zoutpansberg.

Many place-names in Southern Rhodesia are repeated in the Zoutpansberg, e.g. Makonde, Nzhelele, Thengwe, &c., and there is no doubt that, whatever their pre-Rhodesian history might have been, they sojourned in Southern Rhodesia for a great many years and lived closely allied to some of the groups which are now collectively termed Mashona. Lestrade[3] found informative data regarding this period of their wanderings. He says:

'Some interesting points relative to the history of the wanderings previous to the immigration from the Karanga country are to be found in the evidence

[1] Gottschling, E., 'The Bawenda: A Sketch of their History and Customs', London. *J. Roy. Anthrop. Inst.*, xxxv, 1905, p. 365.

[2] Stubbs, E. T., Pamphlet (Grahamstown, 1912).

[3] Lestrade, G. P., 'Some Notes on the Ethnic History of the BaVenda and their Rhodesia Affinities', *South African Journal of Science*, vol. xxiv, p. 491.

HISTORY

collected by the Transvaal Natives Locations Commissions of 1907–8, and in that of 1910, and quite independently collected by Mr. C. N. Manning, whilst stationed in the Zoutpansberg district. These accounts mention the names of tribes with whom the original BaVenda are said to have been in close contact, and from one of which they are stated actually to have descended. Two such names are the BaNyai and the BaLozwi (BaRozwi), the former allied to the Karanga group, the latter, according to Mr. Manning's informant, the tribe with whom the BaVenda were intimately connected: "While Mpefu's people were settled in what is now Rhodesia", he says, "some of the BaLozwi people visited us there and presented us with a leopard's skin, saying that we were of the same stock originally as they".'

My own informants confirmed this very close connexion with the BaRozwi.

There is no evidence of any sudden crisis which instigated a hurried migration into the Transvaal. It seems probable that small hunting parties were the forerunners of larger migrations, and it is possible that the disruption of the Monomatapa Empire was in some measure responsible for their movement south.

The golden age of the BaVenda was probably during the reign of Thoho-ya-Ndou, but at his death jealousy and family feuds disintegrated the tribe through internecine warfare, which continued intermittently until the country was brought under European domination.

Mr. G. Wessman of the Native Affairs Department, Sibasa, has compiled genealogies of the chief branches of the royal houses with traditions and other interesting information connected with them. I am indebted to this compilation for most of the following information concerning the history of the BaVenda after the MaKhwinde occupation.

Vele Lambeho had many sons of whom the four eldest were Popi (who after his father's death became Thoho-ya-Ndou), Tshisebe, Raluswyelo or Tshivhase, and Bele; these four sons were appointed to be petty chiefs at Nzhelele, Makonde, Phiphidi, and Vuba respectively. When Thoho-ya-Ndou became chief, the other three, jealous of his power, prepared to make Tshisebe chief by force. Soon after Thoho-ya-Ndou disappeared, as has already been described, the other three declared themselves independent chiefs, Tshikalanga or Rampofu, the son of Thoho-ya-Ndou being elected chief at the Nzhelele river in his father's place.

After Tshikalanga's death the succession was again disputed. This

HISTORY

resulted in his second son Tshigebeti, with the assistance of a large force of Malaboch allies, establishing himself as chief and receiving the name of Ramapulana, the treacherous. Ramapulana was succeeded by his son Makhado, who became famous as the 'Lion of the North', on account of his long and determined stand against the European occupation. Makhado was succeeded, after disputes among his sons, by his second son Mphephu, who was driven out of Vendaland by the Dutch and settled, with a considerable number of his people, in Southern Rhodesia. He was allowed to return after the Anglo-Boer war, but a number of his followers remained behind in their new home. When Mphephu was driven out his brother Senthumule was recognized as chief, and when he returned his country was divided up among the three brothers Mphephu, Senthumule, and Khuthama, all being recognized as independent chiefs, governing the country of Ramapulana. These BaVenda are often called the people of Ramapulana. Mphephu died in 1924 and was succeeded by his son Mbulahene, who is chief to-day, Senthumule and Khuthama still being supreme in their own comparatively small locations.

Tshivhase, the third brother of Thoho-ya-Ndou, declared himself independent chief in the east of Vendaland. He became wealthy and powerful and was succeeded by his son Mukesi Tshivhase. Mukesi's reign was occupied with battles with his neighbours, his arch-enemy being Ratsibi Mphaphuli, an independent chief living close to him. Mukesi lived to an old age and at his death was succeeded by his son Legegisa, who before his death removed his kraal from Miluwani to Mukumbani, where it is now situated. He was succeeded by his son Ramaremisa, the present chief Tshivhase.

During Mukesi's reign one of his brothers, Popi Rambuda, deserted him and declared himself independent, building his head kraal at Dzimauli. He collected a fairly large following and on his death was succeeded by his son Vele Rambuda. Vele had two sons, Bele and Tshikose, who on their father's death fought for the chieftainship. Bele was killed in the struggle, but his son Khaku was elected independent chief of Madala, where his father had been a petty chief. Tshikose Rambuda died in 1924 and was succeeded by his minor son Ratsibvumo Rambuda. Khaku died in 1923 and his minor son Tshitongani was appointed chief.

The three lineal descendants of the second and fourth sons of Vele Lambeho are head-men under Chiefs Tshivhase and Mphephu.

To-day the important independent chiefs of the MaKhwinde sib

HISTORY

are Mbulahene Mphephu, Senthumule, Khuthama, Tshivhase, and Rambuda. These chiefs are all recognized as rulers in their respective locations by the European administration. Mbulahene Mphephu and Tshivhase have the largest territories and the greatest wealth and power.

The third section is that of Mphaphuli, always an independent chief. Mr. Wessman says that:

'Shamboko Mpafuri is said to have been an independent chief at the time of Vele Lambeho, who was a close friend of his. It is not certain whether Shamboko came from Rhodesia, or whether he had already established himself at Tshitomboni (now forming part of the Knobnose Location) when Vele Lambeho came to this district from Bukalanga (i.e. S. Rhodesia). It would, however, appear that Shamboko was the Mpafuri or Mpafudi, the son of the great Ndebele chief Musi, as this Mpafuri is said to have fled from the "Musi" kraal towards Rhodesia on account of tribal wars, and further that Shamboko was in no way related to Vele Lambeho.'

There is another tradition that Shamboko entered Rhodesia with a horde of marauding Swazis and later attached himself to Vele Lambeho as one of his court officials, and after the migration south set up as an independent chief, in more or less his present position. The subsequent history of this group is one of perpetual quarrels between brothers as to the succession, it being a recognized tradition that every heir must fight and conquer his intriguing rivals before he could consolidate his claim to the chieftainship. There was also constant war against the Tshivhase chiefs, large expanses of land continually changing from one to the other. Ratsibi Mphaphuli was succeeded by Makwarela after the latter had killed his brother Tshikalanga. Makwarela died in 1927 and was succeeded by his son Paswane, in spite of a most persistent attempt by another brother to obtain recognition in his place. The Mphaphuli line of chiefs have adopted the goat as their totem animal, in emulation of the great MaKhwinde sib, hoping thereby to enhance their prestige.

Two other chiefs of probable non-Venda origin are Madzivhandila, now living on the farm Goedverwachting, whose ancestors lived at Mutali on the Levuvhu river, and Lwamondo, whose ancestors fled from Balauri and were appointed keepers of the chief's cattle by Tshikalanga Mphephu, becoming independent during the Anglo-Boer war. Both of these are probably of Sutho stock. In the western area there have been several small BaSutho settlements, which have become absorbed into the Venda group.

HISTORY

All the non-Venda elements have left their mark on Venda culture, although, generally speaking, they have received more from it than they have given to it. To-day MaKhwinde and Vhatavhatsinde and all the other sections of the people that live in Vendaland are proud to call themselves BaVenda, while those whose origin can be traced to other tribes are inclined to resent a reference to their foreign ancestry.

There is one group which is an exception to this tendency, and which does not share the Venda pride of race nor wish to sink its cultural and physical individuality in the tribe among which it lives. The BaLemba are found scattered in small villages or single kraals throughout Vendaland, more particularly in the west, without chiefs and without any political bond of union. They possess marked Semitic characteristics, and are the metal-workers, traders, and business men among their Bantu brethren, wandering among the BaVenda, indeed, anywhere among the tribes from the Zambesi to Pietersburg, absorbing the language of the people among whom they have settled and maintaining by endogamy (at any rate until recently) the purity of their race. The life and customs of this peculiar people are strangely reminiscent of the wandering Jews of medieval times. They are rapidly losing their individuality since European traders have robbed them of their heritage.

The BaVenda have been able to maintain their supremacy in the Zoutpansberg, and on many occasions have been saved from annihilation by their mountains. In the past they were subjected to constant raids from outside, and although there was never a combined effort against the raiders, each independent chief harried the enemy from his mountain stronghold and let him pass on to the next, where he was similarly treated, so making settlement impossible except by peaceful arrangement.

Gottschling[1] mentions two outstanding raids by the BaPedi and Zulus respectively.

'In the beginning of the nineteenth century the BaPedi under Tulane, the grandfather of Sekukuni I, invaded the country of the Bawenda, but the mountains secured the victory for the Bawenda. . . . After the Matabele kingdom in Mashonaland had been established by Moslekatse in 1838, they were troubled by the Zulu hordes crossing their country in order to follow the Matabele to Mashonaland. About 1840 a Zulu horde under Ngoano played havoc amongst the Bawenda, and was followed by a strong Zulu force

[1] Gottschling, E., 'The Bawenda. A Sketch of their History and Customs', *J. Roy. Anthrop. Inst.*, 1905, p. 366.

HISTORY

led by Songandawe, but the latter went over the Limpopo and joined Moslekatse. The mountain fortresses again saved the Bawenda from destruction.'

Their hereditary enemy the BaThonga also continually harried them, particularly the Knobnose branch. Another section, under the leadership of Albasini, a renegade Portuguese, was a continual source of trouble and acted as a convenient buffer between the BaVenda and the Transvaal Republic, which was not then in a strong enough position to subjugate this last obstinate opposition to their authority.

The BaVenda were most antagonistic to European settlement, and until 1872 no missionary was allowed to settle among them. Yet even prior to this date, they made use of the white man for their own ends, in spite of their hatred of him. In 1859, when Ramapulana was struggling for the chieftainship against his brother Ramvuma, he asked help from the independent Dutch Republic at Lydenburg, and returned to his capital with Commandant Potgieter and a strong Boer commando. The Boers remained near Dzanane and founded the prosperous village of Schoemansdal, where they traded for ivory with the natives. This settlement supported Makhado's claim to the chieftainship on Ramapulana's death. In 1867 Makhado raided Schoemansdal and annihilated its inhabitants, for a time freeing his country from the steadily increasing influence of the white man.

The native power in the north was a constant menace to the Transvaal Republic, and it was not until 1899, after various ineffectual attempts to subjugate Ramapulana's section of the tribe, that General Joubert finally succeeded in driving Mphephu into Rhodesia, thus breaking down the last obstinate resistance to European domination. This war has been described by Mr. R. Wessman[1] who took an active part in the proceedings.

After the Anglo-Boer war the whole country was divided into Locations under white administration, a large part being demarcated for white settlement.

[1] Wessman, R., *The Bawenda of the Spelonken*, London, 1908.

III

PHYSICAL AND PSYCHICAL CHARACTERISTICS, CLOTHING, AND DECORATION

Physical Characteristics—Psychical Characteristics—Clothing—Ornaments
—Beads—Personal Decoration—Scarification

Physical Characteristics.

IT is impossible to dogmatize about the typical Venda facial characteristics, as the constant absorption of other peoples that has taken
place from very early times, particularly the intermixture during the
last century with Sutho people, has resulted in a tribe of very varied
appearance.

There is the flat-faced, broad-nosed, thick-lipped MuVenda,
possessing all the common negroid features and varying in colour
from light to very dark brown. There is also a much more alert-faced
individual with sharp well-defined features, clear-cut pointed nose,
and moderately thin lips, presenting a distinctly Hamitic appearance,
which is accentuated among the old men by the fact that they wear
long undressed beards; this type is on the whole more uniformly
dark brown than their less aristocratic-looking brethren. Between
these two extremes are to be found every shade and degree of Bantu
facial type. They are of medium stature and in general physique
inferior to the coastal peoples, though strong and wiry and capable
of great physical endurance and strain. An interesting feature is the
fairly common occurrence among them of soft hair, which they call
by a special term, *hulele*, which differs considerably from the ordinary
more typical ulotrichous hair; this may possibly be derived from the
early Arab colonists, who are known to have mixed with the peoples
of Southern Rhodesia, probably at a time when the BaVenda were
living there. Small ears, small hands and feet and small dark brown
eyes are common among them.

Of 168 men and 56 women whom I measured, the average stature
was found to be 167·6 cm. for the men and 153·9 cm. for the women.
Head-measurements show them to be dolichocephalic, the average
cephalic index being 75·2. The nasal indices give an average of 92·3,
placing them well up in the platyrrhine division. Although these
measurements were determined from such a negligible proportion of

CLOTHING AND DECORATION

the population, they were taken in various different localities and serve as a fair indication of what results might be expected from a more comprehensive study. A complete list of the measurements from which these results were compounded will be found in Appendix II.

Psychical Characteristics.

The nature of the BaVenda is in many ways more complicated and difficult to understand than that of most of the Bantu tribes. This complexity is due to the variety of races and influences that have united to form their intricate character, especially the strong Hamitic strain so evident amongst them.

The old MuVenda is (Plate VIII) conservative and very suspicious of all innovations, cleaving to the customs and beliefs of his ancestors with a passionate tenacity. He is polite and hospitable, following the most elaborate etiquette in all his dealings. To the casual wayfarer he appears pleasant and an excellent host, but he never speaks of any but the most trivial matters to strangers; as soon as a visitor appears to evince a more than casual interest in his affairs, he, while retaining the outward forms of respect and attention, becomes suspicious and secretive, trying at every turn in the conversation to lead it into less personal channels. He replies to his visitors' interrogations with any answer but the real one, deliberately lying with all the outward appearance of speaking the truth; if his integrity is questioned he becomes dour and secretive, lapsing into a sullen reserve which is reflected in the black looks that he darts from time to time at his inquisitor. Much of this suspicious secretiveness is probably the outcome of the scandalous exploitation of the BaVenda by some of the early European settlers, which has made it almost impossible to persuade them that all their dealings with Europeans are not bound to result in their discomfiture.

In spite of this stubborn reserve the MuVenda is a cheerful, good-natured, pleasant fellow, always ready to take part in a dance or jollification. He is an inveterate conversationalist, possessing a dry humour which reminds one of the Scotch, always appreciating a joke even if made at his expense. He is slow to take up his weapons and will argue and talk and gesticulate in the face of extreme provocation, when a Zulu similarly provoked would have half-killed his aggressor. He is not a warrior, performing nearly all his warlike deeds by stealth and intrigue, rather than direct combat.

22 PHYSICAL AND PSYCHICAL CHARACTERISTICS

It is generally agreed by people who have lived for long amongst them that the average MuVenda is lazy but honest in his dealings. The former characteristic is partly due to the excessive heat and prevalence of fever in the summer months, making it hard to work without a very strong stimulus. Added to this, his industries, which occupied him in the old days, have been largely abandoned since the advent of the European trading stores, where for a few mealies he can purchase all commodities, such as clothing, ornaments, baskets, &c., that he once had to make for himself. He is now in the transitional stage, half-way between the old order of things and the new, cleaving tenaciously to the old, which is nevertheless inevitably giving way before the new.

In spite of the persistent conservatism of their fathers and their women, the young men have already lost interest in the old rites and traditions. Perhaps, when this difficult transitional period is over and the time for readjustment arrives, bringing with it new occupations and interests and improved methods of agriculture, this laziness, which is to-day one of the MuVenda's most outstanding characteristics, will give place to a new life of activity and interest.

Clothing.

Soon after birth a string of wild cotton is tied around the baby's waist, *ludedi*, which serves as a belt. Similar strings are also tied around its wrists, ankles, and neck. This is all the child wears until it begins to walk, when the clothing worn by boys and girls is differentiated. At this time the boy is given his first *tsindi*, an oblong strip of leather, made of goat's skin and sewn on to the *ludedi* in front; while he is very small it simply hangs down in front, but later is passed between the legs and fastened round the waist. The *tsindi* must be treated with care, and one sometimes sees a mother wearing this curious little garment around her neck, so that there is no danger of her little son mislaying it while he is at play; she is most particular to teach him the correct way to wear and care for it. A grown man's *tsindi* is made from the skin of a goat, klipspringer, or duiker. The whole skin is used excepting the lower ends of the front legs, which are cut off before the skin is softened; all the hair is removed, except two small patches on either side of the back and that on the ends of the hind legs. It is worn tied around the waist by the legs, the skin hanging down in front and being then passed between the legs and tucked into the belt behind; when it is fastened in position, the patches of

PLATE VIII

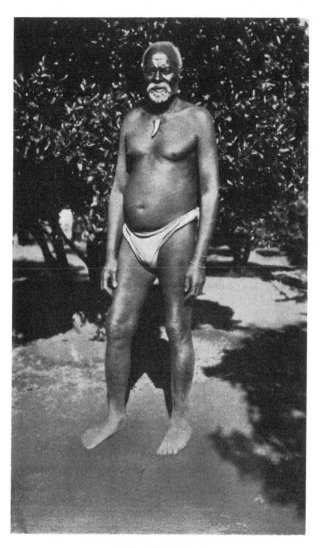

MUVENDA MAN

PLATE IX

MUVENDA WOMAN

CLOTHING AND DECORATION

hair that were not removed come over the buttocks. A man is always particularly careful of his *tsindi*, having been trained to this from his babyhood; when an old one is replaced, the discarded one is disposed of secretly, so that no enemy may discover the whereabouts of the garment that has had this intimate association with its wearer. In the old days it was the privilege of the very old to wear the *tsindi* hanging loosely in front as an apron, *mpinzhe*. The *tsindi* is the only essential garment of a MuVenda man but often, especially in cold weather, it is supplemented by a cloak, *nguvha*. This garment is made by the young men from a complete goat's skin, and by the old from a complete calf's skin, and is worn thrown over the back and tied round the neck by the two front legs.

Sandals, *thovho*, may be worn when travelling or working in the lands; they are made from strong, flat pieces of hide, projecting slightly above the foot on either side; small slots are made in the projecting pieces and a thong is passed from under the big toe, through one slot, across the instep, around the back of the heel, through the slot on the other side; it is then knotted over the instep and passed down again beneath the big toe where it is tied. To remove the sandals the loop behind the ankle is simply slipped down. Sandals must always be removed and carried in the hand before crossing the threshold of any village, as it is strictly tabu to wear them inside the village. It is becoming increasingly difficult to find a man or even a boy over 9 or 10 years of age dressed in his native costume; all wear a heterogeneous assortment of European clothing.

At the age when the small boy receives his first *tsindi*, the little girls have a small square of skin, taken from the stomach of the sheep, sewn on to the *ludedi*, which hangs down in front as a small apron. This is the first *shedu* and it is replaced, when the child is 4 or 5 years old, by a much longer strip, which is brought between the legs and tucked into the *ludedi* behind, where it hangs down in a flap over the buttocks. To-day the *shedu* is almost invariably made of cloth.

All married women wear the *tshirivha* (Plate IX). It is also worn by girls during part of their initiation ceremony. The *tshirivha* is made from the skin of a sheep or a goat. The neck and part of the front legs are cut off in a straight line and the skin is thoroughly softened; the softening is done by rubbing a mixture of cow-dung and water all over the surface of the skin and then well shaking and stretching it; it is stretched broadwise, being pinned down with *mutuni* thorns, three little gussets being cut and sewn up on either side to help

24 PHYSICAL AND PSYCHICAL CHARACTERISTICS

to shorten and flatten the garment; the hair is left on the skin; each leg has a small strip cut down it for ornament, and all the inside of the skin, which is worn uppermost, is decorated with innumerable small shavings, cut with a knife and left hanging in shreds; the ears of the goat are made up into small studs and fastened at the shoulder part of the skin on the decorated side, where they act as the 'eyes of the *tshirivha*'. The garment is considered to be very badly made if strict attention is not paid to all the details of stretching and decoration. It is worn around the waist, hanging down over the buttocks and the backs of the legs and sewn to the *ludedi* by the two hind legs, so that the tail and front legs with their two cut strips all hang over slightly, showing the hair, which is worn next to the skin. It is always made by the father, husband, or betrothed of the wearer. The *tshirivha* of a chief's wife is *tshiluvhela*. In the old days the *shedu* of a chief's wife was often made of *masila* cloth, the cotton material woven by the old BaVenda.

Old women, past child-bearing, wear a skin, similar to the *tshirivha* but made with the goat's skin complete with head and neck. This garment, *pale*, is stretched lengthwise instead of broadwise and the gussets are also cut lengthwise. The skin, when properly prepared, reaches nearly to the ankles.

Women used to wear a cloak of cattle or buck skin slung over one shoulder. This garment is never worn to-day, its place being taken by the *mwenda*, made of European cloth. It is a dark blue striped piece of cloth measuring about 3 feet by 6 to 10 feet, and is worn by the young girls wrapped around the chest, or more often pulled down and tucked around the waist, and by the older women generally fastened over one shoulder. Often blankets are worn in place of the *mwenda*.

Babies are carried on their mother's backs, secured by the *ngozwi*, which is a goatskin sling. The complete goatskin is used with the hairy side next to the baby. It is fastened round the mother's waist by the hind legs, and the forelegs are tied over the chest, one passing over the shoulder and the other under the opposite arm, and secured so that the child is held tightly against the mother's shoulder. The smooth side of the skin is ornamented with shredded strips larger and more roughly cut than those on the *tshirivha*. It is strictly tabu for a woman to remove the *ngozwi* from her back in any kraal except her own. If she is visiting, and puts the baby down on the ground to rest, she must tie the forelegs of the *ngozwi* round her waist. This is to avoid the possibility of leaving any hair from the *ngozwi* in a neigh-

CLOTHING AND DECORATION

bour's home, for danger might be brought to the child through magic practised on its essence left behind where the *ngozwi* had been put down.

Ornaments.

The BaVenda women do not wear a great variety of ornaments, being content with quantities of wire bracelets and anklets and strings of beads. At the first naming ceremony many children are presented with the *maphungo*, a waistband made of pieces of ostrich egg-shell, about ¼ of an inch in diameter, carefully rounded, pierced, and threaded. This is not an essential feature in the dress of a Mu-Venda girl, but it is usually worn by the families of chiefs and headmen and often also by ordinary people. Many girls wear a heavy beaded waistband, *tshiphunga*, from which long cotton fringes hang at either side, reaching the knees. The *thahu*, a curious funnel-shaped object sometimes seen tucked into the back of the waistband, will be described fully in connexion with the girl's initiation. The women all wear copper and iron wire bracelets and anklets, the wire being now purchased from the European traders and rolled into bracelets for the women by their men. These bracelets were made of twisted grass before wire-work was introduced to the BaVenda by the BaLemba, and, for some time after, only the chief's wives were allowed to wear copper-wire bracelets. These bracelets are the medium through which the Venda woman gratifies her craving for a change of fashion. Sometimes fashion decrees that 100 iron bracelets shall be worn next to the ankle, and 200 of brass or copper up the leg; at other times the numbers may be reversed; and changes are made from time to time in innumerable different combinations. Wives whose bracelets are old fashioned importune their husbands to make them new ones, so that they may feel well dressed and happy.

Young men often wear from two to four of these bracelets on each leg, just below the knee.

The wife of a chief used to wear ivory bracelets made from elephant's tusks, *malinga*. These are very rare to-day. She often wears a round flat piece of shell, *ndalama*, from the end of the conus mollusc; it is worn on the nape of the neck, usually forming a clasp to one of her bead necklaces. This shell is sometimes seen copied in ivory, and both the shell and the ivory models are very greatly prized by the wearer as they are unobtainable to-day. A porcelain imitation is sold by the traders, which is now worn by commoners as well as royal women.

26 PHYSICAL AND PSYCHICAL CHARACTERISTICS

The *ndalama* (possibly from *u dalama*, to live long), is similar to those worn by Ba-Ila chiefs and by members of innumerable east coast tribes. The Tshikaranga word for the same object is *ndarama*, which Lestrade thinks is certainly derived from the Arabic word for money. Among the old BaVenda it was only worn by royal women, on the nape of the neck, and no woman ever wore more than one.

Royal women also used to wear two white headbands to distinguish them from the common stock; the one made from ostrich egg-shell, like the *maphungo*, and called *ngoma* (drum) was always worn with a plain cotton string *mulisa* (shepherd) which was supposed to protect the *ngoma*; these bands are often seen to-day, but are no longer kept exclusively for the royal family. Old cowrie shells are greatly prized and are worn interspaced with beads on necklaces; the old variety are very scarce, but others can now be obtained from the traders.

Beads.[1]

The BaVenda are not great bead-workers and the common traders' beads are not so popular among them as they are among many other Bantu tribes. They possess, however, several different varieties of old beads which are of considerable interest; these are greatly prized by their owners on account of their age and rarity and are handed down as heirlooms.

Vhulungu ha madi (beads of the sea) are tiny, pale blue, translucent beads, generally worn only by the wives of important men and by women of the royal family. Netshitumbe, the BaNgona priest, possessed several strings, containing many hundreds of beads in all. He valued them so highly that he refused to part with a single bead at any price whatever. These little blue beads are the most highly prized of any, and are said to be very, very old.

Vhulungu ha mukuvhibvu are small, opaque red, beads.

Vhulungu ha tshimbandambanda are small and opaque, striped blue and white.

Limanda (powerful ones) are long, white, and opaque.

Matombo a Venda (Venda stones) or *mavadwa* are large, white or blue, translucent beads from $\frac{1}{4}$ to $\frac{1}{2}$ an inch in diameter. Some are white and opaque, speckled with tiny black spots.

Vhulungu ha denga are dark blue, cylindrical beads, almost opaque, about $\frac{1}{4}$ of an inch long with fairly regular facets cut over the surface.

---

[1] Many similar beads have been found by Miss Caton-Thompson at Zimbabwe and other Rhodesian ruins.

CLOTHING AND DECORATION

Beads of the smaller varieties used to be found among the Ba-Karanga, and are still found among Majaji's people and other groups in the Northern Transvaal. I heard rumours that some of these beads were of very ancient origin, Roman or Early Egyptian, but Flinders Petrie, who kindly examined some of my specimens, thinks all of them are post-Roman and show no Egyptian influence, except, perhaps, the dark-blue faceted beads. These, he says, might be either Byzantine or an imitation of Byzantine. However that may be, we know that the early Portuguese traded enormous quantities of beads with the natives of Monomatapa. Schofield,[1] in an article on the 'Ancient Workings of South East Africa', says that 'Father Moncharo in 1572 calculated that the profits on importing beads from India and selling them to the Kafirs for gold amounted to 3,000 per cent.'. Bent[2] speaks of 'large Venetian beads, centuries old', which he obtained from the BaKaranga near Zimbabwe. Possibly some of the Venda beads originated in India or Venice. The BaLemba all speak of journeying south trading beads and other luxuries, doubtless getting their supplies from Arab and Portuguese gold seekers.

Personal Decoration.

In the old days every man left a long tuft of hair to one side of the top of the head, to which, in war time, the badge, *tshiala*, of his particular group was attached. To-day the young men in eastern Vendaland generally shave all their hair behind a line taken from ear to ear, from just in front of the ears over the top of the head; this is *tshigula*. In the western area, where Sutho influence is strongest, the hair is usually shaved across the forehead and round the ears, *ndovho*.

Girls and young women shave all around the outside of the head, leaving an oval crown on the top, *tshivhundu*. The stylish young women let the hair of the crown grow long and comb it to the edge of the crown, smearing it down with fat into a thick rim. The hair is also beautified by being rubbed with charcoal and fat.

The men in the old days were all bearded, but to-day only the very old men keep their beards, nearly all the younger ones being clean shaven. Both sexes pluck out all the hair from the armpits and the pubes.

[1] Schofield, J. F., 'The Ancient Workings of South East Africa', *N.A.D.A.*, No. 3, 1925, p. 9.

[2] Bent, J. T., *The Ruined Cities of Mashonaland*, London, 1896, p. 296.

28 PHYSICAL AND PSYCHICAL CHARACTERISTICS

Scarification.

The only scarification that is done for purely decorative purposes is on the upper arms of the women (*philiphisi*). A piece of dried goat's dropping, or a mealie pip, is made very hot and put on to the chosen spot on the outside of the upper arm; the spot has first been prepared by smearing with ash, and when the arm has been thoroughly burnt the hot object is knocked off, taking with it the piece of skin that it covered. Usually from two to four marks are made horizontally or perpendicularly along the arm.

IV

THE VILLAGE, AGRICULTURE, AND DOMESTIC ANIMALS

Village—Huts—Agriculture—Cattle—Dipping—Other Domestic Animals

Village.

BEFORE the present peaceful conditions were established the BaVenda lived in large villages. Each village was ruled by a chief or petty chief and formed a strong, compact community, living inside an enclosure and ready at a moment's notice to mobilize in full strength to protect itself against surprise attacks of enemy invaders. These large villages exist no longer; the modern village is the residence of the chief and his family, important officials, and a few followers; it still serves, however, as the centre of all the public life of the district. When I visited Chief Mbulahene Mphephu's village there were 33 men, 73 women, and 113 children living there. The men included the chief, his officials, some of his subjects, who liked living under his protection in the capital, and two unmarried lunatics. The women included 10 of the chief's wives, 52 wives of his councillors and subjects, 9 royal widows (one being a widow of Chief Makhado and very old indeed), and 2 widows of commoners; 24 children belonged to the chief and the remaining 85 to the other inhabitants. In Chief Senthumule's village there were 33 men, 62 women, and 102 children, distributed in much the same proportion as in the village of Mbulahene Mphephu. Most of the important villages have about the same number of inhabitants. The above figures and information were obtained by visiting each hut in the two respective villages.

In some places dozens of homesteads are built in fairly close proximity to the chief's kraal, while in others an isolated kraal may be separated by many miles from its nearest neighbour. There is an increasing tendency for individual families to live farther from the chief, where they are more independent of him and can live their lives as they please, only attending the chief's village when specially summoned by him. Another new departure, made possible by the discontinuance of war, is for the people to leave their villages, perched on inaccessible sites on hill-tops or precipitous slopes, and build homes on the plains, where cultivation is easier and all the commodities of

30   THE VILLAGE, AGRICULTURE, AND

life, such as wood, water, and grazing, are more conveniently placed. Chief Mbulahene Mphephu's village is easily reached by a comparatively good road.

In the old days the site chosen for a village was always in some almost inaccessible position on a mountain slope or elevation, (Plate X) affording a wide view of the surrounding country, while remaining itself practically invisible. Kraals were also erected in the middle of dense bush, the builders making such apt use of the natural surroundings that a passer-by might go within a few yards of the dwelling unaware of its proximity. Even now the only approach to many villages is by a long, arduous, winding foot-path, zigzagging its way up the mountain side for three or four miles, the only water being a couple of miles away. The villages of Rambuda, Thengwe, and Lwamondo are all in such precarious sites. The entrance gate, *mafhoro*, opens usually into a large open courtyard, *khoro*, which may be 50 yards in diameter in villages built on the plains. The *khoro* is the playground and dancing place, law court, and reception hall for visitors; it is there that all the public affairs of the district are carried on. The *khoro* of a village on a mountain slope, where stones are plentiful, is usually enclosed by a stone wall; where stones are unobtainable a stout palisade is made from thick wooden stakes, *phupu*, dug into the ground almost touching each other and making a very efficient enclosure. The stakes forming the palisade round the chief's kraal are always pointed, but this is tabu to a commoner. A large long stone is sometimes embedded in a vertical position on the top of the stone wall, similar to the phallic stones on the wall of the acropolis at Zimbabwe; there are two such stones on the wall of the *khoro* of Milaboni's village, one engraved with concentric circles (see Plate VI, facing p. 8). One or two large trees are left standing near the middle of the *khoro* to provide shade. The cattle-kraal, *danga*, is generally on the left side of the *khoro*, with kraals for calves and goats, *zwitumba*, on the right, and open stables for horses and mules in any convenient place. At the far side of the *khoro* a gate, *tshivhana*, leads into a maze of passages, yards, huts, granaries, and beer-huts. Where the walls dividing the huts and yards are made of upright stakes close together, the bottom half is often plastered with a thick layer of mud projecting sometimes a foot or more.

Within the village each family is more or less self-contained in its own enclosure; each wife is responsible for her kitchen, *tshitanga*, large hut, *ndu*, and yard, *muta*, and keeps the latter well plastered with cow-dung and sometimes painted in a geometric design in white and

PLATE X

NETHENGWE'S VILLAGE

PLATE XI

HUTS IN COURSE OF CONSTRUCTION

DOMESTIC ANIMALS

red ochre. The chief's granaries and beer-huts, &c., are in any convenient place behind his hut; he has also a special stamping-ground, situated generally just through the *tshivhana*; this hut varies in size and is made of thick poles one or two feet apart supporting a thatched roof; from four to twelve wooden stamping-blocks are sunk in the floor. In many kraals on the left of the *khoro* there is a well-protected path leading to a private hut, *thondo*; this is the small boys' school and sleeping-quarters and is always strictly guarded. There is also another hut of a more or less public character, *tshivhambo*, which is built in its own yard near the *khoro* and is surrounded by a stout fence of stone or wood and earth; this may be used as a meeting hall, a guest-room, or for any other purpose for which an additional hut, in comparative privacy, is required. Sometimes a small sleeping-hut, *khombo*, is provided for the bachelors, to the left of the stamping-hut.

The chief's hut, *pfhamo*, is always the richest and largest in the village and is usually decorated in crude colourings with red ochre and charcoal. It has a side veranda and the best outlook over the country. Towards the back of the hut, on the right side, there is a small and very private roofed yard, *vonga*, where the chief's meat is hung and cut up; only the chief himself, his sons, and his chief wife may enter it. At the present time many chiefs have susbtituted European houses of brick and iron, entirely spoiling the picturesque, unsymmetrical, yet harmonious character of the group of huts.

Smaller kraals of individual families are miniatures of the larger communities. Only the chiefs have the *thondo* and *tshivhambo*, but a courtyard, cattle and goat kraals, a beer-hut, and granaries are found in nearly every kraal, and every wife has her own hut and yard, and often her own kitchen.

Huts.

Before making any preparations for hut-making, the prospective builder, having selected an apparently suitable position, consults a diviner. If the dice show that the site he has chosen is unfavourable, he will select another, until his choice is pronounced by the diviner to be propitious. The medicine-man then marks the site with sticks specially prepared for the purpose of warding off evil. Four sticks, *mbambo*, are rubbed in a mixture of the powdered roots of the *mutavhatsinde* tree, the *tshiralelo* tree (*u rarela*, to surround), the *murombe* tree (*u omba*, to peg), and the *muzwile* tree (*u zwila*, to take away all power, or hypnotize); these sticks are laid north, south, east, and west.

32 THE VILLAGE, AGRICULTURE, AND

Another specially prepared stick, *luvhambo*, which is rubbed in the powdered root of the *mpeta* tree (*u peta*, to fold up) is nailed down at the entrance gate, *mafhoro*, so that every person entering or leaving the village must step across it. Sticks and grass from the old building must on no account be used as material for the new. After the medicine-man has been paid with a goat or beer, the house building may begin.

The work is shared by the men and women, all wood-cutting, timber-work, and thatching being done by the men, while the women cut the grass and do the plastering. Sometimes the ground is marked out in a circle by a string, one end of which is attached to a peg knocked into the ground and the other attached to a man's foot, and drawn around the peg at full length. If the ground is hard, a trench is dug along this line, and the uprights, stakes about 6 feet high and 3 or 4 inches in diameter, are put in position close together, and the trench stamped down. When these are in position, flexible sticks are placed around the inside and laced with withies to similar sticks placed on the outside in three places, at the bottom, middle, and top, making the structure firm (Plate XI).

The framework of the roof is made separately on the ground. Four long poles about 5 inches in diameter are tied together near one end where they are nicked to keep the bark string from slipping. The other ends are then pulled apart wide enough to stretch across the framework and overlap about 3 feet. Between these four poles other thinner ones are arranged, and concentric circles of smaller boughs are laced around this structure a foot apart, a branch running inside and outside and being tied with bark with the same technique that is used in making the wall. The framework is then pulled about to make a rough circle, lifted on to the wall, and adjusted until it fits. The roof is not tied to the wall structure but fastened to uprights fixed about 3 feet outside the wall to meet the 3-foot overlap of the roof poles, forming a veranda. The wall framework is next plastered by the women, the plaster being usually a mixture of puddled ant-hill, cow-dung, and ashes. Sometimes the plastering is only done on the inside, but more often both inside and outside.

The hut is then ready for thatching. The long thatching grass is tied into small bundles, which are themselves tied together in a line 20 or 30 feet long. The whole is fastened around the lower end of the roof, with the uncut ends pointing towards the peak and reaching about half-way up; then similar bundles of smaller grass are tied

DOMESTIC ANIMALS

together in the same way and fastened on starting from the bottom and working upwards in a spiral to the top; this method of thatching gives the bottom of the roof a double layer. The cap is then fitted; it is made by inserting a stick 2 or 3 feet long into the middle of a tied bundle of grass, letting it stick out about a foot at one end; the lower end of the stick is thrust down the peak of the house, and the grass pulled out, part of it making a waterproof cap, and the rest being tied neatly around the stick spire, which is so characteristic of Venda huts.

In the huts of important persons a veranda wall may be built up 2 feet from the ground with mud plaster. The floor of the hut is made with ant-hill earth, which is well watered and beaten hard with sticks. A door is often woven with sticks and withies, and put across the entrance at night.

The fire, *tshivhaso*, is made in the middle of the kitchen; occasionally a special fire-place may be built, slightly raised from the level of the floor in two or three concentric circles. The three cooking-stones, *matswia*, are always beside the fire. Two poles, *mitambi*, are fastened horizontally to the top of the wall opposite the door; in front of them there is a small rack for food, *vhurala*; there is always a forked wooden peg, *tshifhande*, just inside the door, on which the man of the house can hang his hat. The sleeping-mat, *thovo*, hangs on a stick that is fastened between the left-hand pole and the forked peg. One or two wooden blocks, *mituli*, in which grain is stamped, are sunk in the floor on the right of the door. The pots, baskets, and calabashes that are in daily use are kept by the wall on the right of the door.

In the sleeping-hut, *ndu*, there is sometimes a small fire-place just to the right of the door. The man's sticks and axe are kept against the wall just beyond the fire, and beside them his spear and sacred objects. Fat and dried meat are kept in this hut. Poles and a rack are fixed under the roof as in the kitchen. The man's washing-bowl, *sambelo*, and plate, *ndilo*, are kept on the rack. Drums and other large possessions may be kept outside the hut, under the veranda. A great many pots and calabashes are kept in the beer-hut, *sosa*, ready for use. In fine weather it is customary for the women to transfer the kitchen fire to the yard outside and there to cook the morning meal. Occasionally huts, and even yards, are painted with geometric designs, concentric circles, lozenge and chevron patterns, and in some cases with more complicated designs, although no information is forthcoming as to the symbolic meaning of any decoration. The decoration on huts is done by painting

D

34 THE VILLAGE, AGRICULTURE, AND

the mud walls with red, black, and white or yellow colouring. The black is simply charcoal mixed with water, the white a watery clay, and the red and yellow colourings are made from ochre.

Agriculture.

In common with most other Bantu people of South Africa, the BaVenda economic life is influenced by a mixture of the pastoral and hoe cultures. Whilst being great lovers of cattle they regard them more as a source of wealth than as a means of livelihood and depend for subsistence almost entirely upon agriculture. Fortunately, arable land is plentiful and every man can obtain the usufruct of as much land as he requires for himself, his wives, and other dependants.

The chief and head-men have large cultivated areas worked by the compulsory unpaid labour of their subjects. The ordinary people have only small gardens, varying from $\frac{1}{2}$ an acre to 2 or 3 acres, a man's piece always being larger than that of any of his wives. People living in the hills and mountains make use of every available patch of ground, planting their mealies in among stones and rocks and on precipices, where no European farmer would attempt to clear the ground or plant. In many parts of the country wild animals and birds play havoc in the lands; the only means of preserving the crops is to watch them night and day, scaring away intruders by shouting and singing (Plate XII). Overlooking many lands, on a prominent rock or ant-hill, small shelters, *dzitumba*, are erected which give protection and shade to these watchers. Sometimes the dangers to the crops are so great that whole families migrate into temporary houses in the lands, living there altogether throughout the planting and reaping season.

Where there is enough water for irrigation, crops can be grown throughout the year. The fertility of the soil and the general climatic conditions make the production of crops comparatively easy, except to the north of the Zoutpansberg range where the rainfall is small. In spite of these natural advantages the slothful character of the average MuVenda prevents him from doing more than the minimum amount of work necessary to maintain life and enjoy occasional festivities. The same land is used for many successive seasons, there being no idea of the rotation of crops, although sometimes a plot of ground is left fallow for a year and a piece of virgin soil cultivated in its stead.

Where one family is living in isolation the land may be hedged in with thorn bushes, but in other parts, where the lands of different members of a community are side by side, there are no enclosures. In

PLATE XII

LOOK-OUT FROM WHICH THE CROPS ARE WATCHED

GRANARIES

DOMESTIC ANIMALS

these places the live stock is always herded, the different lands being divided from each other by deep furrows, grass baulks, or stone beacons. There is no regularity of size or shape in the plots; each individual knows his own boundaries and respects those of his neighbours. There is nothing to prevent a foot-path going right through the lands. Everything on each plot belongs exclusively to its owner, who may leave large logs of valuable wood or bundles of reaped mealies without any fear of their being appropriated by some one else. The clearing of the lands is done by men, who cut, burn, and prepare the ground for tilling. The tilling is done mainly by women, who simply turn up the ground with hoes; but a man who owns a plough usually ploughs up his wives' lands as well as his own. A man does a certain amount of work in his own garden, assisted by his male relations. He calls his wives and womenfolk to help with the tilling and expects them to keep the garden free from weeds. He may enter his wives' gardens at will and take whatever he wishes from them, but he is expected to pay for anything he obtains from them apart from his food. In times of scarcity he allows them to eke out their produce with the help of his own, but his stores are generally kept in reserve until the women's are all exhausted. Each wife is solely responsible for the cultivation of her own garden. The youngest wife, until after the birth of her first child, has no garden of her own, but works in her husband's. No wife may enter her husband's garden without permission. Wives often barter the produce of their gardens among themselves.

Clearing, weeding, and harvesting is often done in a semi-communal way. A large quantity of beer is prepared and any neighbour may join in the work, and afterwards in the beer-drink. This is a popular and efficient way of lightening the arduous work and appears to be a fundamental factor in the Venda agricultural system.

The usual time for planting the main crop is in October or November after the first rains. The staple crop is maize, *tshikoli*, which is grown extensively. Kafir corn, *makhaha*, is also very popular. Both are used for beer-making, but the favourite beer is made from eleusine, *mufhoho*, which is the indigenous Venda cereal, and, although only scantily grown in some parts, is used whenever possible for the beer of the great harvest festival.

Besides these, millet, sweet potatoes, beans, pumpkins, water melon, vegetable marrow, and monkey-nuts are all cultivated in considerable quantities. The grain seeds are scattered broadcast; often two or three varieties of cereals may be seen growing together. Lately missionaries

THE VILLAGE, AGRICULTURE, AND

have introduced oranges, paw-paws, and bananas; these are all well suited to the climate and are slowly gaining popularity among the less conservative people. The following is a list of the staple crops and the times of sowing and reaping:

Crops.	Month of Planting.	Month of Reaping.
Maize, *tshikoli*	October to February	May to July
Kafir corn, *makhaha*	September to December	May to July
Mixed seeds, *mavhele*	October to February	May to July
Eleusine, *mufhoho*	November to December	May to July
Millet, *luvhele*	October to February	June to July
Beans, *nawa*	November to February	May to July
Pumpkins, *phuri*	November to February	April to July
Water-melon, *mabvani*	September to November	April to July
Marrow, *maranga*	October to December	April to May
Monkey-nuts, *nduke*	October to January	May to July
Ordinary ground-nuts, *phonda*	December to January	May to June
Single round ground-nuts, *nduhu venda*	December to January	May to June
Small potatoes, *matambale*	October to December	May to July
Gourds (big), *tshikumbu* (small), *phafana* (double), *mukumbu*	October to January	March to July
Sugar-cane, *impye*	October to December	January to May
Tobacco, *fhola*	October to February	January to May

When the crops are ready for reaping, the women collect all the cobs or heads in large baskets, which they carry back to the granaries (Plate XII) near the homestead. Large quantities are often carried long distances on a V-shaped sledge, made from the fork of a tree, and drawn by oxen. The corn is threshed on a specially prepared earthen floor; the heads are tied together and then beaten with a small wooden flail about 18 inches long, made of a smooth piece of wood roughly triangular in shape; the debris is cast aside and the seed brushed up ready for stamping.

Granaries. Maize is stored in a variety of ways. The cobs may be tied together by the covering sheaths and slung across a horizontal pole, raised about 2 feet from the ground. Sometimes the cobs are stripped of the covering sheath and put into a circular crib without a roof, also raised 2 feet from the ground. Mealies are shelled by rubbing the cobs against flat stones; they are often stored in large funnel-

DOMESTIC ANIMALS

shaped pits below the cattle-kraal. To make these pits a hole about 3 feet wide is dug down for a few feet, and then gradually widened, until at its base it is some 7 feet in diameter. The pit is dried out by a fire kindled inside it, and the whole is plastered with mud. The mealies are then thrown in and the mouth is covered over with boughs, plastered with cow-dung, and finally covered with earth at the level of the cattle-kraal. When mealies are required the mouth is opened and then resealed. These pits vary in size and are sometimes large enough to store 100 bags of mealies. Wessman[1] says: 'the chief Pafuri once secured a band to perform music in such a store-hole, all the black musicians finding room below ground'. Kafir corn is stored in the open. A platform is erected on forked sticks, and on this the corn-heads are packed very tightly. The whole is then covered with grass, and a thorn fence built around the stack to keep off fowls and other domestic animals. It is stacked with sufficient pitch to enable the rain to run off freely, and the free access of air keeps it in good condition for some time. Millet is also stored in a miniature hut, 3 feet in diameter, with mud floor and walls and movable grass roof, the hut standing 2 feet above the ground. The heads are packed down tightly, and removed as required by lifting up the roof. Pumpkins are put on the ground of the veranda; they are sometimes cut into slices about an inch thick and the seeds scraped out, and the rings of fruit are threaded on to a stick and hung up. They will keep in this way for a long time.

Cattle.

Before the coming of the European only the chiefs and important headmen owned cattle, the ordinary people using hoes as the medium in the lobola of wives. According to early hunters and travellers in the middle of the nineteenth century, cattle were subject to the ravages of the tsetse fly, although the scourge was then rapidly disappearing from the Northern Transvaal. In 1896 the Venda herds were further depleted by the great outbreak of rinderpest which devastated the cattle over nearly the whole subcontinent. Since that time they have been steadily increasing, until to-day practically every man has at least one or two head of cattle, and many, particularly the chiefs, have large herds numbering several hundred head. In spite of sporadic outbreaks of East Coast fever, and the frequent years of drought, the cattle are still showing a steady yearly increase. There is

[1] Wessman, R., *The Bawenda of the Spelonken*, London, 1908, p. 23.

38 THE VILLAGE, AGRICULTURE, AND

now a distinct danger of the country becoming overstocked with these very inferior animals.

Possibly when the BaVenda migrated across the Limpopo to the Zoutpansberg district they were still a fully pastoral people, possessing large herds of cattle, which did not respond favourably to the new environment and died in great numbers, until only the powerful chiefs could still afford to keep them. The people then developed their agricultural work, to which their new country was eminently suited, absorbing into their tribe the indigenous people who were probably agricultural. For a time hoes, the emblem of agriculture, were substituted for cattle for the payment of lobola. But in spite of this easy absorption of an agricultural culture they retained their love of cattle and, as soon as conditions improved, commenced to re-establish their herds. Cattle once more became the insignia of wealth and the medium of lobola. Probably during the interval many of the tabus and regulations associated with the Hamitic culture of a pastoral people were lost. To-day women may possess cattle as well as men, and they are not bound by as many rigidly enforced tabus in their behaviour towards cattle and milk as most Bantu women are; it is customary for the man to do all such work as herding and milking, but when there is no man at home a girl may take his place and fulfil all his duties with the cattle, except during menstruation or after an abortion, when it is feared that the contact might cause the cattle to be sterile.

Venda cattle are of the common long-horned, straight-backed type, small but sturdy animals well adapted to the rugged mountainous country and to the bushveldt. They are able to exist in times of drought, when there is practically no grazing, on the nourishing shrubs and trees with which the country abounds. The *mupani* tree, which contains a high percentage of turpentine, flourishes in some districts; there the cattle thrive and have particularly fine and glossy skins. If some new breed could be introduced it would be possible to raise up fine herds, using the native cattle, which are acclimatized to the conditions, as a nucleus. As it is, they are economically of little value, giving very little milk and being too small for good meat, their sole virtue resting in their sturdiness. There is no method of selective breeding, the cattle running indiscriminately with each other, although sometimes a man may send some of his stock to a friend for a time, and in this way the danger of constant inbreeding is unwittingly avoided. This custom of exchanging cattle probably originated for the

DOMESTIC ANIMALS

39

purpose of decreasing the danger of loss from disease or enemy raids. The people all have an innate affection for their cattle, and generally distinguish each animal by name. They distinguish the different colours, shape of horns, &c., with unerring accuracy, and an owner can tell by one glance at his herd whether an animal is missing. The BaVenda do not depend on their stock for subsistence, and the poorer people, who can seldom afford to kill an animal, collect them for the sole purpose of lobola; the richer people gain prestige by the possession of a large herd. Chiefs and important people often kill an animal for feasting; they also always present an honoured visitor with a beast, driving several animals in front of him so that he may choose the beast that he favours; the visitor is then given a gun and cartridge and asked to shoot it on the spot.

The cattle are seldom sent out to graze before 11 o'clock in the morning, and during the early part of the day suffer a good deal from heat and flies, standing penned up in the kraal. The BaVenda explain that they have found that ticks are most troublesome in the early morning and that cattle sickness is caused when the cattle eat grass before the dew is dry. Some insist that during the hottest part of the day the ticks go underground, and that by keeping the cattle penned up until late in the morning they manage to minimize this dangerous evil. While out grazing the cattle are in charge of boys, who are responsible for their well-being and for keeping them from straying into the lands. After reaping they are allowed to feed among the stalks. Where water is easily obtainable they are driven down to drink daily, but where it is scarce the animals are often only watered every two or three days. At sundown they are driven back to their kraals. The calves are herded separately near to the kraal, the very young ones remaining all day in the cattle-kraal or *khoro*. Milking is done in the morning, just before the cattle are sent out. If a cow is inclined to be wild a string is passed through the nose and around the back of the horns and the animal held by a pointed stick. The cows are milked into large wooden, mug-shaped pails. The milker sits on his haunches on one side of the cow and holds the vessel between his legs. When the milking is finished the young calves are allowed to drink. For the first few days after a cow has calved the milk is boiled and eaten by the herdsmen in the cattle-kraal and not taken to the house. There is no tabu on the milk from a cow that has aborted, or whose calf is born dead, although the cow is usually left to dry up. Twin calves with their mother are always given to the chief.

THE VILLAGE, AGRICULTURE, AND

To-day castration is practised fairly extensively, the wound being rubbed with ash or salt. Oxen are used for riding, ploughing, and haulage. Cows and bulls are often yoked with oxen to the plough. When training oxen the BaVenda sometimes treat them very cruelly, beating them severely and even burning grass round them, or pouring water over a stubborn animal that refuses to get up from the ground.

Very little is understood by the BaVenda about the diseases of cattle, and epidemics are quite beyond their control. There are a few general methods of treating the more ordinary illnesses. If the placenta fails to come away after the birth of a calf the cow is given a drink of cow-dung mixed with water. Cow-dung is also rubbed on the mother's teats to prevent her calf from sucking. A cow that dies while calving may not be eaten by women. Ophthalmia is cured effectively by the application of the milky sap of the *musose* tree. Sometimes, to assist in diagnosis, the top of the animal's ear is cut off, or a few slits are made in it, and the blood given to a medicine-man to examine. A new kraal is built if disease is constantly appearing amongst a herd of cattle, and the medicine-man concocts medicine of the roots of the *mutavhatsinde* and *mpeta* trees, which the owner mixes with water and sprinkles over the cattle as they enter it for the first time; some of the medicine is also rubbed on the stick which is buried in the entrance of the kraal to keep away disease. A broken leg is put into a rough splint, and if this treatment is not effective the animal is killed.

Killing cattle. There is in most important villages a cattle slaughterer. Although the position is often hereditary, he must have a reputation for successful killing, and if the meat of cattle killed by him is bad or tasteless his office will be transferred to a man who can succeed in producing good sweet meat. In small kraals any man may act as slaughterer. The actual killing is associated with a good deal of ceremony. The slaughterer with one assistant approaches the doomed animal; it is tabu for any one else to take part in the killing as there is always a chance that an onlooker may have bad blood which might contaminate the animal's blood and so turn the meat bad. The animal is killed by a spear-thrust behind the shoulder from a spear that has, been rubbed in a mixture made from dried blood of steenbok and the powdered root of the *u-kona-nguluvhe* tree (to beat the pig); some of this mixture is forced into the animal's mouth; as the spear strikes home the slaughterer holds his own nostrils and mouth tightly shut

DOMESTIC ANIMALS

so that by sympathetic magic the animal will have difficulty in breathing and so die quickly. If there is a MuLemba living in the village he quickly comes forward and cuts the animal's throat while it is still breathing, as it is tabu for the BaLemba to eat the flesh of any animal unless its throat is cut before it dies. As soon as the animal is dead the slaughterer cuts off the small pieces of skin round the navel; this is later stuck on the pointed stick at the entrance to the *khoro* to bring good luck and fertility to the cattle. After this all the men of the village gather round the carcass. Women may not approach until a piece of fat has been taken from the stomach of the animal (cut out through the skinned patch at the navel), mixed with the leaves of the *vhova* tree, and passed down the length of the animal, symbolizing the cutting in half of the danger. A fire is always lighted near the carcass as soon as the animal is dead; before skinning, the lower lip is cut off and roasted at the fire for the slaughterer. Three or four men generally help in the skinning and dissection. The two front and one back leg are first cut off, the helpers taking a small strip from each as their perquisite. The carcass is then opened and all the internal organs, except the kidneys, are removed. The skin is then put down inside a hut and all the meat arranged on it ready for distrbution.

Division of Meat. One hind leg is sent as a present, *musumu*, to the district chief; it is put in a *mufharo* basket with a lid; no commoner is allowed to have his food carried in a basket with a lid. The other hind leg and the head are sent to the owner's father; this is also called *musumu*. The neck is sent to his mother's brother (if a child has a short neck the mother's brother is supposed to be able to lengthen it by massage). The chest, stomach, intestines, and udder go to his mother, as the BaVenda associate these parts with the relation of mother to son. One foreleg goes to the father's brother. The meat extending from the ribs to the inside of the thigh on one side goes to the chief wife; the corresponding part on the other side goes to the father's sister; these parts are considered the daintiest portion of the animal. The kidneys go to the mother's mother, or failing her, to the mother's father, or to the mother herself. The tail and the four hoofs and the meat surrounding the heart and lungs go to the cattle-herd. What remains of the carcass belongs to the owner; he gives the liver to his children and may distribute the remainder among his and his wives' relatives; sometimes the family is so large that the owner has hardly any left for himself. If another man tans the skin he receives the hump as payment.

42 THE VILLAGE, AGRICULTURE, AND

Dipping.

The severe outbreaks of East Coast fever among the native cattle have necessitated the compulsory dipping and hand-dressing of all cattle in or near the infected area. This regulation is threatening the social value of cattle to the BaVenda. The whole system of dipping is consequently regarded with bitter hatred and antagonism, the individual owners being quite unable to understand the danger of an outbreak of the fever, except in the few districts where it has practically wiped the cattle out. The grievances are many, and to a large extent justifiable. In the first place, on fixed days all the cattle must be driven to the nearest dip, which is sometimes as much as five miles from the kraal, and the owner must wait about for several hours until it is the turn of his cattle to go through. The complete day is therefore taken up with journeying to and from the dip, leaving the cattle no time for grazing. Whenever an outbreak of the disease occurs the district is in quarantine for 15 months, and the frequency of dipping varies between 4 to 14 days. In districts where 4-day dipping is in vogue the cattle that have to be driven from a distance lose 7 days' grazing in every 28 days, invariably resulting in their losing condition and becoming unable to stand the strain of dipping. This, combined with the shortage of food in the dry season, results in a great many deaths. Another grievance is that cattle rushed to the dip, overheated from ploughing, contract chills, or get blistered by the dipping solution and the hot sun. Additional dipping tanks are being built as quickly as possible in convenient positions, but many natives have already suffered severe losses through the enforced dipping before there were an adequate number of dips. The dipping expenses have to be met to a large extent by the natives. In the locations the dipping-tax has been merged into the general tax, payable by every adult, it being taken for granted that sooner or later every man will possess cattle and make use of the tank. A levy of 5s. per annum is made on natives in crown territories, whilst on private farms anything from 1d. to 6d. per head is charged. This appears to the native a money-making scheme on the part of the white people. Added to all this, no cattle may be moved from one area to another without a permit, which can only be procured with difficulty from the local dip inspector on certain specified days; permission to remove cattle is often refused. All animals which have died or been slaughtered for food must be reported and portions of the carcass sent to the local inspector for analysis. The infringement of any of these regulations

DOMESTIC ANIMALS

is severely punished with a fine or imprisonment, so that the keeping of cattle is becoming a burden, as they are a constant source of expense and trouble. Money is growing in importance as a medium of exchange and is steadily taking the place of cattle in various transactions. Cattle which, in the ordinary way, would change hands in the payment of lobola or fines, are now obliged to remain in the kraal of the original owner, although they are no longer his. The new owner gets no benefit and, when the same cattle change owners two or three times, the system becomes complicated. In parts of the country the usual lobola is compounded by the payment of £40 or £50 in money, and this custom is spreading. The old custom of sending a black bull annually to the Matoba Hills in Southern Rhodesia as an offering to the deity, Raluvhimba, in propitiation for rain, has been abandoned, as the movement of cattle across the Limpopo was forbidden. The core of the bracelets, which every MuVenda makes for his wife, is composed of the tail hairs of cattle, and, owing to the enforced clipping of tails, these are no longer obtainable. Thatching-grass may not be moved without permission for fear of spreading the infection. The whole system is regarded by the natives as a new method of extracting their money, and they insist that quite as many cattle die through the effect of the dip as ever did through the disease itself. The new Chief Phaphuli, on his accession, sent a particularly thin ox as a present to the Native Affairs and Police officials at Sibasa, apologizing for its extremely bad condition, but explaining that it was owing to the dip. The gift was accepted, and a message of thanks returned by the officials, who added that they too were sorry the animal was so thin, but were nevertheless very grateful to have it at all, as, if it were not for the dip, it would most certainly have been dead!

The MuVenda does not and cannot understand that the country has probably reached the limit of its cattle-raising capacity, therefore, when unusual drought periods occur, local losses are bound to be severe, and although dipping undoubtedly does account for many deaths, these would have occurred in any case owing to the drought. Some localities have been particularly unfortunate, but on the whole figures show that the cattle are still increasing steadily. For instance, the official figures obtained from the Sub-Native Commissioner at Louis Trichardt show that in Mphephu's location the total number of cattle in 1924 was 2,767; in 1925, 3,038; and in 1926, 4,058, the last in spite of a severe drought. Possibly, had a cordon been placed around the whole country and the movement of cattle

44 THE VILLAGE, AGRICULTURE, AND

beyond it been prohibited, a great deal of discontent would have been avoided. Instead of the rigid enforcement of compulsory dipping, which is so disliked, the natives would have continued free movement as before within the cordon, and would have been obliged to work out their own salvation with the East Coast fever. Sooner or later the disease would have reached such menacing proportions that assistance would have been solicited from the European authorities and the dipping system could then have been established.

Other Domestic Animals.

Sheep and Goats. Both sheep and goats are kept by the BaVenda. The former are not numerous, but every one possesses goats which among the poor people take the place of cattle. Goats are milked into a clay pot, held in one hand, while the milking is done with the other. They are usually kept in a small kraal behind the cattle-kraal and are herded during the day by very young boys. In some kraals the left side of the kitchen is fenced off with wooden stakes to make the goat-pen. The goats are of the long-haired type and very hardy; they fulfil a number of uses, providing meat, clothing, and milk, and serving as lobola and as sacrificial animals. A goat has its throat cut with a knife that has been smeared with the same mixture as that used on the spear with which cattle are killed. The stomach is punctured and the meat is then considered fit to be eaten; after being skinned the parts of the goat are disposed of in the same way as those of cattle, except that none is sent to the chief. Women are not allowed to kill cattle or goats, but they may kill pigs.

Pigs. The pig is a modern introduction and is still scarce, its flesh being considered a great delicacy by all the BaVenda, although it is strictly tabu to the BaLemba. Pigs are fattened by being imprisoned in small pits in which they are only just able to move; they are killed by having the throat cut. To facilitate removing the animal's hair a hole is dug in the ground and lined with grass; the carcass is put into the hole and covered with more grass; boiling water is then poured over it, and the hair is plucked off easily.

Fowls. Fowls are said to have been introduced by the BaLemba. There are two types, the common small hybrid variety and a curious tailless bird found in various colours and quite different from any known domestic fowl; these birds have an upright poise, the head, neck, and back being in one straight line like an Indian Runner duck; they have no trace of a tail, and are said to be the result of the ordinary

DOMESTIC ANIMALS

fowl interbreeding with wild birds; the eggs are very small. Fowls are left to fend for themselves, although occasionally they may be given a handful of mealies. They usually roost in trees near the kraal. Few chickens can be reared in the summer months on account of the diseases and lice, so that the eggs are eaten at that time, while in the winter they are left to be hatched out.

Horses and Mules. Horses and mules are a comparatively recent introduction; most of the chiefs possess some. Horse sickness is so prevalent that horses require a great deal more care and attention than the BaVenda seem able to provide. The late Chief Mphephu had at one time fifty horses, and it was customary for him to travel the country on horse-back, followed by a large mounted retinue in single file. To-day Mbulahene has only three left out of his father's stock.

Dogs. Dogs of the long, lean mongrel type are very popular, and with proper handling can be trained as excellent and trusty bush-dogs; some hunters keep a pack of them. Periodically medicine-men treat them magically, rubbing medicine on eyes and nose to quicken their senses. A dog that gets its teeth into a buck and then lets go has his teeth well rubbed by the medicine-man to prevent a repetition of the disaster. Frequently the dogs get caught in traps set for wild animals and soon learn to remain perfectly still until their owner discovers and releases them. Usually the first pup of a litter is killed, as there is a vague idea that otherwise the mother will not be able to feed her other offspring.

Cats. Cats are regarded with suspicion and fear and are rarely killed by adults; a man will often take his cat far away into the bush and leave it there to go wild rather than kill it.

V

FOOD AND NARCOTICS

Food—Beer—Snuff—Smoking

Food.

THE staple food of the BaVenda is porridge, *vhuswa*, made from maize meal (mealies). It is generally accompanied by a supplementary dish, *tshisevho*, made from meat, green food, or some other delicacy, which is served on a special dish and always contains the salt.

Maize, for the daily porridge, is prepared by the women at the expense of much time and labour. The grain is slightly moistened and then stamped with wooden stampers in a hollowed block of wood sunk in the kitchen or yard. In the chief's village there may be special huts with several of these stamping-blocks (Plate XIII); often two women stamp together in one block, sitting on the floor in their customary position, and brushing the meal into the hole with small grass brushes; they thump alternately in the wooden block with great force and energy. The grain is then winnowed in large flat basket lids, being tossed up and down repeatedly, so that the fine grain separates from the coarse. The husks are removed and the grain sorted and the stamping and winnowing repeated, the whole process taking several hours. The meal is then put on the roof of the hut to dry and bleach; the finished product is cleaner and finer than the meal of any of the neighbouring tribes, being quite as fine as our flour and pure white. The meal is cooked by stirring it into a pot of boiling water and simmering it until it is of the consistency of thick porridge; it is then shaped into thick oval cakes, piled on to large wooden platters, and left to cool; when cool the cakes are easily separated and eaten with the fingers. Whole or crushed maize is also boiled for food and the green mealies are very popular in the season. The *tshisevho* may be prepared from any food-stuff other than cereals. Monkey-nuts are ground up and baked into hard cakes; beans and all sorts of green foods, including stinging-nettles, black-jacks, figs, berries and wild apples, are boiled, or sometimes eaten raw; other delicacies are caterpillars, locusts, crickets, and ants. The favourite caterpillar is a fat hairy variety, the *mashonzhe*, which is prepared by squeezing out the inside and burning off the prickles, the rest being dried and boiled as required; during the season, when the grub is plentiful, parties go out collecting it,

PLATE XIII

STAMPING

WINNOWING

FOOD AND NARCOTICS

47

leaving patches of charcoal dotted over the bush, where they have been removing the prickles. Locusts and flying ants are also collected in large quantities when procurable, and after the wings have been removed are boiled and dried and then used as required. Crickets and small insects are eaten by the children, either raw or slightly roasted; they irritate the creatures by pricking at their holes with small pieces of grass, and pounce on them as soon as they emerge.

Milk, mafhi, when sour, makes a popular *tshisevho*, goats' milk being preferred to cows'. Cows' milk is transferred from the wooden vessel into which it is milked into a clay pot, to which more is added every day, until it is quite sour. Sometimes the pot is supported on a stand, and a small hole made in the bottom to allow the water to run off, leaving the solid curd. Goats' milk is warmed in the small clay pot, into which it is milked, and then left for a week to sour.

Eggs, kumba, are hard boiled and eaten fresh. They are not eaten by women.

Meat, nama, is consumed in enormous quantities in almost any degree of decomposition. People will travel for miles in the hopes of obtaining a piece of meat or some blood, the fact that an animal died of disease in no way deterring them. It is cooked by roasting on a stick, and only boiled when it is desired to extract the fat. Where game is plentiful the men obtain wild buck or birds fairly frequently; they are particularly fond of cane-rats and ant-bears. Every part of an animal may be eaten except the valves of the heart, which are always cut out and thrown away. The following animals are never eaten: the lion, leopard, cheetah, lynx and all animals of the cat species, the dog, hyena, jackal, mongoose, crocodile, and all snakes. Certain birds are also tabu, noticeably the vulture, eagle, hawk, owl, crow, stork, hammer-head, kingfisher, secretary-bird, heron; also the bat. The intestines of the ant-bear and porcupine are not considered fit to eat, as the one is very earthy and the other very bitter. The intestines of the pig are seldom eaten, as the pig's anatomy is considered to be very similar to that of the human being.

Fish, khovhe, is not popular, and probably used to be entirely tabu; the old people still regard it as a type of snake and never touch it. To-day a woman will not have it brought near the house and will never eat it, although it is often caught and eaten by young boys.

Salt, muno, is plentiful in the soil in some parts of the country. It used to be extracted by putting the salt-containing earth in pots, and pouring water over the earth, which trickled through holes in the

48 FOOD AND NARCOTICS

bottom of the pot into another receptacle; this liquid was then evaporated. Where it could not be obtained in this way it was exchanged in trade. It is considered an important and essential article of diet, and to-day is always bought from the European stores.

Fat, nona, is used for smearing the body and as the basis for many medicines and ointments, but not for cooking. There are two ways of preparing it; animal fat may be boiled down, or butter made by collecting cream in a calabash and shaking it up in a pot.

Beer.

Beer, *halwa,* is consumed in enormous quantities in times of plenty, doing service as both food and drink to the average MuVenda. It is an essential factor in their diet, and to the question, 'What is your favourite food?' every MuVenda returns the same invariable reply, '*Halwa!*'. The whole social system of the people is inextricably linked with this popular beverage, which is the first essential in all festivities, the one incentive to labour, the first thought in dispensing hospitality, the favourite tribute of subjects to their chief, and almost the only votive offering dedicated to their spirits. Every host prepares beer for his guests as a token of his friendship and goodwill. If an unexpected visitor, whether a friend or a stranger, calls upon him and he has no beer ready to offer his guest, his first words are profuse apologies for being obliged to give his visitor such an inhospitable reception. At reaping or harvesting time large quantities of beer are drunk, and no one rumoured to have prepared beer need fear any shortage of labour in his lands; everybody who is able hastens to his assistance and willingly does a share of the work, in joyful anticipation of the beer-drink to follow. A favourite song after emptying the beer-pots runs: 'Joyful! Joyful! The world is full of pleasure.' The men's beer, *mutetshelo,* is served in a special large pot brought to them by the youngest wives of the host; the bearer tastes it, to guarantee its quality, and hands it to her husband who has a long drink before passing it on to his most important guest or relative; it is passed round the assembly, more or less in order of seniority and status, each man taking a long draught before passing it on to his neighbour. Only very old and highly respected women are permitted to drink with the men from their pot. The women's beer, *musendelo,* is brewed separately and served in special calabashes and never drunk by the men. When they collect together to drink at sowing and reaping, it is considered a gross breach of etiquette for men to intrude on a women's beer-drink, and vice

FOOD AND NARCOTICS

49

versa. On all festive occasions at least five pots and calabashes of beer are provided, a pot for the head-man and his chief councillor or relative or honoured guests, a pot for the old men, a pot for the young men, a calabash for the old women, and a calabash for the young women; at very large gatherings a pot and calabash is provided for each age-set. The beer is to-day often ladled out in long-handled cup-shaped calabashes which are used as cups, but this is a modern innovation. There seems to be no limit to the capacity of the BaVenda for drinking beer, pot after pot and calabash after calabash being consumed as long as any beer remains. The effect is exhilarating and exciting, making the drinkers quarrelsome and argumentative rather than intoxicated. Excessive beer-drinking partly accounts for the lazy, slothful character of the average MuVenda and for the heavy dropsical frame of the typical middle-aged chief. Beer can be made from most grains, the fruit of the *murula* tree, the leaves of the prickly pear, or the sap of the fan palm. *Mufhoho* (eleusine) beer is the most popular, and when there is not much *mufhoho*, maize or other grains may be used for the foundation and a little *mufhoho* added for fermentation. This beer is made in the following way: The heads of corn are beaten on a clean smeared place and the corn carefully winnowed to remove all the dust. It is then soaked for two days in covered pots of water and put into baskets until it begins to germinate, when it is spread out in the sun and stamped; this part of the process is *u tomba*. The following day it is mixed with water and boiled for most of the day and then left to cool; this is *u bika* (to cook). At this stage a small quantity of grain which has been set aside to germinate is added to the bulk, and the whole mixed thoroughly and closed up in a large pot for a day, when it starts fermenting; this is *u sutshela* (to mix). The next day it is strained through a sieve into other large pots; this is *u tuda* (to strain); in another day it is ready to drink.

Murula beer is made by chopping up the fruit and putting it into small pots of water, and squeezing all the fruit up inside the water; all the pips are removed and the concoction left for a day; the white scum is then taken off, and the beer put into large pots, which are covered with leaves and sealed with cow-dung; after four or five days the pots are opened and a little earth made by white ants is added to give it strength; it is then ready to drink.

The prickly pear, *mukonde*, makes a strong, highly intoxicating drink; it is greatly relished, but is taken in moderation as it causes acute diarrhoea. It is made as follows: Quantities of the fruit of the prickly

E

FOOD AND NARCOTICS

pear are collected and laid on the ground, and the fine hairs, which cause intense irritation to the skin, are carefully scraped off with the help of soft leaves. The fruits are then cut open and the fleshy part put into a big pot where women squeeze them into a soft pulp with their hands. This is left till the following day when it is strained through fine branches into clean pots which are lightly sealed with cow-dung and the beer left to ferment for three or four days, when it is ready to drink.

Palm wine, *vhutshema*, is made from the sap of the *mulala* tree (the fan palm) which is very rare in the Zoutpansberg but plentiful in Southern Rhodesia; the wine is made in large quantities by the BaVenda living there. The leaves are all removed from the top of the palm-tree, the tip cut off slantwise and a small groove made at the lower end of this cut. The sap runs off this groove and trickles into a horn or calabash that is tied under it; this is emptied two or three times a day and at the same time another piece is shaved off the top of the tree. The sap is protected from flies and the sun by a basket inverted over the top of the tree. The wine may be drunk immediately, but if it is left for a day or two it becomes very strong and intoxicating and is greatly relished.

Snuff.

Tobacco has been grown by the BaVenda for a very long time, but until quite recently was only used for the manufacture of snuff, *fhola*, and was never smoked. Snuff is used freely by everybody after puberty, and is either inhaled up the nose or put between the lower lip and the front teeth. It is prepared in a special clay pot, *luwiende*, with rough incisions on the inside, giving it a rough surface. Dry tobacco leaves are put into the pot and ground up with a stick, the ribs of the leaves are removed and the rest ground very fine, and then mixed with charcoal obtained from a special tree, *tshitavhamisi*, and the mixture again ground up together, resulting in a strong black concoction which is dried by the fire, damped, and put away to dry finally. Many different receptacles are used for holding snuff, the most popular being the hard, egg-shaped fruit of the *mutusa* tree.

Smoking.

Hemp is smoked, but not very extensively. The Venda pipe consists of an ox-horn partly filled with water, into the mouth of which is placed a hollow reed attached to a clay or stone pipe-bowl. It is unlike

FOOD AND NARCOTICS

the usual pipe of that type, where the reed and bowl are actually attached to the horns towards the pointed end. The smoker inhales by placing both hands over the opening and around the reed and drawing through the aperture made by slightly parting the hands. The smoke passes through the water at the bottom of the horn. It is taken in huge breaths, and exhaled with great coughing and spluttering. Usually about half a dozen of these mighty draws are sufficient to produce the desired somnolence.

VI

INDUSTRIES

Pottery—Calabashes—Woodwork—Basketry—Wirework—String—
Weaving—Skin-dressing—Ivory—Iron—Copper

Pottery.

THE art of pottery is almost entirely in the hands of the BaLemba women, although to-day there are also a few Venda potters who have learnt their trade from the BaLemba. The pots are of a simple type and well made (Plate XIV); although made by women, men may help in the firing. They are modelled out of clay, mixed with water and sand, and well-puddled to the required consistency; the potter models her new pot on an old potsherd, smoothing it as she works with a piece of moistened leather; the top is shaped by the addition of small strips pressed into shape with the fingers. The larger type of pot is built up from the base with small lumps of clay. Both types are completed by being rubbed inside and outside with wet leather. A pot may be simply decorated; often a line is traced with a thorn, about 2 inches from the lip, and sometimes a small pattern of dots is pricked around the line. The newly-made pot is left for a couple of days to dry and then fired in a slow fire kept burning around it for a day. Glazing is sometimes done with graphite and the smoke and soot, which are rubbed into the pots when in use, give them a glazed and shiny appearance. After the firing the pot may be further decorated, the strip above the dotted line being often blackened with charcoal. There are six types of pot:

Nko, the big beer-pot is between two and three feet in diameter; a large size can hold five gallons of beer. This type is only used for storing beer, and is kept in the special beer-hut. (Some chiefs also keep stores of beer in large holes sunk in the ground and lined with clay, which can contain many gallons).

Mvubelo is a beer-pot of a size that is convenient for carrying; it is the type of pot in which beer is always served, and for that reason it is often decorated.

Khali and *tshidudi* are smaller than *mvubelo* and used for cooking, the former for porridge and the latter, which is slightly smaller, for green foods.

Tshidongo is flat and saucer-shaped, measuring about a foot in diameter. It is used for serving the *tshisevho,* never for cooking.

PLATE XIV

POTS
1. *Mvubelo* 2. *Khali* 3. *Tshidudi* 4. *Tshidongo*
5. *Luwiende vha fholi*

CALABASHES
1. *Tshikumbu* 2. *Khavho* 3. *Tungu*

INDUSTRIES 53

Luwiende vha fholi is a small, wide-mouthed pot about 8 inches in diameter, serrated inside; it is used for crushing tobacco for snuff. This type of pot is often known by the Sesutho word *tshisilo*.

Sambelo is a large shallow wide-mouthed bowl, decorated by a line pattern round the circumference inside and out; it is the man's wash basin.

Calabashes.

The calabash, *tshikumbu*, is used for holding water and beer. The vessel is made by cutting off the stalk-end of a suitably shaped calabash to form a mouth 3 to 4 inches in diameter. The seeds and soft pith are removed leaving an extremely light receptacle varying in capacity from $\frac{1}{2}$ to 3 gallons. The very largest type makes a resonator for the *deza*, a BaLemba musical instrument. The smaller drinking-vessel is called *pafhana*.

Another type, *khavho*, has a long narrow neck and is used for ladling out beer and as a drinking-vessel. It is made by cutting a circular hole in the side of the calabash, leaving the long narrow neck as a handle. A small hole is often pierced in the end of the handle to hold the string, by which it may be hung up.

A fourth type, *tungu*, is shaped like a cottage loaf with the opening made in the top; it is only used for sacrificial beer.

Snuff boxes are made out of a very small round calabash about $1\frac{1}{2}$ inches in diameter. A small hole is made in one end and a wooden stopper inserted. (The fruit of the *mutusa* tree is often used instead of the tiny calabash; some old men possess this type of snuff-box covered with lead foil.)

Woodwork.

Woodwork is in the hands of specialists who inherit the art, the son learning from his father; they are not differentiated by any social distinction. There is generally a woodworker living in the vicinity of the chief's capital, who is responsible for executing his orders. The most important article of woodwork is the drum.

Drums. There are two types of drum, the *ngoma* and the *marimba* (Plate XVII, facing p. 56). The *ngoma* is large and bowl-shaped; the top is about $2\frac{1}{2}$ feet in diameter, curving into a small saucer rim at the base. It is carved out of a solid piece of wood from any soft-wooded tree such as the *murula*. On the upper part of the outside of the drum, six, or sometimes only four, twisted handles are carved in loops crossing

INDUSTRIES

over and under each other, thus forming corners. Decorative carving in curved lines, chevrons, and circles is done between the handles. The inside is hollowed out leaving the shell about 1 inch thick all the way round. All the work is done with an axe and a small sharp adze, and entails considerable time and patience on the part of the artisan. A small hole is burnt in the base, and holes are burnt around the mouth about 3 inches apart, to hold the pegs by which the skin is attached. An ox-hide is stretched across the mouth, the hair only being removed from a small patch in the middle. A narrow strip of hide, 1½ inches wide, is put round the edge over the holes, and small pegs hammered through this strip and the skin underneath keep the tympanum in position. Before the tympanum is attached a few pebbles or other small objects obtained from the medicine-man are put inside. The larger drum with the six handles is played strung from a simple wooden framework, and the rather smaller instrument with the four handles is slightly canted and played on the ground.

The *marimba* is also carved out of a single block of wood. It is of the tube type, 6 to 9 inches in diameter at the tympanum end and about 2 feet high; it has a long handle and is very similar in shape to the large wooden milking vessels. It has a tympanum of ox-hide stretched over the mouth and secured with wooden pegs, like the *ngoma*. The bottom end is generally open and slightly smaller than the mouth end; sometimes instead of the opening, there may be three or four holes burnt in a closed end.

Milk jugs. The *khamelo* is made from a solid block of wood, 18 inches high and 6 inches in diameter, with a thick handle running down the whole length. The jug tapers slightly at the base, which is finished off with a small projecting rim (Plate XV).

Round Wooden Platter. The *ndilo* is cut from a solid slice of a tree about 4 inches thick and 12 inches in diameter, cut down to a fairly solid plate with a slight lip around the edge.

Cups. The *tshiashi* is occasionally carved out of wood with a long handle, and is similar to the long-necked calabash.

Spoons. The large wooden spoon, *lebula*, similar to our own, is a modification of this wooden cup, having a shallow bowl. I am told that these spoons are an old Venda craft and were made long before the European occupation.

Porridge Stick. The *lufheto* is made from a wooden stick about 2 feet long; at one end two holes are bored about 2 inches apart, at right angles to each other; wooden pins about 4 inches long are inserted

PLATE XV

PLATTER AND SPOONS

MILK JUG

PLATE XVI

WOODEN DOOR FROM TSKIKOBAKOBA'S KRAAL

INDUSTRIES

through the holes. An ordinary branched stick is often used instead of this more complicated utensil.

Stamping-block, mutuli. A solid block of wood, about a foot in diameter and 18 inches high, is sunk in the floor of the hut so that the top is level with the ground. A hole about 5 inches in diameter and 4 inches deep is hollowed out in the middle of the block which, with continued stamping, becomes wider and deeper until the whole block is worn away when it is replaced by a new one.

Stamper, musi. The corn is stamped in the *mutuli* with a heavy wooden stamper about 3 feet long with a club end to give it additional weight. The Venda method of grinding corn differs from that of all their neighbours. The BaThonga use a wooden mortar and stamp, but the mortar is not sunk in the ground and the stamp is longer than the Venda type. In their case the work is done by the women standing, whereas the Venda women stamp in a kneeling position.

Wooden door, vhoti. The Venda wooden door is cut out of a solid block of wood; it is about 4 feet long by $1\frac{3}{4}$ feet broad, and from 1 to $1\frac{1}{2}$ inches thick. The door is cut with two small projections, one at either end, which fit into two sockets, one in the floor and one on the wall above the doorway, making a swivel joint for opening and closing the door. One face is engraved all over with large concentric circles, spirals, chevrons, diamonds, dots and triangles. These doors are very rare. I was fortunate in discovering three at the kraal of Tshikobakoba, near the Presbyterian Mission at Gooldville (Plate XVI).

Carved Divination Bowl, Ndilo ya lufhali. This also shows fine workmanship and will be described in detail in connexion with magic.

Wooden Models. The only other wooden manufactures of importance are the images of man, woman, goat, and leopard, and the short sticks used in the *domba* ceremony. Considerable skill is shown in the carving of these models; at one time the man and woman were sometimes made out of ebony, although to-day they are made of any wood. Although roughly carved, a certain scrupulousness of detail is observed, the outstanding characteristics of each object being faithfully reproduced and in some cases exaggerated. The bodies of goats and leopards are often considerably elongated. The short sticks consist of the upper half of a man or woman about a foot long carved quite realistically in the solid wood, tapering below the hips and buttocks to a fairly stout stick, the whole being about 2 feet long. The models reproduced in Plate XXXI belong to the Chief Mphephu; they are fairly small, the man being 18 inches and the woman 24 inches in

56 INDUSTRIES

height, while the leopard and goat are about 12 and 10 inches long respectively. Markings are either burnt on, or painted in red, white and black.

Basketry.

There are two types of basket among the BaVenda. Men make the *mufharo* basket and those of similar technique (Plates XVII and XVIII). These are of true Venda origin, differing entirely in method of construction from the *tshirundu* or *dani*, made by women, which are the same type as those made by a great many other Bantu. Both types are beautifully made, the *mufharo* being particularly striking on account of its well-fitting lid and the unlikely material from which it is fashioned. The *mufharo* basket is made of thin slivers of wood from branches of the *muluvho* tree. Pieces of branch are cut off the length that is required for the height of the basket, and other longer lengths for the circumference, the pieces being about an inch in diameter; from this material quantities of strips are shaved off with a sharp knife, the edges being cut parallel. These slivers are interwoven in a diagonal check pattern, one strip going over and under two, to form a rectangular mat, the length depending upon the size of the basket required. The ends are then brought together and the projecting strips interwoven, forming a belt with one end drawn into a slight waist; the ends are so neatly interlaced that they leave absolutely no sign of the method of construction. A smaller square mat is woven in a similar fashion to form the lower part of the basket; the edges of this square are drawn up into a hoop made from a twig of the *mulambila* (or *mufharo*) tree, to which the mat is bound with bark string; this part of the basket is called the *thahu*, the name of the funnel-shaped object worn by girl initiates for a week after their first initiation. The *thahu* is then soaked and manipulated to form a nicely rounded base, one foot being used to force it into the required shape. The waist end of the belt is eased into this base portion, and another hoop fitted inside, opposite to the one already attached; the two hoops are then tied firmly together, fixing the two parts of the basket in position. All the ends are cut off and trimmed and the two hoops are bound with the help of a small awl. The open end of the basket is bound to another hoop, the rough ends cut off, and bound with bark. Throughout the process the material is damped, eased and forced into the required shape, resulting in a strong rigid basket. Sometimes the basket is decorated by the substitution of two or three black wefts, making diagonal line patterns.

PLATE XVII

BASKETS AND SLEEPING-MAT
1. *Mufharo and Luselo*   2. *Tshirundu tshakholomo*
3. *Tshidani*   4. *Mutudo*   5. *Thovo*

DRUMS
1. *Ngoma*   2. *Marimba*

PLATE XVIII

BASKET-MAKING

INDUSTRIES

The black weft is a strip of the same *muluvho* tree from which the white strips are made, but it is cut from the heart of the branch and on being soaked turns black. A lid is made in the same way, a woven mat being bound to a hoop and manipulated and carefully adjusted until it fits the basket tightly.

Lids are often made separately and are used as trays and winnowing fans. There are three different sizes, *luselo*, the largest size, *tshiselo*, the next size, and *tshiselowana*, the small size.

A large basket, *tshirundu tshakholomo*, is made with the same technique; this type is used for carrying corn. In the old days these baskets were made very big indeed, and one filled with grain could be exchanged for a head of cattle; they have no lid or waist, the hoop being fixed at the base of the basket with the sides coming straight up.

The *dani*, *tshidani* and *tshisisi* are chiefly used for carrying grain, and are of the coil pattern common throughout Africa, the Venda having imitated the Thonga type. This type of basket is made from withies of the *tshiumbiumbi* and bound with the fibre of the *musese* tree. The work commences at the base, and the withies are coiled round and round, until the basket is of the required size. Each coil is stitched to the following coil by bark fibre, with the help of a small awl. The sides are gradually worked up from a small flat base, increasing in size regularly up to the wide mouth. The base has a slight upward depression to facilitate its being carried on the head. The work is done very finely and neatly, some of the baskets being practically watertight. Often a piece of hide is stitched over the base to give it additional strength. Both types are made in a number of sizes, from a quite small basket, 9 inches in diameter, to a very large grain carrier, which may be over 2 feet across the top. The *tshivhanga* is a small square basketwork bag, made from the dried leaf of the *mulala* palm, with a long loop attached at either end of the opening; this is drawn through the top of the well-fitting cover, which is slightly larger than the bag itself; to open the bag the cover is slid along the string. These bags made in several different sizes are favourites with the traveller; they have been copied from the BaThonga among whom they are very popular. The *tshisenga* is a large, approximately round basket, probably of BaSutho origin; it is used for storing mealies after they have been taken off the cob; it is made of grass coils bound with bark and is about 4 feet in diameter, slightly flattened at the bottom with a small mouth about 6 inches in diameter at the top. When full of mealies this mouth is closed with cow-dung.

INDUSTRIES

The Beer Strainer, mutudo, is also woven from the *mulala* palm. It is made by men with the same technique as the *mufharo,* the leaves being woven flat and then twisted into a long narrow tube 18 to 20 inches long and 3 inches in diameter, tapering down to a closed end.

The Sleeping Mat, thovo, is of the usual Bantu type, made from long flat leaves of the *jesi* which are tied in twos and threes and laid flat, and then all laced together by string sewn across the ends and the middle.

Wirework.

Copper wire for making bracelets used to be obtained from the BaLemba, but now all wire, whether iron, copper, or brass, is obtained from the European stores. Bracelet-making is not very difficult; (Plate XIX) every man makes bracelets and anklets for his wives, the extent of his affection being assessed by the number of bracelets he manufactures for her. Several hairs from the tails of cattle are twisted into a circle of the required size, forming the core over which the wire is wound; the wire runs through a split stick to prevent it from kinking and to keep it fairly tight; it is then started by a couple of twists round the hair, made with the hand; holding the wire in the left hand and placing the hair-ring on a flat board, a roughened end of horn is drawn firmly over the initial twists towards the worker's body, revolving the core; at the same time the left thumb keeps the wire pressed firmly in position and controls the operation. In a very short time the whole hair core is covered and the end of the wire is nipped off and neatly fastened. In this way a good artisan can make from 60 to 100 bracelets a day. Sometimes arm bracelets are ornamented by having small copper or metal beads inserted at intervals.

String.

A number of different materials are used for making string, but the most common and probably the best is made from the bark of the *muvhuyu* tree. Long strips of bark are cut from the main tree, and the fine fibres are twisted together by being rubbed rapidly between the hands and the thigh, the movement always in the same direction. Two threads made in this way are again twisted together, forming a strong pliable cord, capable of standing a considerable strain. Lengths of string are wound neatly on wooden spools ready for use when required.

Weaving.

Weaving is now a dead art. A fine cloth, *masila,* was formerly woven on a simple loom, from thread made of the seeds of the *mudala* tree,

PLATE XIX

WIRE BRACELET-MAKING

PLATE XX

BELLOWS

AXE, ADZE, HOE-HEAD

INDUSTRIES

59

a species of wild cotton. This cloth was a favourite article of trade. To-day small pieces of the cloth are greatly valued and kept as heir-looms.

Skin-dressing.

This art is also dying out, as European clothes become increasingly popular. The fresh skin is pegged down on the ground and cleaned and dried. It is next scraped with a knife and rubbed with a stone, and then worked between the hands for several hours until it is soft and pliable. Skins to be used for clothing or karosses are sometimes tanned. A mixture made from buck fat and the fruit of the *mutanzwa* tree is rubbed on to the skin. Strips of skin are soaked and softened and used as reims. Often a great many small skins may be tanned and cut evenly and sewn with sinews to form karosses, which are used as blankets at night. Occasionally small pill-box-shaped caps are made out of fine skin. The manufacture of the skin clothing and sandals has been described in connexion with clothing.

Ivory.

There is no trace of skilled work in ivory to-day, although it is probable that it was practised at one time in the making of bracelets, as the BaVenda carried on a very extensive trade in the raw material, which their hunters collected in great quantities. It was sold to Europeans until the destruction of Schoemansdal. It is used to-day in the manufacture of divination dice.

Iron.

Iron smelting among the Venda is extinct, but it used to play an important part in their industrial life; they probably brought the art with them when they first came to the Zoutpansberg. Although the BaLemba were the chief metallurgists and themselves insist that they taught the art to the BaVenda, it seems probable that the BaVenda understood it even before these two peoples became interdependent, as, when it was first observed in Vendaland, there were two methods of smelting. The one described by Junod[1] is the built up kiln method, and the other, described by a very old and respected MuLemba, Ramazhizhi, living near Louis Trichardt, is a method of smelting in big earthenware pots. Some idea of the old art of metallurgy can be obtained from the descriptions of people who encountered it at an earlier date. Junod says: 'These Bveshas—the word is said to be a

[1] Junod, Henri A., *The Life of a South African Tribe*, London, 1927, p. 138.

INDUSTRIES

Thonga corruption of Venda—built their furnaces in ant-hills, . . .
They excavated three holes under the furnace and blew into them by
means of bellows made of skin, the air being expelled through an
antelope horn. The ore, broken in small pieces and mixed with
charcoal, was smelted, crushed, melted a second time, crushed again
and made into hoes and axes, &c.' Ramazhizhi described the furnace
made of earth beneath a large clay receptacle which contained the
iron ore, the blast being obtained from bellows made of cow-hide.

Bellows, mvuto. The Venda bellows are made out of the whole skin
of a goat or buck. When the bellows are to be made of goat's skin the
animal is skinned alive, as this is thought to strengthen their power.
The head and legs of the animal are chopped off and the holes left
by the forelegs and one of the hind legs are sewn up. A wooden pipe
or horn about 18 inches long is fixed into the hole left by cutting off
the other hind leg; this is the nozzle which goes into the furnace. The
tail is left on the skin. The hole at the neck is trimmed and
strengthened by the inside of the skin being turned over for about an
inch on to the outside; through the double thickness a loose leather
thong is threaded and knotted, and in the middle of the back of the neck
it passes loosely through two holes, 4 inches apart, in a flat wooden slat
about a foot long and $\frac{3}{4}$ of an inch wide, made from very hard wood.
The bellows are always worked in pairs; the operator squats on his
haunches, a hand through each of the wooden slats, steadying both
bellows by a foot on each of the projecting tails; he works the bellows
alternately up and down and the wooden slat acts as a valve, causing
the complete closure of the hole at the neck between each blast and
so preventing an escape of air and waste of energy (Plate XX).

Iron-work all over Africa is associated with tabus, secrecy, and
magical practices. The ambivalent attitude of contempt and fear so
typical of a Hamitic pastoral people towards a people who work with
their hands is still preserved towards the BaLemba, but little of the
inner life of the ironworkers or of their art has survived. Beuster[1]
writing in 1879 says:

'they restrict themselves chiefly to the making of iron hoes. The iron stone
is brought by carriers in return for a certain quantity of corn fixed by the
people of those mountains. It is then melted and handed over to the smith
for the making of hoes; he understands how to make quite serviceable implements with his primitive stone hammer, working on a stone that serves as an

[1] Beuster, C. L., 'Das Volk der Vawenda', *Berlin. Zeits. Ges. Erdk.* 14, 1879,
p. 239.

INDUSTRIES 61

anvil. According to ancient custom the smith mixes human flesh in with the molten metal to make good hoes, or if there is none handy he will use the flesh of the dead. In earlier times these hoes were exported in thousands to neighbouring districts; at the present time, however, the trade seems to be diminishing.'

Wessman[1] also described the Venda forge. He says:

'The ore was derived from the so-called iron mountains on the other bank of the Lewuwu river, and was carried in baskets to Bavendaland, where it was treated. The furnaces are about 5 feet in circumference, and built (of clay) right into the ground. By means of small holes at the bottom and bellows, a blast was sent into the furnace enabling the temperature to be raised and maintained at white-heat, though a small proportion of the iron was always lost in this process, the bulk was found finally in the shape of a layer block at the bottom of the furnace. Thus the raw material for making different articles was obtained. Communal workshops were used, mostly situated near the public road, and consisting often merely of a shelter against the sun, supported by a few props. The interior of the forge was very primitive, a large, flat-topped stone serving as anvil; other stones as hammers; and wooden sticks had to take the place of tongs. Charcoal, which was used for forging, was obtained from specially suited kinds of forest trunks. Thus all agricultural implements and moreover axes, arrowheads, assegais, knives, &c., were produced in the Bavenda country until European industry with its cheap productions killed the interesting and ancient native iron industry.'

The chief iron manufactures were large hoes, which formed an important medium of currency and were traded in quantities with the neighbouring tribes, particularly the BaThonga, who were not iron-workers. Axes, adzes, spears and arrowheads were also made extensively. Native-made iron weapons and implements are to-day so rare that they are generally regarded as sacred objects by their owners and thought to possess some of the personality of the dead ancestors who originally used them; they are jealously guarded and small pieces are often used for the manufacture of powerful charms. The implements were made by allowing the molten metal to run into rough clay casts, being afterwards hammered into the required shape.

The Hoe, dzembe, is about 18 inches long and 6 inches wide at the broadest part; the implement is roughly diamond-shaped, slightly rounded at the working end and tapering into a spike at the opposite end. A faint rib is visible running up the centre of the blade.

The Axe, mbado, is a flat, triangular-shaped implement from 9

---

[1] Wessman, R., *The Bawenda of the Spelonken*, London, 1908, pp. 28–9.

INDUSTRIES

to 12 inches long and 1½ to 3 inches wide at the base, tapering to a spike.

The Adze, mbadwana, is a similar but smaller flat triangular-shaped implement about 5 inches long and 1 to 1½ inches wide at the base, tapering to a spike.

The hoe, axe, and adze are all inserted by the spike into a hole burnt through the rounded end of a heavy wooden handle, the blades of the hoe and adze being set at right angles to the handle (Plate XX).

The Knife, lufhanga, is shaped like a small spear-head; it is about 6 inches long with a tang just long enough for a hand grip and bent over at the tip to form a ring; it is carried around the neck by a string passed through this ring. These knives are the rarest of all the old native-made iron implements.

The Scythe, luvhida, is a short curved blade 2½ inches broad, ending in a spike which is driven into the end of a wooden shaft 2 feet long; it is a very popular implement, but is to-day always bought from the European stores. The battle-axe, spear and arrowhead will be described in connexion with warfare.

Copper.

Copper work, which, like iron, has to-day been superseded by European manufactures, was practised by the BaLemba (Plate XXI). Most of the work consisted of the making of bracelets and ornaments, although at first only the chief's family and the BaLemba themselves were permitted to wear the ornaments. The BaLemba were feared on account of their superior intelligence and were never allowed to work in the chief's lands but were obliged to pay tribute in pots and copper ornaments in lieu of service. Many parts of the Zoutpansberg are rich in copper. Mr. J. M. Calderwood, M.I.M.M., kindly sent me the following interesting manuscript entitled 'Notes on Ancient Workings for Copper Ores at the Messina Mine', which I here quote in full.

'At the Messina Mine situated in the extreme north of the Transvaal near the Limpopo River, extensive ancient workings for copper ores extending over a considerable area have been traced from the Limpopo southward for a distance of over 25 miles. On these workings are located the present-day mining operations at Messina and their existence led up to the discovery of copper ores in this section of the country. In the same neighbourhood evidence still exists of the copper ores having been smelted by the ancient workers. The bases of crude furnaces, broken clay pipes, slags, ashes, and small pieces of ore have been found, and small copper castings have been obtained from natives residing in the district, which it is claimed were the

PLATE XXI

A MULEMBA

INDUSTRIES

products obtained by crude smelting operations by the old time workers. The smelting appears to have been carried out on an extensive scale at M'Singalele Kop about 2 miles east of Messina, where most of the relics have been found. At Messina and on the adjoining farm Vogelzang several lines of workings have been located along the fissures in the granite and in which the copper bearing lodes have been found and the lodes are now being worked to a depth of 2,000 feet at Messina and 1,200 feet at Vogelzang. The old workings are claimed to be more extensive than anything so far found either in the Transvaal or Rhodesia.

'The workers appear to have extracted all the rich ore found at surface and to have continued down by inclined excavations to a depth of about 80 feet in many places. It is not clear why work was stopped at a given depth, as several workings when cleaned out exposed good copper ore, but in the deeper workings it is probable that the easily smelted carbonate ores gradually changing to sulphide or copper glance made smelting operations difficult, or it may have been that water level obliged the workers to suspend mining at greater depth. Some of the workings are quite narrow where the width of the lode is small and sometimes intervening country rock has been left standing. Small round vertical shafts have been found, put down through the overlying strata to cut the copper lodes below, and in some cases connected with the larger inclined excavations. These old workings appear to have been systematically filled in by hand with loose debris right up to the surface. At Messina, the richest ore shoot so far discovered lies immediately underneath an extensive old excavation which at surface had a length of about 200 feet by 20 feet to 40 feet in width, and is known locally as the Bonanza Lode, and has proved by present day mining to extend to over 2,000 feet in depth, yielding remarkably high grade massive copper ores of chalcopyrite, bornite, and glance.

'The old workers appear to have employed fire to heat the hard rock faces, then cracked the rock by throwing water on the heated surfaces, using short roughly made iron gads, operated by the aid of unshapen rounded stone hammers without handles, to break down the ore. These crude implements have been found at surface, and also buried in the debris in the workings. When the ore was carried to surface, it is evident that it was broken up and cobbed down to eliminate waste rock, making thereby a rough concentrate which was ultimately carried to the smelting furnaces. Large heaps of this broken waste have been found around the excavations.

'It has been difficult to obtain reliable information locally regarding the history of these ancient workings. It is probable that the same race which worked for gold and copper in Rhodesia also worked at Messina before the time of the modern natives. Local chiefs and headmen of the BaVenda tribe in this district appear to think that these old mines were formerly worked by a tribe subject to Ramabulana and that he was afraid that the richness of these possessions would lead to depredations by the Zulus and therefore ordered all workings to be closed down and filled in. The legend of Chaka's

INDUSTRIES

expedition to obtain copper seems to agree with this contention as it is obvious that the workings have been filled in by hand. What has become of the quantity of copper produced by the old-time miners cannot be accounted for, as several thousand tons of copper must have resulted from the hundreds of excavations made throughout the district. It has been stated, however, by investigating authorities that ancient records prove that years ago a considerable export of copper took place from the south to the north of the East Coast of Africa, in a similar way to the export of gold. If these records are correct, doubtless some of that copper must have been derived from these ancient mines.'

According to Sikau, an old MuLemba who lives near Mphephu's village, nearly all the copper used by the natives before the European occupation was obtained from the Messina district. When he was a young man the industry was carried on extensively by the BaLemba, working under the protection and patronage of a MuVenda petty chief, Makhusha. I was fortunate to meet another old man who had been a copper-worker, and he described his methods to me. This old man, Netshisaula, is a petty chief of Chief Masekwa; he is a real veteran and knew Ramapulana and took part in the raid of Schoemansdal. He is a MuVenda but learnt his trade from the BaLemba near Messina, and did not practise it after the accession of Makhado, which more or less marked the end of native iron and copper work in the Zoutpansberg. The following is his description: The copper-ore was first cobbled into small pieces. The kiln for smelting was prepared by making a small circular impression in the ground, about 1½ feet in diameter, and lining it with clay and ashes; on this base a circular clay wall was built up to a height of 1½ feet and reinforced on the outside with stones. A layer of dry leaves of the *mukwiliri* or *mulamvhira* trees was put into the bottom of this kiln to a depth of about 2 inches to help in the kindling, over this was put a thick layer of charcoal and then more leaves. A small hole was made at the base of the kiln to give entrance to the nozzles of the bellows, and the charcoal was fired; as soon as it was red-hot another layer of copper was added and then a final layer of charcoal until all the copper was melted, when the worker proceeded to break down the wall of the kiln. All the debris of dirt, charcoal, and ashes was brushed away, leaving the copper in the clay-lined impression in the ground. The copper was left to cool and then again hammered into small cobbles and resmelted in a potsherd about 7 inches in diameter, which was put over the impression in the ground, so that the molten copper could be manipulated easily

INDUSTRIES 65

and poured out into the moulds prepared for it. The usual moulds were made in the ground with a stick about ½ an inch thick. The copper rod was then ready to be beaten into heavy copper bracelets or ear-rings (the latter are only worn by BaLemba women, never by BaVenda) or made into wire. The complicated process of wire-drawing is done with the help of the *magoka*, an iron plate with six or more holes, each one a little larger than the one before it; the copper is drawn first through the larger and then the next and so on until wire of the required thickness is obtained. The juice of an unknown plant is often rubbed on the copper to give it a bright yellow brassy appearance. Lead,[1] *mutobvu*, was obtained in the early days from the Portuguese and added to the copper; later ordinary solder, also called *mutobvu*, was used. Ordinary copper is called *mesina* or *musuku* and with solder it is *mundalila*. This mixing of solder with copper is important, as objects made of inferior bronze discovered in parts of the country that have been inhabited by these copper-workers may be their handiwork and are not necessarily of very ancient origin.

The following implements (Plate XXII) are used for wire-pulling in addition to the *magoka*. The pincers, *mabako*, is a very heavy iron implement about 10 inches long resembling our pincers; the two ends are held together by an iron ring, *tshongolo*, and wedged tight to hold the piece of wire by an iron wedge, *luvhimbi*. The hammer, *nyundo*, is of rough stone, and the bellows, *mvuto*, have already been described. A small iron staple with two lines engraved across the face, called *muvangwa*, is used for cutting copper wire into short lengths for making large copper studs on bracelets. To draw the wire the *mabako* is wedged firmly into the fork of a tree or into a slot cut for it; one end of a copper rod is heated and pointed and forced through a hole in the *magoka*; it is then clamped tightly into the *mabako* with the help of the ring and wedge; a forked stick is used as a lever and placed against the *magoka*, between it and the *mabako*; with this stick the *magoka* is levered around the tree, drawing out the wire and winding it around the tree; the copper rod, which is sticking out on one side of the *magoka*, is slightly heated from time to time to keep it pliable. The whole process may be repeated, the wire being next pulled through a smaller hole in the *magoka*; in this way it may be pulled to the degree of fineness that is required. When very fine wire

---

[1] Professor J. L. Myres tells me that the adding of lead to copper to make it softer and so easier to work is not unknown in other tribes. No doubt the BaVenda used it for this reason, as the softer alloy would be a great advantage in wire-drawing.

F

INDUSTRIES

is being drawn the *magoka* may be held on the ground by the workman's two feet while he draws the wire through the required hole, rolling it straight on to a stick with his hands.

The musuku. The BaLemba use the term *musuku* for copper and all objects made of it, while the BaVenda usually call copper *mesina*. and use *musuku* for one copper object of peculiar interest, which I shall call by this name (Plate XXII). These objects are only possessed by a few important chiefs and certain BaLemba; they are becoming very rare and are guarded jealously by their owners. The one shown in the photograph belongs to Mbulahene Mphephu. It is a rectangular object, $4 \times 3 \times 3\frac{1}{2}$ inches, with a rough rounded edge, projecting in a flat margin for about an inch all around the base; on the top there are four rows of small protuberances, containing 7, 8, 9, and 8 studs, *nhundi*, respectively; these studs are cylindrical, and about $\frac{1}{4}$ of an inch in diameter and $\frac{1}{2}$ an inch high, the gaps between the studs varying from $\frac{1}{4}$ to $\frac{1}{2}$ an inch. Each row is just under an inch apart. The whole object appears solid and is cast in pure copper. The objects are not uniform in size or shape, some being considerably smaller than the one described, cylindrical and with fewer studs, whilst others are reputed to have been made so large that it took two men to carry them. Dicke[1] describes two which he tested and found to be hollow and filled with sand, and it is probable that they are all similar in this respect. Four broken ones which I examined were hollow. Dicke also describes another copper object which is like a 'giant pipe, straight stemmed', found in the Palabora area of the North Eastern Transvaal low country. He says: 'I am now of the opinion that the pipe-shaped ingots are the commercial type, meant for bartering purposes, and that the shape illustrated (*musuku*) is the ceremonial type, and was made for religious purposes, or purposes in connection with the sacrifices made by the natives.' He also suggests that its curious form is an imitation of the now extinct sacred cactus, which was the representative of their ancestors, and is said to have been similar in shape and appearance. Stow[2] also suggests that the *musuku* had a sacred character. He gives three coloured plates which he describes thus: 'Copper castings (exact size). By the Magaliesberg Bakuana. Apparently made in three castings. Found near some old

[1] Dicke, B. H., 'A Bavenda Sacred Object', *South African Journal of Science*, 1926, vol. xxiii, pp. 935 and 936.

[2] Stow, George W., *The Native Races of South Africa*, London, 1905, opp. p. 518 *et seq.*

PLATE XXII

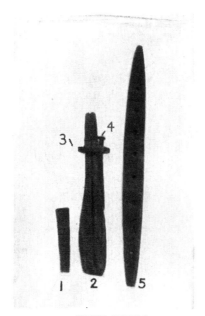

IRON TOOLS

1. *Muvangwa*   2. *Mabako*
3. *Tshongolo*   4. *Luvhimbi*   5. *Magoka*

MUSUKU (BELONGING TO CHIEF MPHEPHU)

INDUSTRIES 67

copper-workings in the Transvaal. It appears to have been a *madula*, or phallic charm.'

Dr. A. C. Haddon [1] describes the Palabora type of ingot and also discusses Stow's illustrations. He says that 'from his (Stow's) illustrations they seem to be simply the casts of the funnels used for making copper rods, the broad flange, which he takes to be a separate casting, being merely the overflow of the molten metal on the surface of the ground around the edge of the funnel. If this view be correct 14–25 rods would be cast at the same time'.

To-day every *musuku* is a sacred object; many have been cut up to make bracelets and charms, which are considered to possess some of the spiritual power of the wearer's ancestors, but this is no indication of their original sacred character, as nearly all heirlooms are now considered sacred. Their peculiar shape and hollowness does suggest that they might be unsuitable for trading, but on the other hand, it is unlikely that a purely ceremonial object should vary so much in size and in the number of studs, which would be unnecessary in this case and make their construction more difficult. I could not find any trace of a cactus similar in appearance to the *musuku*.

The hollowness and sand may be explained in a much simpler way. The crude method of casting, in which the hot molten copper was poured rapidly into the prepared moulds, resulted in the formation of a hollow space inside the *musuku*, and this space would often be almost filled with the sand that dropped down from the side of the mould during the process. (The moulds were made in dampish sand, little holes being pricked at the bottom with a stick for the studs.) My informants were unanimous in describing the objects as being mediums of barter, and said that the studs represented the approximate value of copper in each *musuku*; it is no more curious for the copper-workers at Messina to have used this peculiar shape than for those at Palabora to have used the equally curious pipe shape.

I think, then, that there can be no doubt that the *musuku* was used for simple trading purposes. A description of a *musuku* in the Bulawayo museum gives the following information: 'A *musuku* with only one stud is valued at 5*s*., with two at 10*s*., and so on. The *musuku* was smelted into sticks which were hammered down to be turned into bangles. One hundred of the bangles were valued at £10 or the price of a cow, and in that way used to pay lobola or marriage price of a wife.' Values seem to differ; Ravengai, a MuLemba living near

[1] Haddon, A. C., 'Copper Rod Currency from the Transvaal', *Man*, 1908, No. 65.

INDUSTRIES

Belingwe in Southern Rhodesia, told me that a *musuku* with 4 *nhundi* was of the same value as a cow or 20 bracelets or 10 anklets. Sikau, who possesses a cylindrical *musuku*, says that they were made of various sizes, some times a foot long with 3, 4, or 5 rows of studs, the number being an indication of how much wire could be made of that particular object. He said that the BaLemba presented them to the chiefs so that they might always have a reserve of copper from which bracelets could be made.

VII

WAR, TRADING, TRAVELLING, AND HUNTING

Weapons—Warfare—Travelling—Trading—Hunting—Fishing—
The Crocodile

Weapons.

*T*HE *Bow, vhura,* was the principal weapon of the BaVenda, although many had also the spear and shield. The Venda bow is the simple long type. The stave is round and is about 1½ inches in diameter in the middle, tapering uniformly at both ends into points ⅓ an inch in diameter, and measuring, when strung, 4½ feet from point to point. There is a slight shoulder at each end about 1½ inches long. It is strung by the direct attachment method with a twisted stout leather thong, fastened at the lower end by a double string slip-knot around the lower shoulder and attached by the same method to the upper shoulder, a fairly long piece of superfluous string being wound around the top of the bow stave. The bow is kept constantly strung and is never loosened, although the tension can be adjusted by loosening the slip-knot. The same bows are used for hunting and fighting, all being more or less the same size; miniature toy bows are used by the small boys for shooting birds. The bow is made from any hard wood, being patiently cut with an axe and a knife and finished off by being rubbed with fat and polished.

Arrows, masevha, are either iron-headed and unfeathered, the type used for warfare and big game hunting, or wooden-headed and feathered, the type used for shooting small game and birds.

Iron Arrow-heads may have two ½-inch barbs, measuring about 2 inches from barb to point, with long tangs often over 6 inches in length; another type of arrow-head resembles a miniature spear-head, the head measuring ½ an inch by 2 inches, and the tang being as much as 12 inches long. These arrow-heads are inserted directly into shafts made of bamboo, about 30 inches long and ½ an inch in diameter, the head being kept in position by a very tight leather sheath. Arrows of the iron-headed type are usually poisonous. Arrow poison, *vhutulu,* is often made with a mixture of dried *lutema matanda,* a species of mouse which is supposed to kill anything it touches, and the powdered seeds of the long pods of the *mudulu* tree. The poison is mixed in the gummy bark of the *muembe* tree (wild rubber) and placed on the shank just below the arrow-head.

70 WAR, TRADING, TRAVELLING, AND HUNTING

Wooden Arrow-heads may be simple knobs tapering at one end into a long tang which fits into the shaft. Another type is made of a long pointed piece of wood, which at a distance of about $1\frac{1}{2}$ inches from the point is carved all round into minute barbs for a distance of 2 inches. The base of the wooden arrow-head is inserted into a bamboo shaft and bound firmly with sinew. In order to stabilize their flight, these arrows have a whole feather attached just below the nock, tied by fine sinews at its top and bottom, in such a way that the rib is on the side of the arrow when it is strung ready for shooting. All the arrows have simple nocks about $\frac{1}{2}$ an inch deep. The BaVenda made quivers to carry their arrows, but they are now very rare.

The Spear, pfumo. Spear-heads are of two types, one being slightly broader than the other, and both having a slight rib running down the centre. The commonest variety has a blade 9 inches by $\frac{1}{2}$ an inch, the broader type is 10 inches by 3 inches. Each has a long round tang pointed at the tip, the tang being at least 6 inches long and often very much longer. About half the tang is hafted into a round wooden stick about 1 inch in diameter and 5 feet long. It is bound firmly with copper or iron wire-work or a tight-fitting sheath of hide. The stick has often a slightly clubbed end to give the spear balance.

The Shield, tshitangu, made of hide, similar to the Zulu type but round instead of oval, was used in conjunction with the spear. Probably both spear and shield were adopted by the BaVenda after contact with one or other of the alien tribes absorbed into their ranks. There are no shields to be found to-day.

The Axe, mbado, is rarely found now. Two which I examined were of the crescent-shaped battle-axe type, with a very narrow blade and a 6-inch tang hafted to a wooden handle at an angle of 45°. The crescent is sometimes made with one spike much longer than the other so that it can be used as a stabbing weapon as well as for its specific use.

Clubs are not considered as weapons by the BaVenda, but are carried by them for protection when on the road. The usual club is a small baton about 2 feet in length, with a round or club head carved into a man or woman's head, or some other simple design.

Warfare.

The BaVenda are not a tribe of particular military talent like the Zulus or Masai, and they do not have a highly organized system for

PLATE XXIII

OLD WARRIOR, SHOWING *TSHIALA*

WAR, TRADING, TRAVELLING, AND HUNTING 71

carrying on warfare of the bold, attacking type. Their campaigns were more in the nature of plundering raids, generally on a comparatively small scale, for stealing cattle or for revenge. Their usual tactics were to launch surprise attacks at the enemy, under the cover of darkness, to capture the cattle, women, and children, to kill as many men as possible, burn the kraal, and beat a hasty retreat to their own territory. All lived in a perpetual state of petty internecine war. One raiding party, returning home successfully, immediately prepared for the approach of a retaliatory raid. Makhado often sent small cattle-raiding expeditions into the BaKaranga country and was continually making raids on one chief or another.

This state of affairs persisted among the BaVenda until the Boer War, when all their weapons were confiscated and peaceful conditions enforced under white administration. On the death of a chief there was nearly always a disputed succession, which led to one or other claimant being driven from the district and setting up as an independent ruler, often with a large following. This so broke up the whole tribe that there could be no possibility of concerted action against a common foe. At one time or other nearly all the chiefs and petty chiefs have fought against each other, the ones living in close proximity being in an almost continual state of hostility. Probably the biggest battles ever fought were those just after 1840, when the Swazi raids took place; there were constant bickerings at this time with different small detachments endeavouring to pass north to Matabeleland to join Moslekatze. In Venda battles a death roll of ten or twelve was considered very heavy.

The chief was not supposed to make an offensive expedition without the consent of his councillors. All the petty chiefs and old warriors were summoned to the chief's *khoro*, where the projected campaign was discussed. When war was decided on, the war-note was beaten on the drums and messengers were sent to all the different kraals, crying out to the people to put on their war-dress and take up their arms. All the army then assembled at the chief's kraal, carrying their weapons ready for the fight. The age-sets were drawn up, and every soldier had to wear a new piece of leopard or goat skin; the different regiments were distinguished by the distinctive emblem, *tshiala*, tied to the little tuft of hair that each man left long for the purpose. NeKungula, an old warrior belonging to the *mazulu* age-set, was the only man I saw with this curious tuft of hair, although it used to be characteristic of MuVenda warriors (Plate XXIII). The emblems of

72 WAR, TRADING, TRAVELLING, AND HUNTING

the different age-sets were ostrich feathers, skins of the meerkat, mongoose, white goat, squirrel, strips of leopard skin, and a special red cloth.

In the chief's *khoro* the most important medicine-man prepared the charms which were given to the leaders of each regiment. These charms were catskin bags filled with the powerful war-medicine which would protect the fighters and bring them success. Every great medicine-man had his secret recipe for this medicine; it was made in the following way: The heart of the *tshirugvhe* bird (hammerkop) was dried and powdered and mixed with the dried roots of the *mpeta* tree (*u peta*, to fold up or dissolve), the *mukundulela* tree (way of force), and the *bweri* (soft watery porridge). Before the army set off, the men destined to stay at home to protect the chief made a large fire in the middle of the *khoro*; some of the war-medicine was then thrown on to this fire to help the raiders to overcome their enemies as successfully as the fire consumed the medicine. A special war-axe, *tshirovha*, was brought forward and anointed with the same medicine. Some of it was also added to a large *sambelo* pot of water which the warriors drank; the medicine-man also dipped a hyena tail into the pot and sprinkled them as they set off to the scene of the campaign, led by a man carrying the sacred axe; the leader often carried a hyena's tail, that had been anointed with the medicine, as a *tshirovha*, instead of the sacred axe, and when approaching a village waved it violently to make a big wind blow up to hide his men from the enemy.

The expedition was under the control of the chief's brother who had the chief's power of life and death in the field; under him were the *dzikhwali*, each *khwali* in charge of his age-set. The chief always remained in his capital protected by the boys in the *thondo* and a small body-guard of older men. When the raiders arrived in the vicinity of the enemy, the general directed the different age-sets under their respective leaders, spreading them out to surround the objective and take possession of outstanding strategic points. The general, surrounded by his guard of tried warriors, stayed in a commanding position in the rear with the axe-bearer, who stood facing the enemy and swinging the axe continually towards the fighters; if the enemy was overpowering the army, this guard would go to its assistance, led by the bearer of the sacred axe. If by some evil chance the sacred axe was lost, a second axe was immediately consecrated, medicine being poured over it from one of the catskin charms.

The experienced warriors always bore the brunt of the battle, the

WAR, TRADING, TRAVELLING, AND HUNTING 73

younger men being kept as far as possible in the rear. The chief was kept in constant touch with the fighters by messengers, and the keeper of his cattle was always in readiness, so that if the army was being defeated he could, at a moment's notice, take charge of the cattle and the chief's womenfolk and children and drive them all to a secure hiding-place. Whilst the fighting was in progress everything had to be absolutely quiet, particularly at night; all stamping was done during the day, and there was no sound of work or revelry until after the battle. The battle continued until as much destruction as possible had been perpetrated, the attacking force burning and ravishing indiscriminately. The great objective was to destroy the enemy's capital and plunder their cattle. No men were taken prisoners; all were killed and left where they fell, their weapons being looted and made use of by the victors. The latter, whenever possible, brought home their own dead for orthodox burial. Captive women, children, and cattle were sent back to the chief, who, after the battle, distributed them among his warriors and headmen. The man, whatever his rank, who first opened the gate of an enemy cattle-kraal, was usually given a couple of head of cattle as a reward for his daring, to stimulate his enterprise on a subsequent occasion. The result of the action was always kept a secret until after the return of the warriors. If the campaign had been successful the victory was celebrated in a great feast and dance. At this war-feast any man who had proved himself a coward was decorated with the lungs of an ox hung around his neck and was dressed in women's clothes. He was then forced to eat portions of the lungs mixed with manure, and was paraded in front of the women and ridiculed by all the people. Any man who had killed an enemy was honoured and had a ring painted around one eye or a stripe painted on his forehead, an additional mark being added for each victim slain. If a man had killed ten of the enemy, he was privileged to sit on the big drum and to stop the dancing for a moment. If a warrior thought that the number of his kill had not been witnessed or might be discredited, he brought the right arms of his victims home as proof of his prowess. This feast was also an occasion for a rite designed to inculcate bravery in the young generation; portions of the dead bodies of the enemy, of hands, hearts, livers, testicles, and all the different limbs, were cut up and mixed with beef; to this was added the powdered flesh of the *luvhimba* (eagle); the mixture was put on a big basket lid in which two holes had been pierced and a string drawn through; the lid was then dragged around the *khoro*

74 WAR, TRADING, TRAVELLING, AND HUNTING

by a spear attached to the string; all the young men grabbed at the concoction of meat on the lid, and an old man beat them with a switch of the *mukhala* tree while they were eating it; this experience was supposed to cure them of all fear.

Women and children captured in war were generally treated by their new owner in every way as his own family, although the chief might keep them as his slaves and was considered the owner of all the children born to the women.

At one time a great deal of trading in rifles and ammunition was done with the Portuguese; these weapons used to strike terror into the hearts of the enemy, although they created more noise than bloodshed. When ammunition could not be obtained the Venda ironworkers cast crude bullets for the rifles.

Travelling.

The BaVenda are not great travellers, many of them in the old days rarely going far from their mountain homes. When it is necessary to make a journey the traveller arms himself with a protective charm to hang around his neck, or procures a small staff which the medicine-man treats magically. On the road tribal etiquette is rigorously observed. There is a proverb, *Mulomo ndi khaladzi ya ndila* (The mouth is brother or sister on the road), indicating that a traveller, in the absence of brothers and sisters who are always ready to help in an emergency, must, on the road, depend upon his own resources.

Before approaching the kraal he is visiting, the traveller twists a piece of grass around at the cross-road, and places a stone on it to keep it down, in this way ensuring the presence of his host on his arrival. A weary traveller, fearing that darkness will be upon him before he reaches his destination, places a stone in the fork of a tree, hoping that as the stone is caught in the tree so the sun will be caught and linger in setting. A similar practice is found among the Masai and other East African peoples.

Hospitality is never refused to a traveller, no matter who he may be, and in this way natives of foreign tribes may pass through the country receiving hospitality and food and shelter at night, without any payment being expected or offered. Before reaching the kraal where he desires to spend the night the traveller generally protects himself from the danger of being attacked by the dogs of the kraal by putting a piece of grass between his lower lip and teeth, thereby

WAR, TRADING, TRAVELLING, AND HUNTING 75

rendering himself immune from danger. On arriving at the kraal he stands in the entrance to the *khoro* and says, 'The sun has gone down while I was on my way'. This is a recognized formula, always used when desiring shelter for the night, and generally receives the desired response. One of the inmates of the kraal asks him whence he comes, and tells him to wait until the headman is informed of his arrival. His weapons are then taken from him and put away in an empty hut, and he is taken into the presence of his host, whom he salutes with great respect. The headman then tells his wives to prepare food for the stranger and then to take him to a hut and provide him with a sleeping-mat and kaross. The visitor often shares the mat and blanket of the owner of the hut in which he sleeps. In the morning he again salutes the headman and is escorted to the entrance of the *khoro*, where his weapons are returned to him and he goes on his way. Generally before retiring for the night the visitor is entertained around the *khoro* fire by the men of the kraal, questioning, yarning, and comparing experiences with goodwill and cheeriness. If the stranger happens to be a member of an unfriendly tribe he generally hides the true identity of his kinsfolk. No MuVenda is ever at a loss in the invention of plausible stories that will give satisfaction to his hearers. Guests and hosts are both inordinately polite, vying with each other in expressions of flattery. No MuVenda ever travels without an axe, on account of the bushy, mountainous country and the constant danger from wild animals.

Trading.

There are no recognized market-places; nearly all the people are self-sufficing with regard to food, and often when shortages occur an exchange between neighbours is readily arranged, but in the case of an exceptional drought the people are compelled to seek grain in distant parts. There used to be a constant interchanging of such commodities as pots, baskets, and *masila* cloth, which were hawked around and exchanged for each other or for mealies. Before trading in this way permission had to be obtained from the local chief, who usually received a handsome present from the trader.

When hoe-smelting was a flourishing business hoes were made in great quantities. The iron-ore was traded for mealies, and then taken to the smiths who manufactured the required articles in exchange for a fee. Two hoes were worth one goat, and later a hoe was valued at 5*s*. There was a very big trade in hoes with the BaThonga, who

76 WAR, TRADING, TRAVELLING, AND HUNTING

were unable to obtain them in their own country. Pots, baskets, and basket lids are still traded, all being exchanged for the amount of mealies they contain. To trade a wooden plate it is put on a large *luselo* lid and covered with mealies, then turned over and covered with more mealies until it is quite concealed; it is exchanged for all the mealies used. A big calabash is exchanged for mealies measured in a big *luselo* lid, and a small one for mealies measured in a small lid. Hunters used to hawk skins, particularly those of the jackal and wild cat, and also meat. *Masila* cloth, the making of which was a specialized trade, was of considerable value. Most transactions were done by barter, the wares being traded for mealies, corn, goats, or occasionally cattle.

During the middle of the last century, when the Boers first came in contact with the BaVenda, an extensive ivory trade grew up, with Schoemansdal as the trading centre. Before that time ivory trade with the Portuguese was carried on for many decades. To-day most of the native trade has been eliminated by the appearance of European native trading stores all over the country, selling every commodity. The natives often bring mealies in the season and exchange them for luxuries, ornaments, and clothing, and when food becomes scarce are obliged to buy back their mealies at two or three times their original value. Iron pots (taking the place of the BaLemba earthenware), machine-made hoes and axes, paraffin tins for gourds and baskets, machine-made cloth, bracelets, and blankets are becoming increasingly popular and accessible. The people, deprived of the necessity of pursuing their natural industries, become correspondingly idle and degenerate, or go to Johannesburg to work on the mines, where they rapidly lose their semi-communal point of view and tend to become mercenary individualists.

Hunting.

After warfare hunting was the most important occupation of the Venda men, their traps and snares being made with considerable cunning and ingenuity. Although game is much less plentiful to-day and the game-laws make hunting a dangerous pastime, there are still a great many clever hunters. The spoils of the hunt are used for meat, clothing, blankets, and musical instruments. Certain animals are very useful to the medicine-man. In the days when elephants were still to be found, an adept elephant hunter was honoured and respected by all men; only the very dexterous and courageous men dared to

WAR, TRADING, TRAVELLING, AND HUNTING 77

attempt the capture of this great animal. A party of these adventurous men would stalk their game for hours, often taking refuge behind an enormous ant-heap, and there waiting patiently in the hopes of finally coming to close quarters with the elephant. As soon as the animal came within striking distance two of the huntsmen darted forward and ham-strung it with their axes, so that it could not move, and the rest of the party finished it off with spears and arrows. The tusks of a dead elephant were always considered to be the exclusive property of the chief, who traded the ivory and exchanged it for beads, guns, &c., brought by adventurous traders from Delagoa Bay. It was tabu for the chief to see the elephant's trunk.

The lion and the leopard, particularly the latter, are a constant source of danger and anxiety, frequently lurking around the goat-kraals and stealing the stock. They display extraordinary cunning and audacity, so that their capture is always an occasion of great rejoicing. A simple trap was made in the following way: A large cage with a partition down the middle was made of strong stakes. A live goat was tethered in one side as bait, and a door at the other end held above the entrance by a catch made of rope and a trigger-stick. The leopard, on entering the trap, touched a cross-stick, releasing the door and imprisoning himself; he was then killed by spears thrust between the poles which formed the side of the trap. Another trap is made by an archway of poles, above which a log, often weighted with a heavy stone, is supported; a trail of meat is dragged through the arch to entice the animal under it; as the leopard goes through he releases a cross-stick which in turn releases the overhead log, which crushes him beneath it as it falls. Before the BaVenda guns were confiscated leopards were frequently done to death by trap-guns. The lion is seldom hunted, except with a gun, although he is usually frightened away by dogs and followed for some distance by huntsmen armed with spears and axes; a hand to hand encounter is rarely ventured. The skins of both lion and leopard used to be the property of the chief, although to-day they are often sold directly to Europeans.

Buck are hunted in many different ways. They are often tracked down by dogs, especially after rain when the spoor is easy to follow, the men following the dog until the exhausted beast is cornered; it is then killed with a spear or axe. The buck belongs to the man who first wounded it or to the owner of the dog who first put it up and gave chase, but the meat is generally divided among the huntsmen.

78 WAR, TRADING, TRAVELLING, AND HUNTING

Sometimes the buck is trapped in a snare, made from a noose and slip-knot. A strong sapling is bent over and secured to the earth by means of a string and wooden peg; the peg is placed so that the lightest touch on the cross-piece of stick, to which it is cunningly secured, releases the sapling, which flies back, drawing tight the noose which has been placed across the path and strangling the animal; the noose generally catches the animal around the neck. These traps have been responsible for the untimely death of a great many donkeys. The traps are generally set within hearing distance of the kraal, and the hunter, on hearing the trap recoil, or hearing the cry of the captured beast, hurries out with his axe to make sure of his prey.

In the old days many animals were trapped in a large pit, full of pointed stakes and covered with grass. To protect tilled fields, pointed stakes are sometimes put just inside the fence, so that the buck, leaping the fence, becomes impaled on the other side.

Bush-pigs, which are considered to be the most cunning of all field raiders, can only be caught by being driven into a noose-trap. Young boys, out herding, set miniature nooses in which they capture anything from small birds to guinea-fowl and hares.

Certain hunters specialize in the capture of rock-rabbits, and train dogs to assist in the hunt; the dogs are sent down the holes and crevices in the rocky ledges, while the hunters wait with sticks at a hole where the quarry is expected to appear. When the dogs fail, a piece of iron rod bent into a hook at one end, is inserted into the hole, and an endeavour made to hook the rabbit out by its skin. Sometimes a pointed stick is jabbed into the animal and twisted round and round until the rabbit is dragged out, pinioned on the stick. The flesh is popular as food, and the skins make excellent karosses.

Small birds are caught by smearing sticks with an adhesive gum. The sticks are spread about at the birds' drinking-places, or put into a bush beneath which the hunter hides, hissing in imitation of a snake and enticing the birds into the snare.

Rats, snakes, and other small game are caught in a simple and ingenious trap, as shown in the diagram on the opposite page. The trap is set in the fields or near the river-bank and is very effective.

A great deal of hunting of both large and small game used to be done with the bow and arrow, the arrow often being poisoned. Later guns were used by a great many of the people. To-day both these weapons are forbidden, except to the chiefs, who are allowed the use of one gun, and with it slaughter game in great numbers. All the

PLATE XXIV

PART OF OLD HUNTING-NET

TRAP

WAR, TRADING, TRAVELLING, AND HUNTING

men of the kraal have a huge drive through the bush, the chief shooting the game at close range as it is driven into the open in front of him.

A favourite method of hunting small buck in the old days was with a hunting-net (Plate XXIV). The net was woven with a 4-inch mesh, about 8 feet high, and some 20 to 25 yards broad. The hunter fastened the ends loosely to two sticks across a likely opening in the bush and hid himself close by and waited. As soon as a buck touched the net

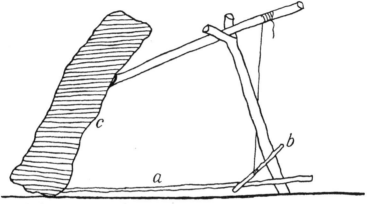

If pressure is put on cross-stick *a*, the trigger *b* is released and *c*, the heavy stone, will fall.

the sticks gave way and the creature became entangled; while it was struggling to free itself the hunter dashed out from his hiding-place and killed it. These nets are never seen to-day in Vendaland, but I saw one at the kraal of a MuKaranga, near Chibi in Southern Rhodesia; this particular net had not been used for some time and had been eaten in half by rats.

A hind leg of every animal killed near the chief's kraal is sent to him. The tail belongs to the man who organized the hunt, and, if suitable for the core of wire bracelets, is considerably valued, especially now that owing to the East Coast fever cattle regulations and the enforced clipping of the tails of all cattle, a large source of the supply of tail hairs is removed.

Apart from its commercial value, the tail is regarded with superstition, and must be cut off and set aside as soon as the animal is dead; it may not be touched until after the meat has been consumed or disposed of. The idea is that a tail, which is wagged before the meat

80 WAR, TRADING, TRAVELLING, AND HUNTING

of the animal to which it belongs is eaten, will bring a violent internal disorder upon the consumer. Another curious ritual behaviour in connexion with dead animals is the severing of the point of the heart; there is also a rigid tabu on the valves of the heart, which must always be thrown away and on no account eaten.

The manis, *khwara*, is the property of the chief; this animal is seldom encountered except after rain, and if it is offered a small present, a knife or a bracelet, it will stay where it is while its discoverer calls his friends to help him capture it and to carry it to the chief. The hunter must beware of a chameleon, as it never loosens its hold on anything that it grips; the only way to kill it is to cut off its head. A roan antelope, *thwandalila* (wound me and I'll cry), is always a source of trouble and brings death to the village of the huntsman who kills it without the punctilious observance of certain tabus. Apparently this animal, when wounded, always falls with one leg sticking up in the air; as long as it remains in this position it is quite impossible for any one, even a lion, to skin or damage it. The hunter may not touch it, but goes quickly home, and there he picks up a small pot or other small object and throws it on to the ground crying, 'I have no father! I have no mother! With whom shall I eat this thing?' By this action and exclamation he redeems the sin of killing the animal. All the family know that he has killed a roan antelope and follow him back to the bush where he left it lying. As soon as the leg falls down they may bring the animal home.

Fishing.

Fishing is a favourite pastime of the young boys, although it is disliked by grown men, and entirely tabu for women, who make any boy who smells of fish wash his hands in cow-dung before he comes into the hut. Fish are caught in various ways.

A fence may be erected across the stream, with one opening, in which a large basket (*mhorna*) is placed. This basket is a trap made of river-reeds; those at the mouth are inverted so that the fish cannot escape when it has entered the trap.

A popular method of fishing is shooting with the bow and arrow. The shaft of the arrow is a long thin reed and the head is a long sharp thorn; sometimes two or more thorns are inserted parallel to each other, forming barbs. When the river is low a rudimentary net, made of thick, bushy branches, is used. The fishers form a semicircle and drag the river, working all the fish enmeshed in their branches towards

WAR, TRADING, TRAVELLING, AND HUNTING 81

the bank, where they are pounced upon. I encountered one small fisherman using an ingeniously fashioned rod; he had scraped away all the thorns, except the very end one, from a branch of the *wag 'n bietje* tree; the end thorn pointed upwards, the whole forming hook, line, and rod combined; the child was fishing in a very remote part of the Nzhelele river, and I wondered whether he had obtained the idea of his rod from observing the white man fishing, or whether it originated independently in his own small brain. He landed a great many fish successfully, using tiny grubs as bait.

The Crocodile.

The crocodile infests all the rivers and pools, and is a constant danger to men and to their cattle. It is regarded with fear and reverence. No MuVenda will kill a crocodile or take part in its destruction. If a dead crocodile is encountered, stretched out on the river-bank, the discoverer will push the body back into the river with a stick. He is afraid to touch it with his hands, as, if his action was witnessed, he would most certainly be accused of being a *muloi* (wizard). The brain of the crocodile is thought to contain a strong and deadly poison, the smallest fragment of which, secreted under the finger-nail of the poisoner, could easily be dropped into his enemy's porridge or beer, and would cause immediate and painful death. Thoho-ya-Ndou is supposed to have discovered this secret, and to protect himself from such a fate forbade any of his people to touch the crocodile, on pain of death or banishment. The chiefs swallow stones from the crocodile's stomach to prolong life.

This peculiar veneration of the crocodile, which is not of an altogether totemic nature, is common to a great many southern Bantu. Bullock[1] says: 'A Mashona is averse to killing animals associated with witchcraft. He is especially afraid of the crocodile, whose dung is sent by sorcerers to injure people. It is the sign of witchcraft and its emblem appears on one of the divining bones. The soap-stone beams with the bird perched on the end, found at Zimbabwe, have this emblem on the back of the beam.' Stow[2] suggests that probably all South African Bantu who share this attitude are subdivisions of peoples originating from the same stock.

The appearance of the crocodile is so uncouth and repulsive and its method of attack so subtle and dangerous that it produces an attitude

[1] Bullock, C., *The Mashona Laws and Customs*, p. 88.
[2] Stow, George W., *The Native Races of South Africa*, London, 1905, p. 518.

G

82 WAR, TRADING, TRAVELLING, AND HUNTING

of repulsion and fear in the minds of all men. This attitude reacts either in the veneration and avoidance of the subject of fear, or in hate and antagonism, culminating in a passion for destroying the hated creature. It is undoubtedly a psychological repulsion, similar to that felt by many people towards the snake, and seems to be passed on from generation to generation and to exist in one form or another wherever the crocodile is found.

VIII

BIRTH AND INFANCY

Pregnancy—Normal Births—Abnormal Births—Twins—First
Teeth—Weaning

EVERY MuVenda woman desires to bear children, and if she does
not become pregnant shortly after marriage her mother-in-law
inquires the reason and advises her son to take his wife to consult a
medicine-man. If the wife is found to have some physical defect.
she is given a drug to mix with her morning porridge. This drug
is made from the roots of three trees: *mudedede* (from *u dededza*,
to lead a child), *mudzidzi* (from *u dzidzi*, to drum the initial beats
of the *tshikona* dance—in this case, the throb of the head in a severe
headache), and *mphimbi*. Portions of these roots are powdered and
well mixed. The powder is also added to water in which the same
species of roots have been boiled; the woman is ordered to drink the
mixture at frequent intervals during menstruation. She may also be
given a python's skin to wear around the waist or neck; it is believed
that a small snake resides within the womb of a woman, whose
function it is to carry the semen into the womb and there build up
the child. Often her barrenness is considered to be due to the malevolent designs of one of her family spirits. When this is the case the
medicine-man, by divination, locates which spirit it is that requires
pacification, and advises the unhappy pair to approach the head of
the family and ask him to perform the necessary rites. These rites
are carried out in the same manner whenever the aid of the spirits is
solicited in cases of sickness and distress, and will be described later.
A few more months are allowed to elapse, and if the woman still shows
no signs of pregnancy the medicine-man prescribes a stronger drug.
If this second visit fails to have the desired effect, the husband consults
a more powerful physician. If the art of this man cannot remedy the
misfortune, and after years of persistence the woman still fails to
produce a child, she resigns herself to her fate, considering that the
gods are against her and that it is useless to struggle longer against
the inevitable. She is pitied rather than despised by the women
around her, and often a child of one of her co-wives is put under her
care in order to lessen her reproach.

Although the non-appearance of the desired child is usually

BIRTH AND INFANCY

considered to be the fault of the woman, occasionally the medicine-man may divine that it is the husband who is impotent and prescribe a drug for him. This is made from the roots of the *murombuli* tree (from *u rumbula*, to impregnate, to make a hole right through) and the *muta-ta-vhana* (from *u tata*, to be afraid, and *vhana*, children).

Although it is the desire of every woman to have a great many children, the size of the average Venda family is small, as a woman may not bear a second child until after the first one has been weaned, which usually does not occur for three or four years. It seems that this restriction on the rate of reproduction became customary when it was found that in time of war it was impossible for a woman to make good her escape with more than one small child dependent upon her. The husband of a woman who bears a child too soon after the previous one, is despised and looked down upon by his fellow men, who say that he is trying to kill his children. Few women have more than four or five children, the average family consisting of two or three; there appears to be a preponderance of girls over boys, although in the absence of reliable statistics it is impossible to come to any definite conclusion. The preponderance of girls is accounted for by the BaVenda in a very simple way, as they believe that with the help of medicine they can readily regulate the sex of their children. To produce a boy pieces of bark must be taken from the east and west sides of the male *mufula* tree (from *u fula*, to pick fruit). The bark is powdered and mixed with water. It must be drunk by both parents morning and evening at the time of conception. To produce a girl the bark must be taken from a female *mufula*.

The infant mortality in the summer months is very high. Some missionaries say that it reaches 60 to 70 per cent.

Pregnancy.

As soon as a woman becomes pregnant she tells her mother-in-law or some other old woman at the kraal, never her own mother, and this woman tells the husband. He receives the news with gratification and orders his wife to take care of herself. She continues her daily life in the ordinary way until about two months before the birth of the child, when, in the case of a first pregnancy, she goes to her mother's home until after the baby has been born. In subsequent pregnancies she stays at her husband's home and is generally placed under the care of one of the old women of the kraal, who is made responsible for her well-being. From the beginning of the pregnancy

BIRTH AND INFANCY

the expectant mother becomes an object of interest and respect to the society in general. In addition to the various food restrictions imposed upon her, there are other tabus and attentions which she is expected to observe to ensure the safe delivery of her offspring. She is regarded as a person of importance in the community, and is often referred to as being a child of Thovela, the mythical ancestor, whose true significance has been lost, but who is still remembered as being a benevolent deity, particularly interested in the welfare of pregnant women. She is saluted respectfully by all men, even her chief. A pregnant woman, going to fetch wood or water, may not turn back until she has accomplished her mission, for should she do so it is believed that the child will also turn back on the day of its birth, causing her to have a dangerous and difficult delivery. For the same reason a stick with an unusual swelling may not be used by her as fuel. Visitors to her kraal, when saying good-bye on their departure, must not salute her, as, should they do so, her life would be endangered. Her whims, if reasonable, are generally gratified. The food restrictions are more in the nature of avoidances than actual tabus. Hot food must be avoided for fear of scalding the growing child, and any blemish on the baby at birth is accounted for by the fact that the mother has been negligent in this respect. Sweet food is generally avoided, mealie meal being soaked for a day and a night to turn it slightly sour. Vegetables may not be eaten at all. Anything sweet is thought to result in sickness. There is no restriction put on the consumption of beer until the last few months, when the woman is supposed to eat very little of anything and to drink only water, for fear that the child may grow too big, making delivery difficult. During these final months she must always eat standing. All the food must be eaten out of a broken pot.

Normal Births.

At the onset of labour the woman secretly tells her mother or mother-in-law, who takes her to the hut and summons one or two old women to assist her. These three people stay with her until the child is born. The doctor is informed that the birth is imminent, and he provides her with medicine to drink and to rub on her legs, back, and abdomen. This concoction is made from the stem of the *luangalala* tree (from *u angalala*, to rise up). The woman either kneels or sits on a stone or wooden block. Often a tight binder is fastened around her abdomen and she is supported behind by one of

BIRTH AND INFANCY

the midwives, while the other one sits in front holding her knees, ready to receive the baby. If the labour is protracted the doctor is again consulted and he endeavours to discover the cause of the trouble by throwing up the dice. The medicine prescribed for this contingency is made from the eel, *khunga*. The skin is cut up into small pieces; some are burnt on a broken pot under or near the patient, so that the fumes envelop her legs; at the same time she is forced to inhale the fumes. Occasionally, in the case of a dangerous obstruction, he may be admitted to the hut, where he rubs the crushed leaves of the *museto* (*u seta*, to rub off by friction) mixed with water, on his hands. He tries to rectify the difficulty by gently turning the child, although manipulation is more often attempted by the midwives. Child-birth amongst the BaVenda is often protracted and difficult, and the mother is subjected to very rough treatment and unnecessary pain at the hands of the midwives. Death at child-birth is very common, abnormal deliveries invariably resulting in the death of the mother or the child, and often of both. Nobody is supposed to know that the birth is in progress, and if the woman makes too much noise she is beaten and told not to behave like a child. As soon as the baby is born the umbilical cord is cut and tied with bark-string and the baby is then washed. No significance is attached to the instrument used for cutting the cord. The placenta is buried inside the hut, or outside immediately next to the outer wall. Boiling water is then poured on the spot to prevent the mother from having after-pains. The baby is given medicine to prevent it from suffering abdominal pain. This medicine is made from the powdered bark of the *muembe*, the custard apple, mixed with water. The mixture is strained and the baby given a few drops to drink immediately after birth. A piece of the plate of the manis, *khwara*, is also dipped into the mixture and rubbed all over the baby's body to give it strength. The juice of the *tutulwa* plant is mixed with powdered potsherd and fat and the mixture is smeared around the cord in order to dry it up, so that it drops off in about four days' time. The cord is then buried with the placenta and hot ashes are placed over the hole and stamped down.

The mother is absolutely secluded until the cord drops off the child. The father is informed of the birth and of the child's sex, but may not see or touch it or its mother until after the seclusion period is over. Infringement of this tabu would inevitably result in the husband being afflicted with a disease of the eyes. During this time the mother is given a liberal diet, and the new baby is fed with a mixture of very

BIRTH AND INFANCY

weak mealie meal and water. After the cord has dropped off the doctor visits the hut. He proceeds to interrogate the mother as to the legitimacy of her child, and it is believed that if she does not answer his questions truthfully the child will be dead by sundown. If she confesses that her husband is not the child's father the husband will claim two head of cattle from his wife's seducer, and there the matter will end, as the child is regarded as being unquestionably her husband's property. Having satisfied himself as to the child's legitimacy the medicine-man proceeds to make small incisions all over it, on the forehead, the front and back of the neck, shoulders, elbows, wrists, thighs, knees, ankles, stomach and buttocks, into which he rubs medicine to protect it against sickness and to enable it to grow into a strong and lusty child. This medicine is made from a piece of the skull of a baboon, ground with the root of the *tshidzimba vhalisa* (*tshidzimba* is the cake made of mealies and monkey-nuts taken for food on the road; *vhalisa* means shepherds). The powder is mixed with fat and rubbed into the incisions and also into the baby's fontanelle. My informant said that the baboon's skull is used for this purpose because it has been observed how very quickly the young of the baboon become strong and independent. The human baby resembles the baby baboon in many ways, and it is hoped that by this sympathetic magic the baby's bones will quickly harden and grow strong, so that it will soon be able to run about and be independent. The mother may now be given the child to suckle. Often before this the mother suffers intense pain, as the midwives refuse to summon the doctor to rub her breasts, so that she may suckle her child, until she has divulged the name of her lover. Sometimes the agony is so great that the mother will say any name that she thinks will satisfy her persecutors in order to escape from her sufferings, although she may be innocent of the indiscretions to which she confesses. If she owns to a lover her breasts must be purified with a lotion made from the powdered root of the *mutshetshete* (from *u tshete*, to be quiet) mixed with water.

After the visit of the medicine-man the mother is ready to emerge from her seclusion. Before she may leave the hut she is visited ceremonially by her husband. He obtains a powder, made from the blood of a menstruating woman, which he rubs on the palms of his hands and the soles of his feet. His wife presents him with a bracelet, *matuvho* (an intense desire). This bracelet must be given to him before he may accept food from her or sit anywhere in the hut where she has sat during the birth of the child. If this purification is

BIRTH AND INFANCY

not duly performed the husband will be attacked by a shivering disease from which he will not recover.

Immediately after the birth of the child the place where it sleeps is surrounded by small twigs, covered with medicine, made from the root of the *mutavhatsinde* tree. This mixture is also rubbed on a long stick, which is laid on the ground outside the hut, a few feet from the door. These sticks are supposed, through the power of the medicine, to act as charms to keep evil away from the infant. The stick outside the door is kept there until the child is brought out, and only old women are permitted to cross it and enter the hut. It is tabu for any menstruating woman to cross it.

After the husband has visited his wife his relations are summoned for the ceremony of naming the child. The older women sit inside the hut with the mother and child, and the old men sit just outside. The younger people may not pass the stick outside the door. Porridge, meat, and beer are provided, and the ceremony is often followed by a feast and dance.

The name is generally given by the father's sister, *makhadzi*, or the father's brother, *khotsimunene*; failing them it may be given by another member of the lineage. The *makhadzi* invokes the spirits and sometimes ties an heirloom around the child's neck. The heirloom is generally an elephant's tooth, a string of beads, or some other emblem belonging to the father's ancestors. While adjusting the heirloom she addresses the child by the name of one of its ancestors saying, '*Wo vuwa zwino ri ri u dzule kha mwana uyu, ri mu vhidza nga dzina lau u mu vhulungu zwa-vhudi*' ('You have risen now, we ask you to come and live in this child, and we call him by your name'). If the *makhadzi* is younger than the father of the child she is not permitted to enter the hut, but must stand in the doorway and tell the old women inside the name that she has chosen. She then presents the old women with a present for the mother. After this the other relatives may give the mother presents, which are handed to her through the medium of the old women. Sometimes the child is given a girdle of beads, *mafhunga*, very often made of ostrich egg-shells.

Although there are a number of names in current use, any peculiarity about the child, its birth, or its parents is generally reflected in the name chosen. Any important event in the life of the tribe, coinciding with the birth, may also influence the name given. Certain names are considered more suitable for boys than girls, and vice versa,

BIRTH AND INFANCY

but most Venda names are given irrespective of sex. One finds in common use such names as Takalani (happiness), Mbulahene (kill me), Tshivhenga (hated thing), Mutshinya (mistake), Phandelani (driven away), Jombere (Joubert), Ratshivhadela (block of wood). The name given in this ceremony is liable to be changed at any time during the owner's childhood. In cases of illness or continued crying, when the parents seek the doctor's advice, it very often happens that he divines the trouble to be due to the fact that the child's name is unfavourable to the spirit of some ancestor, who wishes it to be changed. In such cases a new name is selected, and it is hoped that in discarding the old name the cause of the trouble will be removed. Nicknames are common, and a man during his lifetime may acquire any number of different names, but the two to which he attaches most importance are that given to him by his father's family just after his birth and the one given to him after his initiation.

After this ceremony the child is allowed to be brought out of the hut, *u bvisa ndumi*. It is, however, confined to the yard surrounding the hut for another month. The actual bringing out ceremony, *u bvisa mwana* (to bring the child outside), occurs at the end of this month. In the evening the mother, carrying her new baby, repairs to a chosen spot just outside the kraal; she is accompanied by some of the old women of the kraal, who, if the child is a girl, take with them a handful of seeds, representative of the different crops. They hoe a small patch of ground and order the mother to suckle her child and to plant the seeds in the prepared ground, after which she returns to the kraal with her child, carrying a miniature bundle of wood. If the child is a boy he is taken out with a small axe. Instead of sowing and hoeing the garden, a miniature cattle-kraal is made, and a small bush carried back to the kraal. These rites are symbolic of the child's future activities. As the mother approaches her hut the people in the kraal pour water on to the roof and call to her to run inside as the rain is falling; she runs quickly into the hut, the water falling upon her and her child. This whole ceremony is an appeal to the spirits for their protection, so that the growing child may wax strong and healthy, able to hoe and plant or to clean the land, and may be blessed with successful crops and plentiful rains.

With the conclusion of this ceremony the most dangerous period of the child's life is over. It is necessary, however, for the child to be taken out and shown to the new moon each month, being held upside down. It is believed that this ceremony prevents illness, and

BIRTH AND INFANCY

it is repeated at every new moon until the child has cut its first tooth.
The moon is called the child's *makhadzi*.

Abnormal Births.

The fear of a woman who has had an abortion is deeply rooted in
the mind of every MuVenda; he is firmly convinced that should he
have sexual intercourse with such a woman he will die of consumption.
So great is the fear of this disease that a man will not inherit his
brother's wife if that brother has died of consumption, as he fears that
such a union would bring a similar fate upon himself. In spite of this
dread on the part of the menfolk abortion is by no means uncommon,
often being brought about, with the help of a medicine-man, by
women who have committed adultery and become pregnant by some
man other than their husbands. A man suspecting such an occurrence
will, unknown to his wife, consult a medicine-man. If his suspicions
are confirmed he will demand the name of her seducer and make the
offender pay the usual fine for adultery. After any abortion, before
the man will again have sexual intercourse with his wife, he will take
her to a medicine-man, where they undergo a purification ceremony
together. Small incisions are made, either in the neck or wrist of the
man and woman, and a few drops of blood from the man are rubbed
into the incisions in the woman, and vice versa, signifying that they
are of one blood. A similar infusion of blood is the culminating act
of the marriage ceremony, and this is merely a repetition of that
ceremony, made necessary by the severance of their relations due to
the disaster of abortion. The husband and wife are then placed on
opposite sides of a tree with their backs to each other, and tied
together with a piece of bark-string, the tree being between them.
Both urinate into the same vessel, and the powdered root of the
mukhundandou is added (from *u khunda ndou*, to beat the elephant;
this tree is supposed to be so strong that an elephant cannot break it).
Each is then given some of the mixture to drink; the remainder is
rubbed on their legs; finally the bark string is severed, signifying the cutting away of disease. After this normal relationships may be resumed.
A woman who has had several abortions is considered to be a
dangerous person. Her husband returns her to her father, explains
his misfortune, and demands the return of his lobola.

A baby born in a caul is not regarded with any particular joy or
dread. The phenomenon is supposed to occur when the father of the
child had his clothes on at the moment of conception, the child conse-

BIRTH AND INFANCY

quently being born clothed. It is an interesting example of the idea of like producing like. Babies born feet first and those born with any deformity are killed by having boiling water poured over them by the midwives. The mishap is considered to be the work of an evil spirit. Such children are often buried inside the hut, near the wall, so that their bodies will be in perpetual shade; if the sun ever shines on these remains the mother is afflicted with abdominal pains. All children born dead, or dying shortly after birth, must be buried in a damp place by the riverside.

Twins.

The birth of twins seems to be fairly common amongst the BaVenda, but their advent is regarded as being unnatural and, should they be allowed to remain alive, any misfortune which befalls a family, or possibly even tribal misfortunes, are attributed to them. Unlike so many of the southern Bantu, who kill only one twin, the BaVenda kill both. This is done immediately after birth, by the midwives or mother, by strangulation or scalding. To-day, although some people fear to kill them outright, they are neglected so that they die.

The common method of burial is for the twins to be placed in one pot and buried in a damp place by the riverside. If this procedure is not followed it is feared that there will be a drought in the country. The idea that twins are the carriers of misfortune seems to be deeply rooted, especially among the women. Recently a Christian woman had twins and was persuaded not to destroy them. One died from natural causes but the other lived. This woman's next child was born with diseased eyes and subsequently went blind, which occurrence all the family explained was the inevitable result of allowing twin children to remain alive. Wessman[1] tells how the wife of one of his best labourers, who had twins was admonished to let them live, and assured she need fear no misfortune. One day one of the other children became ill and the mother immediately strangled one of the twins; the child grew better, but the second twin was also strangled as a precaution against further illness.

The arts of magic and medicine are to a large extent intertribal and very often foreign treatments are preferred to the indigenous ones, being less understood and consequently considered more efficacious. This, combined with the mixed origin of the BaVenda, probably accounts for the various methods of purification after the birth of twins.

[1] Wessman, R., *The Bawenda of the Spelonken*, London, 1908, p. 56.

BIRTH AND INFANCY

Sometimes a doctor takes the husband and wife to an ant-hill, through the centre of which he has previously tunnelled a hole. The leaves of the *u kona nguluvhe* (to beat the pig) are mixed with water and sprinkled in the hole; *u kona nguluvhe* is the same tree as the *mubadali* (that which stays the fever); nobody could explain why it should be given this curious name when used in this connexion. Then the wife, followed by her husband, crawls through the ant-hill to the other side; on emerging they are given the same mixture of water and leaves with which to wash themselves. The remainder of the liquid is then thrown into the hole and both openings are covered up, so that the uncleanliness is left inside the heap. In the course of time, when the ants rebuild the damaged portions of their home, it is believed that the evil which caused the dual birth is permanently imprisoned.

In other cases a miniature hut is erected with two entrances opposite to each other. A fire is made in this hut in a hole in the ground and a pot containing the mixture is boiled over it. The parents of the twins walk through the hut one after the other, stepping over the pot, and then walk straight home without looking back.

Another method is for the midwives, after having buried the pot containing the twins in a marsh, to cut a piece of root from the *mukhalu* tree and boil it with water; porridge is made of this liquid and given to the unclean mother to drink; the root is then returned to the tree and reburied in the place from which it was dug up. Incisions are then made in the neck and wrists of the parents in the same way as in the cleansing ceremony after an abortion.

Yet another method is for the parents of the twins to be tied together by a rope, rubbed with fat and the powdered root of the *muramba* tree (from *u ramba*, to call together). The rope is fastened around their waists and the mother is ordered to go into the hut where the twin-birth occurred; the father waits outside. The medicine-man makes a small hole in the back of the hut and hands the mother some of the *muramba* mixture through the hole. She rubs it on to a knife and cuts the string and then burns the end that is around her, while the father burns his end.

An effort is always made to prevent the repetition of the calamity of twins by blocking the old door and making a new entrance to the hut. The clothing and ornaments of the parents are discarded and usually become the property of the medicine-man.

In peculiar contrast to the BaVenda attitude towards twin-children is their treatment of twin-calves. A cow which gives birth to twin-

BIRTH AND INFANCY

calves, becomes the property of the chief; it is often given a separate kraal and all its milk is left for the calves; it is regarded as being favoured and blessed beyond the ordinary cow. Amongst many of the northern Bantu, such as the Baganda and the Bakitara, the advent of twin-calves is considered a great blessing, but among these peoples twin-children are regarded in the same way. On the other hand, the Akamba used to kill one of their twins and they still regard twin-births with apprehension and dislike, but this attitude is reflected in their treatment of twin-calves, which, with the mother, are always killed. Among the Bomvana of the Transkei twin-children and twin-calves are allowed to live and are treated with special ritual.

In communities where cattle and wives are so inextricably associated with one another, the BaVenda conflict of ideas with regard to twin-births is curious, and makes one suspect that one or other is the result of some alien influence. The suspicion that the killing of twin-children is not indigenous to the BaVenda is strengthened by the fact that Takalani, a very reliable informant, and many other older men, assert that long ago twin-murder, when discovered by the chief, was punished by the confiscation of the wives, children, and property of their father, in exactly the same way that the possessions of a murderer are confiscated. They also assert that the parents of twins were specially favoured by the chief, who could ask him to help them with gifts of food and other things.

Assuming that the birth of twins tends to be a hereditary characteristic, and that their murder amongst the BaVenda was indigenous, one would expect to find such births of comparatively rare occurrence, whereas twins are born frequently, although there does seem to be a tendency for them to decrease recently. One informant credited the growing cunning of the medicine-man with the prevention of the disaster! The BaVenda are surrounded by people who kill one twin only, except in the north, where the attitude of the BaKaranga with regard to twin-children and twin-calves is identical with their own, which is not surprising, considering the long sojourn of the BaVenda among the BaKaranga. It is reasonable to assume that the killing of twins has been introduced to both peoples by some alien influence.

First Teeth and Weaning.

Children cutting their top teeth first are killed by strangulation with a reim. These children are called *shenga* (from *u shenga*, to chew), and it is believed that any person bitten by such a child will die. If it

BIRTH AND INFANCY

were allowed to grow up, a girl, on becoming pregnant, would cause the death of her husband, and a boy, on his wife becoming pregnant, would be the cause of her death. A missionary near Sibasa has been approached by mothers of such children, desiring to save their lives, and asked to extract the offending teeth.

The usual time for weaning, *u lumula* (to leave off biting), is when the child is three or four years old, and until this time the mother may not have another child. If she should become pregnant again before this time has elapsed, the child is immediately weaned, the mother obtaining a mixture which she puts in the child's food to induce it to leave the breast. This mixture is made from the roots of the *musenzhe* and the *dundu*. Often a child, although also eating other food, continues to be suckled by its mother until it is teased by the other children for still behaving like a baby, or for some other reason relinquishes the breast of its own accord. It is not unknown for a boy to herd goats all day and then be fed by his mother on his return home. Any weaning rites, which may have been practised, have now completely disappeared.

IX

CHILD LIFE

Boys—Girls—Mixed Games—*Mahundwani*

IN journeying through Vendaland and camping near the villages and kraals one is struck by the whole-hearted happiness and good nature of the young children. Babies seldom seem to cry, but sleep contentedly on the backs of their small sisters or play about the yard while their mothers work.

Boys.

Boys are sent out to herd the goats at a very early age, while the older ones look after the cattle: they spend the best part of their lives playing together in the sunshine while they keep watch over their herds. The age of a man is often reckoned from the time at which he was a herd-boy. They make very good herd-boys, and seem to understand the animals a great deal better than the older men. One little boy of eight or nine years, in charge of a herd of some twelve cows and eight calves, showed an almost uncanny knowledge of the cattle under his care; it was milking time, and he separated the cows from their offspring, putting all the calves together into a small kraal near to the milking operations; as each cow was milked this little boy whistled softly and called its name in an insinuating way; the proper calf separated itself from the group and trotted out of the kraal to its mother; he did this after each cow was milked, and nearly all the calves responded to his call without any hesitation. It is very seldom that a boy returns to his home at night without his full complement of cattle. If he does lose an animal he is sure to receive a sound thrashing from his father when the loss is discovered. Some of the oxen are trained for riding and there are usually two or three such animals in the herd. The boys ride them with skill, and if cattle are driven any distance some of the herd-boys will canter along on the backs of the riding-oxen. In the evening the boys pick up a few pieces of wood on their way home from the grazing grounds and, having safely kraaled the animals under their care, they light a fire and crouch around it until it is time for the evening meal and sing plaintive little part-songs with a great deal of repetition, or imitate the dancing of the older boys.

While out with their herds the boys play a variety of games. Small ones are fond of building miniature kraals, into which they put fruit of

96   CHILD LIFE

the *tutulwa* tree to represent the cows and goats, and small pips to represent the calves and kids; they then spend many hours herding their miniature flocks. They also make clay models of buck, cattle, dogs, and men, and sometimes depict hunting scenes in which the models of the men and dogs are arranged chasing the buck. They are fond of making a wheel with the fruit of the *muramba*, a type of wild orange, which is fastened to the split end of a long mealie stalk, being pinned between the split stalk with a piece of stick; this toy has its facsimile among European children (Plate XXV). They skip with a rope made from a long creeper. Another game, *khororo*, is played with sticks and a ball made of a stone or a hard piece of wood; the players divide into two sides and draw two lines at the opposite ends of a field to represent goals; the respective sides endeavour to hit the ball beyond their opponents' line in order to score a point. Sides are also often taken in *thulwi*, throwing the spear. In this game a round pulpy root is fastened to a tree and the boys have shots at it with spears, made of pointed sticks. It may be rolled along the ground by a player on one side, while the other side thrust their spears at it; to score a point the root must be transfixed in such a way that it can be raised off the ground on the point of the spear. The boys have a system of drawing lots, *madenwa*, to decide who is to perform any work which is particularly arduous or unpopular, such as rounding up the straying cattle. In this instance the boy who went in search of the missing cattle on the last occasion collects as many leaves as there are boys, and breaks one of them in half; he holds them in his hand and each boy draws a leaf in turn, the one who draws the broken leaf having to perform the task. Another method is for one boy to place several short pieces of grass on the palm of his hand; each boy must try to pick up one piece on his tongue; if he picks up more he loses; if all are successful the boy holding the grass on his hand must do the work.

Hunting is a favourite pastime. Boys hunt cane-rats. They trap birds with bird-lime or shoot them with small bows and arrows or with ingenious pistols made from the twigs of trees with a pliable bark; the pith is removed from these twigs, forming hollow tubes about half an inch in diameter; little pellets are cut from a mealie stalk, one being fixed in one end of the tube and another about two inches down the other end; this second pellet is forced against the other one, the pressure created forcing out the lower pellet; one end of the tube is slightly narrower than the other, so that there is a minimum waste of pressure. The boys dearly love to light a fire and roast their prey, spiked

PLATE XXV

BOY

GIRL

PLATE XXVI

GIRLS PRACTISING THE DRUMS

CHILD LIFE

97

on long sticks. No article of food is ever allowed to escape them. If a small boy sees a locust on the ground he straightway pounces upon it, removing the head and wings with two swift movements, and with a third the locust is in his mouth, while a smile of content creeps over his face as he chews the delicate morsel.

Girls.

The little girls generally stay at home and help their mothers to collect wood and carry water, or follow them down to the lands, acting as nurse-maids to their small brothers and sisters. Their games include many very similar to ours, such as hide-and-seek, clap-hands, and tag. Where possible, they seize every chance of playing the drums, (Plate XXVI) and it is quite common for two little girls to spend hours every day at this amusement; they will continue with ceaseless energy, whenever the drums are not required by the older people, and some become very expert. Usually, while the drums are being played, most of the older girls of the village will sit around listening, with their babies on their backs, squatting in their customary position on the knees. They seem to have unlimited patience and continue with the same occupation for an endless time without seeming to become bored or weary. Girls sometimes make clay models like their brothers, an occasional pattern being a woman's breasts. Such models are placed just inside, or outside, the hut, fixed to the wall. (Men sometimes carve the breast pattern on trees.) Sometimes in small families, where there are no boys, the girls may be sent out herding.

In one village, which abounded with cats, the children were allowed to indulge in periodic cat hunts. The grown BaVenda are afraid to kill cats, so avoid the difficulty when their numbers are becoming overwhelmingly great by organizing this hunt for the children, who thoroughly enjoy it; they kill the cats without a qualm and skin them to make ornaments for their dancing dress. To-day the younger boys and girls occasionally play together, but it used to be considered improper for children of opposite sexes to join in each other's games, and the girls, when boys interfered with them in their play, sang, '*Ndole! Ndole! tshitamba na vhasidzana*' (A naughty boy! A naughty boy! He plays with girls). On hearing this song the interloper always ran away quickly, ashamed of his impertinence.

Mixed Games.

Although it is not generally considered seemly for children of both sexes to play together out of doors they are allowed to do so in the

H

CHILD LIFE

evening in the huts and yards, where they are under the supervision of their elders. The game *kubvhe* is like our 'Up Jenkins' and is usually played by boys and girls together. They are sometimes joined by adult women, but never adult men, who consider such childishness beneath their dignity. Two of the players pick sides and these sit facing each other; the members of one side lay all their hands, held cupwise, on top of each other, and a mealie pip is hidden in one of them. Each person then holds up two closed fists and one of the opposition steps forward and strikes the hand in which he guesses the pip is hidden; if he is wrong the person whose hand has been struck says '*Moo*' scornfully, imitating the lowing of a cow; this is repeated until the pip is discovered, when the opposition has its turn. At the end of the game the pip is passed round, and each player bites off a tiny piece before passing it on to the next; this is done to destroy the seed which may not be made use of again. *Kubvhe* is usually followed by an epilogue. A member of one side leaves the party and returns after a short interval, impersonating an old man, covered with ashes and carrying a stick; he performs various ridiculous antics endeavouring to make some one in the opposing side laugh. If he succeeds a point is scored and a member of the opposition then takes a turn as the buffoon. When the players weary of this pantomime all the members of one side touch the three cooking-stones on the fire to signify that the game is ended.

Hide-and-seek, *u dzumbamana* (to hide), is another game played inside the kraal. One side hides in the huts and yards of the kraal; the leader of the seeking party then shouts out, '*tshinoni lidza muludzi*' (bird whistle). When the children who have hidden hear this shout each one gives a short whistle; as they are discovered they are taken to the *khoro*, and when they have all been found the sides change over.

A favourite game is played by a number of girls standing opposite to an equal number of boys. One boy steps forward and with a small stick points to a girl whom he fancies will approve of him. The girl steps out from the line and together they go to one side. If the girl is not pleased with her partner she leaves him standing alone and returning to the group points out a boy of whom she does approve; he must follow her. The process is repeated by each of the boys in turn until only those refused by their partners remain. The fun of the game consists in ridiculing and laughing at these unfortunates for their unpopularity.

There is another game like 'Ring of Roses'. Girls and boys together dance round in a ring, holding each other's hands tightly and singing,

CHILD LIFE

99

'*Tsinga ndedede khatula*' (strong sinew break). They continue dancing round and round until the chain breaks.

These are only a few examples of the numerous games which are played by the children in the evening, and may serve to illustrate the friendly, well-organized family life that is enjoyed by the average Venda child.

Mahundwani.

Mahundwani is the name given to a miniature village built by the children when their parents have finished reaping the harvest. The children build their *mahundwani* and there play at being grown up with a thoroughness and zeal that forms an excellent preparation for life as responsible men and women of their village.

As soon as the mealies have been reaped the children visit the lands and glean all the cobs that have been left behind by their mothers. They then choose a site for their activities. The place chosen is generally a piece of ground a short distance from the village. One of the chief's sons, if there is one of a suitable age, otherwise any leading spirit of the kraal, is appointed chief. In the same way the son of the *mukhoma* (the chief's right-hand man) assumes his father's duties. The children then pair off, each boy taking one or more of the girls as his wife or wives to work for him. When these preliminaries have been settled the children repair to the chosen site and proceed to build their village, which they endeavour to make, as far as possible, a replica of their parents' kraals. The boys clean the ground, cut wood, and fence in the enclosure with thorn branches or mealie stalks. Each little husband and wife build their own grass hut, after having all helped in the erection of a larger and more imposing hut for the chief.

When the village is complete, and each family installed in its small hut, the wives borrow their baby brothers and sisters to act as their children. Everything is now ready for the youngsters to settle down to enjoy domestic happiness. Every morning each little wife takes her mealies to her mother's hut and there stamps and winnows the meal to the necessary fineness. She borrows pots, plates, and spoons and returns to her little hut to cook the morning meal upon her own fire-stones in preparation for her man's return. The boy-husband borrows a dog and goes off hunting like his father. If he catches anything, even a rabbit or a bird, he carries his spoil home to his little wife and presents it to her to cook for him to eat with his porridge. A portion is always sent to the boy-chief. So the day passes, the girl

CHILD LIFE

giving her husband water with which to wash before his meal and paying him all the respect that her mother shows to her father. She cares for the children, sweeps the hut, smears her yard thoroughly, so that if her mother should visit her everything will be in order. Sometimes the mothers walk across to see how their children are behaving, and scold their daughters if the porridge is not cooked correctly or the house properly cleaned. At night all the children go home to sleep, but first thing in the morning return to the *mahundwani*. Life there continues for several weeks, the children holding their court in their miniature *khoro*, obeying their chief and performing all the characteristic acts of courtesy and service that suit their respective parts.

There are generally several of these miniature villages in progress at the same time. Intense rivalry exists between the different groups, and when the time comes for ending the game the members of one *mahundwani* arrange to fight those of a neighbouring village. The boys of the opposing groups line up, and, armed with sticks, fight one another, the victors driving the vanquished from their home and burning it to the ground. The conquerors then fight the next little village, and so on. The final victors return rejoicing, and after great festivities and excitement burn down their *mahundwani* and return to their parents' kraals.

The children who take part in this event are usually between twelve and fifteen years of age and have often been through part of the initiation rites. It is essentially an organization to produce proficiency in domestic and family affairs and, as such, is encouraged by the parents.

On the whole Venda children are well treated by their parents, who give the little girls bracelets and ornaments and the boys a share in any food delicacies. All are allowed a great deal of freedom, although as they grow older the pressure of discipline, which is tribal rather than family, becomes greater, and they are expected to obey the commands of their elders implicitly. When the boys are about seven years old they commence at night to attend the *thondo* school, while the girls are brought more suddenly to a realization of their responsibilities when, on the commencement of menstruation, they receive a severe schooling in the *vhusha*.

X

PUBERTY AND INITIATION

Boys' School (*thondo*)—Boys' Initiation (*vhutamba vhutuka*)—Girls' Initiation (*vhusha*)—Premarital Unions—Joint Initiation (*domba*)—Boys' Circumcision (*murundu*)—Girls' 'Circumcision' (*musevetho*)

The Thondo.

TWO initiation schools for boys exist, side by side, amongst the BaVenda: the *murundu*, which is a circumcision lodge and has been introduced from without, and the *thondo*, the indigenous school through which all young boys had to pass before attaining manhood, and which probably originated with the Vhatavhatsinde. The *murundu* is slowly driving the *thondo* out of existence, and where it occurs the *thondo* is usually absent.

The *thondo* (See diagram on next page) is a permanent institution always in being after its inauguration, with a constant flow of small boys entering and a periodic exit of older boys in groups. The building of the *thondo* is fraught with a great deal of ceremony and secrecy. As with all building operations a special medicine-man (*nganga ya luvhambo*) is called upon to designate the site. If the chief approves, the place chosen is generally on the slope on the west side of the village, opposite the *khoro*, although it varies slightly with the position of each individual village. The medicine-man next plants poles of the *mbambo* and *luvhambo* trees at the entrance, to frighten evil away from the building, and, after planting, smears them with a mixture of butter-fat and the red powder of the *mutavhatsinde* tree. No stones or soil from outside the chosen site may be used in building the *thondo*. The upper end, under the hill, is dug away, and the stones and earth are used for piling up a strong protecting wall at the lower end. Within this enclosure a large hut is built. In some cases the protecting wall is ten or twelve feet in height, so that the hut is not visible from outside. The work of excavating and building the hut and the wall is done by elderly, responsible men of the kraal. Plastering, smearing, and carrying water are done by from four to six specially chosen women. They are sworn to secrecy, and at their inauguration are severely beaten to impress upon them the seriousness of their oath. If a woman dares to divulge any of the doings of the *thondo* to an outsider she is punished by death. These 'women of the *thondo*', as they are called, steal in secretly at night to carry water, harden the floor, and smear it with cow-dung. Their work must be done so thoroughly that not a single crack is visible on the smoothly smeared floor.

When all the building operations are completed the medicine-man is again summoned to open the *thondo*. Accompanied by the chief and the head councillor, he summons all the builders and the initiates to follow him to the newly-erected building. The procession walks in

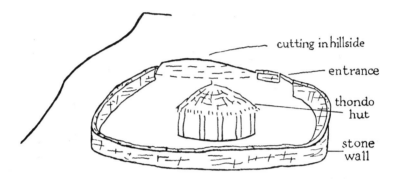

single file to the entrance, where the medicine-man makes the first salute. He goes to the first bend in the wall and salutes again. Inside the hut he falls on his right side and salutes again, leaning on his right elbow in an attitude of extreme deference and respect. All the builders follow, imitating his every action. He then goes to the first space between the supporting poles of the hut and again salutes and walks round the hut from pole to pole saluting at every halt until he returns to the starting-point. Entering the hut again he squats on one of the little wooden stools, which have been specially made for the *thondo*. All the others, having copied him in all his peregrinations, sit down around him.

He then explains to them the rules of the *thondo*, the method of entry, and the names by which everything must be called. He produces a stick of the *mukangala* tree, about two or three feet long and the thickness of a man's thumb, which has been rubbed in cattle fat or castor oil. This stick is used for the chastisement of the initiates. He lights the fire with the fire-sticks and explains that it must never be allowed to go out. With the lighting of this fire the opening ceremony is completed and all the men and youths are called to dance the *tshikona* dance, in order to bring the blessing of the ancestor spirits upon the *thondo*.

PUBERTY AND INITIATION 103

To-day *thondo* schools are held at Thengwe, Makonde, Lambani, HaMulele, Tshikundamalema, Makuya, Tshaulu, Gava, Mbilwi, Mukula, Rambuda, Mukumbani, Vhufuli, Phiphidi, Fondwe, Milaboni, Mubumoni, and Gandanipfa.

Every boy in the district, when he is seven or eight years old, begins to attend the *thondo*, and he continues receiving instruction until he reaches puberty. Boys are released in small batches soon after puberty, and after the initiation ceremony are attached to age-sets. These age-sets are really regiments, and, during war, all members of the same set fight together. At all public feasts and beer-drinks it is customary for the men and boys to sit in their respective age-sets, and they are served in these groups, the youngest group being served first.

It has been said that originally the *thondo* was intended only for the sons of the royal family and members of the aristocracy. There they received a training in the laws and customs of the tribe to equip them with all the knowledge necessary for good chiefs, so that they should not be found unprepared when the day came for them to govern the people. This may have been the case at some very distant date, but for a long time it has been customary for all boys, rich and poor alike, to receive tuition in the *thondo*, and in time of war to act as the chief's body-guard and protect him in his capital while the men were out fighting.

The school is enveloped in secrecy and mystery, no one being allowed to enter the *thondo* unless he is a member. The youngsters are frightened into telling any one wishing to intrude that there is a lion within, who will kill an unlawful trespasser. This rule is very strictly kept, no one except members daring to go near the school through fear of being overtaken by disaster. Boys, disobeying the orders given in the school, or ignoring the law of secrecy, are severely punished, formerly often being killed. Sometimes one of the arms or legs of such a victim would be brought into the *thondo* to frighten the other children into submissive obedience. They would be warned that any one offending in the same way would share their companion's fate. The building is always guarded by one or two of the young boys, who keep a vigilant look-out for intruding strangers.

Every evening, after the usual daily work of herding the cattle and goats, all the boys gather together at the *thondo* for instruction, making it their sleeping quarters. It is essentially a military institution. The boys are subjected to a physical hardening and mental discipline to prepare them for a life of soldiery. The favourite method of warfare

PUBERTY AND INITIATION

amongst the BaVenda is by ambush and night attack. In order to carry out their campaign successfully a good spy-system is essential, so that an important part of the *thondo* training is instruction in stealth and individual daring. The boys are encouraged to steal, and any one purloining a goat from his father's herd is commended. All animals stolen in this way are eaten at a feast held in the *thondo*, and the choicest part of the stolen goods is sent to the chief as a bribe, *musumu* (from *u suma*, to give the chief his part), so that if the owner, suspecting the identity of the thief, searches for his property in the chief's precincts, he will be turned out for trespassing near the *thondo*.

In the school the boys are given tasks to perform, such as mat-making, which tasks must be finished in a prescribed time. All tribal etiquette and rules of politeness are strictly enforced, and any boy, being reported to the head of the *thondo* for negligence in this respect, is punished at night for his neglect.

The school is in charge of the *negota* (the head councillor), assisted by some of the other old men. It is he who metes out punishment to the delinquents while the boys are sitting in a circle round the hut. The delinquent is called forward with an older boy. The *negota* orders the older boy to administer the punishment, first giving the unoffending older boy a severe thrashing with his stick, so that being enraged he will hit his young colleague hard. On occasions everybody receives punishment as part of their training to endure pain. One boy is called out and beaten, and he passes on the beating to the boy next to him, and so it continues all around the *thondo*, each boy thrashing his neighbour. The boys are proud of the marks left by the cane, and display their scars with glee to the admiring youngsters in their kraals. They are trained to instant obedience, and at the sound of the *phala-fhala* horn must leave everything and run to the *thondo*.

A great deal of time is spent in practising dancing, both at night and early in the morning, before the boys are allowed to go off for the day. The school is visited periodically by the chief, who is its supreme head. He joins in the boys' feasting, receives their adoration, and makes a general inspection to see how his embryo soldiers are shaping.

Gottschling[1] in describing the *thondo* refers to certain objects which he states are kept in the *thondo* hut. He says that 'In the "*Tondo*" stands a little round shed on which all the fetishes of the tribe are kept, together with a wood-carved image of their "totem" (sacred animal),

---

[1] Gottschling, The Rev. E., 'The Bawenda: a sketch of their history and customs', *J. Roy. Anthrop. Inst.*, 1905. p. 372.

PUBERTY AND INITIATION 105

and of a man and woman of about 2 feet in height, fairly well carved in ebony. These figures are called "*Votambo*" (feast)'. All my informants deny that any objects of this description are kept in the *thondo*. The figures of which he speaks are shown in the *domba*.

Each boy, when he is aware of his first nocturnal emission, reports the fact to the *negota*, and when a sufficient number of the boys are ready to go through the initiation rite (*vhutamba vhutuka*) they are allowed to leave the *thondo*. Up to this time a boy is called *mutukana* (a small boy), but after his emergence from the school he is *muthannga* (a young man), and would be very insulted if ever again referred to as *mutukana*.

Each boy is given a new name by the old men during his life in the *thondo*. This name is chosen to fit the boy's disposition or to commemorate some current event. The *thondo* name always begins with *ne-*, the abbreviation of *munne* (a man), signifying that he is now a man. It becomes one of the most important of his many names.

After the *vhutamba vhutuka* ceremony the boy's apprenticeship at the *thondo* is over, although he may continue to enter the school freely at any time. He has emerged from childhood hardened and disciplined, ready to shoulder the responsibilities as well as to share the privileges of a fighting man of the tribe. To-day, when military training is unnecessary, the institution is becoming a means by which free labour is obtained for the chief, and often a boy not wishing to attend is allowed to commute his services for money payments.

Vhutamba vhutuka (The washing away of boyhood).

Every MuVenda boy must, on reaching puberty, go through the *vhutamba vhutuka* ceremony. If he is not a member of a *thondo* school he must, when he becomes aware of his first nocturnal emission, inform one of the older boys of his village (never one of his brothers), who passes the information on to the *mukhoma* (the chief's aide). The *mukhoma* waits until there are a number of boys ready and then orders them to prepare a large quantity of snuff. After appropriating a portion for himself he sends some to the father of each of the boys, saying to each that now his son is a young man.

A day is fixed for the boys to attend the *khoro* of the district chief, where they join in the *mathanngwa* dance for two or three nights. On the third morning the initiates must collect a large pile of fire-wood at the riverside and steal, borrow, or buy goats and fowls, which they hide near the pile of fire-wood. In the early hours of the following

PUBERTY AND INITIATION

morning those who were initiated at the previous ceremony, and are now the *midabe*, or instructors, assemble at the gateway of the *khoro*, and with blows and threats drive the initiates to the river. Here they are forced into the icy water, where they must remain squatting for three or four hours, while the *midabe* kindle a fire and feast themselves on the animals that were procured for them, mocking and jeering at the shivering initiates and occasionally derisively aiming a well-picked bone at their heads. On the slightest pretext the *midabe* punish them with the *tshipata*, a neat little instrument of torture dear to the BaVenda, made from four small sticks, which are placed between the fingers of the delinquent and pressed tightly together, causing him acute pain. Stiff with cold and utterly miserable they are at last allowed to emerge from the river and to warm themselves at the fire, before proceeding to the *khoro* again to dance the *mathanngwa*.

All day, after this ordeal, the *midabe* keep a constant watch to prevent the initiates from snatching intervals of sleep. During the day the initiates collect more wood and animals for the delectation of their tormentors on the following morning, when the ordeal in the river is repeated. This continues for six days, and in addition to the physical hardening, engendered by the ordeal of endurance in the river, the boys are given sexual instruction and taught many of the tribal rules of etiquette and mode of life. At the end of the ceremony they are considered to have passed the first stage in their journey towards manhood and are encouraged to indulge in playful familiarities with the girls, which hitherto were strictly forbidden.

The Vhusha.

A girl, at her first menses, is considered to have reached the stage in life when she must discard her childish practices and become a responsible member of the community. The passage from childhood to adolescence is marked by the *vhusha* ceremony. Before this a girl is called *musidzana* (a small girl), and afterwards is always referred to as *musidzana vha khomba*, the term *khomba* meaning 'dangerous', implying that sexual intercourse may now result in pregnancy. Sometimes the term *khomba* is used as an alternative to *vhusha* in referring to the ceremony.

On the first sign of menstruation the girl will inform one of her step-mothers, or one of the elder women of the kraal, of its occurrence. This person will tell the girl's mother, who then tells the father. There is a barrier of reserve which forbids the direct approach of the parent

PUBERTY AND INITIATION 107

by the child in matters of intimacy, especially in affairs in any way connected with sex. This behaviour occurs repeatedly throughout Venda life.

The *vhusha* is held at the village of the district chief or petty chief. The ceremony is often postponed until there are two or three girls ready.

After sundown, on the day that has been fixed for the proceedings, all the women living within reasonable distance come into the chief's kraal in troupes, each troupe heralding its arrival with loud trilling. A fire is lit in the *khoro*, whither the women proceed. All men are excluded, and throughout the ceremony it is strictly forbidden for a man to come anywhere near. If a man is caught in the vicinity he receives a severe handling from the womenfolk and may also be brought before the chief and fined for his indiscretion.

In the *khoro* the women remove their shoulder cloths and *dzirivha* and dance naked except for their ornaments and the *shedu*. The initiates are stripped and placed in the background. All the women, young and old, dance about the fire, to the accompaniment of the drums and the trilling and singing of the rest of the community. No special drums are used at this ceremony, but the ordinary drums are played with a characteristic beat, never heard elsewhere. The singing and dancing continue throughout the night, and at sunrise the party breaks up, the outside women returning to their homes in troupes as they arrived.

The initiates remain at the kraal in the public hut, the *tshivhambo*. This hut is their head-quarters throughout the ceremonies, which continue for six days. They are put in charge of two instructresses, who have previously been initiated, and whose duty it is to direct their pupils. Whenever the initiates leave the *tshivhambo* they are enveloped in a blanket, or wear a *tshirivha* for the first time. They must walk in a crouching position. The instructresses are always naked except for the *shedu*. The initiates are escorted to the riverside each morning, walking in single file, led by one of the instructresses, who beats the drum as a warning to all males that the party is approaching.

At the river-bank a fire is lit and the initiates, still completely enveloped in their blankets, sleep around it for two or three hours. They are then awakened and are taught the tribal rules of etiquette and obedience. Until this time they have been children and their misdemeanours overlooked, but now they are children no longer and must conform to the tribal law in all things. They also receive a

PUBERTY AND INITIATION

certain amount of dancing instruction, although most of this takes place at night. A great deal of time is given up to sexual teaching. They are warned against becoming deflowered before marriage, and are taught how to have sexual intercourse without this occurring. Quite tiny girls are often shown, by an old woman of their kraal, how to stretch the *labia minora*. During the *vhusha* a great deal of time is spent in continuing this practice. To help in the dilatation a bat is killed and cooked, the resulting concoction being rubbed on the parts, so that, as the bat has a curtain across its legs, its essence will facilitate the growth of a similar curtain across the legs of the initiates. Often a stone is tied to the parts to hasten the process. This manipulation results in the formation of a regular apron a few inches in length.

When the sun is high in the sky the initiates are ordered into the river, (Plate XXVII). They kneel in the customary attitude of obeisance, with heads bent right forward in the water. They are then made to fall over on one side and remain completely immersed at the pleasure of their instructresses. In the early afternoon the party returns to the kraal, generally accompanied by a large party of girls who have been down to the river to fetch water. The initiates are often subjected to further humiliations. They may be ordered to lift a heavy stone on to their backs and walk to the kraal carrying it in this position. Sometimes they are forced to pick up hot ashes and hold them for some time. A favourite humiliation is to force them to travel the long distance from the river to the kraal lying flat on the ground, wriggling along with extreme difficulty and discomfort. On the way home the escorting party sings lustily, hitting the lips with the right forefinger and producing a large volume of sound.

The initiates rest until evening. After sunset a drum is sounded, and all the women in the kraal gather around a large fire in the *tshivhambo*. The initiates crouch in the background completely naked, while the older girls sit about the fire playing the drum and singing. Two girls then proceed to dance with great energy between the fire and the initiates. The performance is more in the nature of hard physical exercise than actual dancing. It consists of a series of jumps performed to time and repeated over and over again. When at last the performers are exhausted their place is taken by two other girls, who go through the same dancing procedure. Between each exhibition the initiates put their heads in their hands on the ground in front of them and trill fearfully. After several of the women have danced two of the initiates are dragged forward and attempt to imitate

PLATE XXVII

GIRL INITIATE IN THE RIVER

PUBERTY AND INITIATION 109

the elder dancers. At first their efforts are entirely unsuccessful, and are received with laughter and derision by the older girls, who sing, '*Mutei ndi para-para*' (the initiate is running amok). When the teachers think that they have tried long enough the initiates creep back to their companions and once more kneel down on all fours with their foreheads on the ground. This is repeated over and over again until the initiates begin to show signs of improvement, when a second dancing exercise is started by the older girls. The most skilful dance is one in which the performer stands on her head, and, balancing herself on the palms of her hands, performs a series of leg movements, waving her legs in the air in time to the drums and singing, with remarkable skill and energy. This the initiates find very difficult, and their efforts cause untold amusement to the older girls. The dancing continues until a late hour, when all the company retire to their various huts. The initiates, with their instructresses, curl up and sleep where they are until sunrise, when they are again escorted to the river-bank.

The same routine is repeated for six days and nights, culminating, on the sixth night, in a more general dance which continues throughout the night. The last morning, when the girls are taken to the river, they are washed from head to foot and their bodies smeared with fat, and their heads shaved into the usual crown and smeared with red ochre. Each girl is then escorted to her home, where her parents receive her joyfully, giving her new ornaments and clothes. A curious object called *thahu* is tucked into the girdle at the back, somewhat resembling a tail. It is a small, funnel-shaped object, about 6 inches in diameter, woven from the bark of the *mutanzwa* tree, mixed with the juice of the *muembe*, and thickly plastered with a mixture of red ochre and fat. From the centre hangs a string tassel about 1 inch in diameter and 6 inches long made from the same *mutanzwa* tree. The *thahu* is worn for six days and is then put away until another group of girls from the same area has gone through the ceremony, when it may be passed on to one of them. During this period a newly-initiated girl is bound by very strict laws of etiquette. Except when she is alone she may not stand upright, (Plate XXVIII) but must walk with bent head and stooping shoulders. She must lie right down with her head on the ground in greeting a superior, instead of simply kneeling and putting her hands together, and must in every way comport herself with submission and humility.

I could discover no adequate explanation for the wearing of the *thahu*, but it seems to symbolize the girl's maturity and to manifest

110 PUBERTY AND INITIATION

publicly her changed status. The *thahu* is worn in two other connexions. The chief's youngest wife, called *muta noni* (little bird of the
yard), when she first takes up her residence with the chief, wears the
thahu as part of her dress for some time, probably as a warning to his
officials that she is the chief's property and strictly tabu to them.
Occasionally the baby daughter of an important person has a miniature
thahu tucked into her girdle when she is dressed for a festive occasion,
apparently simply as an ornament.

Amongst the Akikuyu the same word *thahu* is applied to a person
or thing that 'has accidentally become the victim of certain circumstances, or intentionally performed certain acts, which carry with them
a kind of ill luck or curse'. Hobley gives a long list of circumstances
that react in bringing about this state of *thahu*. Possibly at one time
the word was used by the BaVenda in describing a menstruating
woman, who wore the funnel-shaped object as evidence of her condition and was always strictly tabu. With time the word has disappeared from the Tshivenda vocabulary in this connexion, but remains
as the name of the object now worn to declare publicly the fact that
a girl has reached maturity and henceforth will be periodically in a
condition of ceremonial uncleanliness.

In many parts of the country to-day the *vhusha* ceremony ends
with the girl's return to her parents, but the wearing of the *thahu* and
its concomitant behaviour restrictions still persist in some of the more
conservative districts, especially in the eastern area.

A fee, formerly a goat, now ten shillings, is paid by the parents of
each initiate to the chief or petty chief in whose kraal the ceremony
takes place.

Pre-marital Unions.

At the conclusion of the *vhutamba vhutuka* ceremonies the initiates
emerge as *vhathannga* and *vhasadzana vha khombo* ready and eager to
put their newly acquired manhood and womanhood to the test. As
children they took no care of their appearance, but now the young
men try to make themselves look attractive in preparation for their
excursions around the country in search of girl-lovers.

All medicine-men include in their stock-in-trade a number of love-
potions, *ndilela*, for inducing love. The word *ndilela* is derived from
u lela (to cry for). One of the simplest of these concoctions is a powder
made from the root of the *ndilela* tree, which the young man
mixes in his washing-water, thereby making himself devastatingly

PLATE XXVIII

GIRL AFTER THE *VHUSHA* IN THE HUMBLE
ATTITUDE, WEARING THE *THAHU*

PUBERTY AND INITIATION

attractive. Another charm is made from the dried gum of the *muto-gota* tree, powdered and mixed with snuff. Snuff plays an important part in love-making. It may be added to a powder made from a dried centipede mixed with the clippings of the young man's own finger-nails and hair and the scrapings from various parts of his body.

Nearly every girl has several lovers, but she has been warned in the *vhusha* that she must on no account become deflowered before her marriage. So the young people indulge in a pseudo-sexual intercourse (*u davhula*, similar to the Zulu *hlobonga* or the BaThonga *gangisa*). The Venda attitude towards these pre-marital unions conforms with the ideas of most of the Southern Bantu. No misdemeanour is committed unless defloration occurs and pregnancy results. There is a reciprocal term, *mudavhu*, for a man and a girl between whom there exists this *u davhula* relationship, and it is recognized by the rest of the community. A man who is betrothed and has paid part of his lobola may be fully aware of the identity of his bride's *mudavhu*, but as long as she does not become pregnant he does not resent the attentions of the other man. It is customary for a man who is betrothed to a girl to work from time to time for his future father-in law. Her *mudavhu* also works for her father, and it may happen that husband and *mudavhu* may be found working side by side in the father's garden.

A great deal of this type of love-making takes place at the *domba* dance, where the girls display their feminine allurements and the young men vie with each other to receive the favours of the girls of their choice.

The Domba.

The *domba* does not take place regularly. Its occurrence depends largely on the number of girls ready to participate and on the result of the harvest. It is essential that there should be plenty of food to enable the members of the school to have the necessary leisure. It usually lasts about three months, but is often protracted to eight or nine months and sometimes continued for a whole year. Girls always attend on the first opportunity after the *vhusha*. Sometimes if there is no prospect of a school being held near home they may go long distances in order to attend one at the village of some neighbouring chief. It is held in the *khoro* of the village. Everybody, men and women, may attend this very important social function. Those who have not previously attended a *domba* play the important part in the dancing and singing, and are the centre of interest to the elder people,

PUBERTY AND INITIATION

who act as helpers and spectators. It is the duty of the parents of the participants to supply quantities of food and beer for their consumption.

The school is a general preparation for marriage, where boys and girls, who are usually separated, are brought together, and, by means of symbols and metaphors, are together taught to understand the true significance of marriage and child-birth, and by the same means are warned of the pitfalls and dangers that they are likely to encounter during the course of their lives.

The management is in the hands of a man, *nemungoza* or *mme a domba* (mother of the domba), who is chosen for his vocal ability. He is assisted by a woman *nyamatei* (mother of the initiates). These two persons are masters of ceremonies, and are responsible for the arrival of adequate supplies of food and beer and the regular attendance of the participants and their proper instruction, as well as for the general supervision of the whole institution. The *mme a domba*, throughout the school, has charge of three sticks which have been treated with protective medicine. These sticks keep evil away from the school and must always be held in his hand while dancing is in progress. In the intervals he may place them on the drums, but in no other place.

The initiates, *vhatei* (sing. *mutei*), are particularly supervised and instructed by the young people who were initiates at the previous *domba* and who are now the *midabe* (sing. *lidabe*).

Before the *domba* proper starts the girl initiates must take part in two inaugural ceremonies, the *tshikanda* and *ludodo*, taking place on the first and second nights respectively. *Tshikanda* means 'little skin', but I could not discover the meaning of the word *ludodo*, or the significance of either word. At the *tshikanda* all the women, old and young, including the *midabe* and *vhatei*, assemble in the *khoro* and then proceed to the *tshivhambo*, led by *nyamatei*. The *midabe* remove their clothing except the *shedu*, and having stripped the *vhatei* naked, rub them over with red ochre and ashes. Porridge is cooked for the *vhatei* and placed on the earth and they are ordered to eat it, lying flat on the ground and scooping it into their mouths with their hands. In the very early hours of the morning the *vhatei* are sent into the *khoro* in single file, hopping behind one another in imitation of frogs. There they receive their first lesson in the python dance, the central incident throughout the *domba*. When the sun rises they return to the *tshivhambo* and are there entertained by the story of Thovela and Tshishongo. These two mythical heroes are vaguely considered to be

PUBERTY AND INITIATION

the originators of the BaVenda. The story goes that Chief Thovela wishes to have sexual intercourse with his wife's three women attendants. Tshishongo refuses his request and Thovela, in his anger at her refusal, kills her secretly. The three women, on finding Tshishongo dead, decide to consult a diviner in order to discover the cause of her death. Thovela allows them to go and sends a messenger to escort them. They learn that Thovela poisoned their mistress, but on their return find, to their surprise, that she is alive again. They tell her of her husband's treachery and she is filled with anger, hides a spear under her clothing and kills him in revenge. Thovela's messenger, not knowing the part she has played in the death, tells Tshishongo that her husband is dead. She replies that it is a good thing and advises him to consult a diviner as to the identity of the murderer, taking two of her women as escort. On their return, with the knowledge of Tshishongo's guilt, they find Thovela alive again and in turn tell him of the manner in which his wife killed him. After this Tshishongo runs away with her three women.

The moral of this story is obscure, but probably its primary object is to impress on the initiates the futility of committing crimes in the hope that the perpetrator will go undiscovered. The diviner is always able to reconstruct the whole crime and detect the guilty party.

The second night of the *domba* is spent in performing *ludodo* in the *tshivhambo*. The *vhatei* are ordered to sit down one behind the other, each girl with her legs stretched wide apart in front of her. The girls sit close to each other in this position. The women dance and the girls are told to make various movements. They are taught about the signs of pregnancy, the meaning of marriage and child-birth, and are warned that they are now nearly fully grown and will soon have to give up playing at life and their *u davhula* practices. Marriage is not a game but the precursor of child-birth, and, as such, must be properly understood, so that the resultant children will be strong and healthy, uncontaminated by dangers and diseases resulting from improper knowledge and broken tabus. By the time the night is over they have received a thorough introduction to the correct behaviour conducive to successful marriage and parenthood, which information is all going to be emphasized and reiterated, time after time, in many different ways during the course of the *domba*. As the morning dawns each girl is examined by the *nyamatei* to see whether she has been deflowered. Any girl who is found to be guilty is roughly handled by the

PUBERTY AND INITIATION

midabe, who pinch and thrash her and torture her with the *tshiphata*, while the whole assembly of women abuses her.

After the *ludodo* the *domba* proper may commence, inaugurated by a performance of the *tshikona* dance to invoke the blessing of the ancestors on the school and its members. A fire is lit by the medicine-man with the fire-sticks. This fire must not go out while the *domba* is in progress, otherwise the drums must be reversed and all activities cease until the medicine-man relights it with the fire-sticks.

On the third night the women and girls again assemble in the *tshivhambo*, but this time they are joined by the boy initiates, who sit down opposite the girls. Each *mutei*, whether boy or girl, is made to hang by the legs from the cross-beam of the hut, while the *mme a domba* sings, 'Muleme u tamba nga thoho' (the bat hangs with its head down). The *vhatei* reply in a long-drawn 'E—e—e——!' Medicine made from the bat played a part in the dilatation practised by the girls at the *vhusha* ceremony. The symbolization by the *vhatei* of the bat in a sleeping position possibly signifies that as the bat is sleeping so the *u davhula* practices must sleep. Each *mutei* is also made to sit on the drum while the *mme a domba* sings, 'Matunde kwo dzula thenyama'. (The male finch sits balanced). My informants were all very vague as to the significance of these two actions, but they are a necessary preliminary, which the initiates must all perform before learning the secret formulae of the *domba*.

The law of the *domba* consists of a number of words and formulae, which must be used in describing all the places and objects with which the initiates come into contact. The *khoro*, *tshivhambo*, drums, &c., all have their special *domba* names, and it is absolutely forbidden for the initiates to use the ordinary words while at the school. A girl informant, who was learning to write, helped herself to memorize the law by making a list of the more important words. She gave me the following information, which has been confirmed by other informants. Some old people are always gathered at the gate to question every boy and girl wishing to enter. Any who fail to answer the questions put to them are chased away and refused admittance. The young people attending for the first time are brought by their mothers. The first question to be answered on reaching the closed gate of the *khoro* during a *domba* is as to the significance of the closed and open gate. The answer is that the closed gate means pregnancy and the open gate birth. The *khoro* must be called Lake Fundudzi. The right side is *fumi la nanga dza ndou* (ten elephants' tusks). The left side is

PLATE XXIX

THE PYTHON DANCE

PUBERTY AND INITIATION 115

milenzhe (legs) or *fumi la malembe* (ten hoes). The top side is *tshitaha tsha tshi refwe* (nest of the hammerkop). The handles of the drums are *magohna vha lucheli* (a frog's knee). The smooth centre of the tympanum of the drum is *thuvunya ya ngoma ya mwana* (a baby's fontanelle). The complete tympanum is *lukhanda la munna* (skin of a man). The opening at the bottom is *ndila* (vagina, road). The woodwork of the drum is *gumba la poho* (egg of an ostrich). The drum-stick is *tshanda tsha muthu* (hand of a person). The wooden pegs are *munwe* (fingers). The fence around the *khoro* is *lukhanda la tharu* (python's skin). The passage from the *khoro* to the *tshivhambo* is *mulalavhungu* (milky way). The floor of the *tshivhambo* is *tshankhukhu* (threshold). The holes in the wall for tying the door are *ningo dza ngwena* (nostrils of the crocodile). The big beer-pots are *dzinkhome* (pregnant). The pouring out of beer is called *u vhofhololo* (to give birth, untie). The mouth of the beer-pot is *marinini a mwana* (a baby's gums). Many other things have symbolic names, the coals are referred to as 'old women', the ashes as 'old men', the roof poles as 'men', the thatch as 'ostrich feathers', the stick-spire as the 'umbilicus', and so on. Having mastered the law of the *domba* the girls and boys follow a certain daily routine.

Those who join the *domba* during its progress and have not been present at the opening must go through all these introductory ceremonies in the village of their own district chief, so that when they seek admittance at the *domba* they know the law and can take part with the other initiates without further preliminaries.

The python dance (Plate XXIX) is the central feature of the school. The dancers are in a long line, the men in front and the girls behind, the hands of each dancer being placed on the shoulder of the one in front. Sometimes the line is linked by the arms of each dancer encircling the waist of the one in front. There may be other local differences. The dancers are practically naked, the men wearing only the *tsindi* and the girls only the *shedu* and their ornaments. The *mme a domba* appoints drummers. The drums may be played by either sex, but at the *domba* are more often played by girls. There are usually two large drums, the largest slung from a wooden framework, and two small hand-drums. Some men, who have attended the *domba* before, are usually asked to lead the dance for a short time, in order to teach the youngsters. Later they fall out, and the probationers dance on to the beat of the drums, the *mme a domba* keeping between them and the fire and singing at the top of his voice. He sings, '*Tharu ya*

PUBERTY AND INITIATION

mabidhighami' (the python is uncoiling), to which the dancers reply with a long drawn '*E—e—e——*', in a low tone. This and many other phrases are repeated over and over again, while the chain of dancers moves around the fire very slowly, dragging one leg forward after the other, sometimes reversing and making a shuffling movement with the arms, and symbolizing realistically the slow gliding movement of the python.

The words of the song are varied at the inclination of the soloist, who extemporizes at will. When he considers that it is time for the dance to stop, he heralds the conclusion by singing, '*Nowayanga i i a lila u beba ha vhasadzi hungvhe*' (my snake cries that that which is born of woman is always the same). The snake is meant to refer to the small snake that is believed to live inside every woman and is the chief agent in building up the foetus. When the drummers hear these words they know that it is a signal for them to stop playing. As soon as the beat of the drums stops, the dancing ceases.

The python dance is performed for two or three hours before the initiates are allowed to rest. At night some of the girls sleep either in the village huts or in the *tshivhambo*, while the boys sleep around the fire in the *khoro*. Early each morning the *mme a domba* beats the drum and all the initiates are supposed to hurry to the *khoro* and prepare for dancing. There they are counted and any absentees noted. Late comers are beaten, and after being warned to be in time in the future are allowed to join their companions in the dancing. After a few hours' dancing the drums stop, and, after saluting them, the initiates run off to perform small duties, the girls fetching water or grinding meal and the boys cutting wood or hunting. Any person desiring work done can, in exchange for beer, obtain a troop of workers. At the sound of the drums everything is left and there is another rush to the *khoro*, where the dance continues until noon, the dinner hour. The initiates eat together in the *tshivhambo*.

At intervals during the months that the *domba* is in progress instruction is given to the initiates, on the subjects of sex, marriage, and child-birth, and other more mundane matters, with the help of symbols. They are also forced to perform certain feats of endurance to humiliate and to harden them. The symbolic objects, *mitana vha domba*, are kept jealously hidden in the chief's hut, and are only produced when required to illustrate one or other of the anecdotes which are enacted for the enlightenment of the young people. These symbolic representations, *dzingoma* (drums, sing. *ngoma*), are not properly

PLATE XXX

THE *SALI*

PUBERTY AND INITIATION

understood by the initiates for whose benefit they are performed. After questioning a number of informants and making a fairly comprehensive reconstruction with the help of the data obtained, I was fortunate in meeting a man, Abel Mananga, who had himself often acted in the capacity of *mme a domba*. He explained a great deal that had been vague and contradictory and volunteered interpretations as to the significance of many of the *dzingoma*. These often take place at night when the *vhatei* are gathered in the *khoro*. During an interval in the python dance the *mme a domba* tells them to sit in a circle near the fire and bend their heads low over the ground; while the initiates are in this position the *ngoma* is prepared, and when all is in readiness they are told to look up. Others are performed during the day, the time and place naturally depending on the nature of the incident to be demonstrated.

1. *Ngoma sali* (Charcoal). One night the *vhatei* stop dancing and are ordered to lie down and hide their faces for the first *ngoma*. *Nyamatei* goes to the chief's hut and fetches the *sali*, which she places in the centre of the circle of *vhatei*. The *sali* is a calabash-shaped solid object, about a foot high, made from a mixture of ashes, earth and cow-dung and closely studded with mealie seeds. The seeds are of four different colours, red, white, yellow and black. The different colours are arranged in irregular vertical stripes, completely covering the solid core. Two white ostrich feathers are stuck in the top of the object to beautify it. (Plate XXX)

As soon as *nyamatei* has deposited it in the circle she asks the cringing *vhatei*, 'What is before you?' They look up and perceive this curious object with the four colours glowing in the fire-light. They are frightened and, jumping up, they draw back. *Nyamatei* explains the meaning of the symbol. The white seeds represent young men in the full vigour of life, the red, young women of child-bearing age, whilst the yellow and black are the old men and women, nearing the end of their lives. The *midabe* make up a huge fire and *nyamatei* picks up the *sali*, which she brandishes in front of her, dancing wildly about the fire, while all the spectators trill loudly.

2. *Ngoma mavhavhe* (That which hurts, from *u vhavha*, to hurt). For this *ngoma* the *vhatei* are ordered to assemble outside the village and to sit down with legs outstretched straight in front, and hands clasped behind their heads. One or two *midabe* lead, to illustrate the method of procedure. They must shuffle forward for about two hundred yards in this position. It is a very strenuous and difficult

PUBERTY AND INITIATION

ordeal. Any *vhatei* putting hands to the ground to assist them in their progress are severely beaten. The object of this *ngoma* is to humiliate and to harden.

3. *Ngoma nyamudanga* (Vulture). One evening *nyamatei* takes a small pointed stick, a foot long, and sticks it into the ground very close to the fire, singing, '*Nyamudanga lo otsha nama li vho kundwa*' (the vulture has fried meat, but now he cannot unfry it again). She then creeps up to the stick on her knees and grabs it away from the fire with her teeth, while the assembly trill. The stick is replaced and each *mutei* goes through the same performance, the stick being finally burnt in the fire.

According to Abel Mananga, this little pantomime is enacted to impress upon the young people the importance of the fact that a menstruating woman is strictly tabu, and that any man violating this tabu will himself become infected with the woman's impurity and die. As a vulture who has dropped its prey in a fire can never retrieve it, so a man daring to have intercourse with a menstruating woman can never recover from the results of his deed.

4. *Ngoma gali* (Broken pot). For this *ngoma nyamatei* brings a basket tray on which are placed two pots, one containing red and the other white fluid. It is explained to the *vhatei* that the pot containing the red fluid represents the woman, who is tabu for six days and may not be approached by her husband or any man.

This demonstration has practically the same object as the *ngoma nyamudanga*. It is to reiterate and emphasize the strength, and consequently the danger, of a menstruating woman.

5. *Ngoma tsenene* (Tree-buzzer). In this *ngoma* an old man and woman are disguised with grass and leaves, so that it is impossible to distinguish more of their identity than their respective sexes. The *vhatei* are assembled in the *khoro* and ordered to bow down to the ground and hide their faces. When they look up they see the disguised pair, who lie down on a mat prepared for them and are covered with a blanket.

The lesson which is supposed to be taught by this demonstration is the ill-advisability of having promiscuous sexual intercourse in the bush.

6. *Ngoma mutotombudze* (Grasshopper). Some one is disguised as a grasshopper with grass and rushes, and seated on the cross-piece above the *khoro* gate. In the meantime the *vhatei* are lying with their faces hidden, waiting for the orders of *nyamatei*. When the grasshopper is

PUBERTY AND INITIATION

119

ready they are told to look up and, pointing to the creature, *nyamatei* sings, '*Mutotombudze! mutotombudze!*' The assembly answers, '*Rowana shangoni!*' (We found you in the bush). The girl initiates are driven through the gateway and are hit by the grasshopper as they pass. Beyond the gate they are met by four or five men, with thin switches, who give them a sound thrashing. The boy initiates follow and are hit by the grasshopper, but not by the other men.

The grasshopper from the bush is supposed to represent a wife who has come to her husband from far away. She will try to get the upper hand, knowing 'the power of her blood'. The sound thrashing given to the girls outside, which is not shared by the boys, is to demonstrate the futility of her arrogance, and to show that in the end the man will be the most powerful.

7. *Ngoma phalana* (Rooibok). One day the *midabe* stuff a rooibok's skin with grass, making it look as realistic as possible, and hide it in the vicinity of the village. The *vhatei* are assembled at a point that overlooks the scene of the hunt which is about to take place. Two girl *midabe* have strings of thorns tied around their mouths, to represent teeth, and imitate the behaviour of hunting-dogs. They are led by a boy *lidabe*, the hunter. The dogs hunt wildly through the bush for a considerable time, until eventually they discover the stuffed buck. Immediately they begin to bark, and their master rushes up and aims heavy blows at it with his sticks. Having slain it, he commences to carry it back to the village. On approaching the *khoro*, one of the old men demands the dead animal, saying that, by right, it belongs to him. The *midabe* all expostulate violently, declaring that it is theirs, having been killed by one of themselves with the help of their dogs. This dispute ends in a sham fight between the old people and the *midabe*, all using light switches as weapons, the fight always resulting in a victory for the old people. The buck is then carried to the *khoro* by one of the conquerors, where it is cut up and distributed in the same way as a real animal. A handful of grass is first taken to the chief, representing his customary share. The rest of the grass is then apportioned to the various persons present, the skin being taken back to the chief's hut, whence it had been previously taken.

The lesson this *ngoma* is supposed to teach is the prior right of the old people to a share in all the spoils of the hunt. It also impresses upon them the importance attached to the chief's share.

8. *Ngoma tharu* (Python or large snake). This *ngoma* always takes place at night. The *vhatei* lie down and hide their faces while

PUBERTY AND INITIATION

nyamatei brings forward a basket lid, on which is curled the clay model of a large snake, decorated with stripes of red, white, yellow and black. The *vhatei* look up and *nyamatei* explains the significance of the colours as she did for the *ngoma sali*. She asks the initiates what the creature is that is lying on the tray. They all answer that it is a snake. She repeats her question several times and always receives the same answer. She then explains that the girls are like snakes. A woman will be very dangerous to any man who has sexual relations with her after an abortion, until she has been properly purified. The boys are also warned that they will die if they approach their wives when suffering from any infection such as syphilis.

9. *Ngoma kholomo ya duma* (Dwarf cattle). One night the *vhatei* hide their heads in the usual way and *nyamatei* brings in a *mufharo* basket and produces the clay model of a bull. All the gathering trill.

The BaDuma, a BaKaranga tribe, had a very small breed of cattle, and the name '*kholomo ya duma*' is given by the BaVenda to all small cattle. Apparently this model is supposed to demonstrate that a man though quite small is capable of producing a large child. The metaphor is obscure.

10. *Ngoma 'si ngwele'*. The *vhatei* lie in the usual position. *Nyamatei* brings three wooden figures into the circle. They represent a man, his wife, and a young bachelor. Three women manipulate the figures (Plate XXXI) and speak for them in the following drama:

The husband goes out of his hut. Presently the bachelor enters and finding the wife alone says, 'Where is your husband?'

WIFE. My husband has gone out.

BACHELOR. Oh! He will not return for a long time, so that I can make love to you.

WIFE. No, you may not. It is my husband's house.

HUSBAND (*returning suddenly*). What are you doing?

BACHELOR. I am only asking for snuff. (*He goes out.*)

HUSBAND (to WIFE). What was he doing here?

WIFE. He wanted to make love to me.

The following day the bachelor comes again, when the husband is away from home, and this time, as her husband is far away, she is persuaded by him. She cooks for him and gives him washing-water. They have sexual intercourse. The husband chooses this moment to return, and knocks on the door of his hut.

BACHELOR (*on hearing the knock*). Never mind, I must pay him cattle.

PLATE XXXI

Goat   Woman   Man   Leopard

WOODEN MODELS

PUBERTY AND INITIATION

121

HUSBAND (*entering the hut*). What are you doing here?
BACHELOR (*confessing his crime*). I will pay you cattle.
HUSBAND. Yes, yes, you must pay me cattle.

The drama ends with *nyamatei* pronouncing the following epilogue: '*Si ngwele nndu ya sata vhululu a a vhu weli mwana*' (Do not come and fall on me, house of 'sata', because great things do not fall on a child).

The words of the epilogue, the first two of which give the *ngoma* its name, seem to have no connexion with the drama, whose moral is that if wives commit indiscretions with bachelors, in the absence of their husbands, trouble will surely follow and the bachelor be fined.

11. *Ngoma tshivhuyu* (Thick-set, smooth-skinned person). One night a pole is erected in the *khoro* and one of the *midabe* climbs to the top and there fastens a piece of skin, feathers, or porcupine quills. *Nyamatei* orders the *vhatei* to climb the pole in turn, one taking down the emblem from the top and the next one replacing it. After as many *vhatei* as can manage to do so have scaled the pole an old man volunteers to help the remainder, and himself climbs up and retrieves the emblem. This finishes the *ngoma* and the *midabe* take down the pole and throw it into the river.

According to Abel Mananga the pole represents a big well-grown girl, and the emblem on top her breasts. Those who reach the top and secure the emblem are applauded for winning the girl of their choice. This explanation is most unsatisfactory and probably incomplete.

12. *Ngoma mbudzi na ngwe* (Goat and leopard). On the morning appointed for this *ngoma, mme a domba* makes two old men very drunk. He then marches them into the *khoro*, one carrying a calabash of beer over his shoulder. When *nyamatei* sees them approaching she says to the *vhatei*, 'Here are the business men. They are going out to buy goats and will be back before long'. The drunken men depart forthwith, and when they return they are dragging behind them the wooden model of a goat (Plate XXXI). *Nyamatei* gives them more beer, as they are tired. They become still more drunk and pull hard on the string around the goat's neck. *Nyamatei* says, 'You must not do that. You will kill the chief's goat'. *Mme a domba* then makes a miniature kraal, with a dividing fence down the middle, and places the goat in one of the pens. Presently a wooden model of a leopard is unostentatiously put into the empty pen. The leopard makes a small hole in the dividing wall. Suddenly he darts through, pounces on the goat, and kills it.

PUBERTY AND INITIATION

He then makes off. When the people want meat it is found that the goat has gone. The drunken men say that the kraal should have been made stronger. This ends the *ngoma*.

The moral of this is that excessive drinking may result in carelessness and the consequent loss of stock through wild animals.

13. *Ngoma tshi la la ndo ima* (I am standing all night). This *ngoma* takes place on the last night of the *domba* and is one of the great events of the school. Everybody in the district attends the *khoro* on that night. Until midnight the python dance continues uninterruptedly. When the signal to rest is given and the *vhatei* stop dancing they are ordered by *mme a domba* to hold their arms straight up over their heads. They must remain in this attitude for a long time, while the chief, *mme a domba* and *nyamatei* walk around watching them. Any *mutei* who, through sheer exhaustion, drops an arm, is hit sharply on the elbow until it is held up again. Occasionally the chief allows them to rest. *Nyamatei* gives the order, 'Elephants take down your tusks, because people seek to kill you for your ivory'. At this command the *vhatei* drop their arms, and, during the short interval before they are again ordered to hold them up, they resume the python dance. This ordeal continues until morning and is unanimously voted the most arduous feature of the whole *domba*, calling for almost incredible powers of endurance.

14. *Ngoma nyalilo* (She who is crying). On the last morning of the *domba*, the *vhatei* and all the people are assembled in the *khoro*. In the presence of the whole assembly, young and old, a young girl is chosen and ordered to lie down on a mat spread in the middle of the *khoro*, where a boy, often the chief's son, is already lying. The girl generally screams (*nyalilo*) and resists, but is forced on to the mat where the pair are covered with a blanket. They then have ritual sexual intercourse. In the meantime a small calabash of white beer, to represent the semen, is prepared, and some of it thrown on the mat beside them. The ritual is then complete, the blanket removed, and the boy applauded for his manliness. The girl has porcupine quills placed in her hair and is sent to sit with the chief's children. On the last day of the *domba* she is given a goat by the chief. To-day this ceremony is sometimes performed by an old man and woman, at the order of the chief, who pays them for their services.

This is the final *ngoma*, and on its completion burning-beans (a type of red hairy bean which causes acute irritation) are rubbed over the buttocks of the *vhatei*, causing them most excruciating pain. They

PUBERTY AND INITIATION

123

all run down to the river to wash, the boys going to one part and the girls to another. The boys, after washing, have their hair cut, and for them the *domba* is over.

The girls after being thoroughly washed, have their heads shaved, are rubbed with red ochre, and are then examined by some old women to be sure that they have not been deflowered. The virtuous girls are carried home in triumph on the backs of their mothers or the older women, wearing the *tshirivha* and new ornaments. Their return to the family is greeted with trilling and rejoicing. A girl who has been deflowered is spat upon and derided by her companions and the old women. Her bracelets are confiscated and a chain of iron bracelets twisted around her head. She is given a sheep's skin to wear instead of a goat's, and must walk home displaying her shame to everybody. Her reappearance at her father's kraal is greeted with derision, instead of the rejoicing awarded to her more virtuous companions.

After returning home the girls are secluded for six days and remain indoors, doing no work and being lavishly fed by their parents. This six days' seclusion is to-day not enforced as strictly as it used to be.

The mother of each girl must pay one pound or thirty shillings, formerly a goat, to the chief, who, if the *domba* is held in the village of one of the petty chiefs, sends him a proportion of the payment. He also pays *mme a domba* for his services.

There are variations in the procedure of the *domba* in different localities. The symbolic words have different interpretations and the *dzingoma* are performed with local differences. The fire, which is never supposed to go out, to-day may be neglected and the dance continued without fear of consequences. The wooden models of the man and woman used in *ngoma si ngweli* are in some cases merely a source of amusement, in others a method of displaying the different parts of the anatomy. The general break-up in custom and tradition makes it impossible to discover the true meaning of all the demonstrations. The general conglomeration of names and symbols in which Lake Fundudzi, elephant's tusks, babies' heads, and representations of animals are all confused, suggest that all used to have some definite specialized significance. The school is of special importance to the girls, who take the prominent parts in the demonstrations and the dance. The shut door meaning pregnancy and the open door meaning birth, as well as the peculiar form of the dance simulating the activities of a python, are undoubtedly part of a fertility rite. The snake is thought to play an active part in building up the foetus in the womb, and a

PUBERTY AND INITIATION

barren woman is frequently given a girdle of python skin or medicine made from the flesh of a python in order, by sympathetic magic, to stimulate this snake to activity (see Rain and Fertility).

The *domba* completes the transitional period, and supplements the teachings of the *vhutamba vhutuka* and the *vhusha*. Those who have taken part in it are full members of the tribe and fully prepared for immediate marriage. The final act in all three ceremonies is identical. All end with the washing at the river, combined with the cutting of hair and fresh adornment of the body, in this way completing the severance between the old status and the new.

Summary of the Youthful Training of the BaVenda to the Time of Marriage.

From an early age the young boys herd the goats and cattle, and while so engaged have many idle hours in which they acquire, almost unconsciously, a wonderful knowledge of bush-craft. The little girls help their mothers in the performance of their duties, and in so doing achieve a working knowledge of domestic occupations. The economic and domestic training of both boys and girls is continued in the *mahundwane*, which, although a game, serves as an excellent medium for this branch of their training.

In the *thondo* the boys are, for the first time, brought into contact with some of the harder facts of life, learning respect, discipline, endurance, and the arts of war. At the *vhutamba* and *vhusha* respectively the boys and girls receive their first lessons about sex. At the same time the necessity for physical endurance, obedience, and humility are forcefully brought home to them. After these ceremonies the boys and girls are very different beings from the irresponsible children who expectantly entered the schools. They are now members of an age-set, occupying a definite position in the social hierarchy, and possessing spirits, which, in the event of death, for the first time have power to influence their relatives.

At the *domba* the two sexes are brought together, and together initiated into the mysteries of sex and child-birth, as well as being warned about the pitfalls that lie before them on their path through life. Here the training is hard and tedious, but it has to be negotiated. When this has been accomplished the initiates are ready for marriage, and at the birth of the first child have a full status in society.

The mystery and excitement connected with the different schools imbues them with a fearful fascination. The young people enter

PUBERTY AND INITIATION 125

them at the most impressionable time of life, and they are a compulsory part of the training of every MuVenda boy and girl. The training is hard and cruel, especially for the girls, for whom the ordeals and instruction are an almost intolerable burden, taxing their strength both mentally and physically, and making an indelible impression on their unformed minds and bodies, which is reflected in all their future bearing. Often they are terrified and seem to lose every trace of self-expression and individualism, obeying their tormentors mechanically with a docile, unquestioning humility. They have, or until recently had, no choice but to attend the schools, and the fact that a truant is socially ostracized explains the difficulty that missionaries experience in keeping them away. The conclusion of the *domba* is welcomed with relief by all the initiates. Nevertheless, when the tormented become in turn the tormentors, they treat their victims with the same merciless indifference that was shown to them.

The Murundu or Circumcision Lodge.

Circumcision is not an indigenous Venda institution, although it is now firmly established in parts of the country, particularly in the west, where the influence of Makhado and his successors is most widespread. According to Grant,[1] a Native Commissioner in the Zoutpansberg at the beginning of the present century,

'The large extent of the tribe was due to constant accession to their numbers from subordinate tribes who recognised Magato as the paramount chief. The idea of thus enlarging the influence of Magato was said to be due to his redoubtable commander-in-chief, Tromp, who, himself having undergone the rite of circumcision, resolved during the lifetime of Mablaan, while Magato was still a youth, to induce the future chief of the tribe to undergo a similar rite. This was determined on with a view of attracting to Magato other smaller tribes who were known to be circumcised, and the arrangements were undertaken by Tromp without the knowledge of Mablaan, who was uncircumcised. Magato was quietly secluded for a time, and having undergone the operation the fact was duly reported to his father.'

Tromp's nephew, a petty chief of the present Chief Mphephu, as well as many other responsible elders, agree that the recognition of circumcision by Makhado was the beginning of its general adoption by his people.

There is little doubt that the circumcision lodge, *murundu*, was

[1] Grant, Wm., 'Magato and his Tribe', *J. Roy. Anthrop. Inst.*, 1905, p. 267.

126 PUBERTY AND INITIATION

introduced to the BaVenda by the BaLemba, who themselves declare that the BaVenda adopted it for purely mercenary purposes, establishing it with their help and in accordance with their ritual. In Southern Rhodesia a large group of BaLemba, under Chief NeDanga, call their lodge by the same term *murundu*, but it is not the vigorous and comprehensive institution that exists to-day in the Transvaal. The Vha-Pfumbe, the branch of the Venda tribe that did not return to the Transvaal with Mphephu after the Boer War, still practise circumcision. Except for these two small groups it is found nowhere in Southern Rhodesia, being unknown to any of the BaKaranga groups. Harries[1] says that 'the Bavenda ... always get into touch with Maruteng before establishing a lodge and, if possible, obtain the services of a Mopedi to do the operation'. (Maruteng is the head-quarters of the paramount BaPedi chiefs.) My evidence does not confirm this.

Wheelwright,[2] writing in 1905, says that 'the priests who perform the operation are usually Balemba'. This is not the case to-day, when any efficient and experienced operator may perform the operation, but it would be the natural course of events in the early days of the institution, before any of the BaVenda had acquired the necessary skill.

Probably a fundamental factor in the commencement of the institution by the BaVenda was the fact that their near neighbours, the BaSutho, were already vigorous adherents. It can be understood that, although the BaLemba were doubtless the strongest force in its establishment, much of the procedure was borrowed from the BaSutho, whose influence is reflected in many songs, of which the words are Sesutho and not Tshivenda. Possibly the BaLemba were responsible for the introduction of circumcision to all the tribes of the Northern Transvaal. However that may be, there is a general similarity between the circumcision lodges of the BaVenda, BaThonga, BaPedi, and BaSutho.

My information concerning the actual procedure in the school has all been volunteered by BaVenda, non-Christian men, who have themselves been through one of the schools in the Zoutpansberg. It more or less corroborates Wheelwright's description. It is surprising how much of the ritual, especially in the aggregation period, corre-

---

[1] Harries, C. L., *The Laws and Customs of the BaPedi and Cognate Tribes including Native Administration Act No. 48 of 1927*, p. 63, Johannesburg, 1929.

[2] Wheelwright, C. A., 'Native Circumcision Lodges in the Zoutpansberg District', *J. Roy. Anthrop. Inst.*, 1905. p. 252.

PUBERTY AND INITIATION

sponds in almost every detail with the description given by Junod[1] of the '*sungi*'.

The spread of circumcision among the BaVenda was at first very slow. Mphephu and the majority of his people, who were the staunchest supporters of the institution, were out of the country for some years. During this period it stagnated, and it was not until the year 1904 that the numbers of its adherents began to increase rapidly. This sudden impetus was the result of the return of Mphephu, coinciding with the rapid opening up of the country and the increased traffic between the Rand mines and the Zoutpansberg. The rail-head at that time was at Pietersburg. Between that point and Vendaland, there lay a wide stretch of country occupied by tribes who were enthusiastic supporters of the lodge. Any uncircumcised man, venturing near a circumcision school, was likely to be caught and detained by force until he had conformed with all the regulations of the lodge. Many travelling BaVenda must have suffered this fate. The lodge administrators were, in some cases, so formidable that sooner or later capture and forcible circumcision seemed inevitable. The danger and inconvenience became so great that many BaVenda found that the simplest way of solving the difficulty was voluntarily to enter the school before attempting to make a long journey. To the circumcised traveller the lodge is a great convenience. He belongs to the fraternity and has only to repeat the secret formula, which constitutes the password, to be sure of rest, shelter, and hospitality.

The news of these obvious advantages soon spread throughout the tribe, and the more general adoption of circumcision increased. In the eastern area of Vendaland, where the influence of the conservative Tshivhase and Mphaphuli are most felt, the *murundu* is still disliked and discouraged. The lesser chiefs, however, who are more or less independent, are to-day not inclined to oppose any alien introduction which may be a source of wealth to themselves, and often, with the object of increasing their revenue, encourage the lodge in their own districts.

There is no fixed time for holding the *murundu*. It is held at intervals of about five years, provided that at least one of the chief's sons is ready to take part in the ceremony and that a good harvest has been reaped. The school lasts for three months and is always held in the winter. The actual structure is erected in an isolated place, hidden away in the bush and near to a river, where the cold at night is often

[1] Junod, Henri A., *The Life of a South African Tribe*, London, 1927, p. 71.

PUBERTY AND INITIATION

intense. When a suitable site has been selected the usual building preliminaries, including consecration by a powerful medicine-man, are enacted. The ground is enclosed by a roughly constructed thorn fence. At one end a gateway called *vhaloi* (wizards) is built for the use of the initiates, *madzinga* (sing. *lidzinga*—from *u dzinga*, to be deaf), and the set of boys who were circumcised at the previous lodge, *midabe* (sing. *lidabe*). A second much smaller gateway, *tshiwiliwi* (hot place), is made some distance from the *vhaloi* gate for the use of the old men, *vhanna* (sing. *munna*) or *vhoratshihotola* (sing. *ratshihotola*). This gate is near the big huts, *kudi* (little village), occupied by these men. Opposite the *kudi* are the *mpadi,* the badly constructed huts occupied by the *madzinga*. On the same side, but separated from them, are those of the *midabe*. *Madzinga* is the Tshivenda term for the initiates, but they are as often called by the Sesutho word *madikana* (sing. *lidikana*).

All the *midabe* carry sticks, varying in length from 2 to 8 feet. According to Wheelwright the length of this wand signifies the bearer's grade in the lodge. To-day the length has no significance at all.

The *vhoratshihotola* are expected to attend the lodge whenever possible, and particularly should endeavour to sleep there at night. Wheelwright[1] says that during the progress of the lodge 'no business, work, dispute, transaction, marriage, &c., is allowed, and that sexual intercourse between husband and wife is forbidden'. To-day these rules are not strictly kept and the old men continue to live their normal lives, putting in an appearance at the *murundu* from time to time, and occasionally making it their sleeping quarters. They are always treated with the greatest respect by the *madzinga*, who are expected to lie flat on the ground at their approach, and holding one leg and an arm in the air cry out, '*thabela milabo*' (big fish of the river).

The head of the *murundu* is called Ramalia, but what this name means I was unable to discover.

A long fire is lit down the length of the enclosure, called *ndou* (elephant). It is not allowed to go out during the course of the school. Many of the ordinary objects in use in the *murundu* are called by special names, e.g. axe is *goghodo*, not *mbado*, the ordinary term; water is *maghedo* (cutting) not *madi*; porridge is *muhali* (important one), not *vhuswa*; and so on.

[1] Wheelwright, C. A., 'Native Circumcision Lodges in the Zoutpansberg District', *J. Roy. Anthrop. Inst.*, 1905, p. 253.

PUBERTY AND INITIATION

When the chief decides to hold a *murundu*, messages are sent around the country to the various headmen in the district, informing them that the lodge is about to start and commanding them to prepare the boys in their respective kraals. Formerly the boys did not enter before reaching puberty, but to-day little boys, only ten or eleven years of age, may be sent by their parents, on the payment of an ox to the chief 'to make the little boy big'. Sometimes grown men may enter

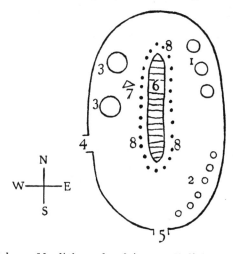

1. Huts of *midabe*. 2. *Mpadi*, huts of *madzinga*. 3. *Kudi*, huts of *vhoratshihotola*. 4. *Tshiwiliwili*, gate of *vhoratshihotolo*. 5. *Vhaloi*, gate of *midabe* and *madzinga*. 6. *Ndou*, long fire, around which the *madzinga* sit. 7. *Makhulu*, pole erected after two months. 8. *Madzinga* sitting around the fire.

the lodge, or are coerced thither and forcibly circumcised. At the end of the lodge men entering in this way are affiliated to whichever age-set is most appropriate to their age, instead of to the age-set of the young newly circumcised boys.

The *midabe* are summoned by the chief at the same time as the initiates, whom they supervise, taking care that their heads are shaved before leaving home. They lead their charges to within a short distance of the entrance of the *murundu*. The operator is seated just outside the *vhaloi* gate, in the centre of a large gathering of the circumcised. A medicine-man is always among the group, with a large horn of water and other medicines. The face of the operator is masked, and the first boy is brought forward amid a tumult of shouting. As he approaches the place of circumcision the *midabe* line up and buffet

PUBERTY AND INITIATION

him along from one to the other. He is seated on a stone, his eyes being covered by the hands of one of the assistants, so that he may not witness the operation, which is performed to the accompaniment of the shouting and singing of the assembly. The noise completely drowns any cries that the initiate may utter. According to Wheelwright[1] the 'prepuce is removed with one stroke and the second skin more carefully removed. The wound is then wrapped up for four or five days in leaves possessing some curative power'. As soon as the operation is over the boy must spit on the ground and shout *'Mafhefhe!'* (from *u fhefha*, to cut). No uncircumcised man may be addressed as *mafhefhe*, but it may be used as a term of address in conversation between the circumcised, and is regarded as an honourable title.

The chief's son is never the first to be circumcised. Usually the lead is taken by the son of a headman. This is doubtless to protect the chief's son from any danger attached to the cutting instrument.

After all the boys have been duly circumcised they are taken a short distance from the scene of the operation. Here their faces are painted with white stripes and they are allowed to rest until sundown, when they are led into the *murundu* for the first time.

As soon as all the participants are inside the enclosure the *vhoratshi-hotola* and the *midabe* form two opposing lines and sing and dance opposite each other, uttering wild meaningless shouts. After a short time one of the old men approaches the opposing line and expresses contempt for the dancers and their singing. The *midabe* reply scornfully that the old men can teach them nothing. This is the signal for the commencement of a fight between the two sections, each endeavouring to drive the other out through the gate set apart for its members. The losers, generally the *midabe*, must pay a goat to the winners.

The next business is to select three initiates for special duty throughout the course of the lodge. One is given the *tshiphata*, or *mbudzi* (goat), as it is called in the *murundu*. This instrument is made from four short sticks, strung together. It is worn by the selected boy slung over his shoulder. It is used for punishing any *madzinga* who commits a misdemeanour. The delinquent, in the presence of all his colleagues, has this instrument placed between the fingers of his clasped hands. The sticks are then squeezed tightly by a *lidabe*, giving intense pain to the unfortunate youth. The boy appointed on the first day to carry the *mbudzi* must take it wherever he goes, and so great is the

[1] Wheelwright, C. A., 'Native Circumcision Lodges in the Zoutpansberg District.' *J. Roy. Anthrop. Inst.*, 1905, p. 253.

PUBERTY AND INITIATION

131

importance attached to it that should he lose it his father must pay one head of cattle to the chief. A second *lidzinga* is put in charge of the *ndau* (lion), a fire-brand taken from the great fire that burns inside the *murundu*. The boy appointed to this office must take the fire-brand wherever he goes and keep a spark always burning. All fires lit outside the *murundu* must be kindled with this stick. Any boy who is burnt by this brand says that it is a lion which is biting him. The bearers of the *mbudzi* and the *ndau* are called *mufari mbudzi* (he who carries the *mbudzi*), and *mufari ndau* (he who carries the lion). A third office bearer is called *vhazhe*. He carries three sticks, each about two feet long, treated previously by the medicine-man, to act as a protective agency, keeping evil from the boys.

When these preliminaries have been arranged the *madzinga* sit, for the first time, around the sacred fire which is the centre of instruction and activity. For two months a regular daily routine is followed. The *midabe* rise early and make up the fire, singing lustily. Then they order the *madzinga* to come out from their huts and to sit in a long line around the fire, each boy being wedged tightly against the knees of the one behind him, the right side being towards the fire. The only explanation that I could obtain for sitting in this position was that the heat of the fire would cause intense pain to the penis if the boys faced it. From time to time the instructors order the initiates to 'kill the elephant', which they do by making a scooping action with one hand into the palm of the other and then throwing it towards the fire, symbolizing the throwing of spears at the elephant.

After this ceremony the boys have their morning meal, which consists of a large quantity of dry porridge. They must eat it cold, with no water. They are expected to consume a prodigious amount, and are flogged if they do not continue eating until all is finished. Throughout the *murundu* the initiates are not supposed to drink water at all. All meals must be eaten in absolute silence. The porridge is prepared by the mothers of the boys at their own kraals. It is brought twice a day to the *murundu* and deposited at a prescribed place, where a stick is put into the ground on which each woman, as she deposits her quota of porridge, places the carrying ring from her head. When one stick is filled another is started and at the end of the school all are burnt. This appears to be a method of checking the amount of food brought. The women, as they approach the school, shout out obscene remarks, to which the *midabe* reply with equal obscenity, thereby signalling to the women that they have right of

K 2

PUBERTY AND INITIATION

132

way to the stick, where the food must be put down. There is no time wasted in depositing the food as it is dangerous to linger in the precincts of the school. Any woman venturing near, unless she is a food carrier, is liable to be caught and very roughly handled.

After the morning meal the *madzinga* are painted all over with white clay, *kedi*, before setting out with the *midabe* to hunt. Each boy carries two sticks and they beat the country in open formation. Towards sunset the hunting parties return home, the *midabe* leading, chanting a warning song at the tops of their voices. All women and uncircumcised persons run and hide themselves, as any one daring to look at the boys is in danger of being killed by them outright. The *madzinga*, during their seclusion in the *murundu*, are exempt from all ordinary tribal restrictions, and are sometimes extremely dangerous.

After hunting the *madzinga* return to their former position by the fire and continue 'killing the elephant' until it is time for the evening meal. During the evening sittings around the fire they are taught the laws of the *murundu*, particularly the secret formulae, the knowledge of which ensures their admission to any *murundu*. The instructors shout, '*Madzinga!*' or '*Madikana!*' The initiates reply, '*Ke byona*' (we are here). The instructors then proceed to chant the formula by which to gain admittance to the *vhaloi* gate. Their words are followed sentence by sentence by the initiates. The formula is as follows:

The Visitor says: '*Kgoabatha, kgoabatha*' (Sandals, sandals). The keeper of the gate replies: '*Matobee*'.

VISITOR. *Ke moeng ke tsoa gole* (I am a stranger from afar off).
ANSWER. *Matobee* (We hear you).
VISITOR. *Ke roele ngata ea malepe* (I have carried a bundle of hoes).
ANSWER. *Matobee* (We hear you).
VISITOR. *Malepenyana-mabedi, godimo ka thatea koeti* (Two hoes here and two hoes here and over this I add some iron-ore).
ANSWER. *Matobee* (We hear you).
VISITOR. *Le mo le mo, la ra kgoedi chaba, kgoedi chaba kudu batho re a feela* (Here and there every month we are to escape, people are fading away).
ANSWER. *Matobee* (We hear you).
VISITOR. *Ri feela moneke moneke molilo va dishu, dishu tsa mongoaga diele diefsoa tsa kgorotlana* (We die of blood, red like fire, fire made of last year's cow-dung).

PUBERTY AND INITIATION 133

ANSWER. *Matobee* (We hear you).

VISITOR. *Kguidishana leda la ra molongoane le ele le e fsoa la tsosha kgetoa. Ra se tsoge basadi le chabe, banna le eme le goge diopo marumo, tsa gopea tsana, tsana ra trsitsane* (That great bush of Ramolongwana burnt up, and an animal rushed out and women ran away and men stood rigidly with their spears in hand).

ANSWER. *Matobee* (We hear you).

VISITOR. *Phururu-mmotlana pele ga barei, barei bo mang* (A rabbit rose just in front of the trappers).

ANSWER. *Matobee* (We hear you).

VISITOR. *Bo-koto le gogoe, le gogeloa kae pele le morago, morago le tsoago ie tsae dibato ga uo re tsetaa* (You old men, where do your legs carry you? You seem to move to and fro therefore, I conclude).

ANSWER. *Tsetaa* (Conclusion).

The second formula is the one that gains admission to the *tshiwili-wili* gate. This starts with the old men exclaiming: '*Macha-macha*' (It is day). The initiates reply: '*Macha*' (It is day). The chant continues: '*Banna ka kgoro a re tsene, re tsena ka se-bidibidi sa mmatse-ngwarsongoana se se amosang ngwana se eme, sa re, ke etsa pogo mathemela thema-thema re ee maote, re o bitsa bo-pelo-ea-sokoe, nnthsu morakabela, a bo-mma ke ramele ngoana, ka re, kitina o eo botsa bo-mma go, ba mkapielo ka pitsana e nwenyane, ka re thu, ka re keleketu, ka re le mpopa modyana na. Mo eantlong ea gotlola. Ramoshi o tsoile legonyini. Macha.*' (We men never enter by the gate, but we enter by the back door of Matsongwarsongoana who allowed the baby to suck while standing, who stood like a fearful bull, Mathemela. He stood and called Theme to proceed, in company with Maote to Pelo-ea-sokoe (the malcontent) the one who is really black. I shall send to call her mother to come and boil me in a small clay pot. Then I shall say to her, 'Do you think me a greedy man?' Any one who goes into the house gives a cough. It is day.)[1]

A great deal of time is devoted to memorizing these two formulae, in which each initiate must be word perfect. These lessons are often followed by dancing, after which the initiates are dispatched to their huts to sleep, and must pass the night in absolute silence.

This daily routine is followed with little variation for about two months. Then, one night, while the initiates are asleep, some of the

---

[1] These formulae in Sesutho, recited by my informant, were written down and translated by Stefanus Dzivani.

PUBERTY AND INITIATION

midabe erect a long pole in the enclosure, while others hide behind the boys' huts whirling *tshivhilivhi* (bull-roarers). The noise frightens the boys, who think that it is a lion whimpering, and do not hear anything of the erection of the pole.

The pole is about thirty feet high and capped with a piece of baboon or rabbit's skin. When it is ready the frightened initiates are brought out and told that the pole is their *makhulu* (grandfather). Early next morning the *midabe* join hands and sing and dance about the pole. One man climbs to the top and shouts a song, in which he exhorts all the uninitiated, *vhashavhuru*, to join the *murundu*, especially ridiculing Chief Tshivhase. The initiates also take part in this dance, any who are able climbing up the pole and shouting from the top.

From the time of the erection of the pole the daily routine is somewhat altered. The *madzinga* change their position around the fire, sitting with the left side towards it instead of the right, as heretofore. The tabu on water is not so strictly enforced, a *lidabe* sometimes permitting a boy to have a sip when he is particularly hot or fatigued. Dancing continues around the pole morning and evening until the end of the school.

Every day, during this month, one initiate, masked and completely disguised with grass and rushes, accompanies the *midabe* when they go to meet the women bringing up the food. This boy, called *lidagalane* (pl. *madagalane*), whistles a tune and dances wildly before them. A few days before the end of the *murundu* two or three *madagalane*, who are particularly good dancers, are taken down to the plains, where all the women are waiting for them. They dance before the women who answer them in song. One of the boys pretends to be mad and rushes about with an axe and a spear, while the others stand aside and laugh at the consternation of the women.

The dancers are not supposed to fall, but should one do so he is covered with leaves by his companions and left for dead. He may only escape after all the women have returned home. This ceremony is exactly the same as the *mayiwayiwane* dance, described by Junod.[1]

The night before the end of the *murundu*, the boys are again distracted by the bull-roarers, while the *makhulu* pole is cut down and burnt. The boys are then called out and, seeing that the pole has disappeared, shout, '*Makhulu* is dead'. On this final night all the circumcised men in the district make a point of attending, and there is a general air of excitement and finality, and much dancing and singing.

[1] Junod, Henri A., *The Life of a South African Tribe*, London, 1927, p. 91.

PUBERTY AND INITIATION 135

Early the following morning, before sunrise, the *vhazhe* takes a brand from the *murundu* fire and a handful of grass from one of the huts and leads the other *madzinga* down to the river. They are not allowed to look back. At the river-bank *vhazhe* lights the grass and hurls the burning bundle with the brand that lit it far into the river. He then leaps in himself, followed by all his companions. The white clay is washed from their bodies; they are smeared with red ochre; their hair is cut; they are given new names and formed into an age-set. In the meantime the *murundu* and everything in it is burnt to the ground.

After this the *madzinga* proceed in a procession to the chief's kraal, walking slowly and solemnly, hands together and heads bowed to the ground, imitating the gait of the chameleon. The old men and the *midabe* accompany the procession, chanting war-songs. On reaching the chief's village all the mothers are assembled to greet their sons, who are returning as men of the tribe after three months' ordeal. Each mother must pick out her own son, the identification being sometimes very difficult, as the feeding and general treatment in the *murundu* changes the appearance of the boys considerably. The difficulty is further increased by the grovelling position which is adopted by the boys at this reunion. Any mother failing to identify her offspring is severely flogged by men specially appointed for the purpose. Each mother then gives her son two strings of beads which he slings one over the left and one over the right shoulder.

Each boy before returning to his home must do labour service for the headman of his district for six days. After this he may put on the clothes that were removed before the circumcision, and return home. He impresses the importance of his new name on his younger brothers and sisters by beating them severely, while shouting it to them repeatedly. His elder brothers, however, may beat him when first hearing the new name.

Concluding Remarks.

At one time it was tabu for any circumcised man to eat meat with one who had not undergone the rite. He was derisively termed *mushavhura* (unclean), and on every possible occasion was reviled and made the subject of obscene jokes and gestures. Unwilling victims are still forced to join the lodge. Cases of assault and manslaughter often result from the opposition of the more determined recalcitrants. One of my uncircumcised informants sleeps with his

136 PUBERTY AND INITIATION

axe by his side in readiness for a surprise visit when a *murundu* is in progress near his home, as it is in the secrecy of the *murundu* enclosures that the frightened initiates are compelled to divulge the names of the uncircumcised.

The rite of circumcision, with the long seclusion in the *murundu*, is not considered a necessary preparation for marriage. It is not even a necessary concomitant to the declaration of puberty, although in many cases the two occasions do correspond. To those for whom it has no appeal it has become a source of terror. Its staunch adherents seem urged more by the social advantages which accrue to its supporters, than by the real Semitic conception of the uncleanliness of the uncircumcised. The fact that BaSutho, BaPedi, BaThonga, BaLemba, and BaVenda may all attend the same school is of great importance, as it is a powerful agent in forming a centralizing inter-tribal bond of mutual interest and friendship.

Murundu Songs.

Most of the songs sung during the course of the *murundu* are in Sesutho, although Tshivenda is being gradually substituted. The following are among the best-known songs, and were written and translated for me by Stefanus Dzivani, an educated MuVenda, teaching at Sibasa. They were sung to him by my best informant, Mafunisa Senthumule. There are many others, some improvised at recent lodges, others that have been chanted for generations. In some cases the subject matter is quite irrelevant and difficult to understand. The singers learn the words and the chant and sing parrot-like, comprehending little or nothing of the substance of their song.

1. *In Sesutho.* This song is sung every morning and evening, throughout the school, before the rite of 'Killing the elephant'. One of the instructors takes the lead and is followed by all the initiates singing in unison. '*Mankekana-kekana, pudi ea lla mogagenu, ea lla e bitsa modisha, e re, modisha nkgokolole, ke o gokolola ke le kae, ke disha lingoe di negala di kgonoa ke botau le bonkue, bagolo ba dingue dibata, ba dutse mo kgathung a tsela, ba bona mpheti a feeta, a feeta le mmpywana tsage, mmpyana tsa maforogotla, sa bo-mmutla se thsoanyana, se re bothomu sa e bo-phasva*' (Mankekana-kekana, the goat is crying at your home. It calls for some one to let it out and cries, 'shepherd, let me out'. 'How shall I let you out as I am looking after the beasts with string around their heads, which can only be killed by lions and leopards, the greatest and fiercest of all the animals. These lie along

PUBERTY AND INITIATION 137

the high road to see a passer-by with his dogs, his fast running dogs. The rabbit's tail is black and white).'

2. *In Sesutho.* This is sung when the *madzinga* are actually 'spearing the elephant'. An instructor sings the solo and the initiates reply.

REFRAIN. *Gotsee.*

SOLO. *Le a dia-ketsa lithsoeni mabele busiu ga di dyi* (It is a lie, it is a lie that monkeys visit the mealie lands at night).

REFRAIN. *Gotsee.*

SOLO. *Thagane-thagane tsa magalakuena* (Thaha birds, thaha birds of the Magalakuena river, visit the mealie lands).

3. *In Sesutho.* This song is the special property of the *midabe* when they are travelling about the country during the *murundu*. It is meant to warn all women and uninitiated persons of their approach. It is the song most often heard, but is strictly tabu at all times except during the duration of a *murundu.*

Si khubhe-khuvhe sa vhasali hogo! hogo! (The hidden part of women ho! ho!)

Tshivhase ra enoli enoli hogo! hogo! (Tshivhase is a coward about circumcision ho! ho!)

Khoshi dzi li rue li wedhze hogo! hogo! (Other chiefs are circumcised ho! ho!)

Li vho Mphephu vha wedzhe hogo! hogo! (Even Mphephu is circumcised ho! ho!)

Famhale vhashimanyana hogo! hogo! (Little boys are circumcised ho! ho!)

Vhashimanyana vha li kuli hogo! hogo! (The goat-boys are circumcised ho! ho!)

Musali gi do nyovha a dzwala ga vhashimanyana hogo! hogo! (I shall pregnate a woman and she will bear boys ho! ho!)

4. *In Sesutho.* The *midabe* and *madzinga* on returning from their hunting expeditions sing this curious song.

He-e! He-e! mmila-a-kgomo! Madikana! (He-e! He-e! The track of a cow! Madikana!)

ANSWER. *Mmila-a-kgomo!* (The track of a cow).

5. *In Sesutho.* This little ditty is chanted in the mornings when a *lidagalane* goes with the *midabe* to meet the women bringing food. It is sung with increased emphasis when all the *madagalane* dance before the women just before the burning of the *murundu.* The boys

138 PUBERTY AND INITIATION

whistle the air and dance, the words being understood and not actually sung, and the women sing their part in reply.

LIDAGALANE. *Thipa kgomo o thipe motho* (Kill a cow, kill a person).
ANSWER. *Iyele-le-le-le-le!*
WOMAN. *O a ea na? O a boa na?* (Dare you go? Dare you go?)
ANSWER. *Iyele-le-le-le-le!*
WOMAN. *Bina botse o a robega!* (You dance and do not break yourself).
ANSWER. *Iyele-le-le-le-le!*
WOMAN. *Mashapo a sa le manyane!* (Your bones are still young).
ANSWER. *Iyele-le-le-le-le!*

6. *In Tshivenda.* This is sung by one of the *midabe* every morning after the erection of the *makhulu* pole. He climbs to the top of the pole and seats himself on the fork, where shaking his legs violently, he shouts the chant. The *madzinga* reply, '*Mafhe-e-e!*' After some time the soloist climbs down and leads the boys through the *vhaloi* gates to the open ground, where they continue shouting the words of the song at the top of their voices.

SOLO. *Vhula vhutshovholo!* (Pitiable ones!)
ANSWER. *Mafhe-e-e! Ri ye haya!* (Mafhee-e-e! Home we go!)
SOLO. *Iyo-wo-wo-o!*
ANSWER. *Mafhe-e-e! Ri ye haya.*

7. *In Tshivenda.* This is rather a pathetic air, crooned by the newly-circumcised boys as they sit by the fire in the evenings, longing for the homes they know they will not see again for many long and weary days. It is addressed to Ramalia, the head of the *murundu*.

SOLO. *Inwi Ramalia!* (You Ramalia!)
ANSWER. *Ho-o!*
SOLO. *Ri iseni haya!* (Take us home).
ANSWER. *Ho-o!*
SOLO. *Ri yo vhona mme!* (To see our mothers).
ANSWER. *Ho-eo!*
SOLO. *Khotsi ri twa nae* (Fathers, we stay with you).

The Musevetho.

The *musevetho*, or *sungwi* as it is sometimes called, is the girls' equivalent to the *murundu*. It has been introduced into Vendaland by the neighbouring BaSutho, where it is called *mula*. The *musevetho* is very popular among a small section of the people, particularly where

PUBERTY AND INITIATION 139

the *murundu* has the strongest influence. Like all similar ceremonies it is deteriorating into a method by which petty chiefs and headmen extract wealth from the people. It is more in the nature of a secret society than a recognized feature of the social organization. The most important part of the proceedings is the operation, which all the initiates must undergo. Children of all ages may attend on the payment of two shillings, quite young children being brought by their mothers.

The function is held in a hut in a small enclosure outside the village. Here *nonyana*, the spirit of the *musevetho*, lives and manifests himself to the initiates. He is assisted by a little girl, *muluvhe*, who is usually one of his own daughters. He also has two or three boy assistants, *vhavhira*, who are disguised in elaborate reed clothing and completely masked in reed helmets, topped with feathers. These boys are sent all around the country to dance and to perform antics for the amusement of the people. They never speak, but carry on all communications between each other and with the outside world by whistling. The object of their peregrinations is to attract new members to the *musevetho*, and to beg gifts for *nonyana* from its old supporters.

Nonyana himself is a man disguised in bark and reeds. He carries a reed pipe in his hand, and is supposed, by the uninitiated, to be the embodiment of a spirit. One end of his pipe is closed with a piece of spider's membrane and, when blown, produces a weird, characteristic sound. At the new moon, when proceedings commence, he is supposed to be thin and gaunt, but, as the moon waxes, he becomes larger and larger, growing with the moon and then again fading with it and dying when it dies.

The initiates, *vhale* (sing. *mule*), on the first night of the ceremony are greeted by *muluvhe*, who calls out to *nonyana*, who is inside his hut: 'Here, *nonyana*, here are many people who come to see you'. *Nonyana* answers, talking through his reed: 'I am glad to see my people'. *Muluvhe* takes an initiate by the hand and leads her into the grass hut saying: 'Feel *nonyana!*' It is night-time and the figure of *nonyana* is vague and shadowy. When he is touched by the initiate he emits a weird noise and the girl rushes out of the hut, terrified. This is repeated by all the girls in turn. Boys, who have been through the *murundu*, are also permitted to visit *nonyana*.

After the initiates have visited the spirit they dance in the enclosure until late into the night. The following morning they are roused by

PUBERTY AND INITIATION

the curious sound of *nonyana*'s pipe. They all dance around him for some time, until he suddenly disappears, when the dance is stopped by *muluvhe*, who says that their *makhulu* (grandfather) has gone and wishes the dancing to cease.

Dancing around *nonyana* is repeated each evening, when there is a moon, for several months, new initiates joining from time to time. The girls are also taught the law of the *musevetho*, which must be repeated very quickly in a monotonous voice whenever the occasion demands.

This secret formula is as follows: '*Ke a reta, ke a reta lenntjakalana, ke retela isina laka. Le apara-kubo, le apara-kubo ka pedi linngwe mathatha makgushakgusha a ba a mo lokishetya, ba mo laile bya bopudi bonya-marokolo. Bya bo-nnku bo ile kae bothitha-minyako bo thithele mitsi ea rare le mitsi ea bangwe? Ke re le ke ea gangeshu ka mo molapong ka'humana mokgopa oa tau bapologa, re bapa oa nnkue re bapa ka moutloa oa mothunu, oa bo noku u i le kae mmapola kubo?*' (I say the law, I say the law, the *lenntjakalana*, I say the law for my name. One who wears two garments and one who is in tatters. Mukgusha-kgusha was never well trained in the good law, but was trained like a goat that brings out droppings. Where is the good law, that of a sheep? As sheep we never go far from the gates of our father's kraals; they will never go to unknown kraals. As I went out to the meadow I found a lion's skin tightly stretched. 'Lion's skin fold yourself!' I said, 'for we want to stretch a leopard's skin, and instead of pegs we use *muthunu* thorns. Why not use the spikes of the porcupine?') I could find no informant who understood the significance of this recital.

Nowadays the girls often only attend at *nonyana*'s hut for a day and a night. They see the spirit and then return to their homes until there are considered to be enough initiates to warrant the operation. On the appointed day the *vhale* are taken to a secluded place on the river-bank, where an old woman performs the operation of cutting the clitoris. At the same time the girls are branded with a mark on the outside of the thigh. The brand is like two inverted U's joined together, or sometimes it may be two round dots. This brand acts as a password on future occasions and proves that its possessor has undergone the operation.

After the ceremony at the river the girls all go to the kraal of the headman who has sanctioned the proceedings. Here they are joined by any boys who have been through the *murundu*. Dancing and singing, with beer drinking, feasting and sexual licence, continues for

PUBERTY AND INITIATION

a fortnight. After this the girls are taken to the river-bank and smothered with fat and red ochre, and brought again to the kraal for a few days' rest. They then return to the river and are thoroughly washed, and when all signs of the ceremony, except the brand, have been removed, they return to their respective homes.

It would be useless to speculate as to the real significance of the *nonyana*, as the whole procedure of the *musevetho* seems to have changed from that of the original institution. For the chiefs and headmen it represents an easy source of income, as they receive a proportion of the entrance fees. The feasting, dancing, and beer drinking appeal to the gregarious Venda character, and often to encourage new initiates, parties of girls travel with meat and beer, dancing and singing, and refusing to allow any one to participate in the merry-making unless she is a member of the society.

XI

MARRIAGE

Lobola—Marriage Arrangements—Marriage Ceremonies—Elopement—
Avoidances—Marriage Irregularities

THE BaVenda, like other African tribes, have a polygynous system of marriage. They possess as many wives as their means allow, the chief often having a great many, while the poorer members of a tribe are obliged to be content with one. Few of the ordinary people have more than two or three wives, and headmen rarely more than six. One would have expected the new conditions of life, due to contact with white civilization, to have brought with them an increasing tendency towards monogamous marriage. There is not such an excess of women as there used to be in the old days, when the ravages of warfare and of the hunt took a heavy toll of the men. Again chiefs who, through force of arms, used to accumulate wealth with which to acquire plural wives, are now limited in their activities. These incentives to monogamy however, are counteracted by other agencies. The protection of the white man offers increased opportunities to the commoner for obtaining wealth by labour in white industries, bringing an ever-growing tendency towards equality. The result of this is that there is less disparity between the condition of chief and subject, and the commoner to-day is better able to support two or three wives than under the old régime. Every MuVenda desires to possess as many wives as possible, for by their labours his lands are cultivated; a man with many wives may reap quantities of surplus grain, with which to brew beer for the entertainment of his neighbours, thereby enhancing his social position and prestige. Generally sons live with their father, unless land is unobtainable or they have quarrelled, and the power of the head of the family depends largely on the number of his progeny. A wife also prefers to share her many duties and welcomes rather than resents the introduction of a co-wife.

At marriage a wife lives with her husband's mother until after the birth of her first child, when her husband builds her a hut for herself and allots to her a portion of land as her own personal property. It is her duty to feed her husband and support her own family, and she may dispose of her surplus produce as she wishes. It is the duty of the man to provide each wife with a separate hut, lands, and granaries.

MARRIAGE 143

The co-wives appear to live very happily together, though petty jealousies sometimes occur, usually about the distribution of land, one wife considering her portion smaller or poorer than that of another. They vie with each other to produce the greatest quantity of grain in order to provide beer for the husband and so obtain his favour. The chief wife has few privileges except during her husband's absence, when she has to preserve peace among the other wives, settle disputes, interview strangers and visitors, and be generally responsible for the well-being of the home. The women seem content with their lot and do not resent their inferior position.

The Lobola.

The Zulu term lobola has been generally adopted in connexion with the cattle which pass from one family to another at every marriage, in place of the unsatisfactory terms bride-price or dowry. The lobola may be regarded as a legitimizing bond ensuring the social status of those concerned and of their offspring, as well as the compensation by one family to the other for the loss of one of its members. It is a medium of exchange, for the cattle acquired at the marriage of a daughter are very soon passed on to another family at the marriage of a son. Amongst the BaVenda the lobola is divided into two parts, the *vhumala* which goes to the girl's father, and the *ndzadzi*, always a cow and a calf, which goes to her mother. The mother's brother, *malume*, formerly had a right to this *ndzadzi*, and to-day, although the mother may keep it herself, she seldom refuses to give it to her brother should he require it.

The practice of obtaining wives by the lobola system is not confined to men. Any woman who has the means may lobola a wife in exactly the same way as a man may do, and although this is not common among the poorer people it occurs not infrequently amongst the ruling classes. Women in a position of authority, such as petty chiefs or witch-doctors, who have been able to accumulate the necessary wealth, often obtain wives in this way, even though they may be themselves married in the ordinary way. A woman may bring three wives to live with her at her own home, and may allow her husband to have sexual relations with them, although he has no rights over them without her permission. These women are really in the position of servants and are obliged to do all the menial work; they may be given to different men for the purpose of obtaining children, but these men, not having paid the lobola for them, have no legal

MARRIAGE

rights over them or their children. In such circumstances the anomalous position may occur in which a woman, whilst being called mother by her own children, is referred to as father by the children of the women for whom she has paid lobola.

There is considerable variation in the amount paid as lobola, depending on the positions of the contracting parties and the local conditions generally. In times of prosperity it rises, while in times of famine, sickness, or adversity it may fall very low indeed. The main portion of the lobola, the *vhumala*, which goes to the girl's father, used to consist of from eight to fifteen head of cattle (now between four and eight) and a varying number of goats, generally eight. The *ndzadzi* is always a cow and a calf. In addition there are numerous small articles, as clothing, bracelets, &c., which are constantly being presented to the girl and to members of her family, until the marriage is complete. Most of these gifts go to the bride's mother. In some of the disputes arising out of the question of lobola, various articles such as blankets, small sums of money, food-stuffs, &c., amounting to a considerable total, exchange hands in the law court. In one such case the plaintiff claimed thirty-five pounds for the miscellaneous presents that he had given to his parents-in-law, in addition to the cattle and goats of the actual lobola, and that sum was handed to him in cash on the spot. A man, in addition to giving presents continually to his parents-in-law, is always expected to help them with labour services. Most of a man's devotion to his parents-in-law takes place during the betrothal period and often diminishes when the bride has been taken to her husband's home, although a good son-in-law continues through his life to treat his wife's parents with great respect, giving them presents from time to time and helping them in times of necessity.

Marriage Arrangements.

Marriages are often arranged in an entirely arbitrary way between the parents. There is a proverb, '*U divha makhulu ndi u vhedzwa*' (to know your parents-in-law is to be told). A great deal of bargaining generally takes place between the contracting parties, and sometimes a man will give his daughter to a friend on the promise that the lobola will be paid at a future date. Sometimes a man betroths a child, or even an unborn babe, to a man from whom he has borrowed cattle. In cases where the whole lobola has not been handed over, a check on the numbers received is kept by both parties. A knot is added to a piece of string after each payment, or a notch

MARRIAGE

is cut in a stick on the veranda post. These sticks or strings are brought out and compared after each payment, and in any subsequent law-suit act as a record. These promises and agreements about the marriage dowry lead to untold complications and form the nucleus of most of their family feuds; the latter may continue for years, being handed down from one generation to the next, as on the death of the head of a family his successor inherits his liabilities as well as his assets.

Marriages are not always arranged in this way. Sometimes a man is attracted towards a certain girl and arranges to meet her in secret. If his feelings are reciprocated he asks her father to arrange a marriage between them, which he is often willing to do in the usual way. It may happen that the girl in question is already betrothed to some one else, and in that case this third party must be taken into consideration and compensated. Genuine love affairs of this kind generally complicate matters considerably and usually end in elopement.

As a rule the marriages arranged between parents are accepted by the young people without demur, although, if the girl expresses a strong dislike to the chosen man, her feelings are sometimes considered and new arrangements made, subject to the consent of the man to whom she is betrothed.

Preliminary proceedings having been arranged satisfactorily between the parents and the lobola fixed upon, the actual marriage negotiations commence. The first step is taken when the man's father visits the girl's kraal, bringing presents of clothing for his son's future wife. As is the custom with so many primitive people, throughout the marriage ceremonies and visits nothing may be given directly to the bride or her family, but everything must reach them through the agency of a third person. This medium, *makhadi*, chosen at the beginning of the proceedings, may be any man or woman from the girl's kraal, who acts as intermediary throughout; if any dispute should ever arise, even at some very distant date, the *makhadi* is always expected to attend the court and give his evidence about the lobola and other presents that were exchanged in his presence. The suitor's father gives the gifts to this medium, who gives them to the girl's mother, who shows them to her husband, and finally hands them to the girl. The man's father then returns home, where his son is busy making wire ornaments for the arms and ankles of his intended bride. On the man's first visit to the girl's home he takes the anklets and bracelets with him, and on his arrival at her kraal sits inside the outer wall and waits. Before long the girl's sisters conduct him to their parent's hut,

146 MARRIAGE

which he finds empty. Through the *makhadi* the ornaments are given to the girl's mother, who shows them to her husband, who consents to his daughter wearing them on the following day. The father then asks the young man to stay the night, and he is given food and drink by the girls of the kraal. He may not see his future bride that day and if he meets her unawares she covers her face. (He may not see or speak with his mother-in-law until after the marriage has been completed). The following morning, very early, after receiving instructions from her mother, the girl covers her face and creeps into the hut in which the man is sleeping, with water for him to wash. This is the first menial duty she performs for her future husband. Later in the day she (with her face still covered) is led by her sisters into the hut where he is waiting. He requests permission to put the bracelets on her, but she refuses until she has been given an additional present. He then stays as an ordinary guest, but may not see or speak to the girl. The night before his departure he asks if he may see her face and speak to her. She demands another present and when this is forthcoming allows him to put his face under her head-covering and speak to her. He returns home on the following day. When he is ready to go the sisters tell the *makhadi*, who informs the parents and conveys reciprocal messages of farewell. The sisters accompany him for a short distance, carrying his weapons, and when he demands his property they laugh and run away, refusing to give up the weapons until he has given one of them a present. On arriving at his home he tells his father that all is well.

After a few months have elapsed the man's father gives him the arranged *vhumala* and one pound in money, and with the help of a friend he drives the cattle to the girl's kraal. The sisters again meet him just inside the kraal and escort him to the hut. The *makhadi* tells the parents that the man has arrived with the cattle, but the father refuses to come out and count the *vhumala* until he has been given one pound, formerly a sheep. It appears that in accepting this gift the father-in-law signifies his final acceptance of the marriage contract, and after this, provided that the arranged *vhumala* is paid, he has no loophole by which he can change his mind and refuse his daughter. Five goats are then presented, the *makhadi* offering them to the mother, who gives them to her husband. The first, *lufhanga* (knife), is to pay for the knife with which to cut up the cattle when they die. The second, *mbado* (axe), is to buy the axe with which to chop up their bones. The third and fourth, *mulomo vha khotsi* and *mulomo vha mme* (the

MARRIAGE

147

mouth of the father and the mouth of the mother), are to enable them to eat the flesh of the cattle, which would be impossible if these goats had not been given. The fifth and last is *thuba ya kholomo* (the switch for driving the cattle). The girl's father in accepting the final goat signifies that he is satisfied with the cattle, and its acceptance acts as a receipt to the man's father.

After another two months have elapsed the man takes another goat, *tsindela mavu* (from *u sinda*, to stamp, *mavu*, ground). He kills this goat at the girl's kraal and takes the skin home. From it he prepares a *tshirivha* for his bride; she is no longer a child to play at stamping, and as soon as the *tshirivha* is ready he takes it with another goat to his bride's home. As he presents this goat he says, '*ndi humbela tshihashi tsha madi*' (I want my calabash of water). By this he means that he has no wife at home to give him water to wash and wishes to take his wife, and this is a sign that on his next appearance he is going to take his bride away with him. The *makhadi* asks the parents if the girl may go and they demand the *ndzadzi*. The bridegroom soon returns with the cow and calf which are given to the girl's mother. The bride refuses to go with him until he has made her a new set of bangles. The long-suffering bridegroom goes home again alone and returns with the bangles and two more goats. One of these goats is *u kanda muta* (to step in the mother's yard), and the other *u tomolo musi* (to pull up the stamp); both are given to the girl's mother. Next morning the girl puts on the bangles and is prepared to go with her husband; her mother and sisters smear her all over with cattle fat, except her face, which is kept covered up. Sometimes the witch-doctor gives her a protective charm which she hangs round her neck or fastens on her girdle. She is examined by the older women to see whether she has been deflowered and is then presented to the bridegroom. He takes her to his father's home, accompanied by three or four sisters or friends. One of the escorting party is given a basket to take to the bridegroom's parents. If the girl is intact the basket contains an unopened calabash and a white bracelet, but if she has been deflowered an open calabash with a black bracelet.

Marriage Ceremonies.

The bridegroom leads the party home, walking a short distance in advance of the girls. At the first cross-roads they sit down and refuse to go farther until a present has been given to one of them. After this the journey continues; the procedure is repeated at every cross-

MARRIAGE

road or river, at each halt the bridegroom giving something to the leader of the escorting party. If the bridegroom is unable to fetch the bride on the appointed day a deputy may be sent in his place, generally one of his brothers or sisters, possibly quite a child. At each halt the deputy must pay a stick or a stone (unless he has been especially provided with a supply of small presents for the purpose) to the leading girl, and these tokens must be accepted by the bridegroom in exchange for suitable gifts. When the party approaches the man's home he says that he is tired of their importunity and is going on alone. He reaches his home alone and tells his mother, who in turn tells his father, of the bride's approach, and a party of girls from the kraal are sent out to welcome the bridal party. As soon as the bride enters the kraal the basket containing the calabash is opened. If the closed calabash is discovered, giving testimony of the bride's virtue, gratification is expressed, and a sheep is sent to the bride's parents as a token of appreciation for their careful upbringing of this daughter. If the calabash is open, there is a general feeling of disappointment and disapproval, and no sheep is sent back.

Before the bride or her companions will perform any actions in the new home payment is demanded. She stops at the gate and refuses to enter until she receives a present, and again before entering the yard and the hut. When inside she sits down with her legs straight out, in an attitude of extreme disrespect, until she again receives payment, when she salutes respectfully; she does the same before she will lie down to sleep. The bride is greased with red ochre and the bridal party is secluded in a hut for six days. About four days after the bride has been taken to her new home her mother and other women from her village quietly approach the bridegroom's village. When the party reaches the fence they suddenly start playing horns, shouting, and making a great disturbance, until one of the bridegroom's family presents the mother-in-law with another goat. She then enters the village, finds her daughter and gives her a last admonishment to behave well in her new life, and then returns home. On the sixth day the girls go out and steal water, which they take round to every hut in the kraal. Every inmate must wash in the stolen water, after first giving payment for it. The girls then proceed to do all the work in the huts, and each separate task is preceded by the correct salutation and payment. On the sixth evening everybody brings their mealies for the girls to stamp the following morning. The girls purposely spoil the mealies by not moistening them before stamping, until they again receive payment

MARRIAGE 149

and consent to stamp properly. The next day the father slaughters a sheep or a goat for them and they return home, taking with them all the gifts that they have received in payment. The skin and hind leg of this animal is given to the bride's parents.

The bride remains at the home of her husband's parents and continues to demand payment for everything she does. All these conciliatory gifts she passes on to her mother. She lives with her parents-in-law for from one to three months and is carefully scrutinized by them. At the end of this probation period the father tells one of his wives, not the bridegroom's mother, to take the girl to his son's hut. At the door of the hut they wait for payment, and after receiving two more presents the girl consents to salute her husband and stay with him. Before the night the woman, *mmane*, and the girl leave the hut again, but early next morning the three proceed to the medicine-man and the *mmane* presents the young couple to him. The medicine-man gives them a clay dish and tells them both to urinate into it, first the man and then the girl. He then mixes drugs and water with the urine. He makes small incisions in the knees, hips, abdomens (just below the umbilicus), and necks of them both, and rubs the blood from the male into the female, and vice versa. He then gives them some of the mixture to drink. After the conclusion of this ceremony the two are husband and wife.

Until this time the bride must always honour the plate of her husband's father, and refer to him as *munna* (husband). She must refer to the bridegroom as *mwana* (child). The bridegroom may not refer to her as wife, but as *mmane*, the term for father's wife.

. This wedding ceremonial, and particularly the peculiar relationship between the bride and the father-in-law, only occurs when the eldest son receives his *musadzi muhulwane* (great wife), who is to be the mother of the heir. Although it is quite understood that the girl is to become the bride of the son, it is the father who pays the lobola and is consequently recognized by the parents as being her legal husband, and he is responsible to them for her well-being.

The BaVenda are like a great many other Bantu in the protracted marriage proceedings that must be observed before the man obtains his bride. Probably the transference of an individual from one family group to another is considered an unnatural process, fraught with danger, so that it must be achieved in short stages with long intervals, bringing the change of status gradually. The prospective bride must keep her face covered, as though to impress upon the man the fact that

150 MARRIAGE

he is acquiring an individual whom he must protect and respect, and not buying a slave. He is constantly reminded of this attitude by her reiterated demands for presents before she will acquiesce to any of his requests. He may not see his mother-in-law, and his visits seem to contain an element of mystery and are hedged around with a host of tabus. This idea of a gulf to be bridged is reflected in the procedure with the cattle at the *vhumala* transactions. Every detail is considered, and the presenting and accepting of the goats symbolize the change of ownership. The cattle belong to another family, and until the rights of the last owner are broken down and the tabus removed by the goats, the two representing the knife and the axe, and the two sanctioning the eating of the flesh by the girl's parents, their passage to the new family is not complete.

Elopement.

However, every Venda marriage is not celebrated in this way, as a young couple often elope together. The preliminaries to elopement are carried on in secret, and after a few clandestine meetings the man asks the lady of his choice to marry him. If she refuses after he has repeated his offer three times he knows that it is useless to pursue her further. If she accepts him, he takes her secretly to his father's home, and informs his father's wife, who tells his father. His father, though momentarily angry at the upheaval of his own plans, generally accepts the position philosophically and immediately communicates with the girl's father in the hope of coming to an amicable settlement. The girl's father demands the immediate return of his daughter and she is sent back with a goat, under the escort of a messenger. If the goat is accepted it is a sign that an amicable settlement may be arranged, and if it is refused trouble is anticipated, although the ultimate conclusion is always the same. The girl runs away and joins her lover at the first opportunity and is again returned to her parents with a goat. After this has been repeated three times a settlement is arranged, and after the *vhumala* and *ndzadzi* have been paid the marriage is recognized. If the full amount cannot be paid at once the man continues giving conciliatory presents to his parents-in-law from time to time. As with regular marriage, the girl is obliged at first to live with her mother-in-law, where she is watched very strictly for a month to ascertain whether she possesses the qualities necessary to make a good wife.

Frequently a man is attracted to a woman for whom he cannot

MARRIAGE 151

possibly collect a dowry, and he proceeds to steal her from her parents. A MuVenda is always ashamed of possessing a woman acquired in these circumstances. It is only after much questioning and circumlocution that he will own to his offence. I heard of a man who possessed two lawful wives and a third whom he had stolen, without having paid any compensation. The circumstances of this union are interesting in demonstrating the strength of the family tie. Twelve years elapsed, the woman living with him all the time and bearing him four children. In spite of promises to pay the dowry no fraction of it had been paid, and the woman's brother, her father being dead, realized that it never would be paid and so demanded the return of his sister and her four children. Although very fond of her illegal husband the woman did not dare to disobey, and during one of his absences returned to the home of her fathers with her children. She occasionally visits her husband, but his authority over her and the four children is transferred to her brother. He will receive nothing of the lobola on the marriage of his daughters, and in event of his wife remarrying her new husband will only pay him one goat. Unless a man pays the required compensation for a wife his marriage is not recognized by the community, and he cannot claim his children, who are not considered his lawful property.

Avoidances.

A man calls his wife's mother *makhulu*. This term is used by a man in saluting a strange woman on the path and is also the term for grandparent and signifies respect. As has already been indicated a man must strictly avoid his mother-in-law during all the marriage proceedings, but by far the most important person to be avoided is the wife's brother's wife. This person is strictly tabu, and if by chance a man finds himself in such a position that he must speak to her, it is always done through a third person, usually a child. His father-in-law is always treated respectfully and only a minimum amount of intercourse takes place between the two. These avoidances apply not only to the man in question, but to all whom he calls brother. This means that when a man anticipates marriage a large number of his male relatives must share in his avoidances; where there are many prospective marriages in deliberation in one family group this may become very troublesome. The difficulty is overcome by the presentation of a goat to the person to be avoided, by the acceptance of which the tabu is removed, not only for the individual who actually presented

MARRIAGE

the goat, but for all those whom the tabu affected. The whole marriage ceremony with its *vhumala* and avoidances emphasizes the importance of the family as a whole as compared with the individual.

Marriage Irregularities.

Adultery is common. Most girls are betrothed when quite small, so that if a girl is seduced by a man other than her betrothed the seducer is answerable to her prospective husband, and if she becomes pregnant, must pay him the compensation of two head of cattle, although all arrangements must be made through the parents. If an unmarried girl dies in child-birth her seducer is fined the usual two head of cattle. Illegal intercourse with a married woman is regarded as a more serious offence, although it is very common. In the old days if a man discovered his wife with a lover he killed him on the spot. To-day the crime is compensated with a cow, and if the woman becomes pregnant, with two head of cattle, the child going to the woman's husband and not to its natural father.

If a woman leaves her husband and takes refuge with her own people she will be returned to him by them unless she has been very grossly abused; the only alternative is for them to return the lobola. If a woman elopes with her lover the husband claims the equivalent to the lobola he paid for her together with all its increase. This often entails considerable difficulties, as the lobola cattle may have been scattered and their increase hard to assess. But if the lover can fulfil this obligation the husband is usually satisfied and allows his younger children to go with their mother.

Barrenness. If a man's wife dies childless she is often replaced by one of her sisters or part of the lobola is returned by her father. There is no obligation on the part of the wife's family to provide another woman, but they generally do so to maintain friendly relations between the families. Failing his wife's sister, the man may be given one of her brother's children or the promise of one when she reaches maturity.

Divorce is unusual. A man cannot return his wife to her parents and receive compensation unless she has had several abortions, committed incest, become an habitual adulteress or thief, or been designated a witch.

XII

FAMILY LIFE AND ETIQUETTE

IT was customary, when there was sufficient arable land, for a young man, after his marriage, to settle down close to his father's kraal. To-day there is a growing tendency to build in more isolated places and for each young family to be self-contained. The head of a kraal is all-important and is treated with deference and respect by all the younger members of the family. The average man lives an easygoing, lazy life when at home, with few definite duties and unlimited leisure. The man rises soon after sunrise and washes in the water placed ready for him by his wife, who has probably been up working for some hours. He then goes off hunting or examining his traps, or he may plough for a couple of hours in the ploughing season, or put in a short spell in the lands, or busy himself cutting timber or erecting a new hut, or doing any little job such as repairing a fence or tanning a skin. He may attend the chief's court to hear a case being tried and possibly speak on behalf of the plaintiff or defend a friend. Some of the men make baskets or wire bracelets. Usually a large part of the day is spent in entertaining or visiting friends and sitting with them arguing happily, consuming large quantities of beer when it is available, or playing *mefuvha*, the ubiquitous stone game. At harvest time, when there is plenty of food and beer, he may assist one of his friends in the reaping of the harvest and receive beer in return. At sunset all the paths leading to the village are swept over, and in the morning are inspected and all new footprints carefully examined. In the old days a guard was always posted night and day. After supper the evening is generally spent around the fire in the *khoro*, gossiping and telling stories, and, except when there is dancing or any other festivity, the men retire for the night fairly early.

Women have a more regular routine and their day is generally arduous. Preparation of the grain for the daily meals is a long and strenuous process. A woman often starts stamping as early as 1 or 2 o'clock in the morning. Staying near a chief's village it is difficult to obtain much sleep, as the ground shakes with the continuous vibration and there is the continual noise of the thudding of the stamps, which can be heard coming from all directions throughout the greater part of the night. Until the first meal at about 11 a.m. the woman is working at her domestic

FAMILY LIFE AND ETIQUETTE

duties, such as fetching water and wood, sweeping the house and smearing the walls and yard, as well as in the actual preparation of the food. She spends a great part of the remainder of the day in her garden, but she must also attend to the fetching of water for the evening, for which she may have to walk a considerable distance. When at the river she usually takes the opportunity of washing herself and her baby and any of the other children who are with her. Wood must also be collected; she can carry a remarkable weight on her head, with very often a baby on her back, as well as a calabash in one hand. On some occasions the preparation of beer takes up most of the day, on others the plastering of newly erected huts or fences. If she has time she may make a basket (if she is one who understands that art), or visit a friend, or do service for a friend in exchange for beer, but generally she is kept busy all day long and seems to have an incredibly short period for sleep.

The women are far more industrious than the men, who do a minimum amount of work and spend a great deal of the day in sleep or complete idleness. This is made possible for them by the industry of the women and the fertility of the soil. The men make few preparations for the future, and when there is a drought or other misfortune often pass through very hard times on the brink of starvation. Such experiences do not make them one whit less improvident, and as soon as the conditions of life become easier they eat and drink with increased relish and continue to enjoy a life of idleness under the sun.

Each wife has her own hut and yard and often her own kitchen. Where she does not have a separate kitchen she cooks in a separate place on her own fire and cooking-stones in her own piece of yard. There are only two regular meals, *tshiswitulo*, the first meal, starting about 11 a.m., and *tshilalelo*, the evening meal. Each mother prepares food for her own family. Everybody, before touching food, is expected to wash the hands. The husband always eats alone in his hut, his food being prepared by his youngest wife and brought to him on a wooden platter. As a rule the mothers gather together for their meal. Each mother has her own plate; her little children eat together from one plate, helped by their mother; if a child is greedy and takes more than its fair share, it is punished by being given its own small portion on a separate plate. The older boys, over twelve years or so, eat separately from a common plate, and the older girls from another. If the co-wives are friendly the children of the different mothers may join together, the little ones eating together, the boys together and all the

FAMILY LIFE AND ETIQUETTE 155

girls, each mother placing her share of the food on the different plates. A married man, visiting his father's home, eats with his brothers. A man, visiting a married brother, may eat from the same plate; but he is often given a separate plate, as the married brother has set up his own home and so become a privileged person. Honoured visitors eat separately inside a hut. If there is no spare hut the father gives up his own to his guest and himself eats outside. A woman visitor is given her own plate, but may eat with the other women.

At night each wife sleeps in her own hut with her small children. All the elder children are separated according to sex, the boys sleeping in one of the kitchens or a hut provided for the purpose, and the girls in another. Formerly the boys very rarely slept at home as all the nights were spent in the *thondo* at the chief's kraal. The husband sleeps alone in his hut where his wives visit him. Often in poorer families the man does not have his own hut, but shares that of his youngest wife, who is always responsible for the care and cleanliness of her husband's hut and for his general well-being. When a visitor passes the night with a family it is customary for one of the women to give up her hut for him and herself share that of one of her co-wives.

The father settles all disputes between his children, who, before they can take independent action in any matter, must first consult him and ask his consent. Although his authority is somewhat relaxed after the son has set up his own house, it is seldom that his orders are not obeyed. Before marriage the sons work for their father in his lands, all the resultant crops belonging to him. To-day, when young men work at the mines and return home with considerable sums of money, the father appropriates the greater part as his right, allowing them to keep as much or as little as he wills. If a man quarrels with his father and wishes to bring about a reconciliation with him, he sends another man, often his paternal uncle, to him, offering him a conciliatory gift, to-day usually one pound. The intermediary explains that the son quarrelled with his father unwittingly and the father is bound to accept his son's offering and end the dispute.

Amongst the sons of the same mother there is communal ownership of belongings. There is a proverb, '*Vhana-vha-munna vha kovhana thoho ya ndzie*' (Brothers share everything, even a locust's head). The idea of individual ownership is unknown to them. A brother, returning home, after offering his possessions to his father, shares what remains with his brothers. For instance, if he has brought back a suit of clothes, provided his father does not desire it, he will divide the

156 FAMILY LIFE AND ETIQUETTE

suit between his brothers, giving one the coat, another the trousers, &c. It appears that little animosity is felt towards a brother who is indolent and brings little home, and little gratitude towards an industrious brother who often brings home the spoils of his labour. Everything is taken for granted between them, the idea being that what a man does for his brother will be done for him on some future occasion. After marriage this system breaks down to some extent, especially as regards cattle, but there always is a certain amount of identity of interest.

A similar communal ownership does not exist between sisters, or between brother and sister, but it is expected that they will always be ready to help each other. Men are also expected to help their brothers in the classificatory sense, that is the children of their father's brothers, but communal ownership does not extend to these persons.

Age plays a very important part in the behaviour of the family. Younger members must respect their elders. If an elder brother is given an order by his father he may pass the order on to his younger brother, who dares not refuse to obey it. Similarly a younger sister obeys her elder sister or elder brother. An elder sister can demand obedience from a younger brother until that brother is grown up, when her sex places her in a slightly inferior position, as women must always respect the men of their family. A curious ceremony is sometimes enacted to repair a quarrel between two uterine brothers, or two uterine sisters, or a brother and sister who are near to each other in age. A medicine-man is called in and told about the quarrel. A goat is killed, from which a long piece of meat is cut off and cooked, and then each of the disputants takes one end of the meat in his mouth and the medicine-man cuts it through the middle; each participant eats up his portion and the trouble is over.

The rigidity of etiquette within the family is often rebelled against, but in the presence of strangers it is strictly adhered to. In the absence of the father the eldest son takes his place and is treated with all the respect due to the head of the family. On the whole, life within the family is happy. The men spend a great part of the day away from home and do not interfere in any way with the womenfolk, as long as there is plenty of beer and the meal is ground to the necessary fineness, and accompanied by some dainty tit-bit. The women work hard, but have considerable freedom, frequently visiting their parents' homes and taking part in every festivity and excitement. They are not

FAMILY LIFE AND ETIQUETTE 157

treated as slaves by their husbands in any way; there is often a genuine affection between a man and his wives and an intense love of both parents for their offspring.

Etiquette.

The BaVenda are very polite. They have a rigid code of etiquette, their method of greeting being different from that of other tribes in the Transvaal. Superiors and elders are treated with respect and reverence, the chief and his sister with obsequious adoration, while the ordinary everyday formalities between husband and wife and their children and friends are strictly defined and rigidly adhered to. *U losha* means to salute or honour, but it has a much more comprehensive meaning; the actual method of *losha* varies according to the sex and position of the person giving the salute; a man greets an ordinary person in one way and a chief in another, while a woman has an entirely different method of greeting. A man always sits to *losha*; he slightly bends his head and shoulders and with eyes looking downwards, elbows pressed to the side and forearms extended in front of him, with finger-tips touching, he claps his hands together very gently; this movement is accompanied by some word of greeting, depending on the occasion, generally '*Ndau!*' (Lion!). He must never *losha* standing. To-day a man always lifts his hat when greeting anybody.

A woman kneels with buttocks on heels, and body bending forward, head bent and eyes on the ground; she places her hands together in the same way as the man, but instead of clapping them lifts the two fore-fingers up and down; she usually accompanies her gestures with a muttered '*Ah!*' On approaching any one on the road she kneels down on one knee, with one hand on the ground and the other hand resting on her bent knee, and with head averted she waits until the wayfarer has passed or motioned her to pass on. If she is carrying a load on her head she simply holds her right hand straight up, with thumb almost touching the ear, and waits. An old woman is addressed by a man as '*Ndau! Makhulu!*' (Lion! Great one!) and she replies, '*Mukwasha!*' (Son-in-law). If two women are passing on the road the younger generally kneels while the older bends her knee and both say '*Ah!*' A woman must always keep her eyes on the ground when talking to a superior; she would be guilty of the grossest insolence if she dared to look up into the face of the man by whom she is being addressed. She must always kneel when receiving anything from any man, and also kneel when giving.

FAMILY LIFE AND ETIQUETTE

To *losha* the chief (called *u luvha* when an inferior is greeting a superior) a man claps his hands together when at some distance, and approaches giving utterance to a number of laudatory epithets while continuing the clapping. When he reaches the chief he squats down with bent knees and leans the head to the right side, turning his hands over to the right at the same time. Occasionally a man is privileged to approach the chief on terms of equality, without doing the *luvha*; this is the highest honour that a MuVenda can attain, and it is only awarded to one who has shown most conspicuous bravery or wisdom. A woman kneels down with her forehead on the ground and her hands together under her face, and always shuffles on hands and knees in his presence or in his hut. The chief's sister is treated with exactly the same respect as the chief himself. Certain other people are treated in the same way, notably a woman possessed of the *molombo* spirit and a man's parents-in-law.

A man joining a party of people must *losha*. If he leaves the party and returns he must again *losha*. When on the road he must *losha* each passer-by, greeting a man as '*Ndau!*' and a woman, older than himself, as '*Makhulu!*' If two men are engaged in conversation the listener is continually interrupting the speaker, interjecting such words as '*Ndau!*' '*Thovela!*' '*Ndou!*' '*Kholomo!*' &c., (Lion! Great one! Elephant! Cattle! &c.). This indicates his interest in the speaker's remarks and has very much the same significance as our '*Yes!*' '*Indeed!*' or '*Is that so?*' If he omits to ejaculate every few seconds the speaker considers that the listener is not giving due attention to his words.

Girls, while attending the *vhusha*, must *losha* continually, especially must they respect the girls who were initiated just before themselves, going (Plate XXXII) down on their knees, with forehead on the ground, when making obeisance to them. A bride must always crawl in the yard of her husband's home, and kneel before she enters the door of the hut, as well as doing *losha* before everything she touches; she continues to behave in this way until after the birth of her first child. If one woman encounters another engaged in some labour, such as smearing, she must *losha* the smearing. Before picking up a baby from the ground or taking it from her back she must *losha*, and again after feeding it. Everybody is expected to *losha* their plate before starting food, and again at the end of the meal; this must also be done by any stranger eating with the family; the only person who need not *losha* at meal-times is the owner of the house, but even he, if he is entertaining an

PLATE XXXII

GIRLS SALUTING, SOON AFTER THE *VHUSHA*

FAMILY LIFE AND ETIQUETTE 159

important visitor, will, after the visitor has done *losha* to his plate, himself salute it.

A person wishing to take a cinder from the fire, even though nobody is present in the vicinity of the fire, is expected to *losha*, out of respect for the person who lit it. A girl must *losha* her elder brother and all married women. Children are taught to *losha* when quite small, but the rules of etiquette are not strictly enforced until after they have entered the *thondo* or *vhusha*. A group of women, approaching the chief's village, always makes a characteristic trilling noise in a high pitch; this is made by rapidly hitting the pursed lip with the forefinger and at the same time hitting the palate with the tongue. On the entrance of the chief to any village or kraal, and again on his exit, the same trilling performance is enacted. If the chief belongs to the royal MaKhwinde sib, the word '*Singo!*' (Elephant's trunk) is interspersed between the trilling.

The giving and receiving of snuff is accompanied by strict laws of etiquette and propriety. The people who take snuff are divided into four main groups; the first comprises the boys and girls, the second the young men and women, the third the middle-aged group, and the fourth the old people. The members of each group may ask their contemporaries or their juniors for snuff, but never a member of a senior group. A senior may give to a junior, who always receives the snuff with extreme politeness. No man is permitted to ask another man's wife for snuff, as it is a favourite medium for the concealment of magical charms; for the same reason it is considered dangerous to accept snuff from a stranger.

There are prescribed sitting positions for different members of the community, and any person sitting in an unorthodox way is guilty of a grave breach of etiquette. The head of the family sits on a stone or a log of wood. Young men and boys sit on the ground with their legs on one side, tucked under them. In the presence of the chief all men sit on the ground, except the most important and influential. Women and girls always sit in a kneeling position, with the buttocks on the heels. Children, however informally they may sit amongst themselves, quickly assume the correct position on the approach of any superior.

The respective importance of different members of a family or of different people in the tribe is reflected in the person used in addressing them. For instance the word '*tshimbila!*' (go!), second person singular, is used in speaking to a little child. The second person plural, '*tshimbilani!*' (go ye!), may be used (*a*) in giving a command to an

160 FAMILY LIFE AND ETIQUETTE

inferior; (*b*) by a father or mother, to a young boy or girl; (*c*) in addressing a company of people. This form seems, in most cases, to be used in addressing inferiors. The third person singular, '*kha a tshimbile!*' (let him go!), is also used in addressing an inferior, e.g. by a father to a grown son. It is more polite than the second person plural. The third person plural, '*kha vha tshimbile!*' (let them go!), is the form used by a child to its parents; a subject to his chief or petty chief; a man addressing a woman and wishing to be polite; a wife addressing her husband; and in most cases where one person wishes to be particularly polite to another. A husband might use the third person singular in speaking to his wife. A child might say '*mmpheni!*' (give ye me!), the second person plural, to its mother, and '*kha vha mmphe!*' (let them give me!), in speaking to its father. The different forms are used interchangeably, except in speaking to a father or chief, when the polite third person plural is always used.

XIII

MORTUARY RITES

Death—Burial—Unusual Deaths—Purification—Mourning

MORTUARY proceedings among the BaVenda show considerable family variations, particularly in the manner of the disposal of the corpse, but as these variations occur more among the chiefs and important headmen than among the ordinary people, they will be discussed more fully in that connexion.

When a man is ill, and all hope of recovery has been abandoned, his kinsmen are summoned to the kraal to await his death. When possible, every relative makes a point of attending the death-bed. Any one failing to put in an appearance, without an adequate excuse, is liable to be suspected of complicity in the death.

In sporadic cases the fear of death is so great that a man who is expected to die is taken away to the bush, so that the hut may not be contaminated; if his death occurs inadvertently within the hut, it is generally burnt down or deserted. Occasionally a very aged person, who has been ill for a long time and is practically unconscious, may be helped to shake off the lingering spark of life; an aged friend, but never a relative, burns a piece of python skin on a broken pot which he holds under the nostrils of the dying man, who unconsciously inhales the fumes and is very soon suffocated. This is done for purely humanitarian reasons in order to lessen the death agony and 'set free the spirit' of the dying man. It has been misunderstood by many observers, who believed that the old people were murdered when no longer of use to the tribe.

The first action after death is to cut a piece from the *tsindi* in the case of a man or *ludedi* in the case of a woman, and roll it up in a piece of grass taken from the roof of the house. The little bundle is hidden in one of the trees outside the hut, ready to be taken by the mourners to the diviner when the time arrives to ascertain the cause of death.

When the deceased is a man the body is arranged in a sitting position, with the right side of the head resting on the clasped hands; if the joints become too stiff to manipulate they are first severed with an axe. The body is secured in this position with a string of the *bhopa vhafu* tree (tie death). A rich man is wrapped in the skin of one of his black oxen and a poor man rolled in a blanket.

MORTUARY RITES

Burial.

The medicine-man divines a site for the grave, generally indicating a place under the fence surrounding the cattle-kraal, or outside the kraal under the cover of bush or trees. Any one may dig the grave, but one of the dead man's brothers must always accompany the party. Great care is taken to conceal the locality of the grave, so that there will be no danger of parts of the corpse falling into the hands of an enemy. The medicine-man also indicates which of the burial party is to be the first to touch the corpse. Burial always takes place after sundown and before sunrise. The body is carried by the male relatives, usually the brothers and the elder sons of the deceased, the eldest sister sometimes helping. The body is placed beside the grave while the eldest sister prepares a rough earth head-rest at one end. The body is then lowered and placed on its right side with the head orientated towards the north-east, while the eldest sister throws the first handful of earth on to it saying, 'You must sleep in peace! You must not be angry with us, for we gave you all that you required and wrapped you in the skin of one of your oxen'. After this the relatives stand aside while the grave is filled in. The eldest son then places a large flat stone at the head of the grave and other stones are laid down by the rest of the party. A branch of the *mutshetshete* (from *u tsheta*, to be quiet) is placed over the head of the grave, to give shade to the dead man. Possibly both stones and thorny branch were originally placed there in order to keep the spirit confined, making it more difficult for it to escape to bring evil to its relatives. The dead man's wooden plate and sometimes an axe or spear used by him during his life are placed on the grave.

When the deceased is a woman her relatives are summoned to help in the interment and to see that all the obituary rites are properly performed. The body is arranged by the old women, who remove all the ornaments, arrange it in the correct position, and wrap it in a blanket. A woman's corpse is never wrapped in a skin. The grave is chosen and the body carried to it as in the case of a dead man, but whereas the man's body is laid down while his head-rest is made, the woman's body is lowered straight into the grave. Her eldest son throws the first clod of earth saying, 'You can rest in peace, my mother. Do not trouble us; I will give you all that you require'. The grave is filled in and the stones and *mutshetshete* bush placed in position. The woman's old stamper, pots, trays and all her bracelets and anklets are broken and placed over the grave by one of her female relatives.

MORTUARY RITES

Unmarried people are buried with little ceremony. The parents of the deceased may attend the funeral, but may not touch the body or take an active part in the burial. Usually the mortuary rites are performed by the old relatives of the deceased. The burials of very young children are left entirely in the hands of the old women of the village, the mother taking no part.

The site of every grave, whether for man, woman, or child, is divined by the medicine-man; after the burial it is always covered with stones and branches of the *mutshetshete*.

After a death all work ceases throughout the district for three or four days, and again on the day the dead man's relatives visit the diviner.

Unusual Deaths.

If a man commits suicide all the relatives are called to the chief's village to determine the cause of the tragedy. It is considered that no man would take his life without some outside provocation, and so the death is regarded as a form of murder. If no adequate explanation is forthcoming the suicide's wives and property are confiscated to protect the rest of the family and to force the culprit to declare himself. If, on consultation with a diviner, the death is discovered to be the work of a spirit, the property is returned, the chief keeping two oxen as payment for his trouble. A suicide is buried in the ordinary way.

A stranger dying away from home is buried in the bush some distance from the kraal. If the body can be identified the relatives are notified, and whenever it is at all possible they are expected to take the body home. Sometimes a man dies away from home and it is quite impossible for his body to be brought back and properly buried. If his spirit becomes troublesome, and requires to be propitiated by a sacrifice at the grave, a fictitious funeral is enacted. A sheep is killed and its head used to symbolize the dead man's corpse; a grave is dug and the head is buried with due reverence in the usual way, together with some of the dead man's clothing or possessions; this grave is thereafter considered to be his.

A leper is isolated in a hut apart from the kraal, and, on his death, the hut containing his dead body and all his effects is burnt to the ground.

A consumptive is buried in a damp place near a river.

A woman dying during pregnancy is buried on the bank of a river and a little channel of water is directed to run over the grave. The baby is generally removed and buried separately.

164 MORTUARY RITES

Purification.

When the burial party returns to the kraal a great lamentation is raised, the women and children wailing and weeping and the wives sometimes throwing themselves about in dramatized paroxysms of grief. The men comfort them by saying that the deceased has gone home. In rich families an ox and a goat are then killed, to follow their late owner to the next world so that he may still have cattle there. The stomach contents of both animals are put on the grave, while the rest of the meat is cooked and eaten, the lion's share being given to the medicine-man. The burial party go through a special purificatory ritual to cleanse themselves from the defilement and dangers of contact with the corpse. They wash in the river, and on their return a heap of grass is lighted in the *khoro*. Their hands and feet are drawn through the fire, so completing the purification. Sometimes instead of a fire the medicine-man makes small incisions on the backs of the thumbs of those who have taken part in the burial. At the time of burial, if the deceased is an important person, the medicine-man extinguishes the fire in the dead man's hut, and any wood that was collected before the death is thrown away, as the fire must die out completely with its owner; the new fire is lit with the fire-sticks. After lighting the new fire the medicine-man dips a branch of the *bhopa vhafu* (tie death) into a mixture that he has brought with him and smears it on the palms and backs of the hands, on the feet, and on the chests of all the relatives. He also gives them a dose of the mixture to drink. All the children of the deceased must go through a special purification ritual. Each child must sit on the spot in the hut where the death occurred, with legs stretched straight out in front, and with the help of his hands shuffle slowly forward to the door. This action is thought to prevent the spirit of the dead man from troubling his children, by removing the contamination of death from the place where it occurred.

Before any grain belonging to the dead person may be eaten, or any of his possessions touched, all the lineage must attend the *dzumo* ceremony (from *u luma*, to bite). All the different varieties of seeds are cooked into a soft porridge and mixed with a powder made from the dried head of the ostrich; each relative takes a portion of the porridge and rubs a little between the big toe and second toe of each foot, and on the knees, elbows, and wrists; a small portion is then taken into the mouth and spat out. If the deceased is a woman her relatives are called and prepare food in the same way, her husband and children also taking part. After the *dzumo* ceremony the seeds of the deceased

MORTUARY RITES

are mixed with the powder and a small portion given to the relatives to mix and sow with their own seeds. This procedure is thought to eliminate the possibility of the spirit of the dead person trying to spoil the crops; when his own seed is mixed with theirs, in spoiling theirs he would also be spoiling his own.

The wives of the dead man are secluded inside their huts for three or four days. The medicine-man then visits the kraal and is given a goat, which he ties to a tree near by. He prepares a purification medicine and then calls out to the wives, '*Ibvani ma dingani*' (Come out of the mud plaster). When the women appear he sprinkles them and the goat with his medicine and the whole party proceeds to the river-bank. The medicine-man orders the wives to wash in the river. While they are obeying him he kills the goat, cooks the contents of its stomach, and adds his medicine to this pottage.

The wives, when they emerge cleansed from the river, drink this concoction, as do the dead man's brothers, some of whom will inherit the women. This concludes the purification of the widows, and after the women have been allotted to their new husbands, each husband and wife, before they can consummate their changed relationship, must visit the medicine-man and have their blood exchanged as in the final marriage ritual.

Mourning.

The mourning period continues until after the cause of death has been discovered and avenged. The day after the burial all the relatives of the deceased shave their heads and shave for a second time after they have visited the diviner. On the first occasion the shaving takes place anywhere, but on the second occasion the relatives are shaved together ceremonially by a member of the lineage, pointed out by the medicine-man. All the hair is collected and rolled up into a ball and put into the nest of the *thaha* bird, which is buried in a hole in an ant-hill. The nest of the *thaha* bird is used for this ceremony on account of the bird's peculiarly shrill noisy cry. The burial of the nest with the hair symbolizes the end of the crying and mourning of the relatives, who are satisfied with the result of the findings of the diviner as to the cause of death. It constitutes the culminating act in the mourning ritual.

XIV

PROPERTY, SUCCESSION, AND INHERITANCE

Property—The Heir—Inheritance of Widows—Heir to Female Fathers

Property.

LAND cannot be owned privately. All the land belongs to the chief, which he holds in trust for his people and cannot alienate. Any person may build on and take temporary possession of any piece of unoccupied land, whether the land has never been cultivated before or is land that has been abandoned. An alien may come to a village and desire to settle near it and, subject to the consent of the chief, he may obtain land on exactly the same conditions. At present there is abundance of land for cultivation, and the problems arising out of the inheritance of land are still questions of the future. There are everywhere communal grazing, water, hunting, fishing, and timber rights, and no man, even a powerful chief, would think of trying to reserve any of these for his individual use.

Every man has indisputable individual rights over the land which he is occupying, allotting different portions to his different wives. His sons, when they grow up, may continue to work their father's land or, if they so desire, may occupy a fresh portion of ground. A man desiring any portion of land simply states his wishes to the local headman. Any controversy occurring about boundaries or the allotment of land is settled by the same person. A thriving *murula* tree may never be cut down; although the owner of the land on which the tree is growing is permitted to make use of the fruit, he must always take a proportion of the beer made from it to the chief or petty chief. Honey belongs to the man who finds it, but he always sends a small portion to the chief or petty chief.

Movable property consists of live stock, household utensils, and the proceeds of agriculture and trade; these are owned individually. A woman may possess movable property as well as a man; the surplus proceeds of her labours are her own and she may dispose of them as she wishes, although she generally discusses their disposal with her husband and would be loth to act without his consent. If she leaves her husband she must leave all the property she has accumulated while living as his wife behind her at his home. The *ndzadzi*, her portion of the lobola, if not already handed to her brother is inherited by her

PROPERTY, SUCCESSION, AND INHERITANCE 167

youngest son, *pedzi*. When this *ndzadzi* has not been given to the wife's family it is often the subject of disputes, the husband being unwilling to allow it to go out of the family, except as the nucleus of lobola for a woman. Any other stock is always inherited by a member of her husband's family, usually her younger child.

The Heir.

The heir inherits the cattle and all the personal property of the deceased. He becomes responsible for all his predecessor's liabilities as well as his assets, and must endeavour in the course of time to fulfil all his obligations. The heir in the direct line, as well as inheriting the personal possessions and the cattle, is the recognized head of the family, and as such he also inherits all the family sacred objects, *zwitungulu*. The heir is the eldest son of his father's great wife. It is the duty of every man to provide the eldest son of each of his wives with a wife. Having done this he has no further obligations towards the other sons, although he often assists them; it is the duty of each son, who has received a wife from his father, to provide his uterine brother next in age with a wife, and this brother acts in like manner towards his younger brother, and so on. If there are many brothers, the youngest, *pedzi*, instead of receiving his wife from the brother next in age to himself, is given his great wife by his mother. The great wife is called *musadzi muhulwane*.

It may happen that a man never receives a wife in this way owing to family quarrels or extreme poverty; these causes may make it impossible for a man to fulfil his obligations either to his son or to his brother. It is the eldest son of the man's first wife who succeeds him on his death in such a case, although he has been obliged through circumstances to lobola her for himself. Of course there is nothing to prevent a man who has not yet received his great wife from marrying other women, and he may acquire one or two other wives before he receives her. In this case, although the previous wives may have grown-up sons, on his death, it is always the son of the great wife who is the heir.

On the occasion of the succession of the heir all the relatives are summoned, and the deceased man's eldest sister, called by his children *makhadzi*, nominates the heir. In her nomination she must be guided by the conditions of succession, and is expected to name the eldest son of her brother's great wife, unless he is absolutely unfit for the position or has disgraced himself in the eyes of the family. In this case the

168 PROPERTY, SUCCESSION, AND INHERITANCE

makhadzi, in conjunction with the deceased man's brothers, may appoint another son, usually the next in age of the same mother. It is always desirable to find an heir who meets with the approval of the whole family, but in the event of a disputed succession it is the *makhadzi* who has the final word, and her nominee must be accepted as the legal heir.

In the event of the great wife not having a male heir, her eldest daughter is recognized as the legal heir, but owing to her sex she is generally debarred from holding the position of head of the family. She has theoretically the right to nominate a brother in her place and is guided by the advice of the *makhadzi*. As a rule the eldest brother by her father's second wife is chosen. In the event of a dispute arising between the deceased's daughter and the *makhadzi*, as to the suitability of the nominee, the wishes of the *makhadzi* will generally be recognized by the rest of the family, and in practice it is seldom that the female heir will question her decision. It now remains to consider what occurs when a man has only female children. When a man has only daughters, on his death his name would die with them, as the daughters' children will belong to their father's family. To prevent this misfortune and to perpetuate the family name his daughter inherits all his property; it is her duty, with its help, to lobola for a woman whom she hands to some other man for the purpose of obtaining an heir. The son born from such a union is, by this fiction, considered to be the son of the brother, who does not exist, and as such the heir to the property. When this child comes of age the female heir passes what remains of the property on to him, together with any lobola she may have acquired at the marriage of her younger sisters. Whenever possible, the man for whom she lobolas the wife to produce her family's heir will be one of her father's brother's sons, whom she calls brother. If for any reason she does not think this desirable, she may give the woman to any other man she chooses. She, and not their physiological parent, is their lawful protector and she is called *makhadzi* by them, and they take the name of her father's family. If the union fails to produce a male heir she lobolas another man in the hope of finally accomplishing her purpose.

When a man dies without any issue his heir is the first son born to his wife by the brother who inherits her. This brother holds the property in trust for his son, until he comes of age. It rarely happens that a man dies without any relatives, but when this does occur his wife may go to any man in the district who desires her, and the first child of this union

PROPERTY, SUCCESSION AND INHERITANCE

will bear the name and inherit the property of the deceased. Should the woman return to her parents and be remarried from her own home, her brother will lobola another wife with some of the cattle from his sister's dead husband's property, and the first child of the union will be heir to the deceased.

Inheritance of Widows.

The wives of a deceased man are inherited laterally by his brothers, subject to certain conditions. His eldest sister has the right of allocating the wives, usually acting on the advice of her eldest surviving brother. If the father is alive, or any of his sisters or brothers, they, in that order, have the prior right in the distribution. The eldest uterine brother of the dead man is given precedence in the inheritance of the widows. 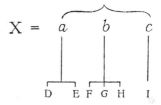 If there is no elder brother the younger uterine brother will receive first consideration before any of his brothers by other mothers. After the claims of the uterine brothers have been satisfied the heir of the dead man's father will have the next choice, the other brothers being allocated widows in a purely arbitrary manner.

Suppose the patriarch X has three wives, a, b, and c, a being the great wife. Suppose a has two sons D and E, b has three sons F, G, and H, c has one son I, and all these sons have wives. On the death of F, b's eldest son, G, has the right to one of F's widows, other than F's great wife (the mother of F's heir), who may not be inherited by any younger brother of the deceased, but must remain at her home under the protection of her eldest son and of G. Usually H would be given a young widow, but he has no actual claim to one. If H died his great wife would be inherited by F, his eldest uterine brother, and G would be given another of the widows. If E died his great wife would be given to D, and if she were too old to bear children he would probably be given a younger woman also. If I, the only son of c, died, D, the heir to the patriarchate, would inherit the great wife. No other brothers may claim the other widows as their right, even though they may be older than D.

As a rule the surplus widows indicate which of the other brothers they would like to marry, and an endeavour is made to distribute them according to their age and character, in a way which will give general

170 PROPERTY, SUCCESSION, AND INHERITANCE

satisfaction to all concerned. If a woman persists in refusing to accept the brother allocated to her and chooses rather to return to her home, all the lobola received for her by her parents must be returned to the heir. Widows who are not remarried continue their lives under the protection of the heir, having children from various lovers, these children becoming the property of their dead husband's heir.

As has been said before, the heir receives all the lobola for his unmarried sisters and provides for the unmarried brothers, according to the customary rules which his father would have followed. The heir refers to his father's widows, other than his own mother, and to all their children as *phulianga* (my slaves).

Heir to Female Fathers.

A woman may also lobola wives, as has been described in the chapter on marriage, and when this occurs she in a sense establishes her own family and as head of that family must have her heir. At her death the eldest son of her first wife will succeed his female father, in the same way as he would have done had she been his real father. If the first wife has no son, but has a daughter, then this girl takes precedence over any of her brothers from other mothers and is the sole heir to the property. It is her duty to procure wives for her brothers, as in the ordinary case, but any cattle which remain at her death go to her youngest child; if she dies childless or is unmarried, the eldest brother by her father's second wife becomes her heir. A woman, who is married and has a uterine son of her own and has also a daughter by a woman lobola-ed by her, usually marries these two to each other.

In reviewing the customs of inheritance it is evident that it is the desire of every man to perpetuate his family and be succeeded by one of his own progeny. The heir must be in the direct line, a brother or uncle not being eligible. If a man dies childless, or with only female children, it is the duty of widow or daughter to make an heir who will adopt his name, inherit his property, and continue the family in the direct line. The ineligible persons, during the minority of the heir, must hold everything in trust for him and hand it over intact when he comes of age. Although in normal circumstances the eldest son of the great wife is the legal heir, this law is by no means rigid, as if the *makhadzi* considers him to be undesirable as the head of the family she may designate any other son, the choice resting entirely with her. Her power in this matter often results in the personal equation influencing her choice unfairly, and sometimes she may, for her own ends,

PROPERTY, SUCCESSION AND INHERITANCE 171

pass over the lawful heir on some trivial and invalid excuse, nominating another son over whom she has more influence. If her nominee is accepted all is well, but this personal element in the appointment of the heir, although theoretically very limited by customary law, is the root of endless family feuds. Indeed in the past the death of almost every patriarch resulted in family disruptions, the deceased man's brothers refusing to recognize the *makhadzi's* nominee and attempting to usurp her power by setting up as head of the family the man whom they considered would best serve their ends.

XV

RELATIONSHIP TERMINOLOGY AND KINSHIP SYSTEM [1]

THE BaVenda kinship terminology is based on the classificatory system, but it is not found in the extreme form in which it exists in Melanesia, and it only applies to those whose relationships can be traced genealogically.

All relations in the generation of great-grandparents, on both father's and mother's side, irrespective of sex, are collectively designated *makhulukuku*. The behaviour of children towards their great-grandparents is of little significance; often the old people who are unfit for work become the nurses of the small children, and there exists a reciprocal attitude of affection and good-fellowship that is common in all societies between the very young and the very old. Grandparents are *makhulu*, and the same term is applied to a man's wife's brother's wife, his mother's brother's wife, his wife's parents, and all their brothers and sisters. *Makhulu* means great or big and signifies respect and, when it is used for mother-in-law or wife's brother's wife, carries with it, in addition to the respect and reverence accorded to every *makhulu*, a rule of avoidance and fear. *Makhulu* on the father's side are more reverenced than those on the mother's side. The mother's parents treat their grandchildren with affection and friendliness, and the children have no fear in asking them for help or food and shelter, when they would be afraid to approach the father's parents.

There is a special term for father, *khotsi*. A man calls all his father's brothers and the cousins whom his father would call brother, in the male line, by the terms *khotsi muhulu* and *khotsi munene*, great father and little father, respectively. He uses the same term for the husbands of all those whom his mother calls sisters, the term for great and little being used according as to whether the sister is older or

---

[1] This chapter was written before the appearance of the revised and enlarged edition of Junod's *Life of a South African Tribe*, which contains a description of the Venda relationship system—vol. i, pp. 302–8. I obtained all my material independently, and on comparing it with Junod find that his account corresponds with mine in nearly every essential. Junod also includes the kinship system of the BaVenda in his list of South African Bantu Kinship Systems, vol. i, pp. 496–503.

RELATIONSHIP AND KINSHIP SYSTEM 173

younger than the mother. A woman calls her sisters' husbands by these terms, as do her husband and her husband's brothers. A father is always greatly respected by his son, who implicitly obeys all his commands. A man in addressing his father and all those of his father's generation and above, will never use the words '*Khotsi*', '*Makhulu*', &c., but if he is bound to address him directly will approach respectfully and say '*Ndau*'. A son only indulges in polite conversation when in the presence of his father, and, although he may approach him personally on trivial matters, in all important crises he will approach his mother, or one of her co-wives, and ask her to convey the message to the father; any irregularity on the part of the son is conveyed to the father in this way, the son only being allowed to explain matters himself to his father when summoned by him to account for his actions. *Khotsi muhulu* and *khotsi munene*, in the father's generation, are also respected and are not directly addressed by name, although there is a freer relationship with these persons than with the actual father; a son who has quarrelled with his father and been banished from the house usually asks one of these relatives to intercede for him with his father. The mother's sisters' husbands are treated with the ordinary respect shown to older people. A woman often refers to her husband's brothers as *khotsi muhulu* and *khotsi munene* because they are the terms which her children use for these people; these terms have no significance. She may also refer to them as *munnawanga* (my husband); in direct address she speaks to them by name.

The mother has a special term, *mme*; she is often called *mavhe* in direct address. All those whom she calls sister are *mme muhulu*, great mother, or *mmane*, little mother; her co-wives and all whom they call sister are called by the same terms. A man calls his elder brother's wife *mmane*, and if she is the great wife he can never inherit her. He may refer to his younger brother's wife as *musadzi vha murathu*, wife of the brother; he can inherit the great wife of his brother next in age, as, according to the system, he is the man who paid the lobola for that woman and gave her to his brother; brothers, however, call each other's wives by name in direct address and converse and mix with them freely; they also refer to each other's wives as *musadziashu*, our wife. The wives all call each other *muhadzinga*, the term for co-wife, thus anticipating at some time becoming wives of the same man.

Every son of one called father or mother is classed with the brothers

174 RELATIONSHIP TERMINOLOGY AND

and every daughter with the sisters. Brothers use a term for each other making an age distinction, calling an elder brother *mukomana* and a younger *murathu*. Sisters use the same term similarly between each other. Brother and sister use an entirely different term, *khaladzi*, which is reciprocal and makes no age distinction. This terminology is used also between children of different mothers. The behaviour practised between members of this group has been described in connexion with etiquette.

The mother's brother, wife's brother, and wife's brother's son are all called *malume*, and a man stands in a peculiar position to his *malume*, of which more will be said later.

The father's sister has a special term, *makhadzi*, and she plays a very important part in Venda life, sharing with her elder brother the privileges belonging to the head of the family. One of the reasons for the position of the *makhadzi*, to which the BaVenda themselves attach great importance, is the fact that she is the primary factor in bringing the cattle into the family, by means of which her brother is able to obtain his wife. She is therefore responsible for the establishment of her brother's family, and consequently the person best fitted to approve of the heir whose duty it will be to preserve the continuity of this family. When a man has not obtained his wife through the usual channels his sister does not have the supreme power over the offspring that she would otherwise have enjoyed; often her suggestions as to the heir and the disposal of her brother's property are completely disregarded, and she is reminded that she was not responsible for the establishment of that family.

The children of the *makhadzi* and those of the mother's brother are classed together as *muzwala* and sharply distinguished from the children of the father's brother and mother's sister, who are all brothers and sisters. A free and easy relationship exists between *muzwala*, who may joke together without restraint and call each other by name in direct address. The child of a *muzwala* is *muzwalana* (little *muzwala*). After marriage with the mother's brother's daughter the *muzwala* relationships are changed.

A man calls all his children *mwana*, and applies this term to all those whom his children call brothers and sisters—that is, his brother's children and his wife's sisters' children, (own and classificatory) but not his sister's children or his wife's brother's children. When necessary the children of an elder brother are further distinguished as *mwana vha mukomanawanga*, child of my *mukomana*, and those of a

KINSHIP SYSTEM 175

younger brother as *mwana vha murathuwanga*, child of my *murathu*; he would further explain if the child was a boy or a girl.

All children two generations below are *muduhulu*, except the wife's brother's son's son, who is *mwana vha malume* or *malume*, and the wife's brother's son's daughter, who is *muzadzana*, little wife. The wife's brother's daughter's children are *mwana*. The generation below *muduhulu* are *muduhulwana* (little grandchild).

The marriage system whereby the eldest son's great-wife, *musadzi muhulwane*, is lobola-ed by his father, and that of the next son by his elder brother, and so on, has been described. Cross-cousin marriage with the mother's brother's daughter is practised whenever possible, and is an essential feature in the society. The only other marriage that is permitted within the family group is with the wife's brother's daughter, under special conditions. Otherwise a man may marry anybody, from anywhere, provided that person is not connected by blood with either the father's or mother's family group. Except in the above cases the rule of exogamy is strictly adhered to and applies to the remotest blood relatives and even to many people in the family group with whom there is no blood relationship at all. For instance, if two unrelated men, A and B, marry c_1 and c_2, who are sisters, and B also marries another woman d, then the son of A and c_1 may not marry the daughter of B and d (i.e. c_2's co-wife) although these persons are absolutely unrelated by blood.

The BaVenda feel very strongly the advantages that accrue from frequent marriage into the same group; there is already a feeling of good-fellowship between the lineage of a man and that of his mother, and many embarrassments and complications are avoided if marriage is continued within this group, further cementing the existing bond in each generation. To seek admission by marriage into an entirely new group is a far more difficult matter, to be avoided whenever the simpler procedure of marriage with the father's sister's son is possible. It is usual therefore for a man to approach his wife's brother when he wishes to give his son a wife, and, whenever possible, his wife's brother is morally bound to agree to the proposed union. If he should refuse his daughter, which rarely occurs, he must return to his sister the *ndzadzi* (i.e. the cow and the calf which his sister passes on to him when she receives it on the marriage of her daughter) and all its progeny, so that she can use it to assist in obtaining a wife for her son elsewhere. In one case a woman, not possessing a brother, gave the *ndzadzi* obtained on the marriage of her daughter to her mother's

176 RELATIONSHIP TERMINOLOGY AND

brother. Her son, when desiring a wife, demanded assistance from that person, i.e. his mother's mother's brother, and was given his daughter.

If a father cannot provide the necessary lobola for his son's wife the latter is often given the girl on the promise of the payment being made as soon as possible. This occurs even in cases where the possibility of payment is so remote as to be dependent on the marriage of a female offspring yet unborn. Sometimes a poor man, wishing to obtain a wife, will ask a rich friend to help him with a gift of cattle for the lobola. When asked for a surety he points to his little toe, implying that the first daughter of the union will be given to the benefactor. If this is agreed upon, although it will be a very long time before the promised daughter is forthcoming, the terminology existing between a man and his father-in-law will come into force immediately the poor man receives his wife. Husband and wife both begin to call their benefactor *mukwasha*, son-in-law, and he calls them *makhulu*; the behaviour between the two families conforms in every detail to the pattern that is followed when the relationship really exists.

In the case where a woman has no daughter, by whose marriage lobola is obtained for the lobola of her son, her brother is morally bound to help the eldest of these nephews; it is considered that in failing to provide a daughter the mother's family has fallen short of its share of the bargain and must compensate for its inadequacy by helping her son. Generally when children are old enough to leave their mother they go to the home of their maternal uncle and live with him for a few years. They always treat him with respect and deference, and must give him any of their personal possessions, as clothes and implements, that he may demand. Even when grown-up the children are bound to help him with his work whenever he demands their services.

In the course of investigating cross-cousin marriage, a few cases of marriage with the father's sister's son were discovered; it is very rare, and may only occur where there is no heir to marry the daughter of the maternal uncle. In this case very occasionally the son of the maternal uncle may marry the daughter of his paternal aunt to maintain the solidarity of the family group. Nearly all informants, however, regard this union as wrong.

A brother calls his sister's husband *mukwasha*, the term applied to the man who brings cattle into the family.

KINSHIP SYSTEM

A man calls his wife's brother's daughter *musadzana*, little wife. The marriage of a man with his wife's brother's daughter takes place occasionally, and was probably at one time a regular form of marriage. To-day, if he has a son, this woman must be given to the son, and only if he has no son is he allowed to keep her himself. The person who pays the lobola for a woman is always regarded by her family as her legal husband and is always held responsible for her.

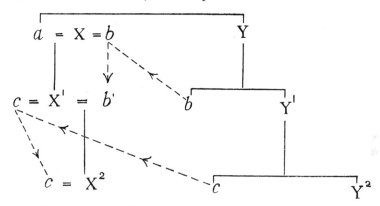

I will attempt to explain with the help of the above diagram why a man calls his sister's son *muduhulu*, the term which is applied to a grandchild, and why a man calls his wife's brother and his wife's brother's son *malume*, the term by which he calls his mother's brother.

Suppose the time has come for X to give his eldest son X^1 a wife. X will approach Y, his wife's brother, for the purpose of obtaining his daughter b, and X and Y will decide upon the necessary lobola and come to an agreement. From this point of view, Y and his family, although they know that b is eventually to be given to X^1 to wife, regard X as her legal husband, he being the man who pays the lobola for her. From the time that the agreement is made until X^1 actually receives b, he cannot call her *musadzi*, wife, but refers to her and all her sisters as *mmane*, the term for father's wife; she during this period refers to X as *munna*, husband; X^1 being her legal husband's child she refers to him as *mwana*, child. So her father Y must call the person whom his daughter calls child *muduhulu*, grandchild, and Y's wife is called by X^1 *makhulu*, grandmother. Even after b has been handed to X^1 by his father, Y still calls X^1 *muduhulu*, and calls X *mukwasha*, as it is he who has brought the cattle into the family and not X^1. If any trouble arises between X^1 and b after the

178 RELATIONSHIP TERMINOLOGY AND

consummation of their marriage and b complains to her father, wishing to leave X^1, her father will approach X on the matter, not X^1. It is only after the death of X that X^1 as his heir is considered as the *mukwasha* by Y. When the marriage between b and X^1 has been consummated, X calls b and all her sisters *mazwale*, the reciprocal term applied to a son's wife; the right which he had of marrying b's sisters then passes to his son. X^1 now calls b's sisters *musadzana*, and if he so desires may marry them. His younger brothers continue to call b and her sisters *mmane*.

A man calls his wife's brother *malume* because, (see diagram), Y^1, like his father, regards X as the legal husband of his sister b, and as such he looks upon X^1 as being her son. Accordingly he regards himself as the mother's brother, *malume*, of X^1, and, regarding X^1 as his sister's son, he calls him *muduhulu*, the term for grandchild, as has been explained.

In the course of time X^1 gives his son X^2 his wife's brother's daughter c to wife, by the same rule as he himself received b; as he, X^1, has now paid the lobola to Y^1, bringing cattle into the family, he is regarded by Y^1 as *mukwasha* as well as *muduhulu*, and c, being his wife he would call Y^2 his wife's brother, *malume*. From Y^1's point of view he regards himself as being X^1's mother's brother, and he is also X^2's mother's brother; in other words X^1 and X^2, whilst being father and son, are both regarded by Y^1 as being his sisters' sons; as such he calls them both *muduhulu*, so that he is in the anomalous position of being mother's brother to two successive generations at the same time. In order to reconcile Y^1's position as mother's brother to X^1 and also to his son X^2, the special term *malume* is applied to Y^1, by both X^1 and X^2.

This curious relationship and terminology is unusual. Seligman[1] found that among the Bari south of the Dinka country the maternal uncle and maternal uncle's son are addressed by the same term; among the Bari, however, a man does not marry his mother's brother's daughter.

Often marriage with the mother's brother's daughter cannot take place, as there may be no daughter or no daughter of a suitable age; in this case a wife must be taken from an outside group. The kinship system of nomenclature is utilized under these new conditions in exactly the same way as would have been the case if the orthodox marriage had taken place; an entirely new family becomes involved,

[1] Seligman, C. G. and B. Z., 'The Bari', *J. Roy. Anthrop. Inst.*, vol. lxiii, 1928, pp. 438 and 440.

KINSHIP SYSTEM

but the relationships between the two groups, once the first barrier of reserve and suspicion is broken down, quickly become intimate.

Amongst many Bantu societies a man has the right to marry his wife's brother's daughter. It has often been suggested that this right has arisen from his claim on his wife's brother's wife, as she was obtained with the help of the cattle provided by him on his marriage; in the event of his wife being unsatisfactory, and there being no other sister to take her place, the cattle, which have helped his wife's brother to obtain his wife, should be returned to him; failing this he may claim his wife's brother's wife, whose husband would be unwilling to give her up and would substitute a daughter in her place. A Venda man has the prior right to his wife's younger sisters and must be consulted before a sister is given to any other man. If he consents to 'untie' his sister-in-law she may marry elsewhere. He may only marry his wife's brother's daughter when there are no sisters-in-law available. It is possible that this woman, who is called *musadzana*, little wife, is called by this term merely because she is a young marriageable woman of his wife's group, but if this were so there is no reason why the wife's father's sister should not also be called *musadzana* and be a possible wife, which is not the case. I would venture to suggest an entirely different explanation.

It seems to me that a man acquires this right over his wife's brother's daughter through a claim on his wife's brother. Except for persons in the generation above the individual concerned, there are no terms to differentiate sex; *makhulu* is applied to grandfathers and grandmothers irrespective of sex; *mwana* is applied to both boys and girls, as is *muduhulu*, &c. In actual practice there is a curious ambivalent attitude towards sex. Where a woman performs the functions of a man she is treated in every way as though she were a man, and is even called by the terms that would be used towards the man whose place she is taking. It would appear that the Venda attitude towards individuals depends upon their function within the family and the society, rather than upon any other factor, even sex. Uterine brothers and sisters are not regarded by the rest of the community as so many individuals, but as one single personality, represented by any or all of the family; a child regards his father and all his father's brothers and sisters with exactly the same feelings, differing in degree according to the distinction in age rather than in sex; he regards his mother and all her sisters and brothers in the same way. The terms *makhadzi* and *malume* are merely sex-denoting. If this idea of the single personality

180 RELATIONSHIP TERMINOLOGY AND

of children of the same mother, irrespective of sex, can be accepted, a man besides having the right to marry his wife's sisters is only prevented by their sex from being able to marry his wife's brothers. The claim over his wife's brother is then transferred to his wife's brother's daughter, whom he calls by the same term that would have been applied to his wife's brother if he had been a woman. In marrying his wife's brother's daughter, he is obtaining a woman of the same group as his wife and of practically the same blood; they have all their relatives in common, which would not be the case if the claim rested on his wife's brother's wife.

To continue with the terminology; a man calls his sister's husband, his daughter's husband, his wife's sister's daughter's husband and his brother's daughter's husband *mukwasha*, the term signifying the man who brings cattle into a family; at family beer-drinks it is customary for a man to seat all whom he calls *mukwasha* together beside him. There is always a reciprocal attitude of respect and deference between *mukwasha*; a *mukwasha* visiting his parents-in-law always takes some present for them, and they receive him with pleasure and gratification and provide him with beer and hospitality.

A reciprocal term, *mazwale*, is used between a woman and her husband's parents and their brothers and sisters, and an attitude of mutual fear and reserve exists between *mazwale*. If a woman wishes to make a complaint against her husband, she will sometimes request his eldest brother to administer a rebuke; more often she will inform her husband's father, but this is always done through one of the persons whom her husband calls *mmane*, and never directly to the father whom she fears more than she does the womenfolk.

A man's wife's sister's husband is either *khotsi muhulu* or *khotsi munene*, according to whether the sister is older or younger than the wife. It has been explained that before a man actually receives his great wife from his father, according to the customary rule, he calls her and all her sisters *mmane*. When he eventually receives his wife this nomenclature changes and his wife, previously *mmane*, becomes *musadzi*, while her sister becomes *musadzana*, little wife, a woman whom he may marry. In the case where a sister is married to some other man the term *khotsi munene* is applied to her husband, the general term for the husband of one called *mmane*. Similarly, he calls his wife's elder sister's husband *khotsi muhulu*, the elder sister always being married before her younger sister, by whose husband she is called *mmane*. The behaviour between sisters' husbands is like that between brothers,

KINSHIP SYSTEM

181

irrespective of the term of address used between them. Whenever possible brothers marry into the same family, an elder brother usually giving his next youngest brother one of his wife's sisters.

RELATIONSHIP TERMS

Great grandparents	*Makhulukuku*

Father's father	
Father's father's brother	
Father's father's brother's wife	
Father's father's sister	
Father's mother	
Father's mother's brother	
Father's mother's brother's wife	
Father's mother's sister	
Father's mother's sister's husband	
Mother's father	
Mother's father's brother	
Mother's father's brother's wife	
Mother's father's sister	
Mother's father's sister's husband	*Makhulu*
Mother's mother	
Mother's mother's brother	
Mother's mother's brother's wife	
Mother's mother's sister	
Mother's mother's sister's husband	
Mother's brother's wife	
Son's wife's parents	
Wife's father	
Wife's father's brother	
Wife's father's sister	
Wife's mother	
Wife's mother's brother	
Wife's mother's sister	
Wife's brother's wife	

Father	*Khotsi*
Mother	*Mme* or *mavhe*
Father's elder brother Mother's elder sister's husband	*Khotsi muhulu*

RELATIONSHIP TERMINOLOGY AND

Wife's elder sister's husband Husband's elder brother Elder sister's husband (w.s.)	*Khotsi muhulu*
Father's younger brother Mother's younger sister's husband Wife's younger sister's husband Younger sister's husband (w.s.) Husband's younger brother	*Khotsi munene*
Father's sister	*Makhadzi*
Mother's brother Wife's brother Wife's brother's son (or *mwana vha malume*) Wife's brother's son's son	*Malume*
Father's brother's son Father's wife's son (step-brother) Mother's sister's son Brother Sister (w.s.) and all a woman calls sister	*Mukomana* (elder) *Murathu* (younger)
Father's brother's daughter Father's wife's daughter (step-sister) Mother's sister's daughter Sister Brother (w.s.) and all a woman calls brother	*Khaladzi*
Father's younger sister's wife Mother's younger sister Elder brother's wife Father's wives (younger than own mother)	*Mmane*
Father's elder brother's wife Mother's elder sister Wife's elder sister Father's wife (older than own mother)	*Mme muhulu*
Father's mother's son's son Father's mother's son's daughter Son	*Mwana*

KINSHIP SYSTEM 183

Daughter
Brother's son
Brother's daughter
Husband's brother's son
Husband's brother's daughter
Co-wife's son
Co-wife's daughter   } *Mwana*
Wife's sister's son
Wife's sister's daughter
Wife's brother's daughter's children
Mother's sister's son's son
Mother's sister's son's daughter

Father's sister's son
Father's sister's daughter
Mother's brother's son (w.s.)   } *Muzwala*
Mother's brother's daughter

Father's sister's son's son
Father's sister's son's daughter   *Muzwala vha mwana*
Father's sister's daughter's son   or
Father's sister's daughter's daughter   *Muzwalazwalana*

Husband
Husband's brother   } *Munna*

Wife   *Musadzi*

Brother's wife   *Musadzi* or *Musadzi vha murathu*

Wife's younger sister
Wife's brother's daughter   } *Musadzana*
Wife's brother's daughter's daughter

Co-wife
Husband's brother's wife   } *Mahadzinga*

Brother's wife (w.s.)
Husband's sister   } *Muhalivho*

184 RELATIONSHIP AND KINSHIP SYSTEM

Father's sister's husband Daughter's husband Daughter's husband (w.s.) Sister's husband Husband's sister's husband Brother's daughter's husband Sister's daughter's husband Daughter's daughter's husband Son's daughter's husband	*Mukwasha* or *Muduhulu*
Son's wife Son's wife (w.s.) Husband's father Husband's father's brother Husband's father's sister Husband's mother Husband's mother's sister Brother's son's wife Wife's sister's son's wife Daughter's son's wife Son's son's wife	*Mazwale*
Father's brother's daughter's son Father's brother's daughter's daughter Mother's sister's daughter's son Mother's sister's daughter's daughter Son's daughter Son's son Daughter's son Daughter's daughter Husband's sister's son Husband's sister's daughter Sister's son Sister's daughter Brother's son's son Brother's son's daughter Sister's son's son Sister's son's daughter Wife's sister's son's son Wife's sister's son's daughter	*Muduhulu*
Great-grandchildren	*Muduhulwana*

XVI

SOCIAL GROUPINGS

Patrilineal Lineage—Matrilineal Lineage—Sibs—Dialectic Divisions—
Age-Sets

Patrilineal Lineage.

EXCLUDING the small family group composed of a man and his wives and children, the most important social grouping is the extended family or lineage. This grouping is unilateral, of the patriarchal type, and includes a man, his brothers and sisters, his children and the children of his brothers (but not those of his sisters) and the children of their sons and so on. The sisters and daughters marry outside this extended family grouping and go to live with the family of their husbands; otherwise all the members of the family tend to live near to each other, each man building his wives' huts close to the house of his father; this aggregation of houses forms a patriarchal group which acts as a single unit in social and religious affairs.

Matrilineal Lineage.

Although descent, succession, and inheritance are reckoned through the father, every individual is also a member of a parallel lineage on the mother's side, very important in social and religious life. This group has a particular significance for the individual, exerting a stronger emotional and personal influence than the more formal patrilineal group. It consists of the mother, her brothers and sisters, her children and the children of her sisters (but not those of her brothers), the children of their daughters and so on, and all the ancestors in the matrilineal line. The functions of this group partly explain the peculiar relationship between a man and his mother's brother, particularly in religious affairs. As its importance is essentially linked with the ancestor-cult it will be more fully discussed in that connexion.

Sibs.

In addition to his being a member of a patriarchal family and of a strong matrilineal group, every MuVenda belongs also to a sib, *mutupo*. These sibs were at one time exogamous and of a totemic character; they are now broken down and have been replaced by the extended family. As the members of a sib increased in numbers

SOCIAL GROUPINGS

small families began to break away from the original stem and to start independent groups in different localities. These new groups often retained the original names of their sib, while gradually ignoring its peculiar character. As the connexion with the original stem grew more remote the rule of exogamy also lapsed. Many old men still express horror at the thought of marriage between a man and woman of the same sib, considering such a union to be incestuous, all siblings to them being brothers and sisters. Among the younger people, however, provided that the interested parties live some distance apart and cannot trace genealogical relationship, these unions frequently occur.

Members of a sib are called by the name of some animal, plant or object, between which and themselves they conceive there is an intimate relationship, and which is always regarded by them with considerable respect. It is difficult to collect accurate information concerning the various sibs and sub-sibs and their totems. The people seem reluctant and almost afraid to mention their sib names, and there are few men who have any knowledge of more than five or six. The difficulty is increased still further by the fact that there are different methods of answering a question about the sib. When possible the name of the totemic animal or object is avoided and the praise name of the group substituted, or the name of one of the original ancestors, or the name of the elder sister of the head-man of the sib, or that of the locality with which the sib is chiefly associated. A man, in taking an oath, always uses the name of his *mutupo*. Many sibs are commonly called by the name of the totem animal with the prefix *vha*; e.g. VhaDau are the people of the lion. Others have the word *ila* interpolated between the prefix and the name of the totem; e.g. *Vha-ila-mbudzi* are the people forbidden the goat. A man has no objection to eating animals which are tabu to another sib, but he usually respects his wives' totems and avoids eating them in their presence, or conforms with the required ritual behaviour. A man whose totem is the pigeon will frighten away any pigeon on his premises to avoid its being killed, but if he catches one in a trap accidentally he is not unduly worried, but gives it to a friend belonging to a different sib to eat. Every sib has one or more honorific phrases, *tshikodo*, associated with it. The *tshikodo* is addressed to a chief when entering a village or when he has performed a noteworthy action; often it is used by a visitor in greeting him as a sign of respect and politeness. A father may reply to the greeting of his child, using the words of the sib *tshikodo*. A woman may use the words in thanking a man for a service that he has rendered her.

SOCIAL GROUPINGS 187

A young man feeling at peace with the world and full of the joy of living may suddenly chant the words of his *tshikodo* as the most satisfactory means of expressing his exuberance.

The following sibs are found in Vendaland to-day; in some cases I was able to obtain the words of the *tshikodo*.

The Vhatavhatsinde, the rulers of Vendaland before the MaKhwinde occupation, are divided into three sibs.

1. *VhaDau* (People of the lion) have their sacred mountain at Maungani. The totem animals of this sib are lions, leopards, and all felines.

2. *VhaKwebo* (People of the dove) have traditional homes on the mountains at Tshiendeulu and Luonde. The totem animals of the VhaKwebo are the dove and the pig.

> *Tshikodo:* '*Mune wanga, MuKwebo, mufha-madi!*' (My lord, MuKwebo, of the dead water).

3. *Ndou* (Elephant). The sib who tabu the elephant have traditional sacred homes at Tshirululuni, Fundudzi, Thengwe, Ha Manenzhe, and Kokwani. The members of the sib, who come from Kokwani, are also forbidden to eat the small figs from the root of the fig-tree.

> *Tshikodo:* '*Ndou ya tavha la muvuda-ngoma la ha Nyamilila mitovha-nombe ine matshele yat ovha zwira Nzhelele la mitanga-omani.*' 'Mountain elephant of the (regular) soft sounding drum, of the cattle-road, true track of the cattle, where to-morrow the armies of Nzhelele with the *mitanga-omani* trees will follow.' (This means that the MaKhwinde will follow them for their cattle.)

This song is particularly interesting as it must have originated in the days when the Vhatavhatsinde were being subjugated by the Ma-Khwinde.

4. *MaKhwinde*, or *Vha-ila-mbudzi* (The people who tabu the goat) have their ancestral home at Dzata. The MaKhwinde totem animal is the goat, which may not be eaten unless it is killed with a special ritual. The skin on the goat's tail must be peeled back and the tail cut off at the root; all blood must be washed off and the animal left standing for a short time before it is killed by having its throat cut. All the important chiefs belong to this, the largest and most honoured of all Venda sibs. Chief Mphaphuli, whose ancestors were not MaKhwinde (I was unable to discover to what sib they originally belonged) now claims to be a MaKhwinde, distinguishing his section of the sib by calling it *Gutame*, the name of one of his father's sisters.

SOCIAL GROUPINGS

There are many other alternative names and praise-names applied to branches of this sib. The great praise-name *Singo* (Elephant's trunk) is used in addressing an important chief. Bullock,[1] in referring to BaVenda sibs, says that 'The *mutupo Singo* is a sharp knife'. *Singo* is not really a *mutupo* and has no connexion with a knife; possibly he has confused the BaThonga word *nsingo* (razor). As far as I can discover, *Singo* is simply a praise-name used in addressing MaKhwinde chiefs. At one time, when the elephant was the great royal animal, it was tabu for the chief to see its trunk.

The less important members of the sib are called *Rambau*. A chief, when in anger and registering an oath to be revenged, prefaces his statement by the word '*Tshavhumbwe!*', the name of the sister of one of his ancestors. The names of other royal female ancestors are also used in this way; questions about this sib may be answered in all manner of different ways.

> *Tshikodo:* '*Khwinde! Khwinde! wa mikondeni, wa bambalani la mitanga-omani mitshena yo tshena Nzhelele i sa li mitshila ya mbudzi i shavha u phumuwa milomo, wa Tshipapa wa tshi Dongololwe.*' 'Khwinde! Khwinde! where the first cakes (slabs) of porridge were cooked, where the young female goats (meaning young unmarried girls) of the white fruit of the *mitanga-omani* tree, loom white in Nzhelele valley, who do not eat the tail of a goat, being afraid to bruise their mouths, of Tshipapa, of Dongololwe.'

The word *Mutavhatsinde* may be used as a praise-name by the MaKhwinde who consider that being the conquerors they may use any name; this further increases the existing confusion about the word. Chief Masekwa distinguishes himself from the rest of the MaKhwinde by using the name *VhaTshishongo*, the name of the sister of one of the early MaKhwinde ancestors; he has also a special praise-name, *MuNdalama* (Man with long life). His people often describe themselves as *Vha-Ndalama*, using the word as their sib-name.

> *Masekwa's tshikodo:* '*Singo, Rambau, Mutavhatsinde vha Tshishongo, Vha Ndalama!*'

5. *VhaLaudzi*, with their sacred mountains at Vhulorwa, Tshingani, and Lwamondo, have no actual totem animal or object; they are forbidden to work in their gardens on the day after they first see the new moon. Those from Lwamondo are of BaSutho stock, from Palabora. Another section of this sib has its mountains at Masia and Tsianda;

---

[1] Bullock, Charles, *The Mashona*, Capetown and Johannesburg, p. 115.

SOCIAL GROUPINGS 189

they have adopted the goat as their totem and practise all the Ma-Khwinde tabus and are probably of BaThonga stock.

The Tshikodo song of the Masia section: 'Mune wanga Khwinde MuLaudzi Ratshinavha tshinavhida Vhavhuya tshi no u fa tsha sinnwa musanda.' 'My Lord Khwinde MuLaudzi (from *u laula*, to point out, smell out) Ratshinavha (*navha*, to stretch out the leg) who stretches out the leg for the good (who receives well the welcome guests) if he (it) dies he is given as a royal tribute to the chief.' (If a Khwinde MuLaudzi dies they must let the chief know.)

6. *VhaDau* (2) (People of the lion). There are several unrelated sections of this sib, all having for their totem animals the lion and all felines. The sib in the Vhatavhatsinde group has already been described. Many VhaDau are reputed to have been BaThonga, although it is impossible to-day to identify this section. There are also VhaDau at Mutali, Tshakhuma, and HaMakhusha, all probably of Sutho stock. A branch at Tshiherni is always careful to dissociate itself from the other VhaDau, as it considers itself to be of pure Venda stock.

7. *Vhatwamamba*, with its important branch sib the *VhaLeya*, have their ancestral home at Tshivhula in the Blaauberg; they were originally of Sutho stock. It is tabu for members of this sib to eat anything that has touched the cooking-stones by the fire. If they are to eat a sheep, it must be stabbed in the back, and while it is dying one of its forelegs must be skinned. They are also forbidden to eat snails. The BaVenda used to carry salt in snail-shells, so that it was tabu for members of this sib to eat anything which had been cooked with salt.

Tshikodo: 'Muthwamamba na vha MuLeya ni ni vhana vha vha tshivhula note.' ('Muthwamamba or MuLeya, you are all children of Tshivhula.')

8. *VhaNyai*, now a Venda sib, were originally a group of people living north of the Limpopo. There are two sections of this sib; one section may not eat sheep unless the shoulder has been cut off before the animal is dead; the other section may not eat porridge that has been touched by the handle-end of the porridge-stick.

9. *VhaKhomolo* are a small sib, with their ancestral mountain in Southern Rhodesia. Their totem animal is the buffalo, and they may not eat the heart of a buffalo or the hoof of cattle.

10. *Mbedzi.* This is a large sib, probably one of the earliest arrivals in the Zoutpansberg from Southern Rhodesia. This group occupies the extreme east of Vendaland and has given its sib-name to that part of the country. The Mbedzi totem animal is the crocodile, and all

190 SOCIAL GROUPINGS

river animals are also tabu to them. There is a tradition among the old MaKhwinde people forbidding their men to marry women of the Mbedzi sib, as such unions are supposed to result in the formation of disfiguring growths on the faces of the husbands. I could obtain no history of this tabu which is gradually being allowed to lapse.

11. *Vhafu-a-madi* (Dead of the water). This was at one time a praise-name of the VhaKwebo sib, but is now the name of a separate sib, which has completely severed its connexion with the VhaKwebo. It is tabu for a member of this sib to eat from the porridge-stick, which must always be put into a pot of water as soon as porridge is ready.

12. *VhaDzivhani* (At the pool). This sib, like a section of the VhaDau, is supposed to have been one of the BaNgona sibs. It is tabu for its members to drink the water of the Mutali river where it runs into Lake Fundudzi.

13. *VhaPfumbe*. Most of the BaVenda who are now living in Southern Rhodesia are called VhaPfumbe; many of them are descended from members of Mphephu's following who remained in Southern Rhodesia when Mphephu returned to the Zoutpansberg after his exile. They are now considered as a separate Venda sib.

There are among the BaVenda some families among whom there is a definite connexion between the original ancestor and the totem. Nemaungani, of the VhaDau sib, whose totem animals are lions and all felines, believes that his first ancestor was transformed into a leopard and still accompanies him wherever he goes, stalking beside him invisible, but always alert and ready to kill his enemies; he is often called Nemaungani vha Nngwe (of the leopard) on this account. Chief Lwamondo, whose village is situated nearly at the top of Lwamondo Kop, belongs to the VhaLaudzi sib, who venerate the new moon. All VhaLaudzi living on the kop have also a very intimate connexion with the baboon, and are to-day generally called the Vha-ila-Pfene (*pfene*, baboon). Junod [1] describes what he considers to be the proper Venda theory on this point in the following way:

'It is believed that these baboons are the Badzimu themselves. Each MuLaudzi, when he dies, becomes a baboon and goes to the sacred hill of Lomondo to dwell there. There is a specially big baboon amongst them. It never utters a cry. It is very old. It is the chief of the flock, and the principal ancestor god. Only when a great misfortune threatens the tribe

[1] Junod, H. A., 'Some Features of the Religion of the BaVenda', *The South African Journal of Science*, vol. xvii, 1921, pp. 218, 219.

SOCIAL GROUPINGS

191

one will hear it coming out of the forest and shouting loudly. Should a member of the clan die away from Lomondo, it is the old baboon which will go, accompanied by others, to fetch the new Mudzimu, who has been transformed into a baboon, and it will bring the new god to the sacred hill. At the time of the first fruit ceremony, the consecrated beer will not only be poured on the back of the ox-grandfather, but part of it will be brought to the forest of the gods and poured on a rock for the baboon god. And when the party which went into the forest returns to the village, one will hear a loud cry. It is the old baboon, who once more has abandoned its obstinate mutism to express thankfulness for the offering. Then all the women assembled in the villages at the foot of the hill will burst into cries of joy, those same peculiar yells with which they greeted Raluvimbi when he visited the country.'

Junod considers that this connexion between the totem animal and the ancestor god is a very unusual conception. In most history origins of the sib the totem object gives birth to a human being from which all the members of the sib are descended. Here there is a belief in the transmigration of souls into the totem animal. Junod does not record the interesting origin of this metamorphic conception, which led to the very natural identification of the baboon with the VhaLaudzi ancestors. According to Chief Lwamondo and several other informants, it happened that during the Swazi invasions towards the end of the last century, the presence of a Swazi impi, stealthily climbing the kop with the intention of attacking the village unawares, was betrayed by the sudden loud barking of a baboon. This timely warning led to the discovery of the enemy impi and to its utter defeat in an encounter which would otherwise have ended disastrously. Surely the ancestors must have been responsible for the opportune bark of the baboon, warning them of the terrible danger at the critical moment! The baboon must then be a reincarnation of their first ancestor, and probably all other baboons on the kop are similarly inhabited by ancestor spirits! The veneration described by Junod readily followed; the conception of metamorphosis is vague, and apparently only applies to baboons actually living on the kop. Chief Lwamondo tells of a European hunter who wished to disprove the sacred character of these baboons; he fired twelve shots at a monster baboon, but of course failed to make a hit! This anecdote, by which a portion of the VhaLaudzi sib have become the *Vha-ila-Pfene*, is a good example of the manner in which a sib-name, through some accidental circumstance, may be changed and an entirely new totem adopted. Possibly many of the overlapping and obscure totems have been the result of similar

192 SOCIAL GROUPINGS

accidents; in time the history origin of the sib-name and totem is forgotten.

Dialectic Divisions.

There are six dialects in Tshivenda. Five of these are associated with certain territorial areas. The names given to these districts on this dialectic basis are used in a half contemptuous way by members of one area in describing those of another. These divisions have no connexion with sib groupings.

VhaMbedzi. The BaVenda living in the extreme east of the country, around Thengwe, Makuya, Mutali, and Luvhimbi, are VhaMbedzi and speak *tshimbedzi*. The name of this district has simply been copied from that of the sib which first settled there.

Vha-ila-furi (Those who are forbidden the pumpkin). The people of the western area, Mphephu, Senthumule, Maemu, Khutama, Mahadulula, and Ravele, are all Vha-ila-furi, and speak *tshifuri*. The influence of the BaSutho has had a marked effect on the culture and language of this group. In spite of their name, given to them in contempt by the more thoroughbred BaVenda, they do eat the pumpkin.

VhaPani (Unclean people). This group lies between the VhaMbedzi and the Vha-ila-furi. *Tshipani* is spoken at Tshivase, Mphapuli, Rambuda, Khaku, Lwamondo, Tshakhuma, Tonnondwa, and Tshiavho. The people have probably been given their name in derision, as many of these do not go to the circumcision school.

VhaRonga. The people living to the south-east of these groups, at Tshimbufwe, Masia, and Tsianda, speak *tshironga*. They are called by this name on account of their close contact with the BaThonga, many of whom are actually living among the BaVenda in this part of the country.

VhaNia. The VhaNia occupy the large dry tract of country in the north of Vendaland at Manenzhe, Madi-mahulu, Nedondwe, Vholovhodne, Khohamela, Malala, and Mapakoni; they speak *tshinia*. *Muniyi* is a tree which grows abundantly in this part of the country, and the VhaNia were called after it, as they are very partial to its juicy fruit.

The sixth dialect, *tshitavhatsinde*, is spoken by the Vhatavhatsinde people; it is not confined to any particular territorial district; strictly speaking, it is more in the nature of a mysterious secret language than a dialect, and it is always spoken in whispers and only understood by thoroughbred Vhatavhatsinde people.

SOCIAL GROUPINGS

193

Age-sets.

Another social grouping, the age-set, *murole*, used to be of very great importance, engendering a strong bond of mutual help and fellowship. Among the boys it was primarily a military grading, all the members of one set forming a fighting unit, and wearing distinctive head-dresses to differentiate them from the members of any other set. The age-set fulfilled another function by sending its members to work as a unit in the chief's lands. The youngest set used to weed, clean, and reap the harvest; the two sets senior to it did the ploughing, planting, and hoeing; the two or three sets above these (the number depending upon the extent of the work) cleaned the land, cut down bushes and trees, and prepared the ground for planting.

In the districts where circumcision lodges are held, the initiates on leaving the lodge are all formed into an age-set, and still recognize many of the mutual obligations involved in this membership; they still work in the chief's garden and take part in all tribal festivities as one unit. Elsewhere the grouping is of little importance; in the districts where mission schools flourish many of the young people are unaware that such a social unit ever existed among their people. Chief Mbulahene Mphephu, the direct descendant of Makhado, the first MuVenda chief to encourage circumcision, is regarded as the head of all circumcision lodges held in Vendaland; he names the age-set of the lodge held under his auspices in his village, and all other lodges held from time to time throughout the country are called by the same name and attach their initiates to this set and fellowship until another lodge is held under his auspices. Since Mphephu's return to the Zoutpansberg just after the Boer War, there have been three age-sets named, giving a new group approximately every eight years. The following is a list of the twelve age-sets in order of their seniority, all together constituting an age-cycle:

1. *Ma-thaha* (The *thaha* is a species of finch).
2. *Ma-rema nga tsanga* (Those who chop with a *tsanga*, a species of battle-axe).
3. *Ma-ntsu.*
4. *Ma-nala.*
5. *Ma-nngwe* (Leopard). Members of this age-set are supposed to show their pluck by catching a leopard unarmed.
6. *Ma-bulana.* This set was named after Ramapulana.
7. *Ma-dali* (Wild cotton). This set was named when wild cotton was used extensively for weaving.

SOCIAL GROUPINGS

8. *Ma-rundela* (*u rundela*, to rape). One of this set broke away from the *murundu* and raped a girl.
9. *Ma-zulu*. This set was named when the Zulus were fighting against Makhado.
10. *Ma-vhegwa* (*u tutuvhedza*, to bring into trouble in war). The word *mavhegwa* came to mean those who are hated.
11. *Ngoma khosi* (The chief's drum).
12. *Ma-ukhu*.
 1. *Ma-thaha*.
 2. *Ma-rema*.

All people in age-sets above the *mazulu* and *marundela* groups are old men; these sets existed before the establishment of circumcision schools, when the young men were formed into regiments as they left the *thondo*. Very few members of the first four sets are alive to-day. The names of the first two sets, *mathaha* and *marema*, have been repeated in naming the two sets formed after *ma-ukhu*, commencing the new cycle. The next set will be *mantsu*.

Girls are put into corresponding age-sets after they have completed their initiation rites at puberty. Among women the sets were never as important a social grouping as among men; women, however, take their place beside men of the same age-set in working in the chief's gardens, and to some extent recognize a bond of mutual interest.

In reviewing the social groupings of the BaVenda it is seen that each individual is a member of several independent groups. Firstly, he belongs to his own domestic family group; secondly, he is a member of the larger family group, the patrilineal lineage, all the members of this group being united by very close social and religious ties; thirdly, he is a member of a matrilineal lineage and is regarded by his mother's family with tenderness and affection; fourthly, he belongs to a sib, sharing with his patrilineal lineage and many other members of the tribe a special regard for a totemic object; fifthly, he belongs to a territorial group speaking a common dialect; sixthly, irrespective of family or sib, he is a member of an age-set, the membership involving mutual obligations and good fellowship; finally, he is a member of an independent community whose members are all bound together by a common allegiance to their chief. These independent communities are, by the cross divisions of social function, loosely connected in a group-conscious whole, the tribe. The disintegrating effect of the contact of the BaVenda with the European seems likely to result in the total collapse of their social system.

XVII

THE CHIEF

Nature of Chieftainship—Officials—The Chief's Wives—The Chief—Death of the Chief—Installation of New Chief—Variation in Burial and Installation Procedure

Nature of Chieftainship.

ALTHOUGH outwardly surrounded with all the trappings of royalty the chief is not absolute monarch. There is a power present behind all his actions, whose authority he must respect and whose wishes he is bound to consider. Metaphorically speaking the chieftainship is a pie which, although carried by one member of the family, has the thumbs of four others embedded in it. The relative importance of the owners of these thumbs must be thoroughly understood in order to appreciate the true position of the chief, the man who carries the royal pie. A chief is succeeded by his son, whose appointment lies in the hands of the *makhadzi* (father's sister) and the *khotsimunene* (father's brother), subject to certain regulations. When these two people appoint the new heir they at the same time appoint one of his sisters to be the *khadzi* and one of his brothers to be the *ndumi*. It is these two persons, the *khadzi* and *ndumi*, who, on the death of their brother, assume the positions hitherto held by the *makhadzi* and *khotsimunene*. The following diagram will illustrate the method of appointing a chief and the relative position of the people concerned:

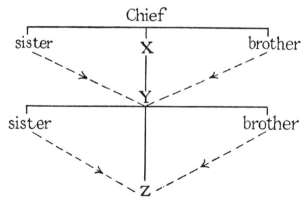

THE CHIEF

X, who has been appointed by his father's sister and brother, dies, and his sister and brother, who were appointed at the same time as he was, and who were his *khadzi* and *ndumi* respectively, now become all powerful and appoint X's son Y as chief, and Y's sister and brother as his *khadzi* and *ndumi*. These two persons, in their turn, do not become important until Y dies, when they have the appointment of Z and his sister and brother in their hands, and so on.

The theory which underlies this method of succession and the mental reasoning of the BaVenda in this respect are important, and help one to understand the somewhat complex system of chieftainship. The chief does not hold his position on account of his prowess in warfare or because he is the most suitable person for that office, but fills his deceased father's position as the sacred representative of his family. To ensure the family's interests being truly represented rather than the individual interests of the chief, when the heir is appointed to be chief a brother and sister are appointed to help him. At his death they represent the family, and as *makhadzi* and *khotsimunene* they nominate the new chief and the new *khadzi* and *ndumi*. All the respect and obedience which was due to the father by his son is transferred on his father's death to his female father and his little father, and until their deaths they have the right to command the person of their late brother's son whom they have appointed to represent their family.

The duties, privileges, and social position of the *makhadzi, khotsimunene, khadzi*, and *ndumi* will now be more fully described in order of their importance in the community.

Makhadzi. The *makhadzi* is generally the late chief's eldest sister by a different mother, usually the eldest daughter of the third wife. All vital matters connected with the state must be referred to her, and if her desires do not coincide with those of the chief he is supposed to follow her judgement. This woman is bound by special marriage restrictions, which are not shared by her sisters, who are permitted to marry any commoner and have no particular status in the country; the *makhadzi* must marry either within the royal family or the son of a neighbouring chief; marriage alliances with foreign chiefs are encouraged and approved; and the *makhadzi's* power does much to remove enmity between the country of her brother and that of her husband; a chief would not make war on the husband of his *makhadzi*, unless the provocation was unusually great, and the husband would be equally disinclined to fight against her brother or nephew, knowing the powerful position she held in her own country. The *makhadzi*

THE CHIEF

generally lives at the chief's capital even after her marriage, where her husband visits her, staying with her as long as he wishes. She occasionally visits his home where she has her own hut and kitchen kept for her. Her children always live with their father. When she is living at the capital she may have her own hut, or if she finds one of the chief's wives a congenial companion she may live with her. She receives a percentage of all taxes, and the chief is bound to gratify her reasonable requests. She is treated with most of the respect and formality awarded to the chief; her approach is heralded by the high trilling of the women who kneel as they pass her or speak to her; even men, to whom all other women kneel, must kneel to the *makhadzi*; her food is prepared, like that of the chief, by one of his wives and presented to her with the same ceremony. All this respect is the outward and visible sign of the real power which she wields in the state. Although she is not present at the meetings of the chief, she has the right to be informed of everything that has taken place, and is consulted before any new measure is imposed upon the people. For instance, if the chief and councillors had decided on war, the campaign could not be commenced until her consent had been obtained. A murderer sentenced to death by the chief might approach the *makhadzi* with bribes of oxen and goats, seeking sanctuary with her, and begging her to alter the sentence; if she considered the bribe sufficient, or the sentence unduly harsh, she could reprieve him, and the people would accept her ruling above that of the chief. If the people are dissatisfied with any measure that the chief has taken, or think that he has been acting unworthily, they appeal to her to use her influence with him.

Khotsimunene. The *khotsimunene* is rarely the uterine brother of the deceased chief, but usually the eldest son of his father's second wife. If another brother has outstanding ability, there is no reason why he should not be appointed. The *khotsimunene* does not necessarily live at the capital, but when he visits it he may sit in the *khoro* and give judgement in the place of the chief. In time of war the general is directly responsible to him and not to his nephew the chief. Like the *makhadzi* he receives a portion of all taxes, and usually the chief will grant him any reasonable request. The chief, throughout his life, treats the *makhadzi* and *khotsimunene* with the same respect and deference which he showed to his father; he generally gives them cattle on his succession and continues to give them gifts throughout their lives.

The relative importance of the three is reflected in the part which

198 THE CHIEF

each receives when a royal beast is killed. The *makhadzi* receives the upper portion of the hip and thigh, *parte*, the portion considered by the BaVenda to be the daintiest; the chief receives the second-best part, the hind leg, *tshisvhi*, and the *khotsimunene* the front leg, *voho*.

Ndumi. The duty of the *ndumi* is to accompany the chief wherever he goes, acting in the capacity of confidential adviser and friend. He lives at the capital, unless he has been made petty chief in another district. He is the *khotsimunene* in the making, and like his prototype he may sit in judgement in the *khoro*. It is the duty of the old *khotsimunene* to teach him the law and how to administer justice, so that, when the *khotsimunene* dies or becomes too feeble for his duties, the *ndumi* can fulfil them without there being any break in the continuity of government perceptible to the people. The *ndumi* is often referred to as *khotsimunene*, and so the identity of the reigning chief's brother becomes confused with that of his father's brother; the people generally recognize little difference in the respective functions of these two people, although the old *khotsimunene*, sometimes distinguished from the young one by the term *vhamusanda*, is the more influential. As the *ndumi* is an integral part of the chieftainship it is the duty of the chief to support him and to give him a portion of all taxes.

Khadzi. The *khadzi* is to the *makhadzi* what the *ndumi* is to the *khotsimunene*. She is often termed *makhadzi*, the elder being distinguished by the term *makhadzi vhamusande*. While the elder *makhadzi* is alive the younger plays little part in the government, although in theory she has the same rights as the elder. She only becomes really important on the death of either the old *makhadzi* or of her brother the chief. Her social position is that of a chief, and she is supported by her brother and given presents by him from time to time.

Officials.

The chief's other brothers and sisters are treated with a certain amount of respect, the brothers being addressed by the courtesy title '*VhaVenda!*' They are only ordinary members of the community and do not necessarily enjoy any privileges above their fellow men. If a chief is fond of a particular brother, or considers one to be a suitable person to put in a position of trust, he may make him a petty chief in a vacant district or keep him at the capital as one of his confidential advisers. A chief's son is always greeted as '*Tshivhanda!*' (Wild beast!), and all his children are called *vhakhololo* collectively.

Nefhasi (Master of the ground) is one of the most important court

THE CHIEF

officials. He has free access to the chief and is consulted in all legal matters; he may act as judge in the *khoro*, fulfilling most of the duties of the *khotsimunene* when that functionary is away. He also supervises the distribution of meat and beer in the capital. He is always an old and trusted favourite, chosen for his personal ability. His portion of meat of animals killed in the capital is the *khwanama*, the soft part underneath the front leg.

Mukhoma (Leader). All the affairs of the chief's household are performed by this official. He is responsible for the smooth running of the capital; he receives visitors and acquaints the chief with their business; complainants refer their grievances to him before they are brought to the judge for consideration; he is responsible for the fulfilment of all the chief's orders; he dispatches and receives all messages; he receives the taxes from the district headmen and gives the revenue to the *khotsimunene*, who passes it on to the chief; he is also responsible for the distribution of land and is supposed to know the boundaries. (In some areas there is a special official appointed to superintend all matters connected with the land.)

The *mukhoma* is entitled to the *mbumbunama* of the royal meat (the part just above the hind leg).

Negota is the chief's head councillor. He sits in the private council and supervises the chief's work outside the village; he is responsible for the correct performance of *vhutamba vhutuka* and other ceremonies; he is responsible for the summoning of dancers to the capital and the correct performance of the dances; he supervises the work of the younger age-sets. In case of trouble in any part of the country he is sent to the scene of the disturbance to settle matters, receiving a fee of one goat from the parties concerned. He is entitled to the *tunda* of the royal meat (the neck). His position is hereditary, descending from father to son.

Nefhasi, *mukhoma*, and *negota* all have a high social status, and any injury done to them is considered a crime only a degree less serious than one against the chief himself, and is severely punished.

Ramadonga (Keeper of the chief's cattle) fills an important post, although he does not enjoy the social privileges of the *mukhoma* and *negota*. He has complete charge of the chief's cattle, and it is his duty to visit the various localities in which the royal cattle are kept and to safeguard the chief's interests; when any beasts are to be slaughtered it is he who makes the selection; he is responsible for branding the cattle with the chief's mark, which no other man may use; he

THE CHIEF

superintends the milking and supervises everything in any way connected with the cattle. He is particularly important in war time, providing the troops with meat and protecting the royal cattle and wives. The position is hereditary.

Nyamita is the man in charge of the women's part of the kraal, *muta*, and of all female labour at the capital. He supervises all plastering and smearing, &c., and the preparation of the chief's beer. The position is hereditary.

There are a number of less important officials.

A *khwali* is at the head of each age-set which he leads in war, acting under the generalship of the *khotsimunene*.

The *maphuga* is the body-guard of the chief and the *khotsimunene*, and is composed of old, proved warriors; these men protect the chief at all times. In war they stand near the *khotsimunene* urging on the laggards, ready to take action wherever the need is greatest.

Phondi is the executioner. The chief used to have two or three of these officials living at the capital.

Nemulambo stands in the *khoro* and calls out all the orders for the day. He combines the functions of a herald and town-crier and acquires a wonderful facility for shouting, with a variety of peculiar intonations, so that his hearers, although not always catching the words that he shouts, understand by the intonation the import of the news he intends to convey. He shouts in this way; 'Ah!—He—e—e—e—e! Ah! He! All the women must bring beer for visitors!' or, 'Ah! He—e—e—e—e——e! Ah! He! So-and-so must come and attend a case!' or whatever his message happens to be. He sometimes visits the different villages, often with a *phala-fhala* horn, to collect people to work in the chief's garden, or to warn them to prepare for war, or for some such purpose.

Malugwani is the leader and instructor in the *tshikona* and *mathangwa* dances and takes his orders from the *negota*.

Vhadinda (sing. *mudinda*) are the chief's messengers. There are generally several in residence at the capital always ready to carry out the chief's commands. If a man lodges a complaint with the chief a *mudinda* is sent to investigate the case; while employed in the chief's business he must be treated with the respect due to the chief himself. He introduces himself by saying, 'How big is your pot? My stomach is big'. This discloses his identity and he is given a goat as a fee; if his investigations are protracted he may be given two or three goats during the course of his visit. Some chiefs have a hereditary *mudinda*

THE CHIEF

who visits the god *Mwari* to ask for rain and one, *nyalumati*, who escorts mourners to the diviner about the murderer of their dead.

Petty chiefs do not have a full complement of officials; generally a *mukhoma*, *negota*, and a few *vhadinda* combine in their persons all the functions necessary to administer the district.

The Chief's Wives.

The important chiefs generally possess a great many wives; a poor chief seldom has less than twenty, and Chief Tshivhase is reported to have at least two hundred. All the wives do not live at the capital; as they become old and the chief tires of them he may send them back to their parents, or send them away to different parts of the country under the protection of petty chiefs. As soon as he is aware of a wife's first pregnancy he sends her to her mother's home until after the birth of the child. He always has a number of wives with him, and often one of the older wives, not necessarily the wife who will be the mother of the heir, acquires a rather special position in the household. In the absence of the chief this woman may receive his visitors and with the help of the *mukhoma* make the necessary arrangements for their entertainment; she supervises all the other wives, keeping harmony among them; she instructs two or three of the youngest wives what food to prepare for the chief and sees that they all perform their different tasks adequately; when the chief demands beer she may indicate to the younger wife, who actually serves it, to whom it is to be given; she has a good deal of freedom of speech and acts more in the capacity of companion to the chief than any other woman in the kraal.

The chief may allow his friends to have sexual rights over one or other of his wives, the children of all such unions being his. Of the hundreds of wives possessed by some of the more powerful chiefs, a great many, even women for whom lobola has been paid, are little more than slaves; the older women have a particularly slavish existence, doing all the menial work for their younger and more favoured colleagues; in many of the large villages one cannot fail to notice numbers of these old, ill-favoured women carrying enormous loads of wood and water and constantly at work about the kraal.

The Chief.

The chief, *vhamusanda*, is the head of his tribe, the father of his people, and the sacred living representative of their far-off ancestors. He is the hub of their universe, all the life of the community, religious,

THE CHIEF

social and economic, revolving around him. His subjects treat him with reverence, awe, and humble adoration. He is responsible for the prosperity of his country; he must see that it is provided with rain and must determine the time for the sowing and reaping of crops; he gives his consent before the inauguration of any event, such as initiation ceremonies and important dances. In speaking of or to the chief many curious euphemistic expressions are used, his most ordinary actions and possessions being described in a peculiar and roundabout way. His door or hut is called the 'crocodile', his mealie meal is 'spider's web', his thatch is 'the broom', his *tshisevho* dish is 'little pups', his porridge spoon is 'the hand', his porridge stick is the 'fire-stick', his stool is the 'big bird', his beer-pot is the 'shade', his water is the 'pool', his seeds are the 'eggs', his salt is 'sand', food left on his plate is the 'leavings of the lion', his dogs are 'messengers'; instead of saying the 'chief is drunk', his subjects say the 'chief has fallen into a pool'; if he is ill, he is 'hot', if he is asleep, he is 'breathing', if he is eating, he 'works', if he is washing he has 'crossed the river', if he is dead he has 'gone away' or his 'star has set', and so on for everything that he has or does.

Unless a chief is particularly active and takes a keen interest in his people most of his life is spent in eating and drinking with his friends who are constantly passing through the capital. Visitors are generally kept waiting a considerable time before being ushered into his presence. A good impression of the manner in which the chief is treated by his people is given by Wessman,[1] describing a visit to the old chief Tshivhase, father of the present chief:

'Suddenly the animated chatter is interrupted by the chief's rather thick voice in close proximity. All eyes are turned upon him, and his large, smiling, full-moon face fits the chequered company exactly. Very slowly, leaning on every prop of the verandah of the house, he approaches, finally stopping at the entrance to the hall, partly in order to shake hands with us, partly to regain his breath; for every movement, even the shortest, has proved a great strain for him, in consequence of his enormous obesity. He is clad in trousers and a shirt, the uppermost button of which stands, on account of his fat neck, immediately below his chin. Slowly he settles down on a mat spread for him on the verandah before the entrance of the hall. He is thus able to watch the proceedings both inside and outside the hall. The moment he squats is the instant of the customary greeting in accordance with Bawenda ceremony. Immediately the assembly shows a dog-like submission. Everybody bows low,

---

[1] Wessman, R., *The Bawenda of the Spelonken*, London, 1908, pp. 15-17.

PLATE XXXIII

CHIEF TSHIVHASE

PLATE XXXIV

CHIEF SENTHUMULE, WITH TWO WIVES AND
SOME OF HIS COUNCILLORS

THE CHIEF

heads nearly touching the floor, and with hands clasped in front they shout in unison for several minutes such salutes as, "God of heaven and earth", "handsome man with four eyes", "lion", "beast", "goat-stable", "cattle-kraal", "ox", "light of the world", "beast of prey", and other similar flattering expressions. In the meantime the chief cup-bearer has filled the large cups and handed them to this or that native without any special selection. The chief has meanwhile made himself very comfortable on his mat. In order, however, that he may not overbalance himself, a nearly nude maiden supports him on her back, whilst another girl serves as his footstool. Still another lady sits in front of him, almost like a wax statue, holding up a tin tray with his own always filled cup, so that he may take a drink in comfort whenever he pleases. On his left, another girl holds his silver snuff-box, from which he now and then allows somebody else to take a pinch. Now and then he takes a long draught from his cup, always closing his bulging eyes as he does so, and every draught being accompanied by enthusiastic shouts from the assembly, such as, "lion", "handsome man with four eyes", "beast of prey", as mentioned before. In the same manner, any coughing or clearing of his throat is accompanied by similar praises and flatteries from his loyal admirers.'

The present chief, Tshivhase, is a faint reflection of his father (Plate XXXIII. He is still feared and obeyed by his people and is the last of the old type of important Venda chiefs, but he is not respected with the humble, unquestioning adoration that was accorded to his father. Every year the power of the chiefs diminishes. Some of them squander their cattle and fortunes in the purchase of European luxuries, in this way alienating the affections of the people whom they are expected to father and protect. A great deal of the administration of justice has been taken from the hands of the chief; he has no longer power of life and death over his subjects. War is a thing of the past, and the chief has little to do but over-indulge himself and waste the fortune collected by his fathers. One of the most depressing aspects of white domination is the way in which the chief, once an absolute monarch, has been stripped of his old authority and is now little more than a figurehead. Nevertheless his life is still associated with considerable ceremony, particularly in connexion with his beer and food. He commences drinking quite early in the day, always sharing the beer with some of his important officials and visitors. The beer is served by one of his younger wives, who brings in a large earthenware pot, shuffling forward on her knees and, after placing the pot on the ground and prostrating herself before the chief, bales out the beer in small gourds. Before handing the gourds to the assembly she drinks a little of the beer herself, and two or three councillors always drink before it is

THE CHIEF

handed to the chief. It is then distributed to the others, the chief's gourd being frequently replenished. The chief is never served first for fear that the beer has been poisoned, as in the old days this was a favourite method of disposing of an enemy, every chief living in constant dread of meeting his death by poison. The chief (Plate XXXIV) eats alone in his own hut, where he is served by one of his younger wives, three or four being detailed off for that particular service; he is always brought water with which to wash his hands before eating; his leavings are given to one of his father's widows. The chief sleeps alone, in the old days with his head pillowed on an elephant's tusk. His sleeping hut is sacred and used to be protected by a stuffed crocodile. The presence of this creature was kept a close secret, and it was never seen by any but his nearest relatives. It is said that to-day the sleeping quarters of one or two chiefs are still guarded in this way. The true significance of this crocodile could not be ascertained, but the crocodile is closely associated with Venda chiefs, and regarded by them as a sacred object.

The chief has various ways of entertaining his visitors besides giving them beer and meat. Sometimes he arranges a hunt for their benefit or orders a dance to be performed for them, or fortune-tellers are brought in to amuse them. He does not spend all his time in the capital but often journeys to different parts of the country to see for himself how his cattle are progressing or to visit his friends. In bad seasons he may move to lands away from the capital, where he may spend weeks or even months superintending the reaping of the harvest, lest the fear of starvation should tempt his hungry subjects to steal his crops. On these occasions the chief used to ride on horseback, accompanied by his *ndumi* and *mukhoma* and a dozen or so of his councillors, the column always journeying in single file along the narrow footpath; to-day he travels by mule-cart or motor. When he is going far he sends some of his wives ahead with beer so that the party can refresh itself en route; at every kraal these women trill in a high-pitched note to warn the people of the royal approach. Women, who are passed by the chief on the roadside, kneel down and greet him as '*Munnawanga!*' (my husband). Possibly at one time the chief had sexual rights over all the women of the tribe, but to-day if the chief commits adultery he is expected to pay compensation to the woman's husband. There are still cases where chiefs, usually young and irresponsible, during their tours about the country, have stolen any girls whose appearance attracted them; in such cases, when the girl

PLATE XXXV

CHIEF MBULAHENE MPHEPHU

CHIEF PHAPHULI

THE CHIEF

205

is betrothed to some other man, her parents are obliged to return any lobola which may have been paid to her prospective husband: these cases are rare and considered to be unworthy of a chief. At night the chief sleeps with a trusted petty chief who has been previously warned of his arrival. His appearance at the kraal is greeted with the high trilling of the women and praises of the men, and at the same time the *tshikona* dance commences and is performed at frequent intervals throughout his stay. If he is in a good mood he will say a few words to his people and beat the big drum. Although a petty chief in his own domain is practically supreme, as soon as the great chief arrives he is of little importance and relinquishes his seat in favour of the chief, sitting at his feet with the rest of the people and joining in the general adulation.

Many of the chiefs (Plate XXXV) are somewhat restricted in their movements by rigid tabus which forbid them to visit certain localities.

MaKhwinde chiefs may not visit the ancestral homes of the Vhatavhatsinde, such as Tshiendeulu, Luonde, and Lake Fundudzi. In addition to this Mphephu chiefs may not visit Ratomba, a petty chief living on a farm at Ratomba. This man hated Makhado and his successor Mphephu, and after an adventurous career of crime succeeded in escaping with his life to his present sanctuary. Having escaped the punishment of his misdemeanours he has never achieved purification and formal readmission to society; he and all his family are therefore considered to be unclean, and the royal MaKhwinde heirs are forbidden to risk contamination by having intercourse with this social outcast. Chepisse, the hot springs about five miles from Mphephu's capital, is tabu to all the Venda chiefs. It was there that many years ago Tshikobakoba, a chief of the Buis people, became very ill. To save his life he was carried to the springs and laid on a bed over the steaming water; he died after a few minutes of this treatment, and Chepisse has since been feared as a place dangerous to the lives of all chiefs. The shadow of Luonde hill falling on a chief will cause his death. Dzata, the old capital, is also associated with vague tabus. The origin of most avoidances is forgotten in two generations, but the tabu continues, and is often obeyed for centuries.

Death of the Chief.

When the chief is seriously ill his condition is kept a close secret. When the people begin to notice he has not appeared for a long time and to ask questions about him they are told by his court officials that

THE CHIEF

he has had a bad cold and must keep in his hut for some time. His special medicine-men attend him and give him medicine and advice, and the *makhadzi* appeals repeatedly to the ancestor spirits for his recovery. When his death is considered to be imminent the medicine-men tell the *makhadzi* and *khotsimunene* that nothing more can be done, and retire from the death-chamber. The death is usually witnessed by the *makhadzi* and *khotsimunene*, one or two head councillors, and sometimes the chief's favourite wife; a favourite brother may also be admitted, but the circle is always very small. It is customary for the dying chief to name his successor, and if the *makhadzi* and *khotsimunene* have predeceased him to suggest who, in his opinion, should be the new *ndumi* and *khadzi*.

After his death the body is shrouded in the skin of his favourite ox and wrapped in *masila* cloth. Burial generally takes place some days after death. The few trusted councillors who witnessed the death dig the grave and line it with cattle skins. Three or four of the chief's brothers are informed of the death and they carry the corpse; possibly, if there are not enough brothers available, some of his elder sons may take their places. They are all sworn to secrecy and are the only people in addition to the few who were present at the death who have authentic knowledge that the chief is dead. Unlike the commoners, who are buried in the crouching position, the chief's body is placed in the grave lying in the extended position on the right side, with the head pillowed on an elephant's tooth and pointing towards the ancient city of Dzata. The corpse is covered with a lion or leopard skin, or possibly cattle skins, and the grave is filled in. The head of the chief's favourite ox is then laid on the grave. Later, after the community is aware of the death of their chief, a small hut is erected over the grave and carefully sealed; entrance to this hut is forbidden for ever. A guard, always a relative of the chief and often one of his sons, is appointed to protect the burying-place and to keep it clean. In the old days the chief's burying-place was faithfully protected and reverenced; to-day, in less than a decade, the hut falls to pieces and the ground is neglected; this is one instance among many of the rapid decline of old customs. If the grave is some distance from the capital a beacon of stones is erected wherever the funeral cortège halts. Every MuVenda who passes such a beacon adds another stone to the pile to show respect to the dead chief; sometimes the beacon is made from twigs instead of stones, in which case twigs are always added.

THE CHIEF

The Tshivhase chiefs used to be buried at Phiphidi, but this custom has lapsed, and they are now buried secretly close to the royal hut and water sprinkled over the ground to harden it and remove all traces of burial.

None of the people are informed of the death of the chief, but when some months have passed and the people begin to grow restless they are told that he has gone away; often a year or more used to elapse between the death of the chief and any recognition of it, but this period is now reduced to three or four months. During the interregnum the *makhadzi* and *khotsimunene* continue the government in place of the chief, so that the continuity of office is in no way broken. It appears that during this interregnum any excitement or attempts at usurpation of power have time to work themselves out before the heir is installed. Everybody has a shrewd idea as to the true state of affairs, although no man dares to speak of it.

Before the new chief is appointed all the councillors are summoned to the capital and are told definitely that their chief has gone away. A medicine-man then extinguishes the sacred fire with water and lights a new fire with the fire-sticks. Each woman goes to the medicine-man and is given fire from the new royal fire with which to rekindle her own, and as she takes her brand she places a bracelet on the ground beside the fire in payment; at the same time she throws away the three cooking stones used for holding the pots on the fire and replaces them by new stones.

All the people are then summoned to the *khoro* to dance the *tshikona* dance. An undercurrent of excitement and anticipation runs through the gathering, as it is tacitly understood that this summons precedes the disclosure of the identity of the new chief. Before the dance begins an interesting ceremony is enacted. All the relations of the late chief collect together and are told the news by the *makhadzi*. An ox is then killed and roasted, and each member of the family, after taking some of the meat in his mouth, spits it out in different directions. It is strictly tabu for any member of the family to eat any food, after they have been informed of the death of the chief, until after this ceremony has been performed. At about the same time all the people are ordered to shave their hair and beards, so that the new hair will grow up with the new chief. This is the only general form of mourning and is a symbol of the cutting of the link attaching them to the late chief and the forging of a new link with his heir. In Phaphuli or Thengwe's area any stranger discovered with an unshaved head when the country is

208 THE CHIEF

in mourning is forcibly shaved and then tied up for a few days until the new hair begins to grow.

Installation of New Chief.

The right of chieftainship is based on heredity, the position descending from father to son, subject to certain qualifications. The chief may obtain wives from anywhere he chooses, not being restricted to women of his own tribe, but the mother of the heir must always be a member of his own royal family. To facilitate this he is privileged to marry persons standing in a degree of relationship prohibited to the ordinary commoner. A good example of this intermarriage amongst royalty is found in the case of Chief Makhado and his son Mphephu and the present Chief Mbulahene Mphephu. Makhado married his father's sister's daughter and she became the mother of Mphephu; Mphephu married his brother's daughter (brother by a different mother) and she became the mother of Mbulahene; he married his mother's sister's daughter. Again, Masinde, the great wife of the present Chief Tshivhase is the daughter of his father's young brother, Pandandilumo. Sometimes a chief's wife is addressed and referred to as *makhadzi* (father's sister), adding another source of confusion to the difficulties that already exist for any one attempting to differentiate the various people called by this term. In this case it is readily explained by the fact that the chief's great wife is often also his sister, and so called by the people *makhadzi*; possibly it used to be a marriage injunction for the chief's sister to be his great wife. As well as belonging to the royal family the woman who is to be the mother of the next chief must have been given to the reigning chief by his father and lobola-ed with the royal cattle; the reigning chief in his turn is the eldest son of the woman given to his father by his grandfather. If the wife designated to bear the heir is barren, or if she dies before bearing an heir, she is replaced by one of her sisters, or the *makhadzi* will provide the chief with a second royal wife.

When the succession is disputed it is the duty of the *makhadzi* and *khotsimunene* to try to come to a mutual agreement that will be satisfactory to all concerned; relationships are traced and every possible factor considered, but in the event of a deadlock ensuing the *makhadzi* has the final word. There are many possible complications preventing peaceful succession: possibly one of the chief's officials commits adultery with the royal wife, who is to bear the next heir, and the chief may disgrace this woman and refuse to acknowledge the legitimacy of

THE CHIEF

her offspring; possibly the heir commits incest with one of his father's wives, which in the old days was punishable by death or banishment. In such cases, after the death of the chief, agreement becomes difficult, and before the lawful heir is proclaimed an ambitious brother may endeavour to usurp his rights, gaining the support of some of the powerful petty chiefs with promises of rewards and high offices. Occasionally the chief may take a violent dislike to the heir and at his death-bed appoint another son to succeed him. In such a case, unless the heir has disgraced himself, the dying man's wishes are entirely disregarded. If the royal wife bears only a female child, this daughter is in theory the legal heir, but she is not permitted to reign; she may, however, in conjunction with the *makhadzi*, designate a brother to reign in her place, often the elder brother of the father's second wife. This situation is liable to lead to disruption as the chief's brothers may consider that some other son would suit their purpose better. The identity of the heir is kept a close secret. When the royal wife becomes pregnant she is sent away to her mother, and the chief will often pretend to neglect her, leaving her for years under the care of her mother or some trustworthy petty chief. The heir meanwhile grows up among his brothers and sisters as one of them, although he is secretly protected by one or two trustworthy elders; he may have a shrewd idea that he is the legal heir, but he cannot be certain until his actual installation. When the time comes for this ceremony a meeting is held around the royal hut, attended by all the late chief's brothers and sisters; his wives are also permitted to attend the meeting but take no active part in the discussion. Here the identity of the new chief is secretly disclosed to them. In the meantime the *tshikona* dance is proceeding in the *khoro*, where the excitement is intense. After the private meeting the *makhadzi* and *khotsimunene* enter the *khoro* and sit down on a pile of skins. The *mukhoma* and some other important officials are ordered to bring the heir and the future *ndumi* and *khadzi* from the gathering. This is done very unostentatiously, and the three are seated together on the skins and completely covered with karosses. The *makhadzi* addresses the assembly, telling the people that their chief, who went away, has returned to them; she praises the new chief and exhorts all the people to be his faithful subjects and orders any man who disputes his authority to leave the country. During the *makhadzi's* oration the people all stand in absolute silence. As soon as she has finished speaking a young girl brings forward a gourd of beer and at the same time the covering is removed from the

210 THE CHIEF

new chief's face. He takes the gourd and lifts it to his lips, and immediately the crowd fall on their knees in attitudes of humble adoration. The men burst unanimously into loud shouts, greeting him with every possible laudatory epithet, while the women trill continuously. After the clamour has in some measure abated the new *ndumi* and *khadzi* are revealed; they also drink and are received with lesser acclamations by the people. After this the dance starts again and is continued with increased zeal. Sometimes as many as fifty oxen are killed and a large quantity of beer is drunk. The feasting and dancing continue for months; all the neighbouring people of any importance visit the new chief, bringing him presents or sending bands of players to sing and dance and make music before him. These visits show the friendly feelings of the neighbours, who in this way acknowledge and sanction his appointment. In the old days the new chief would make war on any subject chief who failed to show him the customary respect. The offerings brought to him are generally cattle, sheep, goats, and wives; the latter he is bound to accept, but is expected to pay lobola of four or five head of cattle for them. A new chief used to be given one beast by each of his subjects, but this is no longer done. The *tshikona* dance is continued at intervals from the day on which the people are told of the death of the chief until the end of all the ceremonies and rejoicings connected with the establishment of his heir.

Variation in Burial and Installation Procedure.

Phaphuli. Among the Phaphuli chiefs, although they claim membership with the MaKhwinde sib, a different ceremonial is observed at death and at the installation of a successor. The dying chief is taken from the royal living hut to a smaller hut near by to die. When he is dead his corpse is wrapped in an ox hide and left where it is lying and the hut is securely sealed up. The people are not told of the chief's death for some time, but when it is known the blowing of the *phala-fhala* horns, so frequently heard in the capital, is forbidden until after the conclusion of the *u pembela* ceremony, which occurs two or three years after the accession of the new chief. Soon after the chief's death the heir is smuggled into the capital and in due course is declared chief. Formerly some of his brothers would immediately force their way into the capital and try to usurp his position while he defended his rights and proved his prowess; even to-day there is always a dispute over the Phaphuli succession. The heir, although he assumes all the duties of

THE CHIEF

chieftainship, is not confirmed in his position for a considerable time; he is not called by the dynastic title or considered to possess the sacred essence of his ancestors until after the *u pembela* (to dance). The exact time for this ceremony is decided by the royal medicine-man, who divines when the late chief is ready to go to his last resting-place and to bestow his full rights on his son. The sealed hut containing the late chief's remains is ceremonially opened by the medicine-man and the new chief is shown the bones of his father. The medicine-man produces a small pebble from among the bones and gives it to the new chief to swallow to give him a long life; the pebble is supposed to have been taken originally from the stomach of a crocodile and is ceremonially swallowed by each new chief when it is recovered from among his father's remains. Another secret ceremony is enacted in the presence of the medicine-man and *khotsimunene* and two or three of the most trusted elders and confidants. The new chief is given a secret medicine to drink to make him impotent; one or more of the elders also partake of this drink in order to keep their chief company in his new life. The person who prepared the drink used to be killed so that his death might give the chief increased strength. Impotence is thought to produce longevity, as the begetting of new life is held to weaken that of him who begets it. After these two ceremonies the late chief's bones are collected and taken to the ancestral burying-place at Muluwani, the old capital, where the remains of the last three Phaphuli chiefs are buried; it is about three miles from the present capital. Two or three days after this burial the new chief with the *ndumi* and *khadzi*, who are now recognized for the first time, are the central figures in a public ceremony; they sit on wooden milking-pots turned upside down and placed on skins in the entrance of the *khoro*, all three dressed in skins and *masila* cloth. The chief is acclaimed by the name of his dead father; the *tshikona* is played, and all the assembly, including many neighbouring chiefs, dance and sing. The chief dances into the *khoro* holding on his back a miniature spear-head, which he has made for the occasion, with all the spears which his ancestors made for similar occasions. This dance, which he performs alone, is *pembela*, from which the whole ceremony gets its name. (*U pembela* is also used to describe any person dancing alone.) As he dances he shouts the new name which he has chosen for himself and which is usually that of one of his ancestors; the people respond, shouting the new name repeatedly, and calling him for the first time by the dynastic title 'Phaphuli'. The ceremony ends with the usual feasting and dancing.

P 2

THE CHIEF

That night the new Phaphuli chief, still dressed in the clothes of skins and *masila* cloth, visits the graves of his ancestors and pours a libation of beer over them, so completing the series of ritual actions which link him inextricably to his ancestor chiefs.

Information about the *pembela* ceremony is far from satisfactory. I was told that to-day it is only practised by the Phaphuli chiefs where the constant disputes over the succession cause long delays; many of the people have only the scantiest knowledge of the ceremony, and are entirely unaware of its significance. Probably, as it occurs to-day, it is only a part of a sacred ritual which, in its entirety, must have been of a most unusual character. It is also possible that this form of burial and succession was formerly practised by all the chiefs of the royal MaKhwinde sib; it is certainly rumoured to have been followed by Makhado's grandfather and also by the father of the present chief, Tshivhase.

Vhatavhatsinde. A form of cremation is used in the burial of the Vhatavhatsinde chiefs. The chief's corpse used to be left in the hut where he died until all the flesh had dropped off the bones, when the bones were secretly removed by night and afterwards displayed before the people. They were then taken by his relatives and laid on a funeral pyre on a flat rock in a river; over this a small open hut was built and the whole structure burnt. The relatives then dispersed, except two or three aged men, who washed the ashes into the river and removed all traces of the cremation. At the present time the same procedure is observed except that the corpse is buried in the cattle-kraal for two or three years instead of being left interred in the chief's hut.

At Thengwe this ceremony is performed in the Tshisivhathu river (burning people), which is one of the boundaries between the Thengwe and Rambuda locations; the bones of the Tshiavho chiefs are cremated on the banks of Lake Fundudzi, and there are other sacred rivers in the Vhatavhatsinde country dedicated to this purpose.

Lwamondo. The chiefs of Lwamondo are (Plate XXXVI) cremated in a similar way, although they are not Vhatavhatsinde but probably of BaSutho origin; possibly they came in close contact with the Vhatavhatsinde and have imitated them.

Netshitongani is a petty chief of Tshivhase living on Tshidzivhe mountain. The method of burial of the heads of this family is most unusual. The sacred forest, Thathe, is supposed to be inhabited by a ferocious lion that is the reincarnation of the petty chief. The body

PLATE XXXVI

CHIEF LWAMONDO

THE CHIEF 213

of the late chief, placed on a wooden framework with a large clay dish underneath, is left on the outskirts of the forest until the flesh drops off the bones and a worm drops from the corpse into the clay bath. The bones are collected and buried in the bush and the worm allowed to escape into the forest; it is supposed to be the spirit of the dead man and to be metamorphosed into a lion as soon as it reaches the forest. The lion which has hitherto possessed the forest, and is the father of the new-comer, is said to disappear for ever, leaving his successor as the sole occupant. The grave where the bones are deposited is marked with large stones and is visited ceremonially by the new chief at each harvest thanksgiving.

XVIII

TERRITORIAL DIVISIONS, GOVERNMENT, REVENUE AND TAXATION, LAW AND JUSTICE

Territorial Divisions.

WITH the exception of the Phaphuli chiefs, whose country has probably always been independent, the BaVenda were more or less united under Vele Lambeho, but on the death of his son Thoho-ya-Ndou the unity of the tribe came to an end. His brothers declared themselves independent; different headmen also threw off the yoke of their overlords, and territorial divisions fluctuated according to the fortune of war and the personality of the individual ruler. The country became divided into smaller independent divisions, *mivundu* (sing. *muvundu*), of varying extent, each under its own petty chief, *gota* (pl. *magota*), several being grouped around the different important chiefs, *vhamusanda*, to whom they owed allegiance. Each *muvundu*, unless it is very small, is subdivided into smaller districts, *zwisi* (sing. *tshisi*), varying in size and importance, each under a headman, *mukhoma* (pl. *vhakhoma*). Although I am using these words, *vhamusanda*, *gota*, and *mukhoma* as above, the BaVenda employ them also in a more general sense; the great chief is *vhamusanda* to all his subjects, the petty chief is *vhamusanda* in his own district and in the sub-district of his headmen. The great chief calls his petty chiefs *magota*; each petty chief calls his headmen *magota*, although to the great chief they will be *vhakhoma*. In this connexion it must not be forgotten that these words, *gota* and *mukhoma*, are also used in a special sense, *negota* as head-councillor and *mukhoma* as the chief's right-hand man.

The political organization of these independent divisions is not unlike the feudal system, the chief having his own district and at the same time being lord over the surrounding country, being in fact *mudzimu vha shango* (the spirit of the place). His country is called by his dynastic title, the prefix *Ha* denoting the place, e.g. Ha Tshivhase, Ha Rambuda (the place of Tshivhase and the place of Rambuda). Each *muvundu* and *tshisi* is called either after the first petty chief or headman to rule over it, or after the name of the conqueror; or it may be called by some word denoting a peculiarity of the place or some event which occurred there, e.g. Tshirembi (back-biters), Thengwe

REVENUE, TAXATION, LAW, JUSTICE 215

(the place of the leopards), Tshivhuyuni (at the baobob trees), Muluwa (at the muluwa trees). By prefixing to the place-name the syllable *Ne*, which denotes a person, it becomes the headman's title: the headmen of the Tshirembi, Maungani, and Thengwe are called Netshirembi, Nemaungani, and Nethengwe respectively.

The positions of the rulers of the different *mivundu* and *zwisi* are hereditary, and many have been ruled by the same family for a long time. When possible, a chief endeavours to place his own relatives in positions of importance, and whenever a recalcitrant leader is driven out he is usually replaced by a member of the royal family. A woman sometimes acts as regent during the minority of her son. There are also women petty chiefs in their own right, e.g. Nyadenga of Phiphidi and Nyakhalavha of Khalavha. When the father of Tshivhase left Phiphidi to make his capital at Mukumbani he made his daughter Nyadenga petty chief in the Phiphidi district; she was his heir, being the only child of his great wife, but being a woman could not succeed her father as a great chief. At Phiphidi she has the full rights of a man and is only subordinate to the chief himself. Her position will be inherited by her eldest daughter. The appointment of Nyakhalavha, petty chieftainess at Khalavha, is in the hands of Netshiavho. Nyakhalavha's son must marry Netshiavho's daughter, who then becomes heiress to the chieftainship at Khalavha.

Government.

There exists a well-developed form of centralized government operating through three councils—the great council, the district council, and the private council. Of these the great council is the most important, and it is there that the deliberations of the private council are discussed and ratified; its decisions operate and are recognized throughout the country. The petty chiefs of all the districts are members of this council and must attend whenever they are summoned, each accompanied by his *mukhoma* (right-hand man). Any of the smaller headmen may attend this meeting if they wish. The council only meets when important measures are proposed, such as direct taxation or some crisis affecting the whole people.

District Council. Matters concerning individual districts are decided by the local chief in his district council.

Private Council. The chief cannot make legislative changes in an arbitrary way but first deliberates privately with certain important persons. The choice of these private councillors is left to the chief; in

216 TERRITORIAL DIVISIONS, GOVERNMENT,

addition to some of the most influential petty chiefs he may take into his confidence any friend or relative, possessed of more than average ability, who will reside at the capital and enjoy the status of a petty chief. The numerical strength of the council is therefore not fixed. An idea of the type of man composing it may be gathered by the membership of the privy council of Chief Tshivhase, which consists of the following people: Takalani and Mukhose (brothers of the chief), Ratogwa (his father's brother), and Mukumbani (a relation by marriage); these are all important and influential petty chiefs, holding large districts. Chief Thengwe, a close ally, also attends. The other members have no districts, but live at the head kraal, and have been chosen for intelligence: Bombi (the chief's mother's brother), Bullok (his father's brother's son), and Nendalamani (an ancient of the tribe), all exceptionally clever men and favourites of the chief. The councillors may be succeeded by their sons, if they can maintain the prestige of their fathers. The chief's *negota* and *mukhoma* always attend, although the latter plays no important part in the transactions but is present on account of his general usefulness and knowledge of the affairs of the chief. This council formulates the policy and has a preliminary discussion on every measure before it is brought before the notice of the great council. All questions are debated, and every member, except the *mukhoma*, has the right to speak and either agree to or amend the chief's proposals. When a final agreement is reached the *makhadzi* is informed of their decision, with which she generally agrees.

Great Council. When these deliberations affect the whole people a day is fixed and the *magota* are summoned to attend the chief's *khoro*. Here the *khotsimunene* or the chief's *mukhoma* tells them the decision of the privy council, after which the *magota* are at liberty to discuss and criticize the measure. Those who agree attempt to win over those who disagree by argument, or they modify the proposals in an endeavour to conform to the general will. The chief is informed of any proposed modifications, to which if they are reasonable he agrees. In some cases a small minority will hold out against the ruling of the others; an arbitrary chief may fine such obdurate dissenters an ox per head, knowing that he has the support of the majority. In the old days a petty chief who persistently opposed the chief was banished from his district. After the discussion each petty chief returns to his respective district, where he summons his headmen to his *khoro* and explains the position to them. The headmen in their turn inform the people under them.

REVENUE, TAXATION, LAW, JUSTICE 217

The power of rulers depends upon their wealth and the numerical strength of their following. This is an incentive to all rulers, of whatever rank, to endeavour to attract new people and to maintain their hold over their present subjects by ruling with equity and justice, acting in all things with consideration and giving wise council. A great deal depends upon the ruler's personality, and often an unwise heir will find a strong heritage quickly weakened, resulting in the lowering of his prestige. '*Mukhoma a tudza, vhalanda vha a ludza*' (If the leader is lame, all his followers also limp). If a leader is unpopular with any of his following, and an individual feels that he has not been treated fairly, or that his overlord is unworthy of the services he is bound to offer him, he has one method of revenge: he can desert his unjust lord and offer his services to another man. This power of achieving retribution by desertion, possibly to join the ranks of a rival, forms a natural check on the absolute power of the rulers and prevents them from indulging too often in arbitrary actions of cruelty and injustice.

Revenue and Taxation.

Venda chiefs are generally rich out of all proportion to their subjects, obtaining a large revenue from their lands, taxation, proceeds of justice, and the fees levied on social functions, as well as many other perquisites. To a lesser degree, all petty chiefs receive the same emoluments in their own districts. The chief generally has large tracts of land close to the capital and often scattered portions in charge of his petty chiefs. He is entitled to free labour for the working of all these lands, both at ploughing and reaping, and also for housebuilding and such work. In like manner petty chiefs are entitled to free labour from their subjects, and when the great chief has strips of land in their domain the people living there are obliged to do double service. The BaLemba are not allowed to work in the chief's lands; instead of doing socage service the men supply him with bracelets and the women supply him with pots.

The chief, at irregular intervals, has the right to augment his revenue by direct taxation, but this can only be done with the consent and approval of his council. The amount of the tax depends upon the decisions of the council, who take into account prevailing conditions and the ability of the people to pay. This tax used to be paid in hoes or goats and is now generally between five shillings and one pound per head. The petty chiefs are responsible for its collection in their own districts and receive a percentage of the tax, the amount depending upon the

218 TERRITORIAL DIVISIONS, GOVERNMENT,

chief's goodwill. All adult men are liable for the payment of such a tax, whether they are resident in the country or, at the time of the levy, are working elsewhere. To-day special messengers are sent to the Rand for the purpose of making the necessary collection from wandering members of the tribe, so that no man shall escape his burden.

Revenue is always trickling in through the fines of justice, the chief or petty chief being entitled to a proportion of all the animals paid by defaulters. Often when a man has won a big suit he shows his gratification by presenting his chief with a few additional head of cattle. In olden times large windfalls were occasionally obtained by the conviction of witches and murderers, when the chief appropriated all the offenders' wives, children, cattle, and other property. Sometimes men guilty of homicide would make their peace with the chief by giving him one or more of their children. Among the smaller perquisites, to which the chiefs and petty chiefs are entitled, are the skins of all lions and leopards; they also receive the hind leg of all cattle and wild game killed in the vicinity of the capital, as well as a share of beer from all *murula* trees. When a cow has twin calves the owner is expected to present it and its offspring to his chief, as it is not considered fitting that such a fruitful animal should be the property of a commoner. It is customary for any man who is blessed with particular good fortune to offer his chief a share of his good luck.

Law and Justice.

The BaVenda have a strong and well-developed conception of justice and, partly owing to the flexibility of their customary law, partly to their inherent sense of right and wrong, it is seldom, except in cases of witchcraft, that the wrongdoer escapes punishment or the innocent man receives an unjust sentence; the rulings of the court nearly always agree with the general idea of equity.

Every MuVenda is *ipso facto* an advocate: all possess amazing powers of rhetoric and oratory and can speak for any length of time on any and all subjects, declaiming with forceful eloquence and convincing argument and appropriate gesticulations. From the time that they are quite young children they begin to acquire the necessary skill in debate, accepting victory or defeat in argument with equal impassivity of countenance; all give evidence when required, without a trace of embarrassment or self-consciousness. The judge generally adapts his verdict to the consensus of public opinion, knowing that in enforcing

REVENUE, TAXATION, LAW, JUSTICE 219

it he can always rely on the assistance of the majority of the people. Some men, such as Takalani, Tshivhase's most important petty chief, achieve a high reputation for the order and equity of their court, and disputants may come from great distances, sometimes even from alien tribes, knowing that they will receive a fair hearing and honest judgement.

There is a sharp distinction made between criminal offences which are non-compoundable and severely punished, in most cases by death, and civil cases which are compoundable by payment. In the latter category a large percentage of the cases arise out of questions in connexion with lobola and are very complicated.

There is a highly centralized legal system, consisting of a hierarchy of courts, corresponding to the hierarchy of headmen. First there is a family gathering, in which an attempt is made to reach an amicable settlement before referring the matter to the *khoro* of the local headman. If, after the grievances have been aired in this court, satisfactory agreement cannot be arranged, the headman refers the complaints to the district petty chief. Here the case is considered in detail, both plaintiff and defendant being given a patient hearing; witnesses are brought and the matter thrashed out and often satisfactorily concluded. In cases where the judgement in the petty chief's court is not acceptable to both parties, the case may be taken to the chief's *khoro*. Here the *khotsimunene* has the full right of the chief and can act as judge. In order to bring a case before this supreme court a fee of three pounds or one ox must be paid to the chief, and any fine imposed by a lower court, whose judgement is upheld here, is always greatly increased after the findings of the supreme court. Certain cases, particularly non-compoundable crimes, are taken directly to the chief.

The procedure in these court cases is extremely interesting and instructive and throws a considerable light on the character and social life of the BaVenda. The most outstanding feature of the court is the orderliness of the procedure, combined with the untiring patience of the judge who listens, sometimes for hours on end, to impassioned eloquence, of which half the subject-matter appears entirely unnecessary and irrelevant.

The case commences with the arrival of the disputants, accompanied by their witnesses and various other supporters, as well as members of their respective families. The parties are greeted at the *khoro* by the chief's *mukhoma*. Most of the elders of the kraal gather together around the chief, who seats himself on a stone, usually under

220 TERRITORIAL DIVISIONS, GOVERNMENT,

the shade of a tree in the middle of the *khoro*; the other people sit about him on the ground in no particular order. The plaintiff is asked to state his case, which he promptly proceeds to do with a great display of rhetoric, scarcely pausing to breathe until he has completed his evidence, when he suddenly stops as abruptly and unexpectedly as he started, saluting the judge and suffixing his oration with the word '*Ndau!*' (lion). During his speech nobody utters a word, except one important councillor, who keeps order. This man squats near the judge and interpolates the word '*Mutavhatsinde!*' or '*Ndau!*' in a high-pitched voice whenever the orator pauses for the fraction of a second. The word *mutavhatsinde* seems to be used in trials of commoners only, *ndau* being substituted for members of the royal family. As long as the speaker's words are accompanied by these interpolations he has the attention of the court, and may not be interrupted by any one. After the plaintiff has stated his case, the defendant addresses the court, and after his statement the witnesses are called to give their evidence. Any man may then ask questions, although most of such questioning is done by the old men living at the kraal, as they are experienced and have great social prestige. If the plaintiff and defendant wish to argue privately over any matter, the *mutavhatsinde* or *ndau* is omitted, automatically suspending the official nature of the discussion, until the argument is concluded and the attention of the court again solicited.

When the whole case has been thrashed out the chief or judge sums up with extreme efficiency, and it is unusual for the smallest detail of the proceedings to escape his vigilance. He declares the customary law and may administer sharp rebukes to offenders who have contravened this law too patently. Judgement is given, unless the case is postponed for further evidence, and the disputants depart to make way for the next case.

Sometimes, when the evidence is unsatisfactory, the defendant may, with the permission of the judge, challenge the plaintiff to consult a diviner as to whether he is guilty of the charge brought against him. The plaintiff dare not refuse, as his refusal would be taken by everybody as proof of the false nature of his charge. The plaintiff and defendant are then sent to consult a diviner, accompanied by an impartial messenger provided by the chief. The defendant pays the diviner a fee for opening his bag of magic dice and another fee for the consultation; if the divination upholds the charge against him the judge orders the defendant to pay the customary fine

REVENUE, TAXATION, LAW, JUSTICE

to the plaintiff; the defendant is also in danger of being branded a witch. On the other hand, if the defendant is pronounced innocent, the plaintiff must pay him an ox for defamation of character. In most cases where a charge fails the plaintiff is obliged to pay this fine for wrongful accusation; this acts as a check on unfair charges, as the price of discovery is too great. A charge is therefore seldom brought up to the court for judgement without good reason and a certain amount of convincing evidence.

All anti-social actions pollute the offender, and until he has been actually cleansed he is a danger to the society in which he lives and may bring the anger of the spirit world upon it. Certain crimes are so grave in their reaction on the group that the only method of purification is in the death or banishment of the offender; in this way only can the danger of contamination be removed and the normal equilibrium of the society restored. Other crimes have a less dangerous effect, and the offender may be cleansed by medicine and sacrifice or by compensating the injured party and then sharing in a ritual meal, in which one of the animals of the fine imposed upon him is eaten publicly in the *khoro* by all the people; the sharing in this meal is a symbol that the crime is expiated and that the criminal is readmitted into society.

All such offences as assault, adultery, seduction, theft, damage to property, &c., are compoundable. The amount of the fine is only fixed in a few cases and generally varies according to the position of the offender, the enormity of the offence, and the culprit's previous record and ability to pay.

Assault. The fine for assault is a sheep, a goat, or an ox. An assault in the chief's capital is considered a serious offence and is more severely punished than if it had been committed on the veldt. In the same way an assault on any of the royal family, or on one of the chief's officials, is treated as being only a degree less serious than an assault on the chief himself. Respect for the old men and superiors is so deeply rooted in the minds of the BaVenda that it is very unusual, and only in the face of great provocation, that an assault would be made upon a social superior or a person of authority. In all cases of assault one animal of the fine imposed is killed and eaten in the *khoro*.

Adultery. Adultery is compoundable by the payment of two head of cattle to the husband of the guilty woman; any child of the adulterous union is his property. Adultery committed with women living in the chief's capital is compounded by three head of cattle. One animal

222 TERRITORIAL DIVISIONS, GOVERNMENT,

of the fine is always killed and eaten in the *khoro*; the remainder, which the injured party receives, are killed and eaten by himself and his relations as soon as he returns home. There is a danger that the guilty woman might at a future date elope with the adulterer, and, if the increase of the fine had reached the number of animals that were in the original lobola paid by her husband, he would not be able to claim the return of his lobola from the adulterer; to avoid the possibility of this complication the animal or animals of the fine are eaten.

Damage to Property. This is usually caused by cattle straying into the lands and destroying crops. If this occurs in the daytime the herd boy is thrashed, and if at night the injured party is awarded one or more head of cattle according to the damage done. All injuries to animals are compoundable in the same way.

Arson. Deliberate arson is punished by a heavy fine; in the old days it was never less than ten head of cattle and ten goats. If the offender is poor his wife is returned to her parents and the lobola paid for her is given to the injured party. In the event of the offender having nothing he may be taken by the chief to be his slave. One animal of the fine for this offence is killed and eaten in the *khoro*.

Theft. For the theft of cattle the thief is liable for any claim the plaintiff likes to make. It is considered a very grave offence and, though the court may modify the plaintiff's claim, the offender is generally heavily fined. The theft of goats, dogs, &c., is similarly compounded. For all other petty thefts, such as food-stuffs and cooking utensils, the fine is heavy, out of all proportion to the crime, as such petty thieving is considered entirely unnecessary and would never occur without an ulterior motive. A portion of the fine is given to the chief.

Theft of Weapons. For the theft of a spear or an axe the fine is an ox and a goat for the first offence and more for a subsequent one. The ox is paid to the injured party and the goat is killed and eaten in the *khoro*. It is believed that a man stealing the weapons of another is, in thus depriving him of his arms, endeavouring to bring about his death.

Failure to obey the Chief's Summons to Work. This crime is punished by the fine of one animal. To-day many of the payments are made in money instead of in kind; a bull is valued at £5 or ten goats, a cow or an ox at £10 or twenty goats, a goat at 10s. or twelve fowls, and a fowl at 1s.; although twelve fowls are given for a 10s. goat, the extra two fowls are thrown in as a makeweight, to pay for all the useless feathers of the other ten fowls.

REVENUE, TAXATION, LAW, JUSTICE 223

The compoundable fines are usually paid at once, but in the rare cases where payment is delayed the headman sends a messenger to the home of the defaulter to remonstrate with him and explain that if he does not intend to fulfil the orders of the court he must go and live elsewhere. The defaulter pays the messenger a goat for his trouble, and if, after this warning, he still persists in ignoring the findings of the court, the chief may order some of his councillors to confiscate the necessary fine and remove any cattle or other property that he thinks fit as a punishment for contempt of court. In the past such an offender would be banished or his home would be burnt down, and he would stand a good chance of being killed by the angry elders.

A certain number of more serious crimes are uncompoundable. These include witchcraft, murder, homicide, incest, and abnormal sexual aberrations, all of which are considered to be crimes against society rather than against the individual and to necessitate the ritual cleansing of the society.

Witchcraft. Persons convicted of witchcraft, or believed to achieve nefarious ends by its practice, are driven out of the country, and their wives and children are confiscated by the chief. Sometimes the women's relatives, objecting to their womenfolk being taken over by the chief in this arbitrary way, will offer him their equivalent in cattle; or sometimes a man may contrive to keep his wives and children by persuading one of his friends, with whom he has secretly left cattle, to lobola for them and then return them to him. Formerly witches and wizards were always killed, with all their family, by being thrown over a cliff.

Murder. Murder is punishable by death or banishment. The family of a murderer is taken by the chief and all his property confiscated as in the case of a man convicted of witchcraft. Occasionally a murderer who has no wives or property may be enslaved by the chief, who is thereafter responsible for him. If a young man without property, living at his father's kraal, commits murder and escapes capture, the cattle and possessions of his father are confiscated by the chief, as the father is responsible for his son's actions. Matricide, parricide, and fratricide are all considered as ordinary murder. In cases of infanticide, the murderer sometimes makes his peace with the chief by handing over to him one of his other children. In no case of murder is the family of the murdered man compensated, although occasionally one of his family may bring the murderer to summary justice by killing him outright.

224 TERRITORIAL DIVISIONS, GOVERNMENT, ETC.

Homicide. Little distinction is made between homicide and murder. If two or three influential persons swear to the dead man as having been the aggressor and to the absolutely accidental character of the crime, the culprit may be released with a fine.

Incest. Incest is a serious crime; the offender is considered to be a dog and is the subject of horror and scorn. He is tried in the chief's court and is punished by death or banishment. Perverse sexual aberrations are similarly punished.

Planning or Conniving the Death of the Chief, if discovered, is always punished by death.

In cases punishable by the death sentence, if the offender tries to escape from justice, he may be followed into the bush by any man detailed by the chief for the purpose and there clubbed to death without a trial. When an offender is sentenced to death he is released and then secretly followed to the bush and there killed or thrown over a cliff by the chief's executioners, whose identity is kept a close secret; his body is left to be devoured by wild beasts, and his death is not announced to his family until all is over.

XIX

CONCEPTIONS OF THE UNIVERSE

Meteorology—Astronomy—Time and the Seasons—Numbers.

Meteorology.

THE earth is thought to be a large flat disk floating in water, roofed by the dome of the sky, *makholi*, which meets the circumference of the disk at the horizon, *sendekamisi* (the place where the stampers are leaned—from *u sendeka*, to lean, and *misi*, stampers). This is practically identical with the BaThonga conception.

Early morning mists and fogs are thought to be clouds leaning down from the sky like bent-up old women and are called *zwikegula* (from *kegula*, old woman). The BaVenda have words to describe clouds in general, a cloudy sky and different degrees of rain, distinguishing between a light drizzle, a downpour, a sudden storm, and hail; also for frost, twilight, sunset, mirage, rainbow, thunder, lightning, &c.

Hail, *tshifhango*, is sent by Raluvhimba as a punishment for evil, and after a hailstorm the chief summons a diviner to discover who was the cause of the god's displeasure. If a hailstorm interrupts ploughing the workers will not continue until the next day for fear the god will think that they are defying him. The rumbling of the thunder, *muvumo*, is Raluvhimba travelling; the loud crash following on a flash of lightning is associated with the lightning, *lupenyo*, and is the passage to earth of a mysterious bird, *ndadzi*. The bird flashes across the sky and strikes the earth with a resounding crash, and as it leaves the earth it often passes through some object and injures it; if the lightning bird strikes its victim on its downward path it will penetrate through it to the ground and be unable to rise again. Where it strikes the ground it is supposed to deposit its *murundo* (urine), from which the young birds hatch out the following year, when the mother will strike the same spot again and release them. It is curious that among the BaVenda the supposed deposit of the lightning bird, highly prized by the medicine-man, is a jelly-like substance, while most Bantu tribes who believe in the existence of this bird think that it deposits small eggs. If a tree or hut is set on fire by lightning in or near a village all the fires in the village are put out, the ashes sprinkled with water, and new fires lit with brands from the fire at the chief's kraal.

Winds. The BaVenda have words for the four winds. The east

226 CONCEPTIONS OF THE UNIVERSE

wind is *mumbedzi*, named after the VhaMbedzi sib, living in the east of the country; the VhaMbedzi themselves call it *vhuvhaduvha* (the place where the sun rises). The west wind is *vhukhovela* (where the sun sets) or *mutalervha*, after a BaSutho tribe living in the west. The north wind is *mukaranga*, after the BaKaranga in the north. The south wind is *murwa*, from BaRwa (the Bushmen). The name given to the south wind suggests that the Bushmen were living to the south of Vendaland when the BaVenda first occupied the country, but there seems to be no history or tradition to substantiate this. All winds are described by these four names; north-east and north-west winds are both *mukaranga* unless they are more east than north, when they are *mumbedzi*, or more west than north, when they are *vhukhovela*.

Astronomy.

Many BaVenda believe that the sun, *duvha*, travels across the dome of the sky from east to west every day and returns to the east again unseen under the cover of the night; others believe that it returns under the water in which the disk-like world floats and arrives at daybreak ready to start its race across the dome again. They appreciate its great heat and think that if Raluvhimba were to bring it near to the earth they would be burnt up. An eclipse of the sun, *tshivhedza*, is an evil omen, either foretelling the death of a chief or a famine or a pest. It is believed that where the sun rises, a bird fancier guards some large and peculiar birds, and that one of these escapes and swallows the sun for a short time, causing the eclipse.

The moon, *nwedzi*, is often called the *makhadzi*, who is the head of the kraal, as the moon is held to be the head of all the stars. There is a riddle, 'My father's garden is full of calabashes, one of which is very large; what is it?' The answer is, 'The moon and the stars'. The moon is supposed to be racing with the sun across the sky, being always left behind, and finally badly beaten in the race when the new moon appears. The new moon is *nwedzana* (little moon); the waning moon is said to be dying or going dark. The waxing moon with the points of the crescent turned upwards is said to be a basin holding all the coughs and colds, and the waning moon with the tips pointing downwards is the basin inverted and upsetting all the colds over the earth.

The stars, *maledzi*, are thought to be suspended from the sky and invisible by day owing to the brightness of the sun. The BaVenda have no explanation for the movements of the planets. They think that a shooting star has become detached from the string attaching

CONCEPTIONS OF THE UNIVERSE 227

it to the sky. Hailstones are connected vaguely with the stars. It is considered unlucky to count the stars, and a child is forbidden to do so, as if he does he will wet the hut during the night.

Two constellations are of particular importance to the BaVenda as they are used to reckon the time to begin ploughing, and so mark the beginning of each year's activities.

Tuda (giraffe) contains the two brightest stars of the Southern Cross (α and β Centauri), called *nsadzi* (female), with the two pointers to the Southern Cross (α and β Crucis), called *ndona* (male).

Tshilimela (from *u lima*, to plough) contains six of the Pleiades.

The time for ploughing is when *nsadzi* is not visible, and *ndona* is just visible over the horizon soon after sunset; at this time *tshilimela* is low on the horizon. These constellations are in these positions at the end of October.

Makhali (rhinoceros) is the only other Venda constellation. It contains the belt and sword of Orion ($\delta\epsilon\zeta\iota\theta$ Orionis) the sword being the rhinoceros' horn.

Sirius is the most observed star. When it appears as an evening star it is *khumbela tshilalelo* (asking for supper). When it is the morning star, rising early in the morning during the winter months, it is called *nanga* (horn). The first appearance of *nanga* each year used to be the signal for the beginning of the harvesting. The first man to spot it climbed up a high hill and blew the *phala-fhala* horn to spread the glad news, and was afterwards rewarded by the chief with the present of a cow. That day the young boys drove all the chief's cattle half a day's journey from the village and then left them unattended. The first animal to reach home safely was greeted with the trilling of the women and there was great rejoicing at the chief's village. The BaVenda are fully aware that *nanga* and *khumbela tshilalelo* are the same star.

Acharnar, when appearing as a morning star, is a sign that the cold weather is about to set in. It is called *tshinananga* (little horn).

Musasi (from *sasi*, door) is Taurus α. It is identified as a morning star in winter and is the first star seen on opening the door, telling the women that it is time to begin stamping.

Khoho motsho (pulling out the dawn) appears in the winter as a morning star and is seen high in the sky in the evening. There was much diversity of opinion about this star, some informants having noted that it did not appear regularly. *Khoho motsho* is the planet Venus, and no doubt the complicated perambulations connected with the transit of Venus account for the difficulty.

Q 2

228 CONCEPTIONS OF THE UNIVERSE

Time and the Seasons.

Months. The year is divided into lunar months, twelve of which are named:

1. *Phando* (corresponding roughly with January).
2. *Luhuhu.*
3. *Thafumuwe.*
4. *Rhambamme* (neglect the mother); in this month the children forget their mothers because there is plenty of food.
5. *Shundunthule* (*u nthula*, to take off, and *tshirundu*, basket); the month in which the women take their baskets from their heads to fill them in the lands.
6. *Fulwi.*
7. *Fulwani.*
8. *Thangule* (*u thangula*, to strip); the month in which the wind strips the leaves from the trees.
9. *Khubvumedzi* (warm).
10. *Tshimedzi.*
11. *Lara.*
12. *Nyendavhusiku* (a kind of locust); swarms of locust appear in this month.

Tshimedzi, the month in which ploughing begins, is really the first month of the Venda year. The moon that appears when the two lower stars of the constellation *tuda* are just below the horizon and the two upper stars just visible is the *tshimedzi* moon.

Between the time of *tuda's* appearance in that position and its reappearance there more than twelve lunar months have elapsed. A lunation is about 29½ days, so that twelve of these, together with approximately 11 days, will make a sidereal year of, roughly speaking, 365 days. This discrepancy may be adjusted by having two years of twelve lunar months and then a year of thirteen lunar months.

Now among the BaVenda there is sometimes a long discussion between the elders and the young men when the new moon appears after the end of *thangule.* The young men declare that the new moon is *khubvumedzi,* but the old men shake their heads and say that it is not, and when asked its name reply 'khangwa vhanna' 'men forget', from *u hangwa,* to forget, and *vhanna,* men). They argue through the debated month, and, if the old men are right and it is the year of thirteen moons, the argument continues into the next month, until

CONCEPTIONS OF THE UNIVERSE

the position of *tuda* shows that it is time to plough, when all agree that the next moon will be *tshimedzi*. Thus the extra moon has come to be called *khangwa vhanna*; it has always been a subject of controversy and never been known by a more specific name. It solves for the BaVenda the old problem of reconciling lunar months and the regularly recurring seasons; the first moon after *tuda* is in the required position, is always *tshimedzi*, and with the help of the movable *khangwa vhanna* the stellar and lunar times are roughly adjusted.

The time of day is calculated by the sun: *nga matshilone*, just before sunrise; *tshi boa* (from *u boa*, to come up), the sun has just risen; *tshi tavha*, the sun is half-way between sunrise and noon; *thoho*, overhead; *mathabama*, middle afternoon; *khovela*, sunset.

To make sure of keeping an appointment some days ahead, notches may be cut in a stick equivalent to the number of days that will elapse and a notch cut off each day.

Numbers.

There are only nine distinct numerals among the BaVenda: *thihi*, one; *vhili*, two; *raru*, three; *na*, four; *tanu*, five; *fumi*, ten; *dana*, a hundred; *khulu*, a thousand; *tshighidi*, ten thousand. All numbers are expressed by these words: 888 sheep will require this complicated expression, *dzinngu dza madana matanu na muraru na mahumi matanu na mararu na taru na raru* (sheep, hundreds five and three, and tens five and three, and five and three). Simple counting is always done with the help of the fingers. Starting with the right hand, the palm facing inwards, the little finger is one; then the little and third fingers are two; the little, third, and second are three; the four fingers are four; the four fingers and the thumb are five. The fingers of the left hand are then added, beginning with the thumb. When the last finger has been put up the hands are clapped to signify ten. The BaVenda have no great arithmetical sense, but the fact that they have words for 10, 100, 1,000, and 10,000 shows a distinct advance on the BaThonga, who have names for 10 and 100 only, besides the basic five.

XX

RELIGION

The Supreme Deity—The Spirit World—Dissociated Spirits—Ancestor
Cult—Sowing and Harvest Rites—Review of Ancestor Cult

The Supreme Deity.

RALUVHIMBA is the mysterious, monotheistic deity of the Ba-
Venda, and has been identified by them with Mwari, the Mashona
god, who reveals himself at Mbvumela in the Matoba Hills of
Matabeleland. Faith in Mwari as an oracle and rain-maker is still
prevalent among the BaVenda and neighbouring tribes in Southern
Rhodesia and the Transvaal, though it is diminishing. The BaVenda
credit Raluvhimba with all the powers of Mwari, and, although it is
probable that at one time they were two separate deities, they have
now become so completely identified that they are referred to indiscriminately by either name; the name Raluvhimba is peculiar to the
BaVenda. Raluvhimba is connected with the beginning of the world
and is supposed to live somewhere in the heavens and to be connected
with all astronomical and physical phenomena. The word *luvhimba*
means eagle, the bird that soars aloft; the BaVenda have a very real idea
of this great power travelling through the sky, using the stars and wind
and rain as his instruments. Beyond this the whole conception is somewhat elusive, especially to the ordinary man, who is more prone to
associate his benefits and misfortunes with his ancestors. In fact Raluvhimba is regarded complacently except under unusual circumstances.
A shooting star is Raluvhimba travelling; his voice is heard in the
thunder; comets, lightning, meteors, earthquakes, prolonged drought,
floods, pests, and epidemics—in fact, all the natural phenomena which
affect the people as a whole—are revelations of the great god. In
thunderstorms he appears as a great fire near the chief's kraal, whence
he booms his desires to the chief in a voice of thunder; this fire always
disappears before any person can reach it. At these visitations the
chief enters his hut and, addressing Raluvhimba as '*Makhulu*', con-
verses with him, the voice of the god replying either from the thatch
of the hut or from a tree nearby; Raluvhimba then passes on in a
further clap of thunder. Occasionally he is angry with the chief and
takes his revenge on the people by sending them a drought or a flood,

RELIGION

or possibly by opening an enormous cage in the heavens and letting loose a swarm of locusts on the land.

There is a cave at Luvhimbi where Raluvhimba was wont to manifest himself. The mountain Tsha-wa-dinda, the place of the messengers, where the cave is situated, was a stronghold of the Vhatavhatsinde people, under Chief Muthivhi. This district was later taken from Muthivhi by Rambura, one of the sons of Thoho-ya-Ndou, who fled from the Nzhelele river at the time of the disintegration of the original tribe; the ceremonies in connexion with Raluvhimba no longer take place there.

At the time when Muthivhi was chief this cave was used as the *thondo*. Raluvhimba visited it from time to time, appearing as a great flame on a platform of rock just above the cave. The appearance of the flame was accompanied by the sound of clanking irons, and the manifestation was received by the people with shouts of joy and trilling, the cries being passed on by the people all over the country. Muthivhi immediately climbed up the mountain to the cave, welcoming Raluvhimba, clapping his hands, and shouting his praises loudly, the claps and shouts echoing for miles around. Muthivhi passed through the cave and climbed on to the platform, where he called on Raluvhimba, and thanked him for revealing himself. He then prayed the great god to give his people rain, felicity, and peace. The chief then returned to the cave and ordered the young men on guard to sound the *phala-fhala* in order to summon all the men to perform the *tshikona* dance. He then went back to his village and told his people that Raluvhimba had visited his children and would bring blessing and rain to the country. The *tshikona* was danced on the following two nights; after the first dance rain fell until noon the following day; the sun then came out, but after the second night heavy rain fell. The story of this cave was told me by Abel Mananga, a nephew of Chief Thengwe, who had heard it from his father. There can be no doubt that Raluvhimba represents some extinct monotheistic cult; he is still at times greeted spontaneously by the whole people in a way that is most unusual among the Southern Bantu. The Rev. G. Westphal of the Berlin Mission was living at Khalavha mission station in 1917 when a meteor burst in the middle of the day, making a strange, humming sound, followed by a crash like thunder. All the people started clapping their hands and shouting with joy, blowing horns and trilling; the cries were taken up by the neighbouring people and swept in huge waves of sound all down the Nzhelele valley until

232   RELIGION

they gradually faded away in the distance. Junod[1] says in this connection:

'The Rev. McDonald told me that about seven years ago he witnessed one of these visits of Raluvhimba. The Gooldville Mission Station is at the foot of a hill which stretches for a long distance in an easterly direction. One day he heard a loud clamour, which arose on the west of the hill and propagated itself to the east. Women were shouting in a way which is peculiar to them, by moving their tongues quickly in their mouths, producing a kind of tremolo on a very high pitch. Men were yelling "E-E-E!" and all of them were clapping their hands. There had just been a slight tremor of the earth. During five minutes the extraordinary clamour filled the air, and it was most impressive! The whole tribe was greeting Raluvhimba who was passing through the country. People say that during the earthquake they also notice a noise in the sky similar to thunder. And whilst they clap their hands, to welcome the mysterious god, they pray. They tell him: "Give us rain! Give us health!" This story of a spontaneous and collective act of adoration of a Bantu tribe towards its god is most curious, and I wonder if such a demonstration has ever taken place amongst Thonga or Souto.'

Raluvhimba is considered to be in some respects particularly connected with the chief, whom he calls *muduhulu*, grandchild; the chief calls the god *makhulu*, grandfather, in the same way as he addresses his ancestor spirits. The link between the god and the chief is not surprising as it is the chief's duty to perform the rites in connexion with rain, which Raluvhimba is supposed to control.

Every year a special messenger, whose office was hereditary, used to be sent with a black ox and a black piece of cloth to visit Raluvhimba, or Mwari, at his place of revelation at Mbvumela in the Matoba Hills. The black ox was set free in a forest to join the god's large herd of black oxen which had accumulated there through these annual offerings. A voice speaking in Tshikaranga, or occasionally in Sendebele, accepted the offering, and the messenger refreshed himself with beer and meat, which he found mysteriously placed for him under the trees. To-day, owing to the East Coast fever restrictions, no cattle may be taken across the border, but messengers are still sent to visit the god, taking money payments and other gifts. No MuLemba ever dares to approach the sacred precincts; if he does he will be seized and tied hand and foot. Old Mphephu, the present chief's father, decided one year that he would consult a new oracle and so consulted Majaji,

---

[1] Junod, H. A., 'Some Features of the Religion of the BaVenda', *South African Journal of Science*, vol. xvii, No. 2, 1921, pp. 209-10.

RELIGION

the famous rain-maker. That year the drought was very bad indeed, so Mphephu decided to return to his old god; Raluvhimba, however, was jealous that he had been neglected for a foreign power, and took vengeance on his people by sending them a very bad drought, which lasted for two years. Since then in years of drought and plenty alike Mphephu, and after his death his son, always sent an emissary to Raluvhimba at Mbvumela. I was informed that last year Mbulahene sent over £100 in cash; his emissaries returned more than satisfied that the god had accepted their offering and would send the required rain, as they had found quantities of beer, game, and snuff lying beside the road, put there by the great god for their consumption. Bullock and Posselt, Native Commissioners in Southern Rhodesia, have both written interesting descriptions of Mwari and his position among the BaKaranga. Bullock[1] says:

'The god of the Mashona is *Mwari*, or, as the Amandebele call him, *Mlimo*; which name in Sendebele is derived from the root *ima*, to be erect, to live. The Chishona name, *Mwari*, means the begetter or bearer, in our terminology creator. This god is not the deified spirit of some remote ancestor, although he is subject to many human weaknesses, but is of a more abstract nature. He is the owner of the earth and provides or withholds the fruits of nature, but is too far from man to be interested in the well-being of individuals; only when some crime is committed against the laws of nature does he afflict the whole race with pestilence or drought. He is not domiciled in any particular spot, although his priests and consecrated women live in the Matombo or Matobo Mountains, and, if approached in proper manner, he will reveal himself in the oracle from the cave on matters of general importance. He also manifests himself through the divine fire on Mt. Rungai and in the shooting stars. When such phenomena occur, men salute *Mwari*, but, as a rule, he is not approached by individuals. They can procure the help they need from lesser beings, but rain, for instance, is needed by all, and, when it fails, they turn to their god, with sacrifices of black cattle and the consecration of chief's daughters to his service.'

Posselt[2] recounts a description given to him by a MuVenda after a visit to the god. He says:

'The following is the account given by Vela, a Mvenda, of a visit to Shango-yima, where Dapa was high priest. Vela had been summoned, among others,

[1] Bullock, C., 'The Religion of the Mashona', *South African Journal of Science*, vol. xxiv, 1927, p. 525.

[2] Posselt, F., 'Some Notes on the Religious Ideas of the Natives of Southern Rhodesia', *South African Journal of Science*, vol. xxiv, 1927, pp. 530–1.

RELIGION

to cultivate the lands of *Mwari* (for the use of the priesthood). "There was a hut with an enclosure under a big rock. Separate entrances to the enclosure were provided for the men and women. After our arrival, a noise emanating from the rock became audible, then voices. Dapa sat with his back to the entrance of the hut and faced the party. A voice came from the hut asking the party as to its health. The party was then dismissed, *Mwari* desiring to sleep. The following day they were given their tasks and a beast killed for their consumption and porridge and ·beer provided. Later, they were called into a courtyard, which was divided by a partition. Food was taken to one portion of the yard, to which the members of the party were not admitted.

"In the evening, the noise from the rock was again heard; then a voice, thin but audible, a long way off. The party was summoned and Dapa commanded to give food. Then the snuff boxes of the party were collected and placed at the door of the hut, into which they disappeared. After a little while, they reappeared. Then the voice commanded Dapa to place a platter with meat for the dogs at the door; this he did in full view. The platter disappeared but shortly afterwards reappeared with different meat, which Dapa was commanded from the hut to distribute. No one was admitted to the hut from whence came the voice except the attendant, who took charge of any goods, and the women who cleaned the floor. The party was dismissed in the evening. The voice from the rock was not heard during the next two days. On the fourth day, *Mwari* took leave of the party. The voice emanated from the top of the rock, descended, and ended in a thud which shook the ground, sufficing to wake a sleeper. The party was dismissed with thanks. On being asked for rain, it replied that rain was unknown and that *Mwari's* throat was dry. But on the second day after the party reached home rain fell." '

The BaVenda, like all other votaries of Mwari, have implicit faith in his power as a rain-maker; this belief is stimulated by the large priesthood connected with the cult, elevation to whose ranks only occurs in response to a definite sign. Posselt continues:

'The *Mwari* cult was esoteric and its details known only to the priests, who carefully guarded their secrets; hence the difficulty of obtaining any reliable data.

'The ranks of the junior priesthood—the *Hosane*—were large. The "divine" call appears to have been signified by fits—whether of an epileptic nature or not is uncertain. The individual was then referred to as a "child of *Mwari*".

'There can be little doubt that the priests, in their duties of interpreting the will of Mwari, imposed on the credulity of the uninitiated by their assumption of mystery, and also resorted to ventriloquism and sleight of hand.'

RELIGION

The following story was related to me by Simpson Vhatu-a-mamba, an evangelist of the Berlin Mission, living at Makonde:

'Once a long time ago, before the Boer War, while Mphephu was still in Rhodesia, I was working in a mine at Selukwe. One morning when we went down the mine we found a fire lit and meat and beer beside it; we did not know who had made the meal, but it must have been put there during the night. The white boss asked the BaKaranga boys who had done this thing, and they all replied "Mwari". Nothing was done then, but when the same thing was repeated on several days, although all the food and beer was destroyed each time it was found, the white boss began to get annoyed and reported the matter to the Native Commissioner. Police officials were sent to the mine to investigate and afterwards Chibi, the chief of that district, was summoned and asked to explain all this nonsense about Mwari which was upsetting the boys in the mine. Chibi replied that it was not nonsense, and that Mwari did send the food, and that his home was at Mbvumela in the Matoba mountains.

'The Commissioner called three police officers and three boys, of whom I was one, and asked Chibi for a boy to act as guide. We set off to find Mwari's home. We went for four days and finally came to a mountain in the Matobas, south-west of Bulawayo. At the bottom of the mountain was one big hut and on the top a large village. The guide led us to the big hut at the bottom of the mountain, and said, "This is Mwari's home". As we came near to the hut we heard a tremendous noise of horn blowing, drumming, and shouting coming from it, and a curious voice crying out in Tshikaranga. The police officers wanted to go in, but we boys were all very frightened and would have liked to have run away. As we came quite close to this hut the noise of horns and drums and shouting became louder. The white men pushed open the door and we went into the hut. There was absolutely nothing there. We stood still very frightened and then heard the noises going on under the floor. Now the hut was built on the solid rock, as are a great many huts in Southern Rhodesia, to keep the ants out, and the white men said that we must see under this stone floor. We looked all over the rock and presently saw a round crack in it. The white men forced an iron crowbar under the crack and levered up a round slab of stone. Underneath we saw a large hole. We lit the lamp and climbed down into the hole and there found a drum. Then we found the hole led into a long tunnel which ran uphill for about half an hour's journey. At the end of this tunnel we came out inside another empty hut in the village at the top of the mountain. All the people in the village ran away into the bush; we caught one man and took him back with us through the tunnel and then back to Chibi. This man told the chief and the white people that it was his business to do these things; people brought him cattle and presents of beer and he did his business. After that there was no more trouble with the BaKaranga in the mine.'

236 RELIGION

My native interpreter was present when this story was told, and it was very interesting to me to note his ejaculations of bewildered astonishment and his shamefaced disgust as he realized that not only he but his chief had been deceived. I had often tried in vain to convince him of the charlatanism of Mwari's priests.

So Raluvhimba and Mwari, whatever they may have originally represented, are to-day used by the clever BaKaranga priests as a means by which they extort untold wealth from the credulous people around them, who will continue to believe in their power until each individual has been present at a similar exposure to that experienced by Simpson Vhatu-a-mamba.

Khuswane is the name given to another deity also vaguely connected with the creation. The story of his origin has been forgotten, but all the footprints formed in the rock at Luvhimbi, Mutali, Mphephu, and other places are supposed to have been left by his foot in the days when the rocks were soft.

Thovela and *Tshishongo*, whose story is related in the *domba* ceremony, are regarded more as human ancestors than as gods.

The Spirit World.

Throughout the country certain places are reputed to be inhabited by spirits, whose sinister presence is greatly feared, and who can influence the lives of the living people. Every chief has, or did have in the old days, a forest or mountain in which the spirits of his ancestors are supposed to abide. Many of these forests are the actual burying-places of the chiefs. The burying-place varies in different localities. A chief used to be buried in the cattle-kraal, which thereafter became a particularly sacred place. The chief's capital would sometimes be changed and the old burying-place after some generations would be forgotten; trees would grow up around it and it would maintain its tradition as a sacred grove, although the reason for its sacred character would be no longer known. Ramapulana was buried in his cattle-kraal, near what is now the town of Louis Trichardt, on a site that is part of the town lands; on the death of his successor, Makhado, his relatives wished to bury him with his father, but were prevented from doing so by the European inhabitants. Makhado was therefore buried in his cattle-kraal in the mountains. Mphephu on his death was taken to the burial-place of Makhado, and Ramapulana's grave is already forgotten by the young members of the tribe, although the site is still regarded as sacred.

RELIGION

A great many spirits also have their abode in rivers and lakes. Lake Fundudzi is essentially connected with the ancestor spirits of Netshiavho, who is the guardian of the lake; it is also supposed to be inhabited by the spirits of other Vhatavhatsinde people. A great many weird beliefs and supernatural phenomena are associated with the lake. At times the waters are supposed to rise and fall at irregular intervals, and often early in the morning trees and shrubs are said to be seen rising out of the water high into the sky and then returning again. At times the surface of the water has a glassy appearance like ice, but on being touched the ice is found to be an illusion. Sheep were once seen grazing in the water of the lake and were considered to be the flocks of the spirits living below. This is an interesting example of how an everyday fact may, by a simple misunderstanding, readily become the basis of a mythological conception; it appears that, at the time when these spirit flocks were seen grazing in the lake, sheep from the flocks of the early white pioneers strayed and, unknown to the BaVenda, lost themselves in the mountains; coming down near the lake these sheep wandered out into the low-lying ground and were marooned when the water in the lake rose; at that time sheep were unknown to the natives, and the phenomenon was readily added to the already numerous peculiarities of the lake. A curious feature attributed to the lake is the fact that the spirits will catch any article thrown into it and cast it out on the bank; there it will be discovered the following morning. Although the lake swarms with fish, no one has ever succeeded in landing a fish caught there. Water, if carried away from the lake in any open receptacle, simply vanishes away. Water sealed up for a day or two will burst the receptacle which holds it, leaving a curious characteristic odour behind it. No man dare wash or swim in the lake, as he will be dragged under by the spirits. Music, sounding like the music of the Venda flutes, is often heard coming from under the water. Netshiavho and his lineage must be particularly careful not to offend the dwellers in the lake, or they will show their anger by hurling stones out of it on to their village. If Netshiavho does not perform his harvest ceremonies correctly the water will rise and all sorts of wild animals leap into the lake, to be found the next day cast up dead on the banks. No chief of the MaKhwinde sib may venture near the lake or disaster will overtake him. In the old days no person was allowed to visit it unless he was taken under the protection and guidance of Netshiavho, who, before taking the visitor down, himself visited it and asked the permission of the spirits. The curious

238 RELIGION

formation and unusual character of this lake make it an object of peculiar awe to the BaVenda, which feeling is greatly enhanced by all the tales and superstitions connected with it. Its association with Netshiavho will be discussed further in connexion with the *tevula* ceremony.

The stranger and the traveller must also exercise care and discrimination when visiting the Phiphidi Falls and Gubukuvho, the large pool into which the falls drop. The spirits of the BaNgona people, the first inhabitants of Vendaland, live there, and during the night these spirits can be heard dancing in the falls. The sounds of babies crying and women stamping and of the big war drum are also sometimes heard. In the old war days, when a big fight was in progress, the water in the river was turned to blood. A particular sound coming from Phiphidi is a certain prophecy of rain. To propitiate these BaNgona spirits everybody who crosses the river must throw down an offering; a man plucks out a tuft of hair and throws it into a small hole in the rocks in the middle of the river above the falls; a woman usually throws down a bracelet or a piece of broken pot; even cattle crossing the river must seek protection from the spirits, and a piece of hair is plucked from every beast and thrown into the hole.

There are probably many other localities associated with some particular lineage or sib, with similar stories of spirits and their mode of life. The small piles of stones or twigs, *tshiawelo* (resting-place), seen scattered throughout the country, are also sacred; these little heaps, which vary considerably in size, mark the place where a burial party has placed its burden while it rested on its journey; every MuVenda passing such a beacon must add a stone or a twig to the pile.

In the Makuyu district, near the mountain Amakahani, also a one-time stronghold of the BaNgona, there is a large *mukononi* tree. Any person getting beneath the shade of this tree is sure to die soon afterwards. Occasionally this tree makes a noise like thunder, and this noise is always the precursor of rain.

Dissociated Spirits.

A great many rivers and mountains are supposed to be inhabited by spirits not directly connected with any particular lineage. They are dissociated spirits, often vague and shadowy in character, but none the less terrifying and dangerous to the traveller. There are mountain spirits, *zwidhadyani*, who are mostly of foreign origin, often BaSutho, but there are a few Venda spirits among them. These creatures, though credited with human reasoning, do not appear in complete

RELIGION

239

human form; one spirit is a leg, another an arm, another a body without a head, another an eye, and another is a monster with one eye, one arm, and one leg. These dismembered monstrosities are all so dangerous to the traveller that if he only catches a glimpse of one of them he is bound to die. In addition to *zwidhadyani*, there are spirits living in streams and pools, a small and warlike people with human form; they are always armed with bows and arrows and, like the *zwidhadyani*, bring death to any one who has the misfortune to encounter them.

Isolated beliefs in the transmigration of the spirit. Although it is by no means considered a universal occurrence, a number of people, particularly individual chiefs, are believed to return to earth after death in the form of animals. The lion is the most usual animal in which a spirit returns to earth, and there are several stories of dead ancestors who wander round their kraals at night, killing cattle and bringing trouble to the people with whom they are dissatisfied. Wessman [1] describes an encounter by natives with five lions. The natives were attempting to kill the lions, but did not dare to pursue them when they took refuge in the bush near by. The chief, hearing of the advent of the lions, forbade his people to kill them, saying: 'The lions are not real lions, but dead ancestors, who have taken the shape of lions in order to visit their children.' Wessman concludes his description of the episode by adding, 'consequently the lions were undisturbed, and after killing many cows disappeared after two weeks' stay'. The head of the lineage of Maungani is said to turn into a leopard at his death. The story goes that the first chief when a child was carried off by a leopard; the child was found alive, some distance from the kraal, with the mark of the leopard's claw on his face. From that day the heir of each chief, when still a baby, is visited by the leopard at night and this mark is imprinted on his face. This shows that he is the rightful heir. At his death he becomes a leopard and walks invisibly beside the living head, accompanying him wherever he goes, and protecting him from danger; this leopard kills any one trespassing in the vicinity of the village and selects as his special prey persons plucking pieces of grass to put between their teeth. Netshiendeulu and Matidza of Luonde have leopards to protect them, which are connected with their ancestors and are propitiated at their lineage festivities; these two headmen belong to the VhaKwebo sib whose totem animals are the pig and the pigeon. The forest of Thathe is inhabited by a lion, which is the reincarnation of the head of the lineage of Netshitongani of the

[1] Wessman, R., *The Bawenda of the Spelonken*, London, 1908, p. 82.

240 RELIGION

MaKhwinde sib. Nephindula believes that his ancestor spirits turn into snakes. Before green vegetables are eaten, a small portion must be cooked and offered to the snakes, who, by eating the offering, signify their acceptance of it. In times of trouble a little porridge may be put outside the door of the hut to appease the snake ancestors. Just before any member of the family dies a snake appears and points to the dying person. No member of this lineage ever kills a snake.

These various animal spirits are in many respects provincial or local gods, as all the people living in their vicinity respect and fear them and often obey the tabus with which they are associated, although they are in no way personally connected with them. It is, however, only the lineage with whom the spirits are directly connected who actually propitiate them. Probably these legends all originated accidentally, in a similar way to that described in the legend of the leopard of Maugani, but except in that case I was unable to obtain the history origins. The people specially associated with such animal spirits are loosely referred to by their neighbours as 'the people of the lion' or the 'people of the snake', and in the course of time the sacred animal is confused with their totem animal, resulting in the formation of new totems, as has already been related in the history of the sacred baboon of Lwamondo Kop in the chapter on social groupings.

Ancestor Cult.

Raluvhimba and these other vague deities and spirits play a secondary rôle in the religious life of the BaVenda. The direct relationship with their dead ancestors is a much more personal factor in their lives and is the basis of their religious ideas. Their attitude is quite rational; to them death is a transition between life on this earth and life in the spirit world, where the dead continue the lives begun on earth, still exerting a powerful influence on their living relatives. The ancestor spirits have themselves experienced ordinary mortal life and so understand the daily trials and difficulties which beset all humanity and their own descendants in particular. The ancestor spirits, *medzimu* (sing. *mudzimu*), have many idiosyncracies, and if they think that they have been slighted by their descendants take their revenge by bringing misfortune to them; they are therefore feared rather than loved. There seems to be a fairly fundamental conception among the BaVenda as to the inherent good of most worldly things, all trouble being associated with the evils of witchcraft or the jealousy and spitefulness of their ancestors. The ancestor spirits which can affect the lives of an

RELIGION 241

individual are divided into two groups, those of the father's lineage and those of the mother's group (mother's brother, mother's mother, mother's mother's brother and sister, and so on). The spirits of the mother's father and his ancestors and the father's mother and her ancestors are unimportant. The relationship between an individual and his ancestors is by its very nature essentially a family affair, and the spirits are only concerned with the members of their own families. But in the event of any national thanksgiving or calamity the chief's ancestors, although actually propitiated by the chief's lineage alone, are felt to be associated with all the people.

In the event of trouble, when a man may wish to make contact between the living and the dead, he first tries to discover to which group of ancestors the angry spirit belongs. The BaVenda are not very curious about the spirit world. Some think that the spirits live a very similar life to that lived on earth, marrying, keeping cattle, and growing mealies in a prosperous and untroubled world; others think that there is no spirit world but that each individual spirit lurks around its grave or former home waiting for an opportunity to bring trouble to its descendants. They think the soul is a combination of the breath and the shadow, as these are both a part of every living creature and disappear after death. It is curious how fixed the idea is among them that a corpse throws no shadow, but the illusion may be explained by the fact that the dead are always buried between sunset and sunrise. The shadow is thought to be an integral part of a living person, who may be dragged into a river by his shadow if he is unwise enough to let it fall in and be seen by a greedy crocodile.

This soul then leaves the body at death and wanders about looking for some new place in which to rest; it may stay in the grave with the body for some time, but sooner or later it will start its wanderings, and it is while the disembodied spirit is prowling around without a home or resting-place that it becomes filled with bitterness towards its earthly descendants. These spirits may reveal themselves to their descendants in dreams, and a person thus visited consults a diviner; he is generally advised to propitiate the ancestor spirit without delay. Contact with white civilization and Christianity has affected the Venda idea of life and death, making it difficult to recapture their original conceptions.

There is one interesting rite in connexion with the spirit world that is still occasionally performed. There is a Tshivenda expression—'*u lubumbukavha?*'—which has the same meaning as the English 'Are you

R

242 RELIGION

daft ?' or 'Are you all there ?'. This word, *lubumbukavha* (simpleton), is also used to describe any young man above the age of puberty who dies before he has been given a wife; he is a poor foolish fellow, having left the world ignorant of the all-important subject of sex and parent-hood, and dying before he has fulfilled the purpose for which he was born. If he is not pacified he may become a source of endless trouble to his lineage. So he is given an old used hoe handle, *gulelwa*, with a cotton string tied near the hole, to symbolize a wife, the string being her waistband and the hole the female genitalia. A girl, never the deceased man's sister, fixes this symbol at a fork in the path in a well-cleared open space where the young man's spirit can clearly see it, with the handle pointing towards him as he approaches his old village (Plate XXXVII). The handle is fixed with four pegs made of the *tshiralala* tree (from *u ralala*, to wander about) or of the *tshilivhalo* (from *u livhala*, to forget). Two are knocked into the ground on each side of the head and tied to it with a string made of wild cotton which has been treated with a mixture made from the roots of the *vhulivhadza* (from *u livhadza*, to make forget) and the *mpeta* (to dissolve or tie up), with powder from the hedgehog quill, *thoni* (bashfulness). These prepara-tions, as can be seen by their names, are all used to confuse the young man's spirit so that it will forget its anger, become bashful and ashamed, and run away before reaching the village. When the handle is properly fixed a woman of the dead man's lineage, generally the *makhadzi*, pours beer into the hole in the hoe, saying: 'To-day we have found you a wife; the wife is here. Do not worry us any more. If you are annoyed with us, come here.' This ends the ceremony, and the spirit of the young man is supposed to be satisfied for ever. A similar rite is, very rarely, performed after the death of a girl dying unmarried, having reached the age of puberty. Such a girl is called *luphofu*, the blind one, as she has died without any knowledge of sexual life. A peg is driven through the hole in the hoe handle that is provided for the comfort of her spirit to symbolize the male organ. The two rites are identical in all else. A hoe handle and two broken pots are placed on the grave of a married man who dies before any of his wives; when a wife has died first he has no need of this equipment as she will be waiting to work for him in the spirit world as she did on earth.

Propitiation of Spirits.

The Sacred Cattle. Before describing the method of communication with, and propitiation of, the ancestor spirits it is necessary that the

PLATE XXXVII

THE RITE OF THE HOE-HANDLE

RANWASHA'S SACRED STONES

PLATE XXXVIII

TSHIKOBAKOBA'S SACRED STONES

AN OFFERING TO THE SPIRITS. THE SACRED SPEARS
AND AXE ON THE STONES

RELIGION 243

ritual objects associated with them should be understood. The spirits are represented collectively either by cattle or river pebbles or goats, and individually by spears or small iron or copper rings.

Many important lineages possess a sacred black bull which is called *makhulu* (grandfather) and is regarded as the embodiment of all the ancestral spirits. Amongst all the chiefs a cow is associated with the sacred bull, in the characteristic Bantu belief that no male is complete without a mate. This cow is not considered to represent the mother's family. The bull is often called by the name of the grandfather of the chief who instals it, or in some cases by the dynastic title of the family whose ancestors it embodies. The sacred bull of Tshivhase is called *Tshivhase*, that of Rambuda is called *Popi*, (his grandfather's name); Mbulahene Mphephu's is called *Ramapulana*, and was installed by the chief Mphephu. These animals, in spite of their very sacred character, enjoy few privileges above the other cattle at the chief's kraal. Their main importance is in connexion with the harvest festival, when thanks are offered to the ancestor spirits collectively. When the bull becomes very old he is killed and a new and younger beast, usually a calf of the sacred cow, is put up in his place. At this ceremony all the lineage assemble, and the head of the family exhorts the bull, saying, 'Oh, *makhulu*, you are now too old and we must kill you, because of your age, but we replace you by a younger animal. Do not take offence at our action but continue to be good to your people'. The bull is then killed and eaten. If the sacred bull is found dead it is feared that the ancestor spirits are seriously angry and a diviner is hastily consulted. He generally finds that headmen of the lineage are quarrelling, or that some important rite in connexion with the ancestors has not been performed; the lineage is hastily summoned, and a new animal put up and the ancestors implored to enter it and to cease being angry with their children. A similar bull cult is found among the Karanga groups in Southern Rhodesia and among the BaLemba, but it is unusual amongst the Southern Bantu.

The Sacred Stones. Every lineage does not own a sacred bull. Most of the poorer lineages have sacred stones instead (Plates XXXVII, XXXVIII). The stones are fairly large, cylindrical, highly polished pebbles; they must be taken from a river-bed and other stones of the same size put in their place in the river. One stone represents the bull and is called *mboho*, and the other, which is rather larger, the cow, *kholomo* (among the BaVenda the female is generally made larger than the male when the sexes are symbolically represented). These stones are embedded side by side near the hut of the headman of the lineage; the ground is always kept carefully swept and smeared for three or four feet around them. A small bulbous plant with a yellow flower, *luhome*, is always planted close to the stones; this plant is very hardy, and grows everywhere and under almost any conditions. The true significance of the plant is doubtful; several informants told me that it represented the shade for the cattle. The male stone, *mboho*, is often addressed as *makhulu* (grandfather) like the black bull, and in many cases the stones

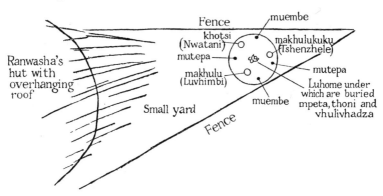

seem to fulfil exactly the same functions as the sacred animals. Ranwasha, a headman living at Luvhimbi, belonging to the Mbedzi sib, possesses three sacred stones, embedded in a circular mud platform 3 inches high and 18 inches in diameter, built around the *luhome*. Four small sticks, two of the *mutepa* tree (from *u tepa*, to bend), and two of the *muembe* tree, are planted near the circumference of the platform, at four points opposite to each other. Powder from the *vhulivhadza*, *mpeta*, and *thoni*, which has been described fully in connexion with the rite of the hoe handle, is buried under the *luhome*. Here the stones represent the father, grandfather, and great grandfather of Ranwasha, who addresses them by name as Nwatani, Luvhimbi, and Tshenzhele, respectively. The *luhome* seems to be a symbol of long life, and the sticks and powder are magic charms to guard and satisfy the ancestors. The Mbedzi sib does not use the stones as a substitute for sacred cattle; apparently they have always worshipped their ancestors in this form.

Possibly at one time the cattle and stone cults were entirely separate and practised by different tribes. As the different Venda elements began to coalesce, members of the bull cult, who found it economically

RELIGION 245

difficult always to keep sacred cattle, copied the stone worshippers and substituted stones for cattle; they continued their own form of worship, endowing the stones with all the properties formerly possessed by their sacred cattle. Confusions and inconsistencies resulted, so that to-day from one to three stones may be set up, all explained by their several worshippers in different ways. Three stones like those of Ranwasha were at one time put up by one of the Karanga groups, and are described by Hall and Neale,[1] from information given by the Rev. G. Cullen H. Reed of the London Missionary Society's station at Bulalima in Matabeleland. 'In every family residence there is a place under a raised platform of poles where three stones are set in a triangle. These are dedicated to the ancestors of the residents. Here, at times of sickness or at the sowing or harvesting of corn, the family gather. A hoe, an axe—and, if the head of the family be a smith, a hammer also—are placed by the stones.' Different forms of association between ancestral spirits and stones are found among tribes along the East Coast of Africa. A comparative study of these stone cults would be of considerable interest.

The Sacred Goat. The spirits of the mothers play a separate and peculiar rôle in the ancestor cult of the BaVenda. As the ancestors of the father's lineage are represented by the sacred cattle, or stones, so those of the mother's mother and her mother and her mother's mother are independently represented by a black female goat. This goat is called *makhulu*, and is first and foremost the mother's mother, but is also the embodiment of all the mother's ancestors in the female line, (i.e. a woman and all her brothers and sisters and their descendants through the female line) giving a type of matrilineal ancestor worship exactly parallel to the patrilineal type. This goat, being essentially feminine, can only be installed and held by children of either sex in the female line, although it is generally held by a woman. The diviner indicates which grandchild, within the group, is to care for the goat; this person is then considered to be specially associated with the mother's ancestors and performs all religious ceremonies concerning these matrilineal spirits. At the time of the harvest festival all the group assembles at the kraal where the goat lives, and a ceremony is performed there similar to that enacted with the bull of the father's lineage. The goat, when it becomes very old, may be killed and a new one installed with exactly the same procedure as is followed

[1] Hall and Neale, R. N. and W. G., *The Ancient Ruins of Rhodesia*, London, 1904, p. 138.

246 RELIGION

in installing a new bull, all the members of the mother's group attending the ceremony. The young goat, whenever possible, is a kid of the old one. When the guardian of the sacred goat dies the animal remains in the custody of her eldest daughter, who performs the necessary propitiatory rites, using the 'mouth' of her mother (in using the 'mouth' of another, the substitute will inform the spirit that she is the person who should be performing the ceremony and calls herself by the name of the orthodox officiant). The ancestor spirits of the mother's group are much more personally and intimately connected with their descendants than those of the father's lineage. They cause far more trouble and are consequently more feared and respected than those of the father. The explanation for this intimacy appears to be the closer emotional and physiological tie between the mother and her children than that existing between the father and his children. The mother, who seldom has more than three or four children, is far less likely to forget them than is the father, who probably has several wives and many children. On the few occasions when single individuals voluntarily approach their ancestors in the event of impending danger, or at the commencement of a hazardous journey, it is always the mother's spirits who are invoked and who are expected to protect their descendants. In connexion with these matrilineal spirits possible reasons for the intimate connexion between a man and his uterine nephew may be discerned, at any rate in affairs connected with religion. They are both associated with the same group of spirits, and either *malume* or *muduhulu* may be the guardian of the sacred goat, necessitating constant intercourse at religious celebrations, or in cases of illness divined to be caused by any of the matrilineal ancestors.

Individual Spirits.

Spears. After death each male member of the lineage, as well as being absorbed into the sacred bull, is represented individually by a spear. It is the duty of the dead man's son, born of his great wife, to provide this spear; it is rarely made immediately after his father's death, but as soon as any illness or disaster overtakes a member of his family, the diviner is almost sure to discover that the dead man's spirit is troubled because his spear has not been put up. The diviner says to the neglectful son, '*Vhusani pfumo la khotsi*' (Awake the spear of your father). The son then hastens to the nearest smith and has a spear made, to-day only a very crude and miniature replica of the

PLATE XXXIX

WOMAN WEARING *MALEMBE* AND SMALL WOODEN CHARM

RELIGION

proper spear. He then takes it to the head of the lineage who summons all the lineage to attend the consecratory ceremony. Beer is prepared, and all the family spears, which are inherited by the head of the lineage, are brought out, and the new one laid down beside them. The officiant holding the calabash of beer goes up to where the oldest spear is lying and says: 'Here is your grandchild; we have given him back to you. Do not worry us.' Then all the ancestors represented by the spears are called upon in order of seniority, and finally the new spear is addressed: 'Here are all your relatives; go to them and leave us in peace, and do not worry us any more.' The beer is then poured over each of the spears in turn. The new spear is put away with all the others and the troublesome spirit pacified. It is thought that the father's spirit will only on rare occasions again worry his descendants.

Each male member of the lineage, except those who die unmarried, whose spirits are pacified by the rite of the hoe handle, has a right to be represented in this way by a spear after his death.

Iron or Copper Rings (malembe) and the *ludo*. Every woman, after her death, may have a small iron ring, made from an old Venda hoe, dedicated to her for the habitation of her spirit, in exactly the same way that every man may have a spear. These iron rings are called *malembe* (hoes) and are made whenever possible from the actual hoe used by the deceased, although only the old Venda-made hoes may be used. There are three types of *malembe*. The first is a plain iron ring about half an inch in diameter and one-third of an inch wide, and is called *tululu*, and represents the generation of the mother; the second which represents the generation of the grandparent, is a similar iron ring with one lip protruding and is called *dzembe* (hoe); the third type has two tangs and is called *lumano* (from *u lumana*—to bite each other), and represents the great grandmother generation. Unless one type of ring is specially designated, all are vaguely and interchangeably described as *malembe*. (Plate XXXIX)

When an illness or misfortune is divined to have been caused by a female ancestor spirit who is worrying because she desires her *dzembe* to be put up, the diviner orders that it shall be made at once, the type depending upon the generation of the deceased. If it is a child who is ill the father immediately reports the diviner's finding to the *malume*; the diviner is then again consulted and decrees who must visit the smith about the making of the required *dzembe*. When it is made it must be put outside the kraal for a night to become cool;

248 RELIGION

it is often put in a calabash of water, and sometimes it is laid on the ash-heap outside the kraal. On the following day all the relatives of the mother's group meet at the kraal of the guardian of the sacred goat to consecrate this new *dzembe*. The goat and all the other *malembe* of the group are brought forward and the new *dzembe* put down beside them. The guardian of the goat then pours a little beer over the new *dzembe* and says: 'Here you are, we give you your *dzembe*. Go in peace now and do not worry your children'. The diviner then again consults his dice, as to which member of the group is to wear the new *dzembe* and who is to tie it on. Very often all the *malembe* of a group are worn by the same person. They are always worn tied round the neck by a piece of string made from wild cotton. If the female ancestor then continues to worry any of her descendants the individual concerned may go to the wearer of the *dzembe* and ask her to invoke the spirit.

The BaVenda who were associated with the Messina area and possess copper of native manufacture usually have their *malembe* made of the old copper.

The *ludo* of the old women is another object of a sacred character. It is a small replica of a hoe fastened into the side of a long stick, at the extremity, in the same way that the ordinary one is hafted to its handle; it may be simply a long, straight iron rod. It is only seen being carried by very old women, and is handed down from mother to daughter, the particular daughter to inherit it being decided by consulting the diviner. If the heiress to the *ludo* is young it is put away in her hut and only brought out with the goat and the *malembe* on ceremonial occasions in connexion with the matrilineal group. It is the particular privilege of very old women, possessing the *ludo* of their ancestors, to use it as a walking stick.

Other Sacred Objects. All old objects belonging to the ancestors are regarded by their descendants with a certain feeling of reverence and awe, particularly the old Venda artefacts which, since the European occupation, are no longer made. In this category are to be found axes, hoes, bows and arrows, *masila* cloth, old horns, copper ingots, iron hammers, pinchers, &c., beads, and indeed anything that was made, used, or worn by their forefathers. There is something extremely pathetic in this reverence for these relics of their ancients, which are all considered to possess some of the spirit and personality of their original owners. They are guarded jealously, and are seldom sold or bartered, even for sums of money several times greater than

RELIGION

the intrinsic value. A MuVenda, on being asked to sell a small dirty valueless bit of *masila* cloth, which lies useless and apparently neglected in his hut, is indignant at the very suggestion that he should part with this last relic of the genius of his ancestors. The loss of an old axe or bow and arrow is a crime, which will undoubtedly bring retribution upon the offender; his outraged ancestor will visit him with some illness or other trouble. The almost invariable response to a request for any old object of Venda workmanship is, 'I cannot sell it, for it is my *tshitungula*'. This word, *tshitungula* (pl. *zwitungula*), is used to describe the sacred bull, stones, goat, spears, *ludo, malembe*, and other indiscriminate heirlooms. It is probably derived from *u tungula* (to throw the bones), suggesting that the heirlooms are mediums through which the living are able to come in contact with their dead. It seems to me that the sacred objects, at any rate the bull, stones, goat, spear, *ludo*, and *malembe* are, more than mediums; the majority of the BaVenda definitely assert that the spirits actually take up their abode in these objects and become identified with them. When these *zwitungula* are used in religious rites they are always addressed in a personal manner as though they were actually the home of the person whom they represent. I asked one woman the meaning of a small charm that she was wearing next to a *dzembe*, and she explained that her *makhulu* had a troublesome habit of leaving its proper home in the *dzembe* and wandering about causing disaster; the diviner, to prevent this, gave her the charm, which contained powder that would keep the errant spirit in its place.

On rare occasions when a particular spirit cannot be pacified it may be irrevocably destroyed by the destruction of the spear or *dzembe* representing it, in a manner to be described later; this seems indisputable evidence that spirits are believed to inhabit the *zwitungula*.

Propitiation of Ancestor Spirits. In religious affairs the medicine-man plays an indispensable part; it is he who, through the power of his magical dice, is able to discover the cause of every trouble. He may divine the source of the trouble to be a spirit, and, if so, by another throw of the dice, he is able to identify the actual spirit concerned; by means of a further throw he divines by what means the angry spirit may be pacified, and informs his client in what he has offended and the best means of propitiation.

It is then the duty of the individual to go through the necessary channels by which the particular ancestor may be reached, unless the diviner should specify some special and unusual procedure. The sister

250   RELIGION

of the head of the lineage, who is so important in its social behaviour, plays an equally important part in its religious affairs. She is the priestess of her lineage, and except on rare occasions paternal ancestor spirits may only be approached through her. Any person requiring her ministrations, in order to commune with an ancestor, must inform the head of the lineage, who summons his sister. If it is quite impossible for her to appear, her brother, the *ndumi*, may act in her place; failing him, the headman may himself approach the spirits, but in either of these two contingencies the substitute must use the name of his sister, the true priestess. On the death of the priestess her daughter or son may act in her place, but always using the 'mouth' of their mother. If she has no child, or if the child also dies, another sister of the headman of the lineage must be appointed by the diviner, so that the office may never go outside the lineage.

The ritual at its simplest, called *u phasa madi* (to spit out water) is as follows: The officiant takes a mouthful of water from a wooden platter and forcefully ejects it, spraying the water over as large an area as possible; she calls the offending spirit by name, followed by the names of all the ancestors as far back as can be remembered, the *phasa madi* being repeated at intervals during the monologue. The wooden platter is then turned upside down on the spot where the water fell, in order to shut in the spirit. Sometimes a pinch of snuff is also put on the ground under the platter as an offering to the spirit. This is the regular method of intercession. A man, slightly worried over a minor trouble, may *phasa madi* himself, using the 'mouth' of the proper officiant, hoping that this will be sufficient to soothe the angry spirit and that he will be saved the trouble of seeking help through the proper channels. If his act has no effect he will at once hasten to the proper quarter, fearing that he may have caused further offence by his arbitrary action. Sometimes in cases of acute disease it may be impossible to communicate with the officiant quickly enough to save life or to get the desired response; in such cases the spirits will probably recognize the urgency of the appeal and will listen to the invocation, provided that it is always made through the 'mouth' of the proper officiant. The only explanation forthcoming for the use of water in this religious act is that water 'cools the spirit'; the spraying of the water is explained in the same way. This idea of 'cooling the spirits' is also evident in the choice of the sacred stones, which must come from the river, so that all the heat will have gone from them. The *malembe* must also be cooled before they are dedicated to the

RELIGION

spirits. If, as is most often the case, it is a spirit of the matrilineal group that is causing the trouble, the intercessor goes to his *malume* as head of the mother's group and he refers him to the guardian of the sacred goat of the matrilineal spirits; in minor difficulties the wearer of the *dzembe*, representing the offending spirit, may perform the propitiatory act, while in cases of dire distress the goat and all the *malembe* are brought together and the act is performed over them all.

The following is a typical example of this rite, when the spirit of the dead mother is being propitiated on behalf of a sick grandchild. The officiant, the child's mother's sister, takes up the platter of water, fills her mouth, and ejects the water, saying, 'Oh, you, my mother, Tshimondima'; and with another ejection of water 'you, my mother's sister, Naridzina, and you my grandmother, Mavhungu'; after another ejection, 'and you, my great grandmother, and even all you unknown ones, hear me when I speak to you. Come all of you and help my child, so that she may be well like other children. Rest in peace! Here is a little snuff that I give you. Now you will be content. Rest well to-night'. She then puts down the snuff and covers it with the platter and the ceremony is over.

Unusual Form of Propitiation. An offended ancestor is not always satisfied with the usual form of propitiation. If the *phasa madi* ceremony has not had the desired result it may be necessary to sacrifice a goat at the grave of the troublesome ancestor. The relatives of the angry spirit take a black goat to the graveside; the diviner accompanies the party and orders one of the relatives to hold the goat by one leg until it urinates. The animal may not be killed until it has urinated, as this act is considered to be a sign from the spirit that it is willing to accept the sacrifice. The party may have to wait a considerable time, but immediately urination has taken place the goat is killed by forcing its mouth and nostrils into the wooden milk jug filled with water, in this way suffocating it. The remainder of the sacrifice is described in detail by Junod [1] who says:

'It is then skinned and cut open. The large intestine is extracted from the body, a part of it is cut and stitched at one end of its extremities so as to form a kind of pouch. From each limb a bit of meat is taken, and quite a provision of seeds of mufoho corn, millet, mealies is brought on the spot, together with drugs. All these kinds of food are introduced into the pouch, this filling up being accompanied by prayer to the ancestor spirit. And whilst the father

[1] Junod, H. A., 'The Religion of the BaVenda', *South African Journal of Science*, vol. xvii, p. 215.

252 RELIGION

proceeds with it, he puts seeds in the goat's intestine with one hand, and, with the other, he takes other seeds and places them apart. These he will keep carefully, to sow them later on; and he goes on praying: "Eat plenty and be satiated," does he tell the ancestor "and leave us some for our use." This part of the goat's intestine has become a person. It is henceforth identified with the deceased grandfather. Thus the god has been fed, duly stuffed. The pouch is then stitched at the other extremity. But now the ancestor must be clothed also! A strap is cut out of the goat's skin, and the sacrificer winds it all round the pouch. Carrying the offering with him he now goes to the grave of the grandfather, digs a little and lays the pouch in the earth parallel to the body which is beneath, and he prays again: "We worship you, grand-father! And we have clothed you. This is your food. Eat and be full and be contented. And leave us food, plenty of food, that we also may be contented and bless the sick child." This is the rite of the "goat with clothes". Really a perfect illustration of Bantu ancestor worship, where sympathetic magic plays an important part.'

To Kill an Ancestor Spirit. Sometimes after a death the diviner, on being consulted, says that it has been caused by a spirit and not by a living person; this spirit must be a *muloi*. Again, it may happen that a child is very ill and the diviner finds the trouble to be the work of a particular spirit; the *phasa madi* ceremony is done, followed by the rite of the 'goat with clothes', but still the sick child becomes worse instead of better. The diviner persists in his diagnosis of the particular spirit as the cause; however, in spite of performing every possible rite with particular care and conscientiousness, the patient dies. The diviner then declares the spirit to be a *muloi*. A *muloi*, whether a spirit or a human being, is a danger to society and must be removed. The spear or *dzembe* of the evil spirit is tied around the neck of a black goat and a large stone attached to it; the goat is then thrown into a deep pool, with the spirit, ridding the descendants of the evil ancestor for ever.

Sowing and Harvest Rites.

Before sowing and reaping the ancestor spirits are invoked and propitiated. These rites, the one of supplication and the other of thanksgiving, are the two main occasions on which the ancestor spirits are approached voluntarily, and as the crops are concerned with the country as a whole, as well as with each separate lineage, the chief's ceremonies are national in character.

The Sowing Rite, u sonda (to sow). In October or November, when it is time to commence ploughing, the headman of each lineage invites

RELIGION 253

the members of his lineage, and the people living in his district, to come to prepare the garden that he uses for the cultivation of *mufhoho* (eleusine indica), the indigenous Venda grain. Any one who cannot attend this ceremony in person will not fail to send a handful of seed to be mixed with the other to be sown for the offering. The women of the lineage cook a pot of seeds, containing *mufhoho*, monkey-nuts, beans, kaffir-corn, and others, and take it down to the *mufhoho* land which has been tilled and prepared for planting. All the lineage and the uterine nephews and nieces having assembled, the pot of grain is symbolically cooked over three cooking stones on a small grass fire. A sacred axe and the *ludo*, to represent the women's spirits, are then brought and placed near the pot, and a little of the mixture from the pot is taken up in a roughly-made spoon and dropped on to these sacred objects. The *makhadzi* then takes up a wooden platter of water and filling her mouth from it performs the *phasa madi* act, saying; 'Here is food for you, all our spirits; we give you of every kind of grain, which you may eat. Bring to us also crops in plenty and prosperity in the coming season'. Some of what is left is served on a platter for the men while the women of the family finish what remains in the pot. The ceremony is concluded in the usual way by a general feast and beer-drink in which all the helpers as well as the lineage participate.

The whole community is summoned to the chief's village for the tilling of the sacred *mufhoho* field. Women prepare *mufhoho* beer and little girls cook a pot of corn, peas, beans, nuts, &c.; on their way to collect the wood and water for the preparation of this concoction the girls arm themselves with little switches and beat every one whom they meet on the road, and any one seeing them come up will cover his face with his hand. In all other details the *u sonda* at the chief's village is similar to that of the ordinary people.

The Harvest Thanksgiving, u lugisa zwitungula (to put right the sacred objects). The harvest thanksgiving of the BaVenda differs considerably from that of many other Bantu peoples. To the Ba-Ila of Northern Rhodesia the harvest is an individual affair, each person placing a mealie cob in the rafter of his house as an offering to the spirits. Amongst the Zulus it was formerly a public festival in which the warriors played an important part and the animals sacrificed as an offering to the spirits were eaten by the participants. The Akamba living in the highlands of Kenya have an elaborate sacrificial feast, in which a goat and corn are placed on the ground at sacred places and

RELIGION

offered to the spirits; certain parts of the goat are eaten by different people according to their social standing. To the BaVenda *u lugisa zwitungula*, or *u tevula* (to pour out), as it is often called, is essentially an affair of the lineage, and its rites express the unity of this important social grouping; it is of special interest in that the offering is held to be eaten by the spirits themselves. The *tevula* of the chief and his lineage must always be performed before the ceremonies of the head-man and the commoners; it is an occasion of national thanksgiving and festivity, and after the completion of the religious ceremonies, which take place in the yard of the chief's private hut and are confined to members of his lineage, all the people from far and near may come to the chief's village and rejoice with him.

I propose therefore to describe the *tevula* as it is performed at the chief's village. It must be remembered, however, that the ritual procedure is, even there, a purely family affair, which is repeated after the chief's thanksgiving by every lineage in the country. Some time before the crops are ready, a species of sugar cane, *impye*, ripens, and the first ripe pieces are given as food to the sacred animals before the cane may be touched by anybody for his own use; when the *impye* is offered to the animals they are invoked as *vhamakhulu* (grand-parents) and exhorted to enjoy these first fruits and leave some for their people. The fact that this *impye* is used ceremonially in this way suggests that it is one of the original foods of the BaVenda. There is no fixed time for the *tevula* festival, but when the *mufhoho* is ripe, some time in May or June, the chief announces the date of the ceremony. The beer for the occasion is prepared from the *mufhoho*. When the *mufhoho* cannot be obtained kaffir-corn, *makaha*, may be substituted, and sometimes these two cereals are mixed. Formerly a MuVenda who dared to reap his *mufhoho* before the *tevula* ceremony had taken place was put to death. The women who prepare the beer for the ceremony must always be naked; no man may approach the vicinity of the brewers, and any man attempting to do so is driven off and may be severely beaten—the women are preparing the beer for the gods and will allow no infringement of this rule. When all the grain is ripe messengers are sent out from the chief's kraal to visit every district and tell the representative petty chiefs that all the young men are wanted at the chief's kraal to dance the *tshikona* for the *tevula*. At sunset the men come in from all sides, blowing horns, or to-day more often whistles that they have brought back with them from the towns, to herald their approach. On their arrival

RELIGION

the *tshikona* starts and continues until midnight, when all the dancers retire to the *thondo* to sleep. All work is suspended throughout the country. Early next morning all the royal spears and sacred objects belonging to the chief's lineage are brought together and placed inside the yard of the chief's hut beside the sacred stones. The members of the chief's lineage assemble in the yard, the older people taking the important places while the children sit in the background; the uterine nephews and nieces may, and generally do, attend this ceremony.

The priestess, *tshife*, who officiates at this service, is generally the *makhadzi*, but the office depends upon the will of the ancestor spirits divulged by the diviner; from time to time, when a member of the lineage is visited by misfortune, it may be divined that the *makhadzi* is not finding favour with the spirits and that her position would be better filled by another member of the lineage, or even by the uterine nephew, who is permitted sometimes to invoke the spirits of his mother's lineage. The sacred bull and cow are now brought into the yard and the priestess calls upon all the dead by name as far back as she can remember, at the same time dipping a tufted bundle of leaves of the *musese* tree into the beer and sprinkling it on the cow and the bull. She says: '*Ndi ni pha mwaha muswa uri ni le ni takale, ni le salaho ndi zwanga na zwiduhulu zwanu na zwone zwi le zwi takalevho*' (I offer you the first grains of the new year that you may eat and be happy; eat all of you; I deprive none amongst you. What remains in the ground belongs to me and your little ones. Let them eat and be happy). '*Ndi nea nothe na lwe tshimudi*' (I give to all of you and even the unknown one). Sometimes the beer is placed on a wooden platter and put on the ground for the animals to drink instead of being sprinkled over their heads, or the party may go with the beer to the cattle kraal and there invoke the animals instead of bringing them into the chief's yard, returning to the yard to continue the ceremony. The invocation is then repeated over the sacred stones and other objects, the exhortation being repeated by the priestess while all the members of the lineage gather round her, sharing earnestly and attentively in the ceremony. The remaining beer is then ceremonially drunk by all the members of the group in turn, the priestess taking the first sip and passing it to her brothers and sisters, and right round the group, until all have tasted it. One of the women then gives a cry of joy, which is echoed by all the women in a loud shout of exultation, while a man sounds the *phala-fhala*. As soon as the party in the *khoro* hear the *phala-fhala* and the cry of the women, a man gives a loud

256 RELIGION

shout as a signal to the flautists, the *tshikona* is played vigorously, and the people dance to encourage (*kunguwedza*) joy. The ancestor spirits have accepted the chief's offerings and every one is joyful. People then crowd into the capital from all parts to dance and sing and drink beer and congratulate the chief. The whole day is one of joy and thankfulness, and consequently of music, dancing, song, and feasting. At sunset the people disperse, each family to its own home, there to prepare for its own lineage thanksgiving.

The rites of the common people, whilst being of the same character, are performed on a much smaller scale. Whenever possible the different members of the lineage assemble at the kraal of their headman, bringing with them any spears or other sacred objects that they may possess. These are placed beside the stones and the same words are used in invoking the ancestors as those used at the chief's kraal. Sometimes when the ancestors are represented by stones the officiant first sips the beer and then pours it over the stones and *zwitungula* as she invokes the spirits; all the lineage and the father's sisters' children kneel down on the ground and lick it up as it flows away. This is almost identical with the procedure of the BaKaranga in their propitiatory ceremony by the sacred stones, described by the Rev. G. Cullen H. Reed, when the spears and other sacred objects are placed on the stones. To quote again from Hall and Neale:[1]

'A pot of beer is brought, and the head of the family, taking some of this in a calabash, and rising, recites words to the effect that they know not wherefore the sickness comes, but fear the spirits are hungry, and he says, "Here, father, is thy food". He then pours the beer on the ground by the stones. The little children on hands and knees suck it up as it flows. This is repeated as often as may be requisite to appease the spirits, said by the casting of bones or dice to be offended. Then all rise and stand round these stones with hands upraised, each hand full of corn. The father then recites a prayer for the cure of the diseased member of the family, or for the prosperity of the crops, as the case may be, and all simultaneously cast the corn down on the stones, where it is left for the birds.'

To-day, when different members of a lineage are scattered, it often happens that the thanksgiving is of a very humble nature, often only a man and his own immediate family participating, sometimes without stones, spears, or sacred objects. Nevertheless, wherever a man may

[1] Hall and Neale, R. N. and W. G., *The Ancient Ruins of Rhodesia*, London, 1904, p. 138.

RELIGION
257

be, or however humble his position, the spirits are never forgotten, and except in cases where the *tevula* is omitted for some specific reason the ancestors are given beer and invoked even if the offering is only poured on to the ground.

After the *tevula* ceremony the graves of the ancestors are visited by some male members of the lineage. These men clear up the weeds and bush and tidy up the graves, and then pour beer over them, thanking the ancestors for all their help and asking that it may be continued in the coming year. Sacred mountains and groves are visited at this time and libations offered to the spirits inhabiting them. In the Tshivhase royal family the beer is conveyed to Gubukubu at the Phiphidi Falls and the offering is made in a sacred grove not far from the top of the falls, where some of the chief's ancestors were buried.

Netshiavho, living near Lake Fundudzi, takes beer down to the lake and there offers it to his ancestors. At the edge of the lake a member of the lineage is rolled in a blanket and tied up tightly with ropes, leaving a long end of rope which is held by the party on the shore. The suppliant walks out into the lake, carrying a calabash of beer; when he has gone some distance he pours out the beer as an offering to his ancestors, invoking them in the usual way. If the spirits accept his offering the beer disappears immediately under the lake, but if they are angry with their living descendants they may refuse it, in which case the beer floats on top of the water and the angry spirits make an effort to pull the suppliant underneath; to prevent this the people at the water's edge quickly pull him to the shore by the rope.

The people who believe that the petty chief of the lineage, or other dead ancestors, are transmogrified into animals, make special offerings to these animal ancestors. NeMaungani pours beer on to a certain rock on his mountain as a libation to his leopard ancestor, who, he believes, comes and drinks it. Netshiendeulu puts different grains on a rock near his home and on the following day the spoor of the leopard is seen amongst the seeds, showing that he has accepted the offering of his people. Those who believe that their ancestors turn into snakes put beer out into the bush for them to drink. At Lwamondo beer is taken up the mountain slopes and poured out for the baboon spirits who live on the kop.

Some of the poorer people think that beer is too precious to be given in this way to their spirits. I heard that sometimes these people tried to deceive their gods by pouring on their graves water instead of

S

RELIGION

beer, the water being mixed with some colour which makes it appear similar to beer.

The *tevula* is held annually unless there have been very bad crops or a member of the lineage has died during the year, when it may be postponed until the following year. Sometimes the *makhadzi*, or other person appointed to officiate at the ceremony, has quarrelled with the head of the lineage and they refuse to meet each other; it may then happen that several years elapse before it is possible to hold the harvest festival.

To a MuVenda the *tevula* ceremonies are the most important events of the year. A man attends that of his own lineage and that of his mother's; in the latter case, if he has married his *malume's* daughter, he is accompanied by his wife. He may also join in the festivities at the chief's village and, by invitation, at the homes of his various wives. In this way he is brought into contact with a considerable number of people, and has an opportunity of meeting a great many friends and relatives whom in the everyday run of life he would never see at all; he is also brought into close contact with his ancestors. On these occasions each individual finds everything that to him makes life worth living—social intercourse and good cheer, abundance of food and beer, music and dancing. It is at these functions that the social, economic, and religious aspects of Venda life are blended into a harmonious whole.

The BaNgona, u lumisa muroho (to bite the green foods). The BaNgona had a rather different ceremony, which took place when the green foods, such as sugar cane, green mealies, pumpkins, &c., were ready to be eaten, and which is still performed in a few places under the auspices of a MuNgona.

Little girls dressed in green leaves pick samples of all the green foods growing in the lands and take them to the priest, *tshife*, who is waiting with all the other children of the district by a rock that is used as an altar stone; taking some of the green stuff in both hands, he bites it and puts it in a hole in the rock, invoking the spirits of the reigning chiefs and those of his own almost extinct tribe. Netshitumbe, the BaNgona priest of petty chief Bohwane at Tshaula, described this ceremony to me. He invokes the spirits thus: 'This is for you, O Bohwane! now chief at Tshaula, and for all your ancestors, and this is for you, O chiefs of the BaNgona;' here he names as many of his old ancestor chiefs as he can remember (he gave the names of sixteen generations without any hesitation). 'Be content; do not let any

RELIGION 259

illness come to your people and no drought, no leopards, no war, no locusts or other plagues. Guard your people and give us plenty.' As he puts the green foods into the hole in the rock all the small boys blow *phala-fhala* horns and the little girls trill, and every one in the whole district knows that the priest is asking the spirits to bless the green foods. This ceremony has been discontinued in many parts of Vendaland, especially where the BaNgona have been completely absorbed into the Venda tribe; in the eastern districts there are still some BaNgona priests like Netshitumbe, whose ancestors have been priests for generations, and who are protected by the chiefs and petty chiefs in whose districts they live, in order that they may continue to perform this ceremony every year. Netshishivhe is the priest of Nethengwe. At Thenzheni, Chief Nethenzheni and Netsinghe both may perform this priestly function; both belong to the VhaDau sib, and are probably BaNgona. At Mianzwi and Lambani the priests of the ceremony are Tshinavhute and Netshauvha respectively. It appears that the invaders, having subjugated the BaNgona, still feared the power of their ancestor spirits who had once lived and sown and reaped in the land; to propitiate these BaNgona spirits one of their descendants would sometimes be encouraged to live near the kraal of the conquering chief; he would act as mediator and would ensure the blessing of the old ancestors on these new masters of the soil.

Review of Ancestor Cult.

On reviewing the ancestor cult of the BaVenda, it appears that the sphere of influence of each spirit depends on the status in society enjoyed by it as a human being before death. Before puberty a child has no status; it is doubtful whether it is supposed to have a spirit at all. The passing from childhood to adolescence, across the barrier of initiation, brings with it a definite status in society. A young man or woman dying after puberty and before marriage has a spirit of his or her own, whose wants can generally be satisfied by the rite of the hoe handle. Marriage brings with it full tribal rights, and the spirit of the married man or woman assumes after death the highest status in the spirit world, and commands the respect of all in a lower one. A spirit has no power to command or torment those of a higher status than itself.

Two important points remain to be considered: (*a*) Why have the ancestor spirits of the mother's group the most powerful influence over the descendants? (*b*) Why do the spirits of the mother's father

260   RELIGION

and, conversely, of the father's mother have little or no influence on their grandchildren?

An explanation may possibly be found by investigating the Venda theory of the composition of the body and its contributing agencies. It seems to be a fundamental conception that the child receives its flesh and blood from the mother and its bones and sensory organs from the father.

(*a*) The BaVenda believe that the cessation of the menstrual flow during pregnancy is due to the fact that the blood is being utilized for the building up of the foetus, and that after the birth of the child the blood continues searching in the womb for some months for fresh life on which to work before it leaves the body again in menstruation. All illnesses connected with the blood, with few exceptions (and those are probably of recent origin), come from the mother's side of the family; hence most bodily disease is attributed to the malevolent spirits of the mother's group, and they are consequently greatly feared and play a greater part in the lives of their relations than do the spirits of the father's side. It is interesting to find that the word *thakhata* (the possessions inherited from the father) is also used to denote aching bones, and the reason may be that the bones come from the father as do the possessions.

(*b*) It follows from this belief about the component parts of the body that a child inherits nothing from its father's mother, and similarly nothing from its mother's father, so the spirits of these two relatives have no influence over it.

We have then two effective groups of spirits, one confined to the father and his ancestors in the male line and the other to the mother and her ancestors in the female line, forming a dual organization whose spirits inhabit respectively the sacred bull and the sacred goat. The instability of the lineage and the constant fission prevent the ancestor cult from being practised systematically and developed to its logical conclusion. Many of the *zwitungula* connected with one lineage are now scattered throughout the country, different groups possessing sometimes a single heirloom. The unity of the lineage could not in any case have been maintained indefinitely, but the normal disintegration has been increased by the influence of the European with his example of individualism, resulting in a growing indifference among the BaVenda to the duties and rites connected with ancestor spirits.

The conception that the child receives its blood from the mother and its bones from the father has probably arisen from the respective

RELIGION

colours of the menstrual flow and the semen, the female contributing the blood and all red organs and the male the bones and white parts, e.g. the hair comes from the father as it has its roots in the skull or brains, which are both white, and it turns white in old age; the teeth and the white of the eye also come from him. This association is borne out by the teaching of the *ngoma sali* at the *domba*, when red and white fluids are explained to represent the woman and man. There is also a phrase used at the *domba*, '*Musuku u toda mutobvu, zwa madzanga zwi a todama*' (copper finds lead, good things find each other), which implies the mixing of red copper and white lead into a superior ore and symbolizes the mixing in marriage of the woman (red) and the man (white). If this is really a fundamental conception, then red should always be associated with women and white with men, whereas men on some occasions are painted with red ochre and women with white colouring; this anomaly appears, at any rate among the BaVenda, to occur only as a ritual act during initiation ceremonies, and these precede the actual coming together of the sexes in marriage. A more comprehensive study must be made of the subject among this and other tribes before it will be possible to establish this theory.

XXI

MEDICINE AND MAGIC

The Medico-Magician and his work—Diseases and their treatment—Witchcraft—Black Magic—Divination—The effect of the Medico-Magician on society—Possession.

IT is impossible to consider the intimately associated subjects of medicine and magic except in conjunction with each other. Although a few of the purely medicinal and herbal treatments are of real therapeutical value, nearly all depend for their efficacy upon the inclusion of a magical element. Magico-medical seems to me the most appropriate term to describe the twofold art which is founded on one fundamental concept, the belief that every object, animate or inanimate, possesses a kinetic power for good or evil. For example, on inquiring minutely into the history of a small piece of wood, worn as a charm round the neck of a MuVenda for protection when travelling, it transpired that this wood was taken from a bough of a tree overhanging a difficult climb in a well-frequented path. This bough was grasped by every passer-by in order to assist him over the difficult place. In this way the power of that particular bough was inordinately increased by helping the wayfarer, and it became the obvious source from which effective charms for the timid traveller could be obtained. Conversely, the history of some powdered wood, possessing a great deal of power to do evil to the traveller, disclosed the fact that in a well-trodden path a small root caused annoyance to every passer-by, being in a spot where it almost inevitably knocked his toe. This root, unlike the friendly bough, became a source of evil power, and its wood was used for charms to bring harm to the traveller.

The art of the magico-medical profession rests in controlling this force; the practitioner mixes the different types of power and directs their energy into different channels. It is the individual skill of the practitioner in his use and interpretation of this force, combined with his knowledge of the specific effects of certain herbs and concoctions, that make or mar his reputation. When once a practitioner has proved his powers and established his reputation he can perform his rites and work his cures with the utmost confidence, believed and trusted implicitly by the credulous people. While the magical element in the treatment is scientifically useless, the personality of the prac-

MEDICINE AND MAGIC

titioner, often combined with undoubted hypnotic powers, and the stimulus and excitement caused by the divinatory ritual, fortified by the implicit faith of the sick person and his relations in the practitioner's powers, so work on the mind of the patient that a cure is effected. The native is immensely susceptible to auto-suggestion, and examples of natives who suffer from supposed illnesses and pine away for no physiological reason, or who die simply through the fear of death superimposed upon them by a more powerful personality, are common knowledge.

The Medico-Magician and his Work.

The medico-magical fraternity among the BaVenda includes two main types. The *nganga* (pl. *dzinganga*) is the medicine-man proper, whose main function is the cure of disease, and the *mungoma* (pl. *mingoma*) is the diviner pure and simple. By far the greatest number of practitioners are *dzinganga*, and they are consulted on practically every occasion when an event occurs outside the natural order of things. Although nearly every *nganga* possesses his set of divinatory dice, he is not generally credited with the occult powers of his more powerful colleague the *mungoma*, who must always be consulted after a death, as he can actually reconstruct the whole scene of the tragedy and disclose the identity of the evil-doer.

Within these two main groups there are a large number of specialists who, while understanding the general principles of their calling, have learnt the specialized treatment of certain diseases or catastrophes, often inheriting the knowledge from a long line of specialist ancestors. A practitioner may know the correct treatment for a very large number of diseases, but he may be skilled in the treatment of one alone; he may simply know the secret of one special medicine, which secret he has inherited from his father and which he preserves all his life, visiting the necessary trees and procuring the necessary animals in the strictest privacy. Obviously the profession is nearly as complicated as our own medical profession, and a patient or client may have to consult two or three different *dzinganga* before his trouble can be cured. The following are some of the more important specialists: *maine vha u fungo*, the finder who sprinkles water, who consecrates weapons and makes new fire and is associated with the bringing of rain and all things connected with the earth; *maine vha u lumulula*, the finder who sucks out with the mouth, who sucks from the body such objects as stones, crystals, lizards, snakes, or other similar objects,

MEDICINE AND MAGIC

which have been diagnosed as the cause of the disease; *maine vha tshipengo*, the finder of madness, who deals with cases of delirium and insanity; *maine vha vhambeu*, the finder of seeds, who works in connexion with fertilizing seeds and crops. There are many other specialists in eyes, dentistry, love-potions, leprosy, &c., and there is also the general practitioner, *maine vha mushongo*, the finder of medicine, who is usually the man to be first consulted in cases of ordinary illness.

As has been said, the *mingoma* are pure diviners, especially skilled in the use of the magic dice and the magic bowl. Among them are the *vhabvhumbi*, the smellers-out, who specialize in discovering articles that have been stolen. There are also fortune-tellers; but by far the greatest number of *mingoma* are *maine vha lufhali*, the diviners who discover the identity of the *vhaloi* (sing. *muloi*), the wizards or witches whose evil machinations are responsible for most misfortunes and nearly all deaths. Practitioners may be skilled in many different branches of their profession and a man may be both *nganga* and *mungoma*, acting in some cases in the former capacity, but when required acting also as the pure diviner or smeller-out. Owing to the secret prescriptions, so carefully guarded in certain families, there is no man skilled in everything, but whether his knowledge is small or great his training and apprenticeship is generally long and arduous.

The medico-magical practitioner, whether *nganga* or *mungoma*, may be of either sex; usually a man inherits his knowledge from his father and a woman from her mother. A woman, having no daughter, may teach her son. Occasionally the normal heir may be deprived of his birthright through a revelation received in a dream; the ancestor spirits may for some reason not approve of the heir and divulge their wishes to the master in this way.

If a man quite unconnected with these hereditary castes desires to become a practitioner he will approach a master of good repute and ask that he may become his apprentice. The master, if he is willing, throws his dice and consults his spirits to discover whether the newcomer is a suitable person to carry on the work; if the dice decide in the negative he will refuse to accept the applicant. Before teaching even his own child he always consults the dice, to be sure of the acquiescence of the ancestors. Provided the spirits agree the apprentice is duly articled, and during his apprenticeship anything he may earn in money or kind is the property of the master. Before leaving the master to practise independently he must pay him at least two head of cattle. The master in the first lesson describes the divinatory dice and orders

MEDICINE AND MAGIC

his pupil to make or procure a set for himself. When the apprentice returns to his master with the dice he is ready to begin his training in real earnest. Before these new dice can have the power of divination they must be treated in a consecratory ceremony. A mixture made from all the roots, powders, &c., in the master's equipment is added to the meat of a white goat and all put into a pot of water. The dice of the apprentice are boiled up in the mixture and are then considered to have received the power of all the different ingredients used by the master. The apprentice is then ordered to eat up the meat and to drink the remainder of the concoction so that he will understand 'inside his heart' how to read the dice. He may then be taught all the secrets of the magical dice and how to interpret the different combinations in which they may fall. This takes about a month to accomplish, When the apprentice understands the dice thoroughly he may prepare the rest of his equipment, and follows his master wherever he goes. The master teaches him all about the different trees, animals, medicines, and magical treatments, giving him samples of all his powders and medicaments and explaining their composition. These medicaments are collected from all over the Zoutpansberg; some cannot be obtained in the Venda country at all and must be procured from very great distances. Obviously the collecting of a comprehensive dispensary is a matter of great difficulty, requiring patience and a real knowledge of the different plants and animals and their habitats. Some of the rare species are traded with foreign practitioners in exchange for other articles. Long after his apprenticeship is over, and it usually lasts two or three years, the budding practitioner continues to consult his master about cases which he finds difficult. The master, if he cannot solve the problem himself, will intercede for the young man with his spirits; if the master's master is still alive he will be consulted and will consult the spirits of the man from whom he learnt his art. All magico-medical practitioners, on occasions when their art seems to be failing them, will ask the help of their doctor ancestors. On these occasions the suppliant spreads out all his dice, bones, medicine, and equipment and does the *phasa madi* ceremony over them, saying, 'O fathers, doctor ancestors, give me more power, that I may be successful in this difficulty'.

I have spoken several times of the doctor's equipment and will now attempt to describe that of an ordinary MuVenda *maine vha mushongo*. The divinatory dice consist mainly of four pieces of ivory, representing the old man, young man, old woman, and young woman respectively.

266   MEDICINE AND MAGIC

These will be described in detail later. Many practitioners have two or even three sets of dice, which are all used together, but each set of four is read independently; this multiplication of sets serves to speed up the consultation and to lessen the number of throws, two or three readings being made possible simultaneously. Every MuVenda *nganga* or *mungoma* has at least one set of these dice, and nearly all have a varying number of supplementary bones and other objects. These supplementary bones have no direct connexion with the dice and have been adopted in imitation of the divination bones of the BaThonga. The interpretation placed on these supplementary objects depends almost entirely upon the individual and is not systematized throughout the fraternity. The other equipment also varies according to the special requirements and knowledge of the individual. This is the stock-in-trade of Mushapa (Plate XL), a *maine vha mushongo* at Luvhimbi. He has two sets of divinatory dice, one made of ivory and the other, the Mashona type, of a dark wood like ebony; he uses both sets together and so can readily satisfy both Venda and Mashona clients. In addition to the dice he has the following supplementary objects: two baboon astragalus bones, one male and one female; two pieces of tortoise-shell, one male and one female; a male wild boar's astragalus bone, the female complement being lost; two fruits of the *murula* tree, one male and one female; and a stone from the sea. All these objects are considered to have a positive and a negative side, whereby Mushapa makes his interpretations.

The baboon's astragalus bones are *dzitenga* (sing. *tenga*) and are taken from old baboons. Falling positively, *tenga* signifies, in cases of disease, that the illness will be long and tedious; in connexion with the village it signifies prosperity; falling negatively it signifies a long journey and a safe return.

The tortoise-shell, *tshibode* (the tortoise), is a good omen in the positive position and a bad omen in the negative for male and female respectively.

The wild boar's bone is *nganga* and is specially associated with the medicine-man himself; the wild boar is always snuffling about among the roots, digging holes and eating everything, in the same way that the real *nganga* does. The same name is used by the BaThonga. The bone is only used with reference to the practitioner himself and has no significance in the consultations of an ordinary person. If it falls in the positive position all is well with the medicine man, but if in the negative it is a sign that another practitioner is working black magic on him.

PLATE XL

MUSHAPA THROWING THE BONES, WITH HIS HORN,
SWITCH AND MEDICINES BEHIND HIM

PLATE XLI

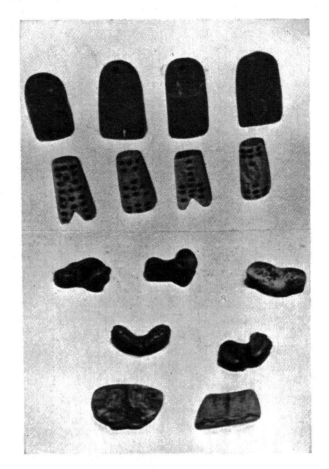

MUSHAPA'S DICE AND SUPPLEMENTARY
OBJECTS

MEDICINE AND MAGIC 267

Mufhula, the fruit of the *murula* tree, is associated with the *vhaloi*. In the positive position it signifies that a *muloi* is coming to interfere with either the practitioner or client; in the negative that all is well and no evil is predicted. If both male and female *vhaloi* are doing evil both male and female fruits will fall positively.

The stone from the sea is connected with all domestic animals and indicates by its position whether a sick animal will recover or die.

Mushapa carries all his bones and dice (Plate XLI) in a basketwork bag with a lid and cord which he slings over his shoulder. Many practitioners make this bag of wild-cat's skin. If a *nganga* loses his bag of bones he is powerless to continue his profession. Mushapa also wears a large eland's horn containing a thick viscous oil obtained from the *mupfiri* tree (castor oil). The seeds of the *mupfiri* tree are crushed and boiled, then crushed again, and all the oil squeezed out; this is used as a lubricant and as the foundation in which a great many drugs and powders are embodied. The cork of the horn-container is made from the *tshiralala* tree and carefully carved. The horn is worn strung on a reim, from which there also dangles an assortment of small pelt containers. Three of these are of python skin, four of the skin of the *turi* (a stoat which is greatly feared by the BaVenda), three of the skin of the meercat and one of the skin of a spring-hare. He also has other small bags made from odd pieces of skin and material. All these pelts hold different roots, powders, or other magico-medicinal equipment. The first one contains a small horn full of ready-mixed powder for the treatment of lung trouble, *mushongo vha mali*, together with a large thorn for pricking the patient's chest before rubbing in the medicine. Another contains a powder mixed ready for the treatment of fever and some other diseases; a third is filled with the powdered and dried head of the *turi*, and so on. These powders will be described fully in connexion with the diseases for which they are prescribed.

Diseases and their Treatment.

Although certain epidemics and illnesses, such as malaria or pneumonia, are cured by specific methods of medicinal or external treatment, the BaVenda attribute nearly all diseases either to the evil influence of the ancestor spirits or to witchcraft. The first step taken in any illness is to consult a *nganga* who will diagnose the cause of the trouble by divination. Occasionally the diagnosis is so obvious that the *nganga* straightway prescribes the necessary treatment without

268 MEDICINE AND MAGIC

recourse to divination, but this is rare. When a client visits the *nganga*, either on his own behalf or on behalf of one of his sick relations, the practitioner immediately throws the dice, at the same time calling on his spirits and asking them to help him to discover the trouble. Occasionally the lie of the dice indicates to the *nganga* that he must not continue the case, and he tells his clients that the spirits are unwilling to disclose the cause of the trouble to him, and advises them to seek help from another source. Much more often the spirits show their acquiescence and the dice are given to the client to throw. Suppose he is a man who is anxious about his sick child: he holds the dice in both hands, claps them together, and then throws them up, saying; 'Tell us about this illness; we want to know if it has been brought about by witchcraft or by the spirits. Tell us, so that our child may recover'. The presentation of the dice is then interpreted by the *nganga*. This procedure is repeated two or three times, unless the *nganga* has two or three sets of dice, when one throw may suffice. In the case of a very serious illness the *nganga* may be called to the kraal of his client, and any near relative may throw up the bones. To ensure intimate contact between the diseased person and the divinatory dice they may be held in front of his mouth, so that his breath touches them. A bracelet in the case of a woman patient, or a piece of string in the case of a man, is breathed upon in this way, before a visit is paid to the *nganga* on his or her behalf. The token is then put among the dice and thrown with them. When the ancestors are the cause of the trouble the *nganga* discovers the reason of their anger and has no more to do with the matter. When the trouble is due to witchcraft, he prepares the magical antidote, and if he does not possess the power to overcome the particular form of evil the client will leave him and consult a *nganga* who has specialized in the necessary treatment. In the case of ordinary diseases, which react to specific treatment, he mixes the necessary herbal or animal decoction, or applies external applications, nearly always in conjunction with a certain amount of magical ritual. The *nganga* is only called to the patient's kraal in extreme cases.

Payment varies considerably. Before the *nganga* will consent to throw his dice at all the client must give him a fowl, nowadays 1*s*., *u luputulula tevheli* (to open the medicine bag). When the case is finished, if the treatment has succeeded, the *nganga* is given the *tshidzimo*, a goat or 10*s*., and this is the final payment except for the *halwa vha totshi* (the beer of the hair of the patient); the latter is taken by the patient to the *nganga* on his recovery, when he goes to have his

MEDICINE AND MAGIC 269

hair cut by him as a final purification, to cut the trouble off for ever. Small jobs are paid according to their worth, possibly by two or three fowls, 3*s.* or 4*s.* If the client has nothing either in money or in kind with which to pay, the *nganga* may accept a bracelet as a token that he will be paid as soon as possible. If the treatment is not considered to have been successful and the patient does not recover the *nganga* is not paid.

Malaria (dali) is prevalent throughout the country, especially in the low-lying districts, and very few escape it in the wet season. These constant attacks of malaria seem to drain the vitality of the people and are possibly a factor in their indolent character and indifferent physique. A malaria patient is often treated with vapour baths. Leaves of the *mushakhaladza* are boiled up with stones and water, the stones being used to keep in the heat. The patient is seated beside the pot and wrapped in a blanket. When he has been steamed for some time he is given a strong emetic and purge. An alternative treatment is to mix a powder made from the droppings of the *tshiruvhi* bird (hammerkop) and the powdered root of the *bwere* tree (*bwere* is soft porridge) with fat, and to rub the mixture into the arms, legs, chest, ears, &c., of the patient. When there is nightmare or delirium a little clay is mixed with this powder and put on the fire and the fumes are inhaled by the patient.

Rheumatism is treated with the above ointment, which is smeared on to a heated round river pebble and massaged with it into the affected parts.

Bleeding from the mouth and nose (nombe) is sometimes treated with vapour baths; more often the powdered root of the *mutanza* tree (*u tanzwa*, to clean) is mixed with shavings from the horn of a barren cow and put into a pipe made from a mealie cob, which is smoked by the patient. A similar cure is effected by inhaling a mixture of the powdered root of the *mutanza*, the hair of the klipspringer, and the excrement of a goat, all cooked together in a pot over the fire.

Pneumonia or any pricking pain in the chest or sides may be treated in the following way: The powdered root of the *mubadali* tree (*u omba dali*, to stay the fever) is mixed with the dried blood of the *thwandalila* (roan antelope), *thaidi* (kreisbok), *phuluvhulu* (steenbok), *phele* (hyena), and *ndadzi* (lightning bird), and this concoction is well beaten up in ox fat. The *nganga* then makes small incisions on the chest of the patient, three on the right side and two on the left, with either a spear-point or the thorn of the *mutunu* tree (*u tunu*, to branch off in all directions). After making the incisions the doctor thrusts the

270 MEDICINE AND MAGIC

spear or thorn into the ground, in order to bury the evil thing that he has taken out of the body. He then massages the fat mixture very firmly into the sides of the chest. After this part of the treatment has been completed the following roots are cut into pieces and boiled for some time in water: *tshipandwa* (from *u pandwa*, to stamp mealies a second time after the removal of the bran), *muhwidzi* (*u hwida*, to pluck), *mutshetshete* (*tshete*, be quiet); the roots are then taken out, mealie meal is added to the water, and the resultant concoction is put into the *tshiselo* dish, the bottom of which is placed quickly on to the affected parts, and the dish is finally placed on the ground. This is done, as in the case of the spear-head or thorn, to draw out the evil and bury it in the ground. This action is repeated once or twice, and the patient is then ordered to eat as much of the porridge as he can manage and to finish the remainder on waking the following morning.

Abdominal trouble (maliso). This complaint is described by the BaVenda as being accompanied with abdominal distension and belching, and is usually divined to have been caused by a *muloi*. It is treated by the following reeds, *luthanga* (reed): *munengeledzi* (*u nengeledza*, to make to disappear in a certain direction), *muvuvhu* (*mvuvhu*, hippo), *mpesu* (*u pesula*, to flick, e.g. tail of bushbuck) and *mudzidzi* (*u dzidzi*, to beat, e.g. of the head in headache, onomatopoeic in imitation of the drum in the *tshikona*), and these bulbs: *dzhesi-khondo* (*dzhesi*, rush—*u honda*, to cry), *mutate* (*u tate*, to be afraid or to drive out), *lutshesena*, which are all collected and cut up into small pieces; all these plants grow near water. The *nganga* next collects the intestines of a python burned and powdered, some powdered belly skin of a crocodile, the root of the *mpeta* (*u peta*, to fold up, dissolve), and the bark of the *mulanga* (*u langa*, to discuss, to manage). These four ingredients are mixed together and put into a piece of cloth. When the two separate concoctions are both ready a goat is killed; a small portion of each part of the goat,—leg, heart, liver, &c.,—is boiled up in a pot together with the first mixture and some water. When this has boiled up the second mixture is added and the liquid poured off from the solid part. This liquid is the medicine for the disease and must be drunk night and morning until the cure is effected. More water is added from time to time as required.

Bone diseases (thakha). Diseases of this nature are rare and are always diagnosed as having been caused by angry spirits of the father's lineage. The treatment is a form of vapour bath. A fire is burned over a piece of ground and put out; the leaves of the *lidevhe la tholo* (ear of the

MEDICINE AND MAGIC 271

koodoo) tree are spread on the hot ashes mixed with the powdered shin bone of the ostrich. The patient stands over the fumes and perspires; he also drinks a thin porridge to which the powdered bone of the ostrich has been added.

Ear trouble. A powder made from the head of the guinea fowl is put in the sore ear of a child, while for a grown-up person the brains of the leopard are used. The guinea fowl and leopard are two inhabitants of the bush with very acute hearing.

Vomiting. The patient is given the powdered gall-bladder of an ox to drink in water.

Consumption (lufhila) is common and is the most dreaded of all diseases. It is thought that a woman who has had an abortion will infect any man who has sexual intercourse with her before she has gone through the necessary purification rites. Once a man is stricken with consumption he is considered to be practically incurable, although the following palliative treatment is generally attempted: *phaladzane* grass is burned and the patient inhales the smoke. This grass is credited with possessing a very disturbing power, and if put inside the house will cause friction between husband and wife. If a mischief-maker were to hide a piece in the ashes on the hearth everybody in the hut would start quarrelling.

Headache and aches in other parts of the body are generally cured by scarification and cupping. The cupping instrument, *mutoho*, is a small piece of horn, three or four inches long, with a hole at the tip. The open end is applied to the part to be treated, and the blood is sucked into the horn. The hole at the tip is covered with wax, in which a small hole is made to relieve the pressure; the process is then repeated. When the treatment is applied to the body the *nganga* often pretends to discover some small object in the blood, such as a worm, frog, lizard, or piece of crystal. An alternative treatment for headache is to inhale the powdered bark of the *mudziwa* tree (*u dziwa*, to be despised) mixed with fat; at the same time two small incisions are made on the front or side of the head and the same mixture is rubbed in. A very large proportion of the BaVenda, particularly the women, have two scars on each temple as a result of this treatment; in fact, these scars are so common that they have often been thought to be the tribal mark of the BaVenda.

Smallpox (thombe). Before the arrival of the Europeans, bringing with them vaccination, smallpox used to take a heavy toll of the people. The BaVenda practised a rude vaccine treatment of their

MEDICINE AND MAGIC

own. If one member of the family was suffering from smallpox, pus was taken from one of the sores and rubbed into scratches made in the arms of the rest of the family; although death did sometimes occur as a result of this treatment, there were fewer deaths than when this prophylactic was not attempted and the disease allowed to run its own course. The BaThonga treat the disease in a similar manner, though more comprehensive and complicated. The whole question of the customs connected with smallpox amongst the BaThonga is discussed by Junod.[1]

Convulsions in a child are treated with medicine made from the powdered head of the baboon mixed with water.

Giddiness. The root of the *tshidzungudza* is cut up and boiled in water, and thin porridge made with this water is given to the patient to eat. He is also ordered to wear a piece of the root around his neck.

Snake-bite. The bites of certain snakes, particularly the night-adder, often result in death, while others are found to respond to treatment. Most doctors have a specific powder always ready in case of need. The powder is made from the baked head and tail of a poisonous snake and the powdered root of the *ndalumwafhi* (where am I bitten?). These two powders are mixed with water and the mixture rubbed into the wound. At the same time the patient is given a dose to drink. When the powder is not available the wound is often scarified and an attempt made to suck out the poison. A third method is to give the patient several doses of a strong emetic. The patient vomits repeatedly, and when he urinates it is believed that the danger is over.

Madness (*tshipengo*) is treated by a special *nganga*. He gives the patient medicine (the ingredients have not been ascertained) mixed with the lungs of a black sheep.

Leprosy (*mapele*) is incurable. The leper is generally isolated in a small hut on the side of a mountain and food &c. taken to him. At death the body is not touched, but the whole hut and all his possessions are burned.

Sprains and stiffness, particularly stiff neck, are cured by the external application of the powdered root of the *mpeta* mixed with fat. This mixture is rubbed into scarifications made at the seat of the trouble by the *nganga*; to ensure speedy cure it must always be applied in the early morning before either *nganga* or patient have eaten. Sometimes the *nganga* cuts his elbow and massages the sprain with his

[1] Junod, Henri A., 'Customs connected with Smallpox among the Baronga', *South African Journal of Science*, 1919, pp. 694–702.

MEDICINE AND MAGIC

elbow, rubbing the *mpeta* mixture and the blood from his elbow into the sprain.

Septic wounds are lanced and the pus is squeezed out.

Toothache, from which the BaVenda suffer considerably, can only be cured by extraction. The aching tooth is levered out by means of a pointed rod while the patient's head is held between the knees of the operator.

Fractures are treated skilfully, the bones being roughly set, anointed, and then placed into a splint. The type of splint is ingenious, made from lengths of bamboo, placed parallel to each other, and bound together at three points by strings made of pliant fibre. According to Bartels,[1] these splints possess a high degree of elasticity combined with the necessary rigidity and are very successful.

All small cuts, sprains, &c., are immediately treated by the application of cow-dung, which cools and heals.

The above are some of the more common Venda diseases. Of course each *nganga's* treatment varies, although most of them have the purely magical element in common. Where the ritual ingredients vary the alternative mixture is generally credited with possessing the same curative possibilities. Nearly every medicine shows the influence of the homoeopathic conception. It was quite impossible in my short stay among the BaVenda to obtain more than a few examples of their treatment of disease, but perhaps these few, collected from three or four different practitioners, will give some idea of the value of their prescriptions and of the mental attitude of both doctor and patient in the treatment and cure of disease.

Witchcraft.

Vhaloi. Closely allied to disease and its treatment is the much-discussed phenomenon of the *vhaloi*. The Venda conception of these anti-social beings closely resembles that of the BaThonga, so admirably described by Junod.[2]

The word *vhaloi* (sing. *muloi*) comes from the verb *u loya*, to bewitch, and is applied to those people who through sheer malignancy, either consciously or subconsciously, employ magical means to encompass all manner of evil to the detriment of their fellow-creatures. They destroy property, bring disease and misfortune and cause death,

[1] Bartels, M., 'Schienen–Verbände für Knochenbrüche bei den Bawenda', *Verh. Ges. Anthrop. Berlin,* 1896, pp. 365–6.

[2] Junod, Henri A., *The Life of a South African Tribe,* London, 1927, pp. 505–36.

T

MEDICINE AND MAGIC

often entirely without provocation, to satisfy their inherent craving for evil-doing. The *vhaloi* may be of either sex, but are generally women. They carry on their nefarious practices by night, sometimes travelling long distances on the back of a hyena or some other animal, and sending snakes, owls, and particularly the *turi* (stoat) into the hut of the object of their spite, to bite the unfortunate person or to enter his body in order to cause disease or death. The family of a *muloi* is always feared and suspected as it is possible that the parent will teach her offspring her evil practices. There are two distinct types of *vhaloi*—the one who acts subconsciously and is quite unaware of the fact that she is possessed of this evil genius, and the other who deliberately attempts to encompass the death of her enemy through sympathetic or contagious magic. Various creatures, particularly those to whom the average person has a psychological reaction of dread or disgust, are the special agents of the *vhaloi*. These are the hyena, crocodile, owl, all snakes (except the python), and the *turi*. The unconscious *muloi* nearly always acts during sleep. It is supposed that the evil spirit of the seemingly innocuous individual leaves the body and goes out into the world to carry on its evil mission. A hideous monster, one of the instruments of the *muloi*, is left in her place. During this metamorphosis the other inmates of the hut are put into a heavy sleep, so that no ordinary person ever sees the disgusting creature that is his bedfellow. The diviners have seen them, however, and when consulted on the subject describe in vivid detail the unpleasant creature in all its grotesque horror. Powerful medicine-men have often seen them engaged in weird happenings which they describe to clients, thereby increasing their own prestige. Several *vhaloi* may meet together for a feast, beat drums, eat human flesh and dance; they may wage war on one another, one group trying to steal the corn of another group. To cross a flowing river a *muloi* may take several sleeping people from their huts and with their bodies build a bridge, and so make a dry passage. A careless *muloi* has been known to enter the hut of a *nganga*, so that he has then been able to take good stock of the intruder. The *muloi* appears as a shadowy human form, always stark naked, having left her clothes behind in the hut to cover her metamorphosed body; her eyes are bright and shining like burning lumps of coal. The *nganga* will rub his anti-*vhaloi* medicine into his stick and proceed to belabour the intruder fiercely. The *muloi* realizes that she has entered the wrong hut and having escaped is very careful not to venture into such a dangerous place again. There are

MEDICINE AND MAGIC 275

numerous stories about the evil-doings of these weird and unfortunate people. The *muloi* is generally intent on murder, but when not busily engaged in death-dealing she plays other mischievous pranks. She is reputed to be very fond of milk and is able to enter a hut and make the owner go into the kraal and milk the cows and give her all the milk; the owner of the kraal performs the milking and all his actions quite subconsciously, his only conscious reaction as he returns to his sleep is a feeling of cold and discomfort. In the morning he wakes, oblivious of the night's happenings, and goes to the kraal to milk, to find to his discomfiture that the milking has already been done, and that all the milk has disappeared. On consulting the *nganga* it is divined that he has himself milked the cows during the night under the influence of a *muloi*. The *muloi* may also obtain milk by sending a *turi* to suck all the cows dry. In the morning the calves refuse to suck, disgusted by the smell left by the *turi* on the udders of the cows; in this case the *nganga* purifies the udders by burning a cleansing herb under them. It may happen that during the day a woman, who is really a *muloi*, is badly treated; in the night in her *muloi* incarnation she will wreak her revenge. Possibly she may send an owl to harm her enemy with an evil charm, or a snake to bite him as he walks unsuspectingly along the road, or a crocodile to drag him into the river, or a *turi* to enter his body.

Before the *muloi* can harm any one it is necessary that the matri-lineal ancestors must be off their guard. The *muloi* knows that these spirits are the great protectors of their descendants; so she waits until her divining dice reveal that the spirits are not on the alert and then shuts them up and has her revenge on her enemy. A *nganga* some-times divines that there is a conflict ensuing between the mother's spirits of his client and the magic of the *vhaloi*. A *muloi* may also act like a vampire, going at night and sucking the blood of her enemies, causing them to become emaciated and anaemic. In fact there is very little that is horrible, revolting, or anti-social that the unfortunate evil genius may not and does not at some time accomplish. The im-plicit belief of the average MuVenda in the reality and power of the *muloi* is amazing. The whole grotesque conception, with its mixture of the human and the animal and its absolute power for evil, is a deep-seated, immovable belief, in which the BaVenda have been born, and which is to them as rational and natural a fact as the difference between night and day. Fear of the *muloi* and her creatures hangs as a sinister shadow over all their doings. Not long ago a native was caught by a crocodile. He was not allowed to return to the village but was

T 2

276 MEDICINE AND MAGIC

permitted to build a hut some distance away, where he lived alone and unattended, food being brought daily and left near the hut; he was considered to be contaminated by witchcraft, if not actually himself a *muloi*. A farmer at Lwamondo told me an interesting story of a somewhat similar nature. He shot a crocodile, and to his extreme concern the bullet ricochetted from its hide and severely wounded a boy some distance away; this boy, when he returned to his village, after recovering from the wound, was straightway dubbed a *muloi*, and he and all his relatives were obliged to leave that part of the country. The people had absolutely no doubt that he was a crocodile, disguised in human form, otherwise the bullet that hit the crocodile could never have hit him as well.

Black Magic.

In contradistinction to the *muloi*, with this dual personality, acting in the day as an ordinary individual and at night as an evil creature, there is a being also called *muloi* who consciously and deliberately, by himself or with the aid of a *nganga*, endeavours to bring about the death of an enemy by magical means; the black magic employed is termed *madambi*. Many *dzinganga* are acquainted with this means of destruction and are willing, for a large fee, to help the *muloi* to carry out his designs. When thus engaged the *nganga* who is supposed to act for the good of society becomes an anti-social agency and himself a *muloi*.

The efficacy of *madambi* is based largely on sympathetic magic, the *muloi* using his magic on an object belonging to his enemy and thereby destroying the enemy himself. It is to prevent clippings of hair and nails from getting into the hands of a *muloi* that they are always carefully hidden away. A very simple way of killing an enemy is for a *muloi* to obtain from the *nganga* a death-dealing powder. Looking in the direction of the enemy he blows the powder towards him, saying at the same time 'You must die!' The closer the powder can be brought to the victim the more rapid will be his death. One woman who had been sent the deadly powder in this way became unconscious of her actions. She went down to the river for water but filled her calabash with sand, and later prepared her husband's porridge with it instead of meal. After acting strangely in this way for some time she died. Sometimes this powder is blown on, or towards, a hare, which runs to the enemy and looks into his eyes; on being chased the hare will vanish, but will soon after again approach the enemy and gaze into his

MEDICINE AND MAGIC

face. After repeating this several times the hare will vanish for good and soon after the unfortunate victim will die. If a man so much as points a finger at another and says in a threatening tone 'You will see', then on any trouble occurring in the threatened man's family the former will be in danger of being called a *muloi*. A *muloi* can, by rubbing medicine on to a climbing shrub, turn the branch into a snake which, at the order, 'Go to that man and let me know that he is dead', goes straight to the victim and bites him.

A clever *nganga* can harness the lightning bird for his use as a medium of death, and may send it long distances to strike his victim. This explains why the body of a person killed by lightning is never touched until after it has been sprinkled with water and the ground on which it fell well soaked with water. Unless the ground is cleansed after the contamination of witchcraft it will always be a source of danger, as the magical property of the lightning remains in the ground until it is removed by the cleansing properties of water. Many *dzinganga* can only command the lightning through the agency of a cock, which is covered with red ochre and flung up into the air while a formula is uttered commanding the lightning to strike the victim. This rite has been taken from the BaSutho. Perhaps the most popular *madambi* is devised with the help of sand from the enemy's footprint. The sand is mixed with poisonous herbs, and by sympathetic magic the owner of the footprint dies from poisoning. This device is employed so frequently that a prophylactic has been devised. A man travelling through a district where he knows an enemy resides will, before starting on his journey, obtain a powerful protective charm from a *nganga*. This charm, if sufficiently powerful, may carry the attack into the enemy's camp; it is a magic powder which is mixed with fat and rubbed over the soles of the feet and sometimes all over the body, so that the wearer is completely enveloped in a magical coat. The *muloi* when he takes sand from the traveller's footprint is unwittingly putting himself into a very dangerous predicament, for not only have the powder and fat placed a barrier between the foot and the sand preventing the traveller's essence from touching the actual sand, but they have infected the sand with the magical power of the powerful *nganga* from whom they were obtained. If this power is greater than that of the *muloi's nganga*, the traveller will pass through the ordeal unharmed while his enemies will themselves suffer the fate that they had prepared for him. In working with the help of *madambi* a formula is always uttered, exhorting the enemy to die, or go mad or fall ill, as may be desired.

MEDICINE AND MAGIC

Powder and fat put into a duiker horn may be blown like a whistle, while such words as 'Oh, you ——, living at so-and-so, die, die, die!' are interpolated between the blasts on the horn.

Protection against the crimes of the vhaloi and other evils. It has already been described how before the building of a house or cattle-kraal, and before childbirth or initiation, sticks rubbed in powerful preventive medicines are placed in prominent positions, so that the danger of the interference of *vhaloi* is minimized. In addition to these general protective measures individuals can obtain preventive charms of a similar nature which protect the wearer in the same way that the sticks protect the household or community. These charms can be obtained from nearly all *dzinganga*. A simple charm may be made from a root taken from a path on which everybody steps; the wearer considers that the wood, touched as it is by the foot of every one who passes along the road, is imbued with some of the essence of every one in the district, including those of the *vhaloi*; therefore, in wearing it, he has a sure protection against them, for in bringing evil to the wearer of the charm they would inevitably bring evil to themselves. A more complicated and more powerful charm is made from the powdered root of the *mukundulela* (the way of force), mixed with the powdered bones of the snake, owl, bat's wing, and *turi*. As this mixture is composed of parts of all the agents of the *vhaloi*, it is particularly powerful in making the wearer invulnerable to their attacks. The fear of the *turi* is very great indeed, the little creature being considered with more apprehension than any of the apparently more horrible creatures. If a man sees one crossing his path he hastens to a *nganga* to obtain an antidote, otherwise the *turi* becomes invisible and enters his body causing a mortal illness. The usual antidote for the danger involved by the sight of the *turi* is an inhalation of crushed *turi's* head.

All medicines used for protection are called *pamba*. These are used for many purposes as well as protection against *vhaloi*, although that is their most usual function. To obtain protection against ordinary disease a charm may be made from the powdered roots of the *vhuli-vhadza* and the *mpeta*, which keeps the ancestor spirits from worrying the wearer. A favourite protective charm is the skin of an ant-bear. (This has a further curious power; if tied round a dog's neck when it is crossing a river it protects the dog from crocodiles.) A powder made from the prickles of the hedgehog, the blood of the duiker, and the root of the *mpeta* tree is worn as a protection against a supposed enemy. There are innumerable similar powders. In most cases the *pamba* is put in a

MEDICINE AND MAGIC 279

small container of horn, wood, or ivory and worn round the neck of the person whom it is supposed to protect. These charms are often loosely referred to as *zwitungula*, but are essentially different both in purpose and composition from the *malembe*, which contain the spirits of the dead female ancestors.

The *nganga* is also skilled in discovering theft, which is, however, not a common crime among the BaVenda. At the time of sowing every garden is protected by an anti-*vhaloi* charm. If a thief gets through this protective barrier and steals, the injured person hastens to the *nganga*, who soon brings the thief to account by putting a powerful poison on the place from which the object was removed, which acts by contagious magic in such a way that the thief, as soon as he touches the stolen object in his own home, will be pricked or bitten by an unseen animal. As soon as he feels this mysterious attack he is compelled by an indwelling force, too powerful to resist, to return the stolen object and confess his fault. He knows that unless he is cleansed by the *nganga* he is bound to die, and his purification is never completed until he has paid a very heavy fine to the man whom he has robbed. The fine is always quite out of proportion to the value of the stolen object, a fine of two head of cattle being imposed for the theft of a few mealies or a fowl. In cases when this simple method does not have the desired effect, it is considered probable that the object has been hidden away by the thief; in this case the *mubvhumbi*, the smeller-out, is consulted. He is always accompanied by an assistant, who is not necessarily a *mungoma* or even an apprentice, and between them they are generally successful in producing the stolen object. The *mubvhumbi* divines the theft with the help of a switch. A pellet of mealie meal and magic medicine is put on the base of the switch and he sniffs the pellet up into his nose so that the power of the medicine will reach his mind; drowsiness overcomes him, and he sits in a stupor thinking deeply. Suddenly the magic compels him to rise and, still in his semi-comatose condition, he goes straight towards the stolen object.

Divination.

Divination by means of the magical dice or the magic bowl to discover the actual identity of a *muloi* is the special province of the *mungoma*. When an illness has been divined by the ordinary *nganga* to be the work of a *muloi*, one of the relatives of the patient pleads with the unknown *muloi* to withdraw the magic. He walks round the *khoro*

280 MEDICINE AND MAGIC

of the village shouting lustily 'Listen, all you people in the village; somebody is trying to kill my child. If the *muloi* does not hasten to remove her evil my child will die, and I shall go to a *mungoma* and discover who is the *muloi*'. This exhortation (*u bembela*) in the *khoro* is supposed to frighten the *muloi* into removing the evil. If the patient's condition does not improve the relative visits a diviner. The *mungoma* throws up his dice calling upon the spirits to divulge the cause of the disease; he interprets the fall of the dice and describes the cause, and then, by another throw, detects the sib of the *muloi* and that of his mother and grandmother. The client is then told to throw the dice, which he does, hitting them together and explaining his trouble to the spirits; by the fall of the dice this time the *mungoma* confirms his previous reading. The relatives may then accuse a possible offender of the crime and threaten to kill him if he does not straightway withdraw his magic, but in doing this there is always a risk of being fined for wrongful accusation. In all villages there are certain unpopular persons, suspected and feared by the other villagers, and the *mungoma* himself has a shrewd idea of the character of most of the people with whom his client has dealings; so it is not difficult to fix upon some unfortunate person and to accuse him. Once suspicion has attached itself to anybody, it soon grows into a fixed conviction, which increases in intensity as the name of the suspect and the history of the crime are passed from mouth to mouth. Once his guilt is accepted fairly unanimously by the other villagers the unfortunate scapegoat, even if innocent, will begin to believe in his own guilt.

The *mungoma* is always consulted after death, except in the case of a very old man, when it is ascribed to natural causes. One or two months after death all the relatives of the deceased collect at the kraal and set off together for the village of the *mungoma*. On this day nobody in the district must do work of any kind. The party must always be accompanied by a special messenger, *nyalumati*, sent by the chief, who acts as spokesman throughout. On the way to the *mungoma* the party must gather at the graveside of their deceased relative, and one of them must remove a stone from the grave, *u vhula mbilu ya mungoma* (to open the heart of the *mungoma*); unless this is done the diviner will not have the power to disclose the whole truth. The local *nganga* accompanies them as far as the graveside, and after the stone has been removed throws his dice to discover in what direction the party must travel to find the *mungoma*. When they reach the village of the *mungoma*, indicated by the local *nganga*, they assemble under the tree

MEDICINE AND MAGIC

281

where he holds his consultations and there wait for him. They bring the *lukhata* (waist-band) of the deceased, also a knife with which to cut it, with all the usual accessories, which are kept by the *mungoma* as perquisites. Before reaching the village one of the party hides something on his person, a thorn in his hair, or a shilling or a bracelet, to test the power of the diviner. As soon as the *mungoma* comes out of his hut to the tree he points out the hidden object; if he should fail in this test the party lose faith in him, and although they usually listen to his divination they refuse to pay him and do not give his findings serious attention. Strangely enough, he nearly always discovers the object without any hesitation. Without more ado he opens his bag of dice and throws them down, saying, 'Here are people in trouble; will you tell us the cause?' He turns to the group and demands the dead man's *lukhata* and the knife, cuts two or three small pieces and asks the assembly, 'Who is crying?' The mother comes forward and receives the dice in her hands. The *mungoma* places one piece of the *lukhata* on top of the dice, and water which has been brought by the party is poured over them, so that the power of the *lukhata* (and so of the deceased) can saturate the dice. During this rite the mother says, 'We cry; we have lost through death one of our relatives. Is it the spirits that have done this, or is it indeed a *muloi*? Tell us, so that we may know'. At the same time she claps the dice together with the *lukhata* and throws them down. The *mungoma* notes the lie of the dice but makes no comment. He picks up the dice, gives them again to the woman with the second piece of *lukhata*, and the performance is repeated. He again reads the dice silently. The performance may be repeated again. When the *mungoma* is satisfied that he has interpreted the dice correctly he tells the mother to return to the group and carefully washes the dice, to cleanse them from the contamination of death, and then puts them away in his bag. He then addresses the assembly. He enumerates all the sibs by name, saying: 'You VhaKwebo, MaKhwinde, VhaLaudzi, VhaDau, &c. . . . Oh, I only see VhaKwebo among these. It is a person whose mother is Ndou and whose mother's mother is of the VhaLaudzi. This MuKwebo killed your relative, putting poison into his beer and causing him to be ill and to vomit blood, and making him speak like a man in a dream. . . .' He continues in this strain, describing the whole illness in detail, and finally ends abruptly with 'That is all that my dice tell me'. He then sits down under his tree and receives his fee of one sheep, two goats, and one ox, or sometimes more than one. He does not vouchsafe another word to the party. The

MEDICINE AND MAGIC

relatives return home again, passing the grave of the deceased; the stone that was removed is rolled into position again and the party pursues its way. At their own village every member of the mourning party must have his hair cut. While this is being done the chief's messenger returns to the chief and reports the whole of the proceedings, including the finding of the *mungoma*. The chief then discovers which MuKwebo in his district has a mother and grandmother who belong to the sibs in question; he and his councillors generally know the sib pedigrees of all the people living in the district. All the people in the district are summoned to the chief's *khoro*, and he asks *nyalumati* to repeat the *mungoma's* finding. As soon as *nyalumati* has finished speaking the chief points to one of the company and says that he is the *muloi*. The accusation is nearly always emphatically denied, and the accused man can demand a consultation with another *mungoma*, or can challenge his accuser to the ordeal. For the ordeal a specialist *nganga*, who can prepare the ordeal poison, must be visited. All the relatives of the deceased, as well as the accused *muloi*, are ordered to drink this secret powder mixed in water. Each person when he has drunk the mixture spits it out, but the *muloi*, if guilty, will not be able to spit it out and will swallow it and die. This ordeal is never practised to-day; the usual procedure is for the accused to accompany the party on a visit to a second *mungoma*, *nyalumati* being again in attendance. This time the accused pays the fee before the proceedings begin. As before, the mother is called upon to throw up the dice, but no *lukhata* is used on this second occasion. After two or three throws the *mungoma* addresses the woman, saying, 'You cry because your child is dead', and then proceeds to enumerate the whole history of the illness, death, visit of the first *mungoma*, and the proceedings in the chief's *khoro*. If his divination proclaims the suspect to be the *muloi*, and he agrees with his colleague's interpretation, he puts medicine on his switch, sniffs it up his nose, and taking a heavy stick and sjambok walks around among the company. When he passes the *muloi* he gives him a fierce stroke with his stick and then belabours him mercilessly. All the people set upon the unfortunate victim with sticks until he flies for his life. The party then returns home and the chief is told all that has occurred. The *muloi* is either killed or banished from the country, and his property, wives, and children are confiscated by the chief. On rare occasions the accused may be given a third chance and allowed to consult a third *mungoma*.

When the second *mungoma's* divination does not confirm that of the first it is usual to believe his interpretation and to disregard the

MEDICINE AND MAGIC 283

first. He may divine that the death was due to an ancestor spirit, or he may discover a different *muloi* and name the three necessary sibs. The proceedings are again reported to the chief, and the man previously accused is compensated for the wrongful accusation. If the relatives are not by this time exhausted with the affair, but still wish to pursue the *muloi*, the chief points out the second accused and another *mungoma* is visited by him. If the second accused is pronounced innocent, he must be compensated. The relatives seldom pursue the case further as they are worn out with the tedious, unsatisfactory business and the loss of wealth entailed in compensating the persons falsely accused.

Nevertheless the death must be avenged, and so when exhausted by unsatisfactory consultations with *mingoma*, the relatives consult a powerful *nganga* and ask him to bring vengeance on the unknown *muloi* with *madambi*. The grave of the deceased is pointed out to the *nganga* and he visits it, sometimes alone, sometimes accompanied by one of the relatives. He places two small twigs, which must be cut from a green tree, on the grave, one at the head and one at the foot, and ties them together with green bark string rubbed in a potion made from the bark of the *musika* tree (*u sika*, to burn), which has the power of killing anybody that ventures beneath its shade; a little of the same potion is also rubbed on green leaves and put under the string. While preparing this, the *nganga* utters a formula bidding the power of the *musika* go out and enter into the *muloi* who killed the person lying in the grave below. The *nganga* then returns to the kraal of the deceased and tells the people that soon they will hear of the death of some one in the neighbourhood; this person is the *muloi*, and if any of his family shed tears after his death they will die too.

My interpreter, Mafunisa Senthumule, told me the following story in this connexion: His mother's mother's brother's daughter died, and the girl's father was very angry; and, thinking that the death must have been brought about by a *muloi* went straight to a powerful *nganga*, without consulting the *mungoma*, and through him discovered the identity of the *muloi*. The *nganga* performed the rites just described and told his client that in three days he would hear of a death. On the second day he heard the sound of weeping in a very wealthy kraal, about a mile away. He felt gratified that he had avenged his daughter's death so satisfactorily, but was surprised to hear that four members of the kraal, including the headman himself, had died on the same day; the following day ten others died. The eldest son of this kraal, hearing

MEDICINE AND MAGIC

that the father of the dead girl had been consulting the powerful *nganga*, guessed that his relatives were being killed by magic. He went to the father and pleaded with him to ask the *nganga* to remove his magic, promising him his sisters and ten head of cattle in payment. The *nganga* removed his charm and no further deaths occurred. Needless to say, the *nganga* received five head of the cattle from his client.

Appeal to a foreign mungoma. When seeking to discover a *muloi* many BaVenda like to consult an altogether foreign *mungoma*, and relatives of a deceased person will travel long distances to consult a man who has achieved a good reputation in this respect. The BaThonga medico-magicians are very popular among the BaVenda. There is one diviner, Phafhuli, living on the Portuguese border, who is greatly sought after. Now that the death or banishment of *vhaloi* is forbidden by the white administration, Phafhuli always shaves half the head of his victim and then sends him home. The unfortunate *muloi* will be disgraced, feared, and avoided for the rest of his life—a social outcast, the butt of all his neighbours' scorn, and suspected of complicity in every theft, assault, or death that occurs in the district.

Divining dice. The divinatory dice used by BaVenda diviners consist of four flat pieces of ivory, the best being made of elephants' tusks, others of pigs' tusks or the ribs of the larger game. The size of the dice varies from $1\frac{1}{4}$ to $1\frac{1}{2}$ inches in length and $\frac{3}{4}$ to 1 inch in breadth. The thickness is generally about $\frac{1}{4}$ of an inch. The shape varies from a rough square to a rectangle, some tapering at one end to a blunt-pointed triangle. The four dice represent the four different stages in the family and are all marked in such a way that the owner is able to identify them readily. The first, *vhami*, represents the old man; the second, *tshilume*, the young man; the third, *twalima*, the old woman, and the fourth, *lumwe*, the young woman. In the Venda sets the two female dice differ from the male by having a notch cut in one end, so that the male and female elements are immediately distinguished. All are further differentiated by the markings on them.

I have examined four independent outfits, the first containing one set of dice among other bones, shells, &c., of the BaThonga type; the second two sets of dice, including one BaKaranga set; the third two sets, and the fourth three.

There are four distinct types of marking on these ivory dice.

1. A circle with a dot in the middle stamped with a hot iron instrument or engraved.

MEDICINE AND MAGIC

2. Two concentric circles with a dot in the middle done in the same way.
3. Plain dots burned or bored on to the ivory.
4. Triangular markings, some very rough, carved out of the ivory.

The BaKaranga set was made of dark wood. The dice were roughly rectangular in shape, but curved at the bottom. The markings were completely different from those on any of the ivory sets and they did not have the characteristic notch in the dice representing the females.

The following is a list of the number and type of patterns on each die, but does not indicate the relative positions of each pattern.

	Vhami (old man).	*Tshilume* (young man).	*Twalima* (old woman).	*Lumwe* (young woman).
Outfit 1.	9 concentric circles with dot	5 circles with dot.	8 concentric circles with dot	4 circles with dot.
Outfit 2.				
Set A.	18 dots.	14 dots.	21 dots.	13 dots.
Set B.	Karanga	Karanga	Karanga	Karanga
Outfit 3.				
Set A.	15 circles.	10 circles with dots.	10 circles with dots.	Entirely different type of marking —5 circles with dots and about 15 tiny pairs of triangular signs.
Set B.	15 circles with dots (slightly differently arranged from *vhami* in Set A).	10 circles with dots.	17 circles with dots.	13 circles with dots.
Outfit 4.				
Set A.	15 circles with dots.	9 circles with dots, the circles almost worn away.	10 dots (this die has only a small nick to make it female; it has been used to replace the original bone with notch, which was broken).	8 dots (3 have vestiges of worn-away circles around them).
Set B.	17 pairs of roughly carved triangles.	28 dots.	30 triangles (more or less in pairs).	11 rough triangles
Set C.	17 pairs of crescent-like carved triangles.	6 pairs of crescent triangles and 8 ordinary triangles.	11 pairs of crescent triangles and 1 ordinary triangle.	10 pairs of crescent triangles.

286   MEDICINE AND MAGIC

It may be seen from the above that the number and type of symbols on each die of the same name do not follow any consistent rule. The slight similarities do, however, suggest that possibly among the Venda sets the markings used to conform to certain rules. The one thing common to all these sets is the notch on the female dice which also appears on the BaPedi set described by Junod[1] and Jacques. In the above list, with one exception, the symbols on the dice representing the old man and the old woman are greater in number than those on the dice representing the young man and the young woman. The relative positions of all these markings vary on all the dice, even those of the same name. (Plate XLII.)

My informants all told me that the symbols had no significance, and that the number, type, and position of the symbols depend entirely upon the individual desire of the maker. I was told that one *nganga* possessed a set of dice without any markings whatever except the notches. He identified them by the slightly different shapes. I endeavoured to ascertain whether special signs were associated with special sibs or families but could get no satisfaction. The various types of symbols—circles, dots, and triangles—are used in all Venda decorations.

Of the sixteen possible positions in which these four dice may fall each has its own name and significance. In describing these positions and their significance I propose to follow the method used by Junod and Jacques in describing the divinatory dice of the BaPedi. In this way it is hoped that similarities and differences between the BaPedi and the Venda interpretations will be readily observed. Possibly the same method will be followed by investigators of dice used amongst other tribes and will be a simple basis of comparison.

Vhami, the old man, will be represented by *M*, *tshilume* by *B*, *twalima* by *W*, and *lumwe* by *G*.

Falling with the markings uppermost, that is on the positive side, the position will be noted by + and falling on the reverse side, that is in the negative position, by —. Each position has its special name, which is uttered by the thrower as soon as he sees the lie of the dice. While arranging the dice in a row he utters the formula and then proceeds to interpret the significance. The formulae and interpretations about to be described were given to me at Luvhimbi by Mushapa, in conjunction with another *nganga*, now a Christian in the Berlin Mission, and were translated for me by the Rev. G. Westphal of the Berlin Mission

[1] Junod, Henri A., *The Life of a South African Tribe*, London, 1927, vol. 2, p. 603.

PLATE XLII

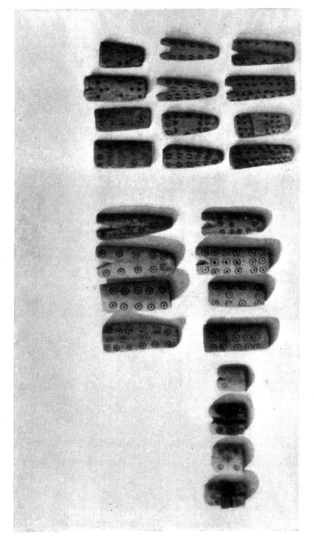

DIVINING DICE

Outfit 1   Outfit 3 (a and b)   Outfit 4 (a, b and c)

MEDICINE AND MAGIC

287

at Makonde. In the following list, (a) is the name of the combination, (b) is the formula uttered, and (c) a smattering of the interpretation.

1. $M+B+W+G+$
    - (a) *Mufhirifhiri* (dissension).
    - (b) *Vhumbedzi ha vhu nga dumbu; vhu sa ungi, mbvula-mubvumbi.* The country of VhaMbedzi is not like a storm; it does not rage, it is drizzle-rain.
    - (c) Fighting in the village, and unsatisfactory people. If it falls continually, fighting with wife. Rain and storms. Enemy to attack from outside. Chief will drive away any one making mistakes.

2. $M+B+W+G-$
    - (a) *Makulela* (that which has grown too big for its power. A thing beyond one's power).
    - (b) *Masunda—phuli mahulu a vho ndoungwana.* The great driver away of slaves is like a small elephant, i.e. He who drives away slaves on a big scale is like a small elephant, very powerful.
    - (c) Always connected with the head of the lineage. In illness the father's spirit is worrying the sick person and the spears must be brought and *phasa madi* done. If there is quarrelling the head of the village *must* be approached at *tevula*.

3. $M+B+W-G-$
    - (a) *Mahe* (Gristle ?).
    - (b) *Ndi na zwimbi; ndi na mela; tshi na muto wa u lala—nawo.* I have got a swelling; I have got a growth; which has a fester for remaining with it (i.e. which will not burst).
    - (c) A good omen. Also connected with the head of the family.

4. $M+B-W-G-$
    - (a) *Hwami* (burden carrier).
    - (b) *Tsha hwami ndi u lalamisa, u vhonisa mmbi ndi halo.* I bring peace into the world, and it also sees war.
    - (c) The time for birth has come. In war the people will be driven from their village. The sick animals will die. Connected with the spirit of father's father.

5. $M-B-W-G-$
    - (a) *Mutangula—(u tangula*, to strip naked, to take away everything).
    - (b) *Wa tangula u sa rwiwi u dzi: tshanga tshi do vhuya.* If you rob and are not beaten, it is 'mine is going to come back' (i.e. if you steal and are not punished you will steal again).
    - (c) Very good sign. There will be no trouble. In sickness recovery will be quick.

MEDICINE AND MAGIC

6. *M — B+W+G+*
    (a) *Murwarwana* (beating each other, i.e. general upset).
    (b) *Lushada—vhalindi—vha—noni, vhalisa mbudzi tshitwela.* Noise of watchers of birds; shepherds of goats are at their pastime, i.e. all noise.
    (c) Bad omen. In illness the *muloi* has sent a *turi* to enter the sick person. A journey should not be undertaken for fear of harm from a snake or other evil thing. Family quarrels are the work of a *muloi.* A man consulting a *nganga* about an accusation of madness, drunkenness, &c., receives confirmation that he is in the condition of which he has been accused. Quarrels between uterine brothers are the work of their wives. Associated with the mother's spirit.

7. *M — B — W+G+*
    (a) *Vhukata (u kata,* to enfold).
    (b) *Tshikatele ndi tshikatele, a tshi na mukatululi—mukoni.* Enfolding is enfolding, and it is not a 'be-able-to-unfold' (i.e. cannot be unfolded).
    (c) Peace in the village. Recovery from an illness, except for women, for whom it portends serious illness. If it falls three times no journey must be undertaken. An enemy will not be successful.

8. *M — B+W — G+*
    (a) *Thamba-dzivha* (the washers in the pool—indicating the crocodile).
    (b) *I ri: 'Nululu!' ndi u wela thivhani: 'Nululu!' ndi u bvela nnda! I fara Mbedzi ya tshigwena—matope.* It says 'Splash!' that is, falling into the lake. 'Splash!'—that is, coming out. It catches *mbedzi,* of mud-crocodile.
    (c) Of no very great significance. Good omen. No illness. A man with no relatives will not be admitted to the village.

9. *M — B+W — G —*
    (a) *Tshilume* (male).
    (b) *Ndi mbandambanda mudini, madiari ndi pfumbupfumbu ya musanda.* He is the man who slouches about in the village (indicating at night-time). Mid-day he is the encourager of the head kraal.
    (c) Sorrow. Connected with lobola. If a girl has run away with a man who has not paid the lobola then child gets sick; it proves that it is because the lobola has not been paid. Child's *malume* must be approached to *phasa* for the child.

10. *M — B+W+G —*
    (a) *Murubi* (most probably *rumbi,* thigh or lap; hardly *marubi,* deserted village).

MEDICINE AND MAGIC 289

(b) *Murubi ndi vhula ha mme.* The lap is the womb of the mother.

(c) Connected entirely with the mother and her side of the family. The mother's spirits are causing trouble.

11. $M+B-W+G-$

(a) *Muhuluri* (something black).

(b) *Ndo vala, nda hona, tsho la mukhoma tsho bvafhi.* I closed (the door). I locked (the door). That which killed the *mukhoma*, where does it come from?

(c) Good omen. Happiness.

12. $M+B-W-G+$

(a) *Tshitangu* (shield).

(b) *Kunga tshitangu ri ende, u sa nge munyadzi wa lwende.* Entice the shield that we may undertake a journey. Don't be like the despisers of the journey (the kill-joy).

(c) Good omen for the traveller. Illness caused by the quarrels of two brothers over their father's cattle. The father of the sick person must end the quarrel.

13. $M-B-W+G-$

(a) *Thwalima* (something dangerous).

(b) *Tshi vhasa mulilo dudndu, musadzi mutsuku ha malwi, ndi tshitangu tsha phaladza—mudi.* It lights fire (*dudndu*—flaring). A red (light-coloured) woman is not lobola-ed. It is the shield (hides the man) of village dispersion.

(c) Very bad omen. Fire. Village is deserted. Danger in everything that is undertaken. One of the women will suffer a great deal and a pregnant woman will give birth immediately.

14. $M-B-W-G+$

(a) *Lumwe* (or perhaps *lunwe*—the other).

(b) *Ndi nga thenga a tsho-nga dzula, ndo nzula nga u tundumala, ndi vha ndi tshi ya ha Tshivhula nda wana muvhuyu wo ima nda felela u posa misevhe, matsina ndi do pfula mukhoma—tshivhula.* I am like a feather that has not got a firm seat. I am poised uncertainly. I was on the point of going to Tshivhula (the chief of the saltpan). I found a Baobab tree standing. I was on the point of shooting an arrow and I noticed that it would have pierced through the *mukhoma* of Tshivhula.

(c) A bad omen. Illness is of the blood or stomach. Be very careful to guard *malembe.* In a dispute between a man and a woman it is the woman who is at fault.

MEDICINE AND MAGIC

15. $M+B-W+G+$
   (a) *Muraru* (the three in one).
   (b) *Tsha muraru a tshi ho kule, tshi mavaleloni a tswinga.* (The sin of) the three in one is not far. It is at the closing point of the *tswinga* (poles for closing the *khoro*).
   (c) Favourable. Prosperity in the village. In illness, the sick person must personally approach the spirits.

16. $M+B+W-G+$
   (a) *Mahe-a-khadzi* (Female gristle).
   (b) *Khasa! woya. Khasa! wo vhuya! madadanye tshi tshi vhuya na vhutala.* Running! you go. Running! you come back. The runner when he comes back comes back on his own spoor.
   (c) Lost property will be recovered. If the wife of a man married to his *malume's* daughter runs away the man must get his cattle back as she will never be any good.

The interpretations of these formulae vary according to the purpose for which they are to be applied by each specialist; a diviner who specializes in detecting witches associates the different combinations with the sibs of the tribe; one who smells out stolen and lost articles interprets them differently; one who is consulted about illness gives them another interpretation, &c.

Divination by dice, which are similar in name and function, occurs among many tribes in southern Africa. A number of plates, taken by Garbutt,[1] representing the divinatory dice used among the 'Mashona, Matebele, and Makalange of Rhodesia, and amongst the Ba-Toka, Ba-Totela, and the Ba-Leya of the Zambesi', show them all to be similar to those of the BaVenda, those of the BaPedi, and those described by Roberts,[2] used among the Malaboch tribes. Smith and Dale[3] mention the occasional use of similar dice among the Ba-Ila, but think that they were introduced to them by the Ba-Rotse on the Zambesi. Dornan[4] briefly compares the dice used by the Matabele and Mashona of Southern Rhodesia with those of the Bushmen, and comes to the con-

[1] Garbutt, H. W., 'Native Witchcraft and Superstition in South Africa'. *J. Roy, Anthrop. Inst.*, vol. xxxix, 1909, pp. 537–47.

[2] Roberts, Rev. Noel, 'A few notes on Tokolo, a System of Divination Practised by the Superior Natives of Malaboch's Tribe in the Northern Transvaal', *South African Journal of Science*, vol. xi, 1914–15, p. 367.

[3] Smith and Dale, Edwin W., and Murray A., *The Ila-Speaking Peoples of Northern Rhodesia*, London, 1920, p. 272.

[4] Dornan, Rev. S. S., 'Divination and Divining Bones', *South African Journal of Science*, vol. xx, 1923–4, pp. 504–11.

MEDICINE AND MAGIC 291

clusion that the Bantu copied the Bushmen in this practice. Miss Bleek,[1] an authority on the Bushmen, does not agree with this theory. She says, 'these dice, or divining sticks, are frequently found among Northern and Central Bushmen, occasionally among those dwelling on the southern borders of the Kalahari. The Colonial Bushmen and those of Griqualand West do not know them. I think they are decidedly adopted from the Bechuana, or other Bantu tribes, as the frequency of their use coincides with the amount to which any tribe has been exposed to Bantu influence. The way the Naron handle them shows they do not know much about them.'

It would seem that the use of the dice is specially concentrated in Southern Rhodesia and the Northern Transvaal. Dice are engraved, among other symbols, on all the magic bowls that I have seen among the BaVenda and also on the one which was found in a cave ten miles from Zimbabwe, depicted on the frontispiece of Bent's *Ruins of Mashonaland*. I am inclined to believe that the use of the dice has spread from the Zimbabwe area and is associated with the old Zimbabwe culture.

The Divining Bowl. Some Venda *mingoma* possess divining bowls, *ndilo ya lupangwa* or *ndilo ya lufhali*, which are only used for the detection of *vhaloi*. The divining bowl varies in size from an object 12 inches in diameter, like the wooden platter, *ndilo*, to a larger bowl about 18 inches in diameter. It is carved from a solid piece of wood to a depth of from $1\frac{1}{2}$ to 2 inches with a broad flattened border. Realistic representations and other designs symbolizing different phases of the religious and magical conceptions of the BaVenda are engraved around this border and in the bed of the bowl. The *muloi* is discovered by the determining of the sibs with which he or she is connected, as in divination with the dice; the sibs are also represented on the bowl. In the centre there is a small protuberance, varying in size in the different bowls, with a large cowrie shell embedded in it; this is the *mukhombo* (umbilicus) and represents the mother's spirits. There is also an elaborate decorative pattern on the back of the bowl, carved around three small legs on which it stands (Plate XLV p. 300).

After a death the relatives may decide to consult a *mungoma* who discovers *vhaloi* by means of one of these bowls, rather than one who uses the more ordinary divining dice. On the arrival of the mourning party the *mungoma* brings his bowl from his hut concealed in a skin. Before any of the party may look at it their eyes must be treated with

[1] Bleek, D. F., *The Naron. A Bushman Tribe of the Central Kalahari*, Cambridge, 1928, pp. 28–9.

MEDICINE AND MAGIC

a white powder, made from the droppings of the kingfisher found under the water; if this is not done they will turn blind. The *mungoma* keeps this powder in a small horn container. After rubbing some on the eyes of all the assembly, he uncovers the divining bowl and they all gather round it. A blanket may be held up on the windy side to protect the bowl and to keep the water that is put into it from being disturbed. It is then filled to the brim with water, which must be carried over the symbol on the border that represents the *khoro*. The *mungoma* next gives the chief mourner from 4 to 6 seeds from the *murutu* tree, which he keeps in a small string bag and uses for this purpose only. He puts scraps of the *lukhata* or *tsindi* of the dead person with these seeds, and, telling the mourner to hold them over the bowl, he pours a little water over them so that it trickles from them down into the water in the bowl, so imparting to the bulk of water and to the *murutu* pips the essence of the deceased. The mourner then drops the pips over the *mukhombo* in the centre of the bowl. The *mungoma* sniffs a pellet up his nose, in the manner described before, and begins to whistle, sometimes blowing through the hollow wing-bone of a vulture, exhorting the floating pips in the same way as that described for the dice. After calling out the names of all the sibs he concludes his exhortation by saying: 'Here are people who are in trouble and want to know who has caused the death of one of their relatives. I want you to tell them clearly whether it is a *muloi* of the mother's spirits or the father's. Show me carefully. Show me the road.' All the pips float around the bowl and the first to touch one of the sib symbols indicates the sib of the *muloi*; the second and third pips identify the sibs of the mother and mother's mother respectively. The *mungoma* watches the pips closely and observes the movements of the other pips as well as the further movements of the three that have revealed the sibs, the symbols at which they touch enabling him to interpret and reconstruct the whole crime. Sometimes the pips hover around the *mukhombo*, showing that the death was caused by the mother's spirits.

When the pips come to rest the *mungoma* removes them from the bowl, often with a small iron spoon made with native wrought iron, and then empties out the water. All the other features of this divinatory rite are exactly the same as those described in connexion with the finding of a *muloi* with the divining dice.

The two bowls shown in Plates XLIII and XLIV belonged to Tshiobi of the Tshilata district in Mphephu's location and Mukharu of

PLATE XLIII

TSHIOBI'S DIVINING BOWL

Iron spoon   Bag of *murutu* pips   Horn containing eye medicine

MEDICINE AND MAGIC

293

the Mukula district in Tshivhase's location respectively. Both are of considerable age, having passed from father to son through several generations. I propose to describe the interpretations of the symbols on these bowls exactly as I received them. Tshiobi described his bowl to me himself, but unfortunately Mukharu did not as he died soon after parting with his bowl; Mukharu's bowl, however was interpreted for me by his friend Mphiri, avowedly well acquainted with this bowl and himself a notable diviner. In the course of my investigations I examined four different bowls in detail. All contained many symbols in common, but all varied in the relative positions of these symbols to each other and in the order and manner of their arrangement. The skill and individual taste of each wood-carver may also account for many variations. The symbols on some bowls are more realistic than those on others; some symbols are very crude and roughly carved while others are complicated in design and workmanship; some designs are continued from the edge of the bowl into the bed. The crocodile on the bed of Tshiobi's bowl is realistically pictured with its head resting on the edge, so that when the bowl is filled with water the body is submerged and the head left resting on a sandbank at the water's edge.

The interpretations of the different symbols also vary and are influenced by the locality in which the diviner lives. Tshiobi had sibs represented on his bowl which are quite unknown to most BaVenda and are really small sub-sibs living near to him. In some cases sibs belonging to alien tribes are represented. There are innumerable differences of this sort both in the designs and interpretations, although all are similar in constructive essentials and in function.

Interpretation of Tshiobi's Bowl. (See Plate XLIII.)

1. The *khoro* over which the water is passed into the bowl. The lines which are continued into the bed represent the *mafhoro*, the entrance gate to the *khoro*.

2. A. ⎫
   B. ⎬ Divining dice representing the combination *murubi*.—See p. 288.

   A pip touching here signifies that the mother's spirits are responsible for the death. The symbol below this in the bed of the bowl represents the hyena, which carries the *muloi* of the mother's spirits.

3. A. Axe, the weapon which kills.

   B. Duiker horn. The hole is the outlet through which the magic formula is uttered by a *muloi* seeking to kill his victim by black magic.

   C. Divining dice representing the combination *thwalima*. See page 289. It symbolizes blood, fire, and disaster.

MEDICINE AND MAGIC

D. Duiker horn, the same as A. but referring to another district.

Section 3 represents the VhaLuvhu sib, who may not eat the small figs growing near the root of the fig tree. It is a small branch of the Ndou sib, with its mountain at Kwakani in Mphephu's location.

4. Divining dice representing the combination *mahe-a-khadzi*. See page 290.

It represents the VhaKwebo sib.

5. Shield.

It represents the BaNgona people.

The symbol between 4 and 5 [g] represents a horn and a hole; the former contains medicine and the latter is used for mixing the medicine. It is connected with 4 and 5.

6. A. Divining dice representing the combination *mufhirifhiri*. See page 287.

B. The door by which the *muloi* entered the hut of his victim.

C. Poles of the door.

Section 6 represents Netshiavho's branch of the Ndou sib, which lives at Lake Fundudzi.

7. A. Man's chest.

B. Elephant's head and eyes.

A pip striking here shows that the father's spirits are responsible for the death.

8. A. Ostrich feather.

B. Stone on which medicine is ground.

C. Hand of the person who made the medicine.

Section 8 represents the Mbedzi sib, living at Luvhimbi.

9. A. Divining dice representing the combination *hwami*. See page 287.

B. Snake, the medicine through which the death was caused.

C. Holes that the snake lives in.

Section 9 represents the VhaNyai sib.

10. A. Divining dice representing the combination *muhuluri*. See page 289.

It represents the VhaKhomolo sib.

11. Divining dice representing the combination *lumwe*. See page 289.

It represents the Vhatwamamba sib.

12. A. Pointed stakes around chief's kraal.

B. Chief's comb.

C. „ bull.

D. „ comb again.

Section 12 represents the royal MaKhwinde sib.

MEDICINE AND MAGIC

13. The thorn used by the *muloi* for poking poison into his victim's meat. The pip touching here shows that the *muloi* is an illegitimate person whose sib cannot be ascertained, and therefore belongs to the *kanga* (forgotten) sib.

14. A. Divining dice representing the combination *mahe*. See page 287.
    B. Thorn.
    C. Comb.
    Section 14 represents the VhaLaudzi sib.

15. A. Bull.
    B. Comb.
    C. Hole from which evil medicine was obtained.
    Section 15 represents the VhaLeya sib, living near Messina.

16. A. The hole in which the crocodile lives.
    B. Head of crocodile (the body being continued in the bed of the bowl).
    C. Sandbank where the crocodile is basking.
    Section 16 represents the Tshigwena branch of the Mbedzi sib.

17. A. Divining dice representing the combination *tshilume*. See page 288.
    B. Heart.
    C. Old man.
    D. Heart of old man.
    Section 17 represents the VhaDau sib, living at Tshiherni.

18. A. Hole through which a man (B) has crawled in order to cause trouble with a MuDau of Tshiherni, symbolizing the creeping into the victim's country.
    B. Man of another branch of the VhaDau sib with evil medicine.
    C. Bundle of medicine.

19. A. Divining dice representing the combination *murwarwana*. See page 288.
    B. Stick carried by the *muloi* at night.
    C. *Turi* sent by the *muloi* to do the evil deed.
    D. Gate pole of the victim's gate. The curved object inside the bowl under this section is the *ludo* of the old woman. See page 248.
    Section 19 represents the BaNgona people.

20. A. Divining dice representing the combination *muraru*. See page 290.
    B. Spear handle (continued on the bed of the bowl).
    C. Road taken by the *muloi*.
    D. Village from which the *muloi* was chased.
    Section 20 represents the Nyasiame sib, a branch of the Ndou, who changed their sib-name after having been driven across the Luvuvhu river as a punishment for witchcraft.

MEDICINE AND MAGIC

21. A. Trees.

    B. Divining dice representing the combination *vhukata*. See page 288. The pip touching in this section shows that the death occurred through intercourse with a woman who was unclean through abortion or some other reason.

The Bed of the Bowl.

Opposite 6 B ⌒ *Tshidhadyani*, dissociated spirit. See page 238. The pips hovering over this sign show that the death was caused by a *tshidhadyani*.

The three symbols opposite 7 and 8 represent the wings of the *ndadzi* bird with the lightning between them. See page 225. A pip hovering over these symbols indicates that the death was due to the lightning bird.

Opposite 13 and 14 the straight line represents

the bull and the circles on either side the bull's eyes, the whole being enclosed by the fence of the cattle kraal. A pip hovering above this shows that the death was caused by the spirits of the father's lineage, because the sacred bull was not installed for them. See page 243.

Interpretation of Mukharu's bowl. (See Plate XLIV)

1. A. The man who shuts the *khoro* gate.
    B. *Khoro.*

2. Baboon.
    It represents the Vha-ila-pfene sib from Lombe, east of Luvhimbi.

3. A. Two symbols supposed to represent the sacred objects of the *zwidhadyani.*
    B. Two *zwidhadyani*. See page 238.

4. Two divining dice representing the combination *vhukata*. See page 288. It represents the VhaNyai sib.

5. A. Cow.
    B. Bull.
    C. Three spears (continued inside the bowl). These symbols all represent the spirits of the father's lineage. See pages 243 and 246. If a pip touches here the father's ancestors brought the death and must be propitiated by the installation of a bull or spear.

PLATE XLIV

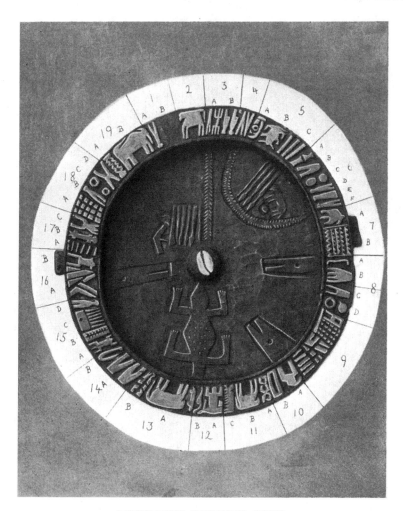

MUKHARU'S DIVINING BOWL

MEDICINE AND MAGIC

297

6. A. Comb of chief's wife.
   B. Divining dice representing the combination *thwalima*. See page 289.
   C. Divining dice representing the combination *mahe*. See page 287.
   D. Chief's daughter.
   E.   ,,   son-in-law.
   F.   ,,   daughter.

   Section 6 represents the MaKhwinde royal sib. The semi-circle in the bed of the bowl opposite 5 and 6 is the fence of the chief's yard. The spears have been mentioned, and the other signs are the chief's dog and the chief's fire.

7. A. Cow.
   B. Explained as being only decoration.
   Section 7 represents the VhaLaudzi sib.

8. A. Root for medicine.
   B. Hand.
   C. Divining dice representing the combination *tshilume*. See page 288.
   D. Hole for grinding medicine and stone for pounding.

   If a pip touches here it shows that the *muloi* is a *nganga* belonging to the MaKhwinde sib.
   Symbol on the bed of the bowl opposite 8 A and 8 B represents the *shedu* of the woman who administered the poison.

9. All the symbols said to represent porcupine quills. ?Represents the sib of the Vha-ila-thoni,

10. A. Zebra.
    B. Only decoration.

11. A. Only decoration.
    B. Lion.
    C. Only decoration.
    Section 11 represents the VhaDau sib.

12. A. Crocodile.
    B. Dogs.
    ? Said to represent the Mangelele sib, living at Mutali.

13. A. Elephant.
    B. Only decoration.
    Section 13 represents Ndou sib.

14. A. Divining dice representing the combination *mutangula*. See page 287.
    B. Snake.
    Section 14 represents a Rhodesian sib Vha-ila-mbila (those forbidden the rock-rabbit).

298 MEDICINE AND MAGIC

15. A. Sacred object of the VhaLovhedzi sib (the VhaLovhedzi are a sib of Majaji's people near Pietersburg).
    B. Only decoration.
    C. Comb.
    D. Man.

    Section 15 represents the VhaLovhedzi sib.

16. A. Only decoration.
    B. Small mud-crocodile.

    Section 16 represents the Tshigwena section of the Mbedzi sib, who tabu this particular crocodile.

17. A. Only decoration.
    B. Man of Vhatwamamba or VhaLeya sib.
    C. Not identified at all.

    Section 17 represents the man of the Vhatwamamba and VhaLeya sibs.

18. A. Only decoration.
    B. Woman.
    C. Stones, used in the old days by the Vhatwamamba and the VhaLeya for grinding corn.
    D. Old dress of women of this sib, with one skin in front and one behind.

    Section 18 represents the women of the Vhatwamamba and VhaLeya sibs.

19. A. Only decoration.
    B. Elephant.

    Section 19 represents the Ndou sib, especially the more powerful and influential branches.

Symbols on the Bed of the Bowl.

Axe and spear opposite 18 and 19 of the father's lineage. If a pip hovers over here it shows that one of the father's spirits caused the death.

Crocodile represents one section of the Mbedzi sib.

The identical symbols opposite 16 A, 8 A and B, and 10 A represent the women's *shedu*—the hole in the centre of the symbol is the vagina— —a pip hovering here signifies that the deceased died from consumption, or from having sexual intercourse with a woman who had aborted or was for some other reason sexually tabu.

Two holes near the axe are where the medicine is prepared. If a pip hovers here it shows that the dead man was poisoned by poison being actually put into his food and not by magical means.

MEDICINE AND MAGIC

Lines in the vertical rim (not visible in the plate) separate the different symbols.

In comparing the detailed designs on these two bowls many curious discrepancies are disclosed. On Tshiobi's bowl 19 C represents the *turi,* and the identical symbol 15 A on Mukharu's bowl is a sacred object of the VhaLovhedzi sib. Again on Tshiobi's bowl the symbols 19 A and 16 C are practically identical, although the former is interpreted as the combination *murwarwana* of the divining dice and the latter as the sandbank on which the crocodile's head is resting. There are other similar examples. Tshiobi's bowl has 12 of the 16 possible combinations of the divining dice and Mukharu's has only 4. When I showed Tshiobi Mukharu's bowl he gave altogether different interpretations to many of the symbols.

All these inconsistencies bear out my suspicion that the present users of these bowls do not understand the real significance of the symbols engraved on them, but that the BaVenda came in contact with them at some early time and adapted them to their own use, gradually forgetting their original meaning and interpreting them to suit themselves. If this is the case, where did these bowls originate? I think that probably, with the divining dice, they are a relic of the ancient Zimbabwe culture.

As far as I could ascertain they only occur in southern Africa among the BaVenda in the Northern Transvaal and the BaKaranga in Southern Rhodesia. Bent [1] discusses a wooden platter of the same type found near Zimbabwe, and I here quote what he says in this connexion:

'One of the most interesting of the later finds in Mashonaland is a wooden platter found in a cave about ten miles distant from Zimbabwe, a reproduction of which forms the frontispiece to this edition. Mr. Noble, clerk of the Cape Houses of Parliament, to whom I am indebted for the photograph of this object, thus describes it:

"In the centre of the dish, which is about 38 inches in circumference, there is a carved figure of a crocodile (which was probably regarded as a sacred animal) or an Egyptian turtle, and on the rim of the plate is a very primitive representation of the Zodiacal characters, such as Aquarius, Pisces, Cancer, Sagittarius, Gemini, as well as Taurus and Scorpio. Besides these there occur the figures of the sun and moon, a group of three stars, a triangle, and four slabs with triangular punctures (two of them being in reversed

---

[1] Bent, J. T., *The Ruined Cities of Mashonaland*, London, 1896, Frontispiece and pp. xv–xvi.

300 MEDICINE AND MAGIC

positions), all carved in relief, and displaying the same rude type of art which marked the decorated bowl found by Mr. Bent in the temple at Zimbabwe. A portion of the rim of the plate has been eroded by insects, probably from resting on damp ground. Altogether, the relic presents to the eye an unquestionable specimen of rare archaism, which has been remarkably preserved through many centuries, probably dating back even before the Christian era. Previous observation and measurements of Zimbabwe, by Mr. R. Swan, established the presumption that the builders of it used astronomical methods and observed the zodiacal and other stars; and this plate shows that the ancient people, whether Phoenician, Sabaean, or Mineans—all of Arabian origin—were familiar with the stellar grouping and signs said to have been first developed by the Chaldeans and dwellers in Mesopotamia." '

The BaVenda know nothing of the signs of the Zodiac and I am not prepared to identify any of the symbols on their bowls as Zodiacal characters. Nevertheless, the connexion between this bowl and those of the BaVenda is quite unmistakable.

The Effect of the Medico-Magician on Society.

There is no doubt that most of the medico-magicians believe in their own supernatural powers, and feel that they are a caste apart from and superior to the ordinary people. All believe implicitly in the efficacy of their therapeutical treatments. Some have undoubted hypnotic powers, fostered by the ease with which the will of the hypnotist is imposed on the weaker minds of his hyper-credulous clients. It is the natural outcome of ancestor-worship that the child of the medico-magician should be endowed with all the special powers of his ancestors, and that the apprentice should imbibe the very essence of his master and thereby have the right to the help of his master's doctor ancestors.

The art of the medico-magician is inextricably woven into the social, religious, and economic life of the whole community; he has an influence out of all proportion to his knowledge and skill; he is in constant and intimate touch with the chiefs, some of whom actually belong to the fraternity. There is no doubt that in some ways the influence of the medico-magician has a salutary effect on the morality of Venda society, acting as a check on the wilder spirits and organizing the rogues and wise men so that their treachery and genius can only find vent in certain specified channels. The magician rules primarily through fear. The implicit belief of the ordinary people in his power to detect evil and to punish the evil-doer has the effect of keeping

PLATE XLV

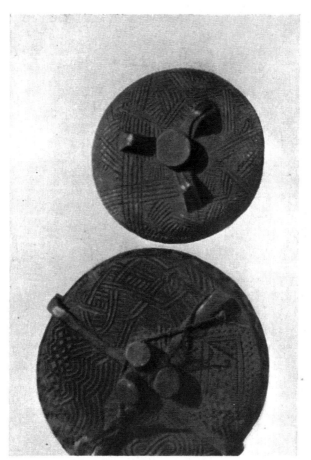

DECORATIONS ON BACKS OF DIVINING BOWLS

MEDICINE AND MAGIC

the people fairly law-abiding. The fear of being divined to be a *muloi* is the greatest check on the criminally intentioned, and is a powerful factor in fostering the courtesy and fair dealing that is so noticeable among the people in general. The position of a MuVenda accused by a *mungoma* of being a *muloi* is certainly unenviable.

As a rule the *dzinganga* and *mingoma* are keen observers, and while they trick people into believing that all their divinations are genuine thought-reading or revelation, they frequently do discover the truth and pick out as the guilty person an undesirable rascal, who is a real danger to the community. The shrewd and intelligent man, who from childhood has been taught by his father all the hidden secrets and family skeletons in the neighbourhood, achieves a very intimate knowledge of the lives, habits, and characters of his clients. In looking closely into the details of the divinatory powers of these practitioners many simple and obvious ruses are brought to light; doubtless some of the more obscure magic is made by equally simple methods. The *mungoma*, when divining the sib of the *muloi* and his maternal ancestors, narrates the whole history of the events leading up to the consultation. But the local *nganga* points out to the party which *mungoma* to consult! He has doubtless primed the oracle with a full account of all the happenings, and his colleague is therefore able to speak with confidence, bringing many pertinent details into his discourse. Again, the *mungoma* protects the water in his bowl from the wind, so that with his hollow vulture's wing he may help to direct the pips on their passage. The man who draws out objects from the bodies of his clients resorts to the ubiquitous trick of hiding the said objects in his mouth or on his person. Many other, to the BaVenda, genuine manifestations of their power can be explained by simple conjuring, sleight of hand, and ventriloquism. A particularly clever person who suspects the trickery of the medico-magician often becomes himself apprenticed to the profession and, while learning all the tricks and counterfeits, absorbs also some belief in their supernatural power. The obvious trickery, combined with an equally obvious sincerity, results in the contradictory character of the medico-magician which presents such a problem to the white observer. Most of the clever brains of the tribe are to be found among the medicine-men. Although most of their medicines and treatments are scientifically useless, until there is some one else to fill their place, whom can the people consult ? After all, it is human nature, when in trouble, either physical or spiritual, to seek advice or consolation from some one. If the most

302　MEDICINE AND MAGIC

intelligent medico-magicians could be picked out and exposed and then, instead of being punished as criminals could be taught a smattering of simple science and medicine and allowed to return to their people, it is possible that they would turn their knowledge to good account. It is impossible and unreasonable to try to stamp out witchcraft without providing some substitute. At present the witch-doctor is driven underground, but his influence is sure to continue until the people are taught from childhood the simple scientific explanation of ordinary natural phenomena.

Possession. Molombo.

The phenomenon of possession was rare among the BaVenda until about 1914. The ancestors, *vhaloi*, and medico-magicians were to them sufficient explanation for all abnormalities, both good and bad, that occurred in the life of the people, while the rare manifestations of Raluvhimba explained obscure meteorological happenings.

The possession-cult was of very small significance until it spread from Southern Rhodesia and proceeded to gain popularity with extraordinary rapidity. At present the cult is focused in two localities, although its votaries extend all over the country. People in the first of these two centres, when possessed, always speak Tshikaranga, the language spoken by the tribe, among whom the BaVenda first encountered the cult. The second centre is at Mutali, and its votaries speak in a mixture of Tshikaranga and Tshivenda; this language is becoming rapidly more Venda-ized, most of the songs sung during the ceremonies being to-day in pure Tshivenda.

The spirit, *tshilombo* (pl. *zwilombo*), which is supposed to enter the host, is usually the spirit of some offended ancestor, sometimes absurdly remote. This spirit will cause its victims illness and subsequent death if it is not pacified. Occasionally this *tshilombo* will have no genealogical connexion with the person into whom it enters; it may be an exorcised spirit, who by the help of a *nganga* has been completely divorced from further contact and communication with its own descendants. Banished spirits of this order wander about full of mischievous intention, in search of any host in whom they can find temporary refuge. Such spirits may enter anybody and generally hide in crevices of trees making weird unnatural noises; a MuVenda, who hears a strange creaking noise emanating from a tree top, and, on looking back at the tree sees a new crack in its trunk, knows that a homeless *tshilombo* has left its hiding place and entered him; this

MEDICINE AND MAGIC

explains why every MuVenda is afraid to look back when he hears an unusual noise. The BaVenda conception differs slightly from that of the BaThonga, who think that all *zwilombo* belong to foreigners. The BaKaranga, among whom the cult is found in a very advanced stage, consider the *zwilombo* may be the spirits of all manner of creatures, human or animal. I came across one MuVenda, recently arrived in Vendaland from Southern Rhodesia, who was said to be possessed by the spirit of a python, from the Karanga country. It seems probable that this cult, which is increasing enormously in popularity, will before very long have as strong a hold on the minds of the BaVenda as it has to-day on those of the BaKaranga.

Among the BaVenda it is generally women who become the victims of the *zwilombo*, although on rare occasions a spirit chooses a man to be his host. Possession is diagnosed by the *nganga*, who has generally been consulted to discover the cause of some strange illness or behaviour of a woman; on declaring that the patient is possessed of the *tshilombo* he tests the truth of his diagnosis by offering her various foods to eat; if she vomits he knows that he is right and advises his clients to summon the assistance of a *maine vha tshele* (diviner of the rattle) who, having himself once been possessed, has become an authority on the subject. If the patient is married her husband quickly visits all the people in the district, especially his wife's relations, and asks them all to come to her help; he borrows drums and summons a drummer who knows the *molombo* beat, and that evening as soon as the beat of the drums begins all the women and many men of the district hasten to the scene, and any persons who have ever been possessed take an active part in the proceedings. A general hubbub arises which gradually settles into some sort of order, when the *maine vha tshele* begins to sing the words of the *molombo* song and to dance wildly to the sound of the drums with a weird exotic tread; each old *molombo* dancer takes her part, sidling up to the drums, gradually quickening the pace until she is whirling wildly round, waving her axe and sometimes stamping on the floor and leaping in the air. All the company sing and shake their rattles and the noise and dust and general excitement increase. The patient is sitting crouched in the hut; she has probably been ill for some days, vomiting and becoming tired, weak and helpless. The *nganga* has pronounced the sentence; she is possessed of a *tshilombo*. She has seen other women in this state and is filled with dread, but she remembers vaguely that it is a condition that brings with it prestige, and that all

MEDICINE AND MAGIC

molombo dancers are treated as a class superior to the ordinary people. She is feeling very ill and hopes vaguely that she may come safely through the ordeal, feel well again, be rid of this cruel spirit, and finally emerge from her trials as one of the elect. Meanwhile the dance goes on; after a time the *maine vha tshele* will stop dancing and go to the patient. She rubs the patient's body with a special mixture and sprinkles the residue on the fence around the hut; the mixture is made from the leaves of the *murandela* and *bunganyuyu* trees, the nest of the *thaha* bird (finch), and a piece cut from the *khumela* (lump on the root of *muvuvhu* tree), all crushed and mixed with water. After this she leads the patient by the hand into the group of dancers, and, stimulated by the prevailing excitement, her strength returns and she dances wildly, obeying every order given by the *maine vha tshele*. Every eye is on her and it is astounding how long the poor creature can keep on dancing before she falls to the ground. Her collapse is the first sign from the *tshilombo* spirit; the noise and clamour continue, the *maine vha tshele* singing and shouting in a frenzied manner and shaking her rattle close to the patient's ear; if there is no further sign the possessed woman is taken back to the hut to rest for a short time, when a further attempt is made to make the *tshilombo* reveal itself, by dancing, singing, and rattling close to her head. Finally, if nothing transpires, she is made to dance again. This may continue for several days during which the patient is urged to go on dancing, until she collapses again and at the same time emits a deep loud grunt like a bull; this is a sign that the *tshilombo* will now manifest itself. After giving vent to this grunt all her joints become absolutely stiff, and she is taken into her hut, laid on a mat and covered with a blanket. The other women gather round the mat and stand gazing at her in expectant silence; the *maine vha tshele* stands close to her head and from time to time she feels her stiffened joints; when these start to relax she bends over the patient and calls 'Who are you?' The answer comes in a weak, childish far-away voice, in Tshikaranga, the words being so faint and indistinct that they are only audible to the *maine vha tshele*, who repeats them to the expectant watchers; 'I am so-and-so' (naming some long deceased ancestor), 'and I entered you when I was walking in a certain place' (naming it); 'you do not treat me well. I want a present, some clothes or ornaments'; she may even demand the spear or axe of her ancestors, or a tail-whisk or kerrie stick. There are four particular types of cloth that find favour with the *tshilombo*, a black cloth described by the spirit as *lutombo* (stone), a red one,

MEDICINE AND MAGIC

tshilemba, a white, *mutshena*, and a spotted black and white, *palu*. All objects demanded are readily promised by the husband and relatives of the possessed woman, although they are not necessarily handed over then and there. Sometimes before the spirit will consent to reveal its identity it must be conciliated with the payment of two fowls. The relatives are often not satisfied with the first manifestation and ask for further details, which the *tshilombo* gives, and which are again elucidated by the *maine vha tshele*. After this the husband kills a goat and cuts it up, giving the *maine vha tshele* a piece of every organ and cooking all of them in a pot with some very sweet medicine (the ingredients were not discovered). The patient is given the mixture to eat and the *maine vha tshele* addresses the spirit saying; 'Here, so-and-so, we give you meat and food. Eat it, and do not make our people ill, so that they cannot eat, but let them eat anything like others'; she continues; 'I am going home now. In future if you desire to dance, you may come back to this person and dance, but do not make her ill.' The *tshilombo* replies; 'I, too, want to go home', but the husband says; 'No, stay for a few days and continue dancing or my wife will get worse.' The *maine vha tshele* then goes home but the patient continues to dance for two or three more days until the *tshilombo* whispers to her; 'I am tired and want to go home, my feet are sore.' Then one of the women brings a basin of water and the patient washes all over from head to foot, and the *tshilombo* escapes. All the presents that the spirit demanded are given to her by her husband, and when she receives them she does the *phasa madi* over them, asking the *tshilombo* not to make her ill again. These objects are all put away in the patient's hut, and whenever she begins to vomit her food and fears that the *tshilombo* has returned, she puts on the clothing and takes the other objects, weapons, &c., in her hand and begins to dance.

When a woman is possessed by the *tshilombo* her husband and relations must treat her with great respect and consideration, saluting her as if she were a chief. She addresses her husband as *muduhulu*, grandchild. After the departure of the spirit the woman generally becomes extremely fat.

If the *tshilombo* kills the patient her husband goes to his wife's mother and says, 'Look, you must be a *muloi*, the *tshilombo* of your family has killed my wife. Give me back my cattle'; his cattle will be returned without demur. If the *tshilombo* reveals itself to be a wandering banished spirit it may be disposed of in the following way: The *maine vha tshele* rubs the knob of her kerrie stick with a special

x

MEDICINE AND MAGIC

preparation and, holding it, dances wildly with the patient; suddenly she darts out of the clamouring crowd, brandishing her kerrie above her head, and declaring that the *tshilombo* is caught up on it; she rushes into the bush and hurls the stick into the fork of a tree where it is caught up; the patient staggers and presently retires to her hut cured. The medicine on the stick keeps the spirit safely secured, unless some unwary person touches it, when he will probably become the *tshilombo's* new victim. Ancestor spirits are never treated in this way, only troublesome or evil foreign spirits. The Mutali district is reputed to be full of these bad spirits, and no one going there will ever pick up any object from the ground or touch the fruit on the trees. Occasionally a very evil *tshilombo* is driven into a sheep, which is driven away into the bush or drowned.

A person, once possessed of the *tshilombo* spirit, is never again the same irresponsible individual that she was before; she belongs to the fraternity of *molombo* dancers, and is always liable to be repossessed by the spirit for which she has once been host; if this occurs the *tshilombo* spirit is pacified with presents and dancing until it departs. All persons who have once been possessed hold dances at intervals to appease their various *zwilombo* and keep them in good humour. They meet from time to time at the kraal of the eldest *maine vha tshele* in the district and, dressed in their *molombo* paraphernalia, dance fast and furiously for several days. These dances, which take place at least once a year, are prophylactic; they also serve to remind people of their relative's *tshilombo* association; *molombo* dancers must be treated with care and discrimination and conciliated by husbands and relatives with frequent presents.

Sometimes an ordinary girl of the tribe with no previous claim to celebrity, after having been once possessed, may become suddenly a *maine vha tshele* of wide repute and extraordinary power. The following episode in this connexion occurred within a few miles of my camp. Mutshitama was betrothed to a man whom she did not like. When the time came for her to go to her husband she became sullen and depressed. She was taken to his village but ran away and returned to her home; her father was very angry and thrashed her severely and she ran out into the bush and disappeared completely for six days. She returned to her father's kraal looking very ill and complaining so bitterly that her father's anger melted and he sent for a doctor, who divined that she was possessed by a spirit who had once been a great doctor and a great diviner. The father decided to wait until her symp-

MEDICINE AND MAGIC

307

toms became worse before calling in the *maine vha tshele*; that night the girl woke her father and commanded him to follow her. He protested, but feared to disobey her as she spoke in Tshikaranga with the voice of the spirit within her. She led him to the river side and, pointing to a dark object in the river which appeared to be a crocodile, she picked up a stone and after rubbing it with her hands told her father to throw it at the creature. He was too terrified to obey, so the girl herself hurled the stone, and the supposed crocodile disappeared with a splashing noise. She turned to her father and said; 'That is no crocodile but a *muloi*. It is that Shangaan woman who lives close by disguised as a crocodile'. The father was so deeply impressed by this evidence of his daughter's newly-acquired powers that he called together all his relatives and told them that his daughter was possessed by a great doctor spirit. The girl told them to follow her to the river where she would prove her powers; she plunged into the river and disappeared for nearly an hour. When she emerged she held a green mealie in one hand and a variety of shrubs and roots in the other. Her relatives on the river bank were amazed, as it was not the time for green mealies, but she explained that Mwari had given them to her and taught her about all the roots and medicines. She returned home, ate the mealies, and, mixing the shrubs and roots that she had brought back from the river bed with dried mealies, pounded and prepared her equipment. She demanded four rattles, of the type used by the *maine vha tshele*, from her father, and forthwith began to practise her new vocation. She is now one of the most famous doctors in the district and her village is always filled with the sound of the dancing and singing of her clients. This girl will probably teach her daughter and a new hereditary line commence.

The *molombo* performance is obviously stage-managed by the *maine vha tshele*, who works herself into such a state of nervous excitement and exhilaration that she acts almost subconsciously. She undoubtedly whispers ventriloquially the words that the *tshilombo* is supposed to utter through the mouth of the possessed woman; and the latter, on regaining consciousness after the long faint which was the climax of her dancing ordeal, is as convinced as every one else that it is indeed the *tshilombo* within her who is speaking. After that she readily accepts the fact of her dual personality, believing that she has begun a new life.

All *molombo* dancers have a strange, intent, staring expression when performing in these orgies; they are pale and thin and appear utterly

MEDICINE AND MAGIC

absorbed in their dancing and singing. The strain of the first exorcism has a lasting effect upon any previously normal woman, and the sound of the *molombo* beat on the drum is generally enough to draw her by a strange, subconscious, psychological reaction to the scene of the excitement, where the whole environment recalls her first experience. The *molombo* dance is regarded with an ambivalent attitude. The people fear it and do not really enjoy it, but it possesses a magnetic attraction that they cannot withstand, so that they all seem to become hypnotized and drawn irresistibly to the scene. A person once possessed is feared and conciliated by her people and is a valuable asset to a kraal, as she brings visitors and presents in her wake. Powerful chiefs like to have a *molombo* dancer among their wives.

XXII

RAIN-MAKING AND FERTILITY OF CROPS

ALTHOUGH the southern slopes of the Zoutpansberg mountains are well watered and the country around Tshivhase's territory exceptionally fertile, there remains a great part of Vendaland that is dry and arid, depending for its whole supply of water on the summer rains. These rains generally begin in October and November in time to soften the ground before ploughing, but they are by no means constant north of the mountains, where droughts are frequent.

When *tuda*, the constellation formed by the two bright stars of the Southern Cross and the two pointers, is in the position in the heavens that indicates the beginning of the new year and planting time, the whole mind of the people is fixed upon the all-absorbing subject of rain. When will the rain come? When the thunder clouds roll past, as they often do for weeks on end without a drop of rain falling, every head is turned skywards and everybody is filled with a sickening dread as the longed-for rain fails to fall. When the position begins to be serious the people look to the chief for help.

The python dance of the *domba*, which has been described as a probable fertility rite, is made clearer when the beliefs concerning drought are understood. In the minds of the BaVenda there is a very close association between the python and rain. It is tabu for any python to be killed at the time when rain ordinarily begins to fall, or during the following six months, which is the time of the planting, growth, and ripening of crops. During the other six months of the year, although the python may be killed, it is tabu to peg out its skin to dry like the skins of other animals; the python's skin is either left unpegged or is stretched out to dry with the help of stones. The head and tail of the python are always buried in the cattle kraal to ensure fertility of the cattle, and the carcase dragged to a river, however far distant, and thrown into it. A chief, on hearing of the slaughter of a python, will often send a messenger to satisfy himself that the python has been deposited in the river, as otherwise rain will certainly not fall. The python is often found lurking around river banks and the BaVenda sometimes call it a water-snake; hence has arisen its association with rain. Without rain nothing can grow or live, and therefore the python must be treated with deference. The connexion between water and

310 RAIN-MAKING AND FERTILITY OF CROPS

fertility is obvious and explains why the python's head and tail, buried in the cattle kraal, make the cows prolific, and why its skin worn around the waist of a barren woman induces pregnancy. For some reason the tail of the hyena is also associated with rain. It is strictly tabu for anybody to possess such a thing, as if it is waved in the air strong winds will follow and prevent clouds from forming; any one discovered in possession of this dangerous object is promptly dubbed a *muloi* and treated accordingly. Twins, all children dying directly after birth or still-born, and all consumptives must be buried near water, otherwise rain will not fall. In the rainy season it is strictly tabu to play the game *mefhuva* with stones, for fear that the rain will be turned to hail; fruit pips are used instead. Another reason for the failure of the rain is the anger of Raluvhimba or of the ancestor spirits of the chief. If the chief has failed to prepare the *zwitungulo* or neglected to perform some sacred ritual the *nganga* may divine that the ancestors have withheld the rain.

There is no annual ceremony in connexion with rain, as if all tabus are observed and all the ancestors satisfied it is considered that the rain is certain to fall; it is the neglect of carrying out everything in its proper order that brings the punishment of drought. Rain may be induced to fall by religious or magical means. A year of insufficient rain is always followed by the dispatch of an emissary to Mwari with presents of oxen and money as has already been described; if, after this, another year of drought is threatened, the chief consults his *nganga* to divine the cause. Possibly the *nganga* will divine that a malicious individual has a hyena tail in his possession, in which case the malefactor is discovered by a *mungoma* and either killed or hounded out of the country. Possibly twins or a consumptive have not been buried by the river-side, in which case the relatives are summoned and ordered to exhume the bones of their dead and see to it that they are immediately re-interred in the correct and proper place. More often than not the failure of rain is divined to be due to angry ancestors. The identity of the spirit is discovered and all the people are summoned to do the sacred *tshikona* dance, either in a village within hearing distance of the grave of the offended ancestor, or in the bush near the grave. Meanwhile the chief, accompanied by his relatives, visits the grave and, having performed the *phasa madi* ceremony, lays the stomach contents of an ox on it. He beseeches the spirit to withdraw his anger and not to let the earth get hot and his descendants starve for want of water. In the old days when the BaVenda were more united,

RAIN-MAKING AND FERTILITY OF CROPS 311

all the chiefs of the MaKhwinde sib, who are now independent, gathered at the ruins of Dzata, and there the chief prayed to his ancestors for rain, while a huge gathering of people danced the *tshikona*. Chief Mbulahene Mphephu still visits the ruins and holds a similar ceremony, but to-day it is a comparatively small affair. Before consulting the professional rain-maker the chief will summon the *maine vha u fungo* (diviner of seeds) to organize the *mudzivho* (*u dzivho shango*, to put the country right). This *maine* is not actually concerned with the making of rain, but he prepares the earth in order to induce an environment favourable to rain. There are two ways in which the *mudzivho* may be carried out. In the first, all the young children, who have not reached maturity, are given branches dipped in a magical fluid; with these they damp out all the fires in their district. A *nganga* lights a new fire in the kraal of each petty chief and each woman must light her fire from it, leaving a bracelet beside the fire in payment for the *nganga*, as she does when relighting her fire after the death of a chief. If the children find any pots of food on any of the fires that they are extinguishing they are allowed to confiscate them. The other *mudzivho* is also performed by the young children. In this case they are each given several small sticks and stones which have been rubbed in medicine and are told to place some at every cross-road, river, drift, and boundary, and on all the paths that lead to the district; the medicine used is made from the crab and *fukwe* bird (the cry of the *fukwe* bird is considered to be the harbinger of rain) mixed with scraps of meal left on the women's stampers and porridge sticks, and with scraps of women's clothing. While some of the children are busy depositing the little stones and sticks, others are detailed to visit the graves of the chief's ancestors and to pour water upon them, thus cooling their anger and showing them that it is water that their people require. When after this the rain still does not come the chief sends to a rain specialist. Some years ago the BaVenda rain specialists, *maine vha mvula* (finder of rain) were renowned in all the country and were consulted by neighbouring tribes, but to-day there are none as famous as Majaji in the Pietersburg district or Musunga in Southern Rhodesia. There are still specialists of some renown practising in their own districts: Masiswe of Lwamondo, Ratshisimbi of Lambani, Mutige of Mutali, Mayeba of Makhuya and Tshisinavhuti, a woman rain-maker at Mianzwi under Tshivhase. Simpson, an evangelist in the Berlin Mission at Makonde, described to me how his paternal uncle, Mutige, produces rain. When the chief's messengers arrive at Mutige's kraal

312 RAIN-MAKING AND FERTILITY OF CROPS

he makes them welcome and tells them to stay in his village for the day. He then powders up some dried crab and *fukwe* bird and mixes it with scraps of refuse disgorged from the river when last in flood; he puts some of this mixture on to a small piece of broken pot over a fire which he lights on the veranda of his hut. As soon as the fumes from the mixture begin to rise from the potsherd he goes into his hut, shuts the door and covers himself up with blankets; before long he begins to perspire and he stays shut in his hut all day, completely enveloped in blankets and perspiring freely. Towards sunset a small cloud appears in the sky, drawn thither by the smoking powder, and presently the clouds increase and rain falls. The idea is that the powder goes up into the sky, and its constituents, all closely associated with water, there form themselves into rain-clouds that form into drops and fall, induced by the violent perspiration of the man in the hut. Another *maine vha mvula* plays a *phala-fhala* horn and dances vigorously until he is bathed in sweat; as the drops fall from him a rain-cloud is supposed to appear and raindrops fall. Each specialist has his own secret method, but they are practically all based, like these, on the principles of sympathetic magic.

Certain *dzinganga* are able to prevent rain from falling and their help is sometimes required in the event of unusual floods. One specialist makes a mixture from the roots of the *mubadali* and *tshitungulo* trees and round monkey-nuts, all mixed with fat to form a paste; this is rubbed on to the end of a stick and pointed at the clouds, while the *nganga* exhorts the rain to cease from falling. Sometimes instead of the stick he rubs the paste on to the end of a spear-head and swoops the spear with a violent cutting movement in the direction of the clouds, thereby cutting off the progress of the clouds, so that they cannot proceed further across the sky. The mixture may also be taken into the mouth and spat out on the ground, where the lightning bird will swoop down on it and carry it off and with it the rain.

To-day the rain-maker with the greatest reputation in the Transvaal is Majaji, and many chiefs send to her for help. Chief Senthumule told me that she is descended from a Portuguese woman, who claimed to have the power of making rain. The original Majaji must have been an extraordinary personality; she is reputed to have pulled out all her hair to conceal the fact of her European origin and to have married a MuSutho man; having borne a daughter to him she killed her unfortunate husband. At her death she was succeeded by her daughter who married her son. The male children of these

RAIN-MAKING AND FERTILITY OF CROPS   313

unions are of no account and the rain-maker is always succeeded by
her daughter. Each successor is supposed to follow the example of
the original Majaji and to kill her husband as soon as she has provided
herself with an heiress. What truth there may be in this story I am
not prepared to say, but Majaji is undoubtedly an outstanding
character in the Transvaal.

Fertility of Crops.

The chief, as well as being held responsible for an even supply of
rain is expected to arrange that the harvest shall be abundant. The
annual sowing rite (*u sonda*) already described, at which the ancestor
spirits are asked to bring a good harvest to their descendants, is the
only fertility rite of a distinctly religious type. From time to time
when, in spite of rain and good conditions, the crops are poor throughout the country, the chief attempts to remedy the fault by magical
means (*u suka mbeu*, to mix the seed). All the people bring a handful
of the different seeds they are sowing to their petty chief, who
collects the seeds, to which he adds a handful of his own and sends them
in a basket to the chief's kraal; here all the baskets of seed from the
different districts are mixed up together with a magic powder by the
maine vha mbeu. The powder, the ingredients of which were not
ascertained, is sometimes obtained from Mwari by a messenger sent
specially to Rhodesia with a heavy payment. Early the following morning a party of women from each district arrives at the chief's kraal,
each party in charge of the *mukhoma* of their district; they hoe a small
piece of land, the *tshirengwarengwane*, and sow it with some of the
magically treated seed. Each *mukhoma* is given back a basket of this
magic seed, with which he returns to the petty chief, followed by all
the women; the petty chief mixes the magic seed with his own and
the following morning all the women under him hoe his *tshirengwarengwane* and sow some of this seed, in exactly the same way that they
did for the great chief. After this each woman who brought a handful
of seed in the first instance, receives back from the petty chief a handful
of the seed that has been mixed with the magic seed. She returns home
with her precious handful and mixes it with her own grain, which she
then plants in her own garden. In this way the power possessed by
the original magic powder is, through contact, imparted to every seed
that is sown through the country.

It sometimes happens that the chief's gardens flourish while those
of the commoners promise a very meagre crop, causing them to suspect

314 RAIN-MAKING AND FERTILITY OF CROPS

that their seed has not received fair treatment at the *u suka mbeu* ceremony. People will sometimes secretly visit a *nganga* with their own seed and ask him to treat it for them; in fact most people employ secret methods for ensuring the fertility of particular crops, quite apart from the national rite. Tobacco is usually specially protected from the danger of contact with menstruating women by the root of the *mutondo* tree, which has a blood-red sap, being spread over the tobacco garden. The powdered bark of the *mulanga* tree is rubbed into the cut ends of the small pumpkin runners (*u lumisa*, to make bite the pumpkins) to make them prolific. There are innumerable remedies and precautions of this sort, every *nganga* having a large stock-in-trade for use in the protection of gardens and crops. Sometimes human flesh is used to aid fertility; in cases of urgent necessity a man may obtain flesh from the corpse of some powerful person who has died recently and secrete it in his mealie pits, so that the power of this great man will be passed on to the mealies.

There is no evidence of human sacrifice in the generally understood sense in connexion with fertility, although an interesting murder case that came before the law-courts some six years ago disclosed the fact that innocent people are sometimes put to death for the good their bodies may do to the country. Ratshivuma, the petty chief at Tononndwa and the eldest son of the present Chief Tshivhase, was charged, together with six other important members of the tribe, with a series of murders. The crops had failed persistently and ordinary expedients had met with no success, so it was decreed (by whom has not been divulged) that the only means by which this calamity could be remedied was by associating the seeds, &c., with portions of freshly killed human beings. No ordinary man's corpse would do; the oracle decreed that the victim must be a lucky man, successful in all his undertakings; he must also be short and very black in colour (the type universally admired and envied by the BaVenda as being the true Venda stock); above all he must have been lucky in his harvests. A likely man was waylaid by Ratshivuma and his chosen band in a desolate rocky kloof near Tononndwa and there killed; certain parts of his body were burnt and handed over to *dzinganga*, others were burnt and powdered and strewn over the lands to help the crops; the skull was buried in a niche in the wall of the mealie pits. Other murders followed, all the victims being small, dark, successful men. The whole affair was brought to light by a man who accidentally witnessed one of the murders and escaped and told

RAIN-MAKING AND FERTILITY OF CROPS 315

the police. It is not known how many victims there were. This incident is a remarkable case of sympathetic magic. The victims were all of the same type, the favoured type, all were successful in their undertakings and all had raised good crops. These murders were not human sacrifices as there was no idea of propitiation; they were committed merely to obtain the essence of these fortunate people so that their power could be passed on to the crops and make them fertile.

XXIII

MUSIC, DANCING, AND SONG

Musical Instruments—Tribal Dances—Other Dances—Songs

MUSIC, dancing, and song are an integral part of nearly all the social activities of the BaVenda. A traveller seldom journeys far through their country without hearing the sound of drums, flutes, or the xylophone emerging from one or other of the kraals in his vicinity, at any time in the afternoon or evening, and especially at night when the moon is full.

The small informal dances which often begin spontaneously towards the end of a beer-drink are generally accompanied by singing, but the important tribal dances are invariably associated with the beat of one or more of the drums and the playing of flutes.

Musical Instruments.

Drums and wind instruments, chiefly pipes and horns, form a band for most dances, and are, with the *mbila*, the instruments of social value, played primarily for the benefit of the community, and not for the aesthetic enjoyment of the musician himself.

Drums. The two types of drum and their manufacture have already been described; they are usually played by women, although anybody is allowed to play them. The large drum, *ngoma*, is beaten with one stick, the tone being modified by pressure of the left elbow on the tympanum. The small drum, *marimba*, is held between the legs at an angle, with the tympanum away from the body; it is beaten by being vigorously struck with the lower part of the palm of the hand and the fingers, giving a fairly high sharp note. A band usually contains two large drums, one considerably bigger than the other and often slung on a wooden framework, and one or two smaller ones. There may be only one *ngoma* and one or two *mirimba*. A special beat of the drums is played to call the people together for war; there is a characteristic rhythm, easily recognizable, for the various dances. Thoho-ya-Ndou was reputed to have a drum which brought death to every one who heard its beat and Makhado to have had human forearms for drum sticks. The big drums of chiefs are often given special names. Those of the MaKhwinde chiefs are called '*u mutula goli*' (to foretell a cloud,

MUSIC, DANCING, AND SONG 317

i.e. to make a noise like thunder which foretells rain). Manenzhe's big drum is always *tundundu*, that of Mutali *dindindi*, both onomatopoeic.

Wind Instruments. Flutes, *dzinanga*, are simple lengths of reed of different notes and are played in bands of ten or more, each player blowing down his instrument in the way boys blow down cartridges. The flutes are made from a special bamboo, *musunoni*, only found in a certain sacred forest at Tshaula in Paswane's location. All the BaVenda chiefs, and even the BaSutho, send to buy this bamboo for their flutes. They are all made in the village of petty chief Bowhane, and twelve flutes are sold for 5*s*. or a small goat. The history of this forest is unknown.

Horns, khwata, are another favourite instrument and are made from kudu, sable-antelope, bush-buck, or water-buck. The sable-antelope horns, *phala-fhala*, are the most important and are played in the *thondo* and around the chief's village. They are blown through a small rectangular hole in the side about 8 inches from the point, to which the lips are pressed as with an ordinary bugle. Horns, *tshihoho*, much appreciated by young boys, are made from the front part of the bush-buck horn. They are about 6 inches long and the boys shout down them, and can carry on a conversation with other *tshihoho* blowers at a great distance; they produce an enormous volume of sound, and the boys have a code of ear piercing articulations in which they converse. Horns are often used to accompany the drums for dances, especially for the *mathanngwa* dance, to produce a volume of base notes. Every chief has a horn-blower, who summons the people to the capital by a specified blast on his horn to dance the *tshikona* or *mathanngwa* or for meetings of any sort. One horn I saw was made out of wood and belonged to a woman. The instrument was about 2 feet long, made from a slightly tapering wooden stick, which was split down the middle, each half being hollowed out separately. The two halves were then replaced in position and bound tightly with iron and copper wirework. The narrow end of this tube was plugged with a lump of copper and the rectangular mouthpiece made about 3 inches from that end. The construction of such an instrument would entail skill and patience, and would probably only be undertaken where horn was unobtainable. This particular instrument was of great age and much valued by its owner as a sacred object.

A species of flute, *tshitiringha*, is made from a length of reed about 8 inches long; it is closed at one end and has four holes, one slightly larger than the other. The player blows through the large hole and

318 MUSIC, DANCING, AND SONG

uses the other three for playing with the fingers. This instrument does not produce much sound; it is chiefly used by herd-boys, who may often be heard fluting in the grazing lands.

Stringed Instruments. Lugube is played by women. It is made from a hollow bamboo about 2 feet long, the ends being connected by a tightly-drawn string made either from the tail hairs of a wildebeest or from a fine sinew. The player holds one end between her lips, her mouth, which is opened and closed to vary the sound, acting as a resonator. She strikes the string at this end with the left forefinger in a to-and-fro movement. The other end is held between the thumb and right forefinger, the backs of the other three fingers of the right hand pressing the string up slightly from below, and so varying the note.

The most ingenious stringed instrument is the *tshijolo* (Plate XLVI), also used by the BaSutho. This is the only instrument played with a bow, and is a type uncommon among Bantu people. It may owe its origin to European influence, and have been brought to the BaSutho by the early Boer settlers, as the word tshijolo is said to be a corruption of the Afrikaans 'viool'. The *tshijolo* is made from a branch of very soft wood, about 30 inches long and $1\frac{1}{2}$ inches in diameter, from which all the pith is removed, leaving a hollow tube; about 6 inches from one end a wide strip is cut off the remaining length, about one-third of the circumference of the tube, leaving the inside exposed; a wooden peg 8 inches long and $\frac{1}{2}$ an inch thick, tapering slightly, is passed through two holes burnt on the top of the lower side in the centre of the circular end, making an angle of $45°$ with the tube; the upper hole is slightly larger than the lower to fit the tapering peg; at the opposite end the groove is cut to a point forming a shoulder, to which the end of a wire is attached, the other end being fastened to the peg which protrudes about 2 inches above the instrument. In order to tighten or slacken the string, the peg is raised and twisted round to the right or left, and again drawn down tight; it is quite impossible for the string to slip. About the middle of the instrument, on the under side, a small notch is cut to fit the thumb and to keep the instrument steady. The bow is a small stick about 6 inches long and $\frac{1}{2}$ an inch in diameter; 2 grooves are cut all the way round, $\frac{1}{2}$ an inch from one end and $2\frac{1}{2}$ inches from the other, to which a dozen or so tail hairs which have been rubbed in resinous gum, are fastened, leaving a loop; the $2\frac{1}{2}$ inch end is held against the palm of the right hand and the thumb inserted in the loop, drawing it towards the palm and making it tense. The *tshijolo* is played by the bow being being rubbed to-and-fro across the

PLATE XLVI

TSHIJOLO WITH BOW

MBILA

MUSIC, DANCING, AND SONG 319

string, the peg end being placed against the mouth, which acts as a resonator, and the string being occasionally stopped by one of the fingers of the left hand.

The common musical bow, *tshivhana*, is fairly often found. It is played by the young unmarried men. It is a one-piece bow, about 28 inches from point to point, made from a piece of wood 1 inch in diameter; the curved ends are cut to quite a thin strip, leaving a solid belt in the back of the bow, with thin tapering ends; at either end the bow is pointed to form a shoulder, to which a wire is strung; the cross-wire is made taut, by being pulled down to the bow by means of a small piece of string. The instrument is plucked with the finger on either side of the string, giving two notes; the mouth is used as a resonator, and the note may be changed by moving the string towards either end of the points of the bow.

A similar bow, *tshikaba*, with a calabash resonator, is sometimes found, but this has been copied from the BaSutho bow. Often several pieces of flat tin, usually scraps of paraffin tins, are attached to the centre of this bow, and vibrate as the string is plucked. This is a Karanga type of instrument.

The *tshizambo* is a combination of the bow and rattle, and gives a lively, infectious sound. It is made like the musical bow, but is strung with a long narrow *mulala* leaf, about ½ an inch wide. A number of nicks are cut on one side of the bow, and these are rubbed vigorously in a to-and-fro movement by a stick about 8 inches long, which has been threaded through two or three *ntusa* pods, or through small calabashes filled with pebbles. One end of the bow is held against the mouth, which acts as a resonator. The *tshizambo* is probably of BaThonga origin.

The stringed instruments are played mostly for the musicians' own amusement, as the volume of sound is extremely weak. They are very popular, and most are played by men and women; the *tshivhana* is played by men only and the *lugube* by women only. Wind instruments, except horns, are not played by women.

Rattles made from calabashes filled with stones often accompany the drums. Many dancers wear leg rattles; these are made by threading two or three small calabashes or *ntusa* pods on sticks about 3 inches long, and then joining the sticks together; the pad is jointed, rather like a cricket pad. A similar rattling effect is obtained by the dancing skirts, copied from the BaSutho, which are made by threading small narrow tubes of bamboo about 2 inches in length, on a string 12

320   MUSIC, DANCING, AND SONG

to 14 inches long; a large number of strings are attached to a girdle by one end, making a fringed skirt.

The *xylophone, mbila,* is of the usual Bantu type (Plate XLVII). It is often a skilfully made instrument, varying in range from one octave to 23 or 24 notes. It consists of wooden slats, 3 or 4 inches wide, often decorated with carving, and very carefully tuned; these slats are tied together with leather thongs, over long bottle-shaped calabashes, which are open at one end and at the narrow end have a small hole pierced and closed with a thin spider's web membrane, to form a tympanum; these calabashes make the resonator. The instrument is played with wooden hammers, the heads of which are made of wild rubber. It may be played by men or women, and very often two players perform together. It is an instrument requiring skill, and is only played by a few experts, who teach the art to their sons and daughters. Players of the *mbila* are becoming increasingly rare; formerly every chief had a player in his village, who, in the evenings, would often amuse the chief and his guests with his instrument. There are various orthodox tunes, including war dances, &c., and often a player travels round giving entertainments at the different large kraals.

The *deza* (pl. *madeza*) was introduced by the BaLemba. It has about twelve metal keys, varying in length and breadth and carefully tuned, all clamped down to a wooden resonator by an iron band strengthened with traces of wire. The wooden resonator is 12 by 18 inches and 2 inches in depth. The wood is partially hollowed out, and the iron slots rest on another iron bar fixed across the breadth of the wood about 1½ inches from the clamp. The *deza* gives a soft, sweet sound. Another type of resonator is made from a large calabash, often decorated around the mouth with shells which make a vibrating sound. A number of players, generally BaLemba, play as a band at the chief's kraal, accompanying their music with songs. Several *madeza* played in unison give a pleasing sound.

Tribal Dances.

There are two tribal dances of special interest and significance accompanied by the music of drums and flutes, the *tshikona* and *mathanngwa.* The initiation dances at the *vhusha* and *domba* which have already been described are accompanied by drums and singing.

The *tshikona* dance is almost sacred in character (Plate XLVII). It is performed at the command of chiefs and petty chiefs and is closely associated with every phase in the life of the people as a whole. The

PLATE XLVII

THE *TSHIKONA* DANCE

MUSIC, DANCING, AND SONG

principal performers, always men, go through a long and tedious apprenticeship in this dance. The second dance, the *mathanngwa*, is performed for the expression of enjoyment and goodwill; it resembles the *tshikona* in construction, but is entirely opposite to it in psychological intention. The *mathanngwa* may be danced by quite young boys who copy the older boys and gradually gain proficiency, at the same time gaining knowledge of the basic steps of the *tshikona*. Both these dances are supervised by a leader, *malugwani*, who must be obeyed implicitly. Each chief and petty chief has a *malugwani* resident in his village, who trains the troupe of young men in the district. The dance is quite complicated, as each dancer plays a flute and must understand his particular rôle in the correct harmonizing of these flutes. One set of dancers is called a *mutavha*, and is made up of at least ten flautists, generally twelve or more. Ten flutes are named individually, while all sizes, larger and smaller than this original ten, are named collectively *mazika* and *mitwilo* respectively. It is probable that originally the number of flutes was ten. The melody is repeated over and over again in endless repetition. The flutes are tuned in semi-tones, and are always made in even numbers. The flutes are named as follows:

Tshikona.	*Mathanngwa.*
1.	1. *palana*
2. *palana*	2. *mpinji*
3. *mpinji*	3. *tshiboho*
4. *takhulana*	4. *tshihunguvhu*
5. *tshihunguvhu*	5. *veve*
6. *veve*	6. *tshiaravhi*
7. *tshiaravhi*	7. *takhuli*
8. *takhuli*	8. *pala*
9. *pala*	9. *tangu*
10. *tangu*	10. *kholomo*
11. *mboho*	

Tshikona.

Mathanngwa.

322 MUSIC, DANCING, AND SONG

When it is necessary to dance the *tshikona* a messenger is sent from the chief's kraal to summon all the dancers in the district, and they all hasten to the *khoro*, each *mulugwani* bringing the flutes for his *mutavha*. Most of the women in the kraal collect round the drums, and two drummers, either men or women prepare to beat the two big drums. One *mulugwani* is chosen to lead the dance and the dancers select their flutes and get into line beside the drums. The leader, standing between the dancers and the drums, as soon as he sees that everybody is ready to start, begins to move his feet in the first steps of the dance, and this is a sign for the flutes to begin. As soon as the flutes are being blown in proper harmony the drums join in, and the dancers take their time from the drums, at the same time keeping an eye on the leader; as the drum-beat changes slightly the theme of the dance changes. As soon as the drums start the players form into a large circle; the first steps are left, right, left, right, then left, right, turn on the third step, and two steps in the opposite direction, and turn again. It is a curious step, something between a fox-trot and a waltz; after dancing round for some time the beat changes and the dancers face the centre and step forward and back, and then round again. The leader signs to the drums and the dancers follow on, each blowing his individual flute with all his might. The dance proceeds with a rhythmic swing. If the *makhadzi* of the village is present she may join in the dance, *u havhedza* (to dance softly). She takes off her shoulder cloth, folds it up and goes forward towards the circle of dancers; on her approach the men squat down and she dances alone in the middle of the circle, sometimes followed by one or two other women who imitate her every movement; an elder holds an ostrich feather, *lukole*, over her head as she dances, to do her honour. When she is tired she kneels down and does *losha* to the drums as a sign that she is content, and, slowly rising, moves away from the circle. The men then continue dancing with renewed fervour and energy. When the leader thinks that it is time for the dancers to rest, he signs to them to dance forward into a group, and then leaps high into the air, followed by all the dancers. He then signs to the drums to stop, and that is a signal to the dancers to rest. Men and women may never dance together in this dance. Each *mutavha* consists of men only, and on occasions when the *makhadzi* joins in the dance the men always squat and simply blow their flutes. The *tshikona* is associated vaguely with the ancestors and is the national dance; it is always performed to inaugurate initiation and other ceremonies, such as the *tevula*, in order to solicit

MUSIC, DANCING, AND SONG 323

the goodwill of the ancestors; it is performed on the death of a chief and on the accession of a new chief, and when rain is required. It is of great social value, as it is the outlet for the tribal emotions and a means of united self-expression. It is danced with solemnity and concentration, and is generally performed, as is our national anthem, immediately on the arrival of a chief at the kraal of one of his subjects, as a sign of loyalty and respect. At close quarters the noise of the flutes is very shrill and discordant, but heard in the distance the sound is toned down, and the different notes following one another in a peculiar rippling cadence make a pleasant melody, sounding very like the chimes of church bells far away.

The *mathanngwa* is different; it is used whenever there is a desire for merriment and collective enjoyment. Often one chief will visit another with a troupe of *mathanngwa* dancers who will stay and dance at the kraal of their host for two or three days. The chief, who has been honoured by the visit, always slaughters cattle and provides beer for the entertainment of his guests. Sometimes a troupe of dancers will make a tour of the country, stopping to dance at every big kraal and always sure of a warm welcome. They always take back to their own chief the hind leg of every beast that has been killed for them, and often use the hides of the slaughtered animals to decorate their flutes. When the *mathanngwa* is being danced in a chief's kraal one or two *phala-fhala* horns may be blown to give added volume to the sound of the flutes and drums.

Other Dances.

Two dances somewhat similar to the *mathanngwa* have been introduced fairly recently by the BaSutho, the *ghiba* and the *vhisa*, and are rapidly gaining popularity. Troupes of these dancers travel about the country giving entertainments; these dances are more lively than the *mathanngwa* and give more scope for solo performances and individual variations. The dancers used to wear distinctive clothes, but to-day dress up in a curious motley of European towels, cast-off clothing, scarves, beads, &c., and present an utterly ludicrous appearance.

All other dances are of a much more homely type. Sometimes informal dances, especially at the chief's village, may be accompanied by the *phala-fhala* horns or by the drums, which may be played by either sex, but more often than not the dancers extemporize their own accompaniment, the leader of the dance shouting the solo part while the rest of the gathering unites in the chorus. Most of the singing is of

MUSIC, DANCING, AND SONG

this antiphonal type, and, except in the dances accompanied by the flutes, dancing rarely takes place without song or song without dancing. In fact nearly every muscular activity is combined with a humming or singing, giving a rhythm to the muscular action, which undoubtedly makes the occupation more harmonious. The men sing as they plough or chop wood, and the women sing over their domestic duties. Movement and melody cannot be separated. Whenever a number of people are gathered together for any purpose, such as work in the chief's gardens, building, or hunting, or threshing, the completion of the task is always made an occasion for beer, which is followed, more often than not, by singing and dancing. Every good mother-in-law, *makhulu*, brings much beer to her son-in-law, *mukwasha*, and he gives her goats in return; these presentations are made the occasion for a general family jollification which is typical of the informal Venda festivities. The *makhulu* and her party are always accompanied on their visit by a man, *tshivhula ya mbudzi* (the demander of the goat), who acts for the woman. The women approach with several calabashes of beer, heralding their arrival with a special song. As soon as they reach the kraal, one calabash is drunk by the men in the *khoro* and a second by the *mukwasha* and his relations in the yard of his hut. A little of the contents of the *mukwasha's* calabash is thrown down for the ancestor spirits. The *makhulu* and her party are given accommodation for the night, and the next day the *mukwasha* summons his friends and relations, and kills some goats or a cow, on which they feast with the *makhulu's* beer. After consuming much beer the company are very excited, and the *makhulu* begins to abuse the *mukwasha* and he to reply with similar abuses.

SHE. 'Where is my goat, the one that you promised to give me every time we met?'

HE (*with his relations*). 'Oh, your beer is but water!'

SHE. 'If my beer is only water, how is it that you are so drunk?'

HE. 'We are happy because you are our *makhulu*, not because your beer is strong.'

SHE. 'Mukwasha, I am very fond of you but I do not like your impudence.'

HE. 'I like your daughter but she dislikes doing what I tell her to do.'

This sort of good-natured raillery is continued for a long time, members of the group dancing from time to time to break the monotony. Each dancer tries to better the one that danced before him, and so it continues, the people all becoming more and more excited, the

MUSIC, DANCING, AND SONG

dancing wilder and wilder and the invective more vituperative. Finally the *makhulu* yells: 'Pigs eat roots because they do not know how to sow,' and then harangues her daughter, telling her that if she is lazy she will have to eat refuse. With this final admonition the party disperses.

Songs.

Songs are extemporized to commemorate almost every incident of unusual interest or significance.

1. The following song, in which an unfortunate girl grieves over her shame, is fairly typical of the manner in which they originate.

Snuffing is Injudicious.

A girl asked a young man, Gabara, for a pinch of snuff, which he gave to her although she was a stranger. As a result of breaking the snuff tabu he became a vicious character and worried her with indecent suggestions until, finally, he committed adultery with her. After that she composed this song, which is well known in Vendaland. It is sung very sadly:

326 MUSIC, DANCING, AND SONG

Fhola li na mulandu!	Snuff is guilty,
Yohve, li na mulandu!	Oh, it is guilty!
Nde ndi tota fhola	As I took a pinch of snuff
Yovhe, ndi mulandu!	Oh, it is guilty!
Tshanda tsha Gabara	From the hand of Gabara
Yovhe, ndi mulandu!	Oh, it is guilty!
La vhuya la senga	It was discovered
Yovhe, ndi mulandu	Oh, it is guilty!

Gabara is now a very old man living at Ngobela, and is well known to his neighbours on account of this incident.

2. This song was composed by Sepuma, a brother of petty chief Manenzhe. He received a severe leg injury at the Kimberley Mines soon after their opening, which left him with a stiff leg.

Tshikwebe, mulangalanga,	The stiff-legged one, sleepy eyes
Tshikwebe nga vholawe!	The stiff-legged one must be killed.

MUSIC, DANCING, AND SONG

3. This is sung by little girls when young boys interfere with them when they are playing; when the boys hear the song they run away ashamed.

Ndole.

Ndole! Ndole! A naughty boy! A naughty boy!
Tshitamba na vhasidzana! He plays with girls.

4. This is sung after emptying the big beer-pots, when the drinkers are feeling particularly pleased with themselves and the world in general. One man sings the '*Mbuhe!*' (Joyful) and the whole assembly join in the '*shango ndi matakadza*' (the world is full of pleasures). During the chorus the soloist stalks around majestically, and at every '*mbu!*' leaps into the air, stamping down heavily at the '*he!*'

5. There are innumerable popular songs sung at beer-drinks such as: *Tshititi tsha Ngamangwana tshi ya tamba mutshakatha.* *Tshititi* (the name of a bird) son of Nyamangwana plays the *mutshakatha* (name given to the rattles tied on the legs for dancing).

6. *Vho mmeanga! salani! ho! salani!*   Mother mine! Goodbye! Ho! Goodbye!
   Nne ndi a fha! salani! ho! salani!   I am dying! Goodbye! Ho! Goodbye!

7. *Vho makhulu vho da vho da u vhona mukwasha.*   The mother-in-law is coming, is coming to see the son-in-law.

MUSIC, DANCING, AND SONG

XXIV

FOLK-LORE

THE psychology of Bantu folk-lore with its songs, tales, riddles, proverbs, and incantations has been well described by Junod.[1] Nearly everything that he says about the BaThonga folk-lore is also true of that of the BaVenda.

The BaVenda are particularly rich in all branches of folk-lore and spend their evenings singing and story-telling over the *khoro* fire. The tales may be told by people of either sex and any age. There are generally two or three persons in every kraal with reputations as story-tellers, but almost every adult has at least one good tale to his special credit, in the recital of which he or she excels.

Nearly all the folk-tales are embellished with songs, which are often repeated three or four times during the narrative. When the story-teller reaches a point in his tale for the song connected with it to be sung all the listeners fall naturally into the parts best suited to them. I heard many of the following tales myself; others, and most of the riddles and proverbs, were collected by members of the Berlin Missionary Society resident in the Zoutpansberg, and are some of a large number published in Tshivenda in a little hand-book, *Ndede*, used as a reading book in the mission schools.

The animal hero of the BaVenda is not the usual Bantu hare, but is *Sankhambi*, whose identity is the subject of much discussion. He is probably the tortoise or some animal of the same species; the BaVenda accept him as a creature wise above all other animals and are not over curious as to his identity.

In the first three stories I have inserted the songs to illustrate the method in which nearly all of them are told.

1. *Song about the Python.*

There was once a man who was very very ill and he had been ill for a long time and no medicine-man could cure him, and one day he heard of a wonderful medicine-man, a python, living in a cave in the rocky mountains. Now the man had five sons, and he sent his eldest son up the mountain, saying, 'Go to the mountain yonder and bring me the *nganga* to cure me of my illness.' When the son reached the cave of the python *nganga* he sang:

[1] Junod, Henri A., *The Life of a South African Tribe*, London, 1927, pp. 177 et seq.

Son.	'Tate wanga vha a lwala, nganga mbuya.'	'My father is ill, *nganga* (make him) better.'
	Vha ri: ndi u vhidze nganga mbuya.	I ask you: you must call *nganga*; (make him) better.
	Tate wanga vha a lwala, iwe nganga.	My father is ill, come *nganga*.
	U vha thodze nganga mbuya.'	Come to cure him, *nganga* (make him) better.'
Doctor.	'Izwi nda da henefho Izwi a u nga shavhi naa.'	'If I come there Won't you run away?'
All.	Ndo pfa! Ndo pfa!	'I heard! I heard!'

FOLK-LORE

333

The python went off to get his calabash of medicine and the boy rushed off home as fast as he could go. When the python did not arrive, the father sent his second son up the mountain, and he sang:

(Here the song is repeated)

When the python went to get his medicine the second son ran away. Then the third son went up the mountain and sang to the python:

(Here the song is repeated)

When the python went to get his medicine he ran away, and the fourth son went up the mountain and sang to the python:

(Here the song is repeated)

When the python went to get his medicine he ran away. The last son then told his father that he would go up and bring the *nganga* to cure him. His father, mother, and brothers all tried to prevent him from going, but at last they let him go and he went off up the mountain and sang very sadly to the python:

(Here the song is repeated plaintively)

When the python said 'Won't you run away?' the boy stood quite still and said, 'I'll never run away.' So the python fetched his medicine and the boy waited. When the python returned he wound himself round the boy's body, and the boy carried him home. When they arrived the man's wife and four other sons all ran away, but the fifth boy brought the python *nganga* into the hut where his father slept. Then the python *nganga* licked the sick man and asked the boy to take him back to his cave in the mountains. At first he and all his family refused, but finally all started to accompany the boy with the python wound around him. The python would not allow the party to go far, and in the end the boy took the python *nganga* back to his cave in the mountains alone. We notice in this and other BaVenda tales that the youngest son is often the hero.

2. *The Python and his Two Wives.*

A python married two wives. The great wife, Nengome, knew very well that her husband was a python, but the younger wife did not, and whenever she asked about her husband she was told not to bother about it.

One night, while the young wife slept, she felt the python moving along by her side, and she woke up singing:

Nda rothodzwa rothodzwa. Vho Nengome!   I am dripping wet, dripping wet. You Nengome!

This was repeated on several nights, and the python husband told Nengome to give the young wife a necklace to comfort her and told her to be silent. Now the morning meal was served by Nengome, the great wife, and the evening meal by the young wife, and both wives

FOLK-LORE 335

had to work in the mealie lands and return at sunset. As they drew near the kraal Nengome sang:

	Ri vho vhuya! Ri vho vhuya!	We are coming! We are coming!
PYTHON.	'*No lima na guma ngafhi?*'	'You were hoeing and where did you stop?'
NENGOME.	'*Ri guma nga mufhanda, mutshetshete u vhukate.*'	'We stopped by the *mufhanda* tree, the thorn tree in the middle.'
PYTHON.	'*Ihi nkadziwanga. Ihi nkadziwanga.*'	'Yes my wife, yes my wife.'

The young wife sings throughout:

'*Dumbu lina guse.*'	'Stomach with wool' (meaning the stomach of a python).

One day as the two women were working in the mealie lands the younger wife said: 'I must go home to fetch my snuff-box which I left at home.' Nengome would not let her go, and said that she would fetch it for her. This happened again the next day, but the third day the young wife ran off to the kraal and found her husband, the python, in the *khoro* catching flies for food.

When she returned to the lands, Nengome called out, 'I told you not to go. Now you have seen the python and I do not know what will happen.' And the python husband slipped away into the deep pool and never returned, and all the streams and water-holes and rivulets and rivers began to dry up, and all the people and animals and cattle cried out for want of water. And the chief consulted all the rain-makers in vain. The only place where there was water was Lake Fundudzi, where the great python lived.

Now Nengome, of course, knew the reason which had caused all the waters to dry up, and she whispered it to the people. So the chiefs gathered together and asked Nengome to tell them all, and then ordered the people to prepare beer so that they could offer it to the python in Lake Fundudzi. And the young wife was told that the only way to save the people was for her to go into Fundudzi with the pot of beer.

When the appointed day came she was given the pot of beer to carry and all the men played the *tshikona* to encourage her on her way.

She stepped into the lake and sang:

YOUNG WIFE. *Khaladzianga salani!*	My sister farewell!
ANSWER. *Nga a lile mavhili, vhili!*	Play with a roaring sound!
YOUNG WIFE. *Vho khotsianga salani!*	My father farewell!
ANSWER. *Nga a lile mavhili, vhili!*	Play with a roaring sound!
YOUNG WIFE. *Vho mmeanga salani!*	My mother farewell!
ANSWER. *Nga a lile mavhili, vhili!*	Play with a roaring sound!

As the *tshikona* was played louder and louder she flung herself into the depths of the lake, and immediately the water in the streams and water-holes and rivulets began to rise, and the people, animals, and cattle drank joyfully. The story is finished.

3. *The Man and his Mbila.*

There was once a man with three wives. He went on a journey, followed by his two eldest wives carrying their baskets on their heads, and left his herd of cattle at home in charge of his youngest wife and two boys. The man took his *mbila* with him. They walked the whole day towards the east. Early the next morning they came to a forest, and there they met the great monster of the bush, who said to the man: 'Put down your *mbila* and play me a song.' The man was terrified, but not knowing what else to do he put down the *mbila* and began to play.

FOLK-LORE

339

2. *Thi a fha nda si a kholomo dzanga!*	I die and leave my cows at the kraal.
Shango la muno a li endi nwana.	This country must not be visited by a child.
Shango la muno li na mavhanda.	This country has a monster.

(The first player plays Part 1, the chorus singing '*Yo wee madandila wee*'.

The second player plays from 2 to the end.)

The monster then devoured the first woman and ordered the man not to cry but to play the *mbila*.

(Here the song is repeated)

The monster then devoured the second woman together with her two children.

He again ordered the man not to cry but to play the *mbila*.

(Here the song is repeated)

After that the man could not play any more, so the monster devoured him too and kept the *mbila* for himself. The story is finished.

4. *The Beautiful Girl who had no Teeth.*

There was once a man who had three sons, none of whom had a wife. One day the father went out to see if he could find a suitable girl for his eldest son, and he found a beautiful girl at a village near by. That night, when he returned home, he called his eldest son and said, 'I have found a beautiful girl for you, and to-morrow I want you to take the cattle to her father.' Early next morning the son went out with five of the best cattle and presented them to the girl's father. On his arrival the girl took his sticks and the young boys took the cattle to the kraal. The girl's father then said, 'Have you come to take my daughter?', to which the man replied that he had. The girl's father then called his daughter and said, 'Here is your husband, you must go with him to his home to-day.' The girl then replied that she was ready and she and the man departed together for his home. On the road home the girl began to sing, 'I am a beautiful girl but I have no teeth.' Her husband became alarmed and said, 'Open your mouth that I may see if what you say is true.' To his surprise he found that what she said was true and that she only had a black ridge where her teeth should have been. The husband then said, 'I was not told of this, and I must return you to your father.' They returned to the girl's

FOLK-LORE

home and there the husband demanded the return of his cattle as his wife had no teeth; and the cattle were returned and the disappointed man went his way home. On his arrival his father asked, 'Where is the girl, my son?' The son replied, 'I could not bring her home because she had no teeth.' The second son, on hearing this, asked his father, 'May I not go myself to see if the girl has no teeth, because I too want a wife?' The father agreed, and the next day the second son set off with the five head of cattle; presenting them to the girl's father, he said, 'I have come for your daughter. I have come early so that I need not sleep here to-night but may return home with your daughter this evening.' The man informed his daughter of the wishes of the young suitor and the girl replied, 'Very well, but I must first give my husband some food.' After the meal the girl suggested that they depart now, and they proceeded along the road. When she and the second son reached the same place on the road as before the girl began to sing, 'I am a beautiful girl but I have no teeth.' On hearing this the young man asked her to open her mouth that he might see for himself. To his surprise he found that what she said was true and he immediately returned her to her father. 'Here is your daughter,' he said, 'she has no teeth and I want my cattle returned.' The girl's father sadly agreed, and the second son returned to his home. On his return his father said, 'Where is the girl?' The son replied, 'I thought my brother was lying, but it is true, she has no teeth and I returned her to her father.' The youngest son now rose and asked his father if he might go and see for himself, and the father agreed. The eldest brother asked in disgust, 'Do you think that we are mad and stupid because we left the girl?' 'No, no,' answered the youngest brother, 'but I should like to see a girl who has no teeth.' The next day the youngest brother took the cattle and went to the girl's kraal, where he presented the cattle and asked for the girl. The old man, seeing such a young man, said, 'You are very young to want a wife, and besides, both your brothers tried but returned my daughter. However, you may take her if you so wish.' Calling his daughter, he told her she must return with this new man to his home. The girl agreed, and after first giving her new husband some food they proceeded down the road. At the same place as before the girl again sang, 'I am beautiful but I have no teeth;' 'Open your mouth,' said the young man anxiously. On seeing the black ridge within her mouth he showed some surprise, but only said, 'Never mind, let us go our way.' On arriving at a river the girl began to sing the same song, but the young man said nothing; when in the

FOLK-LORE

middle of the stream, he called to the girl to come near to him, and, clasping her tightly by the neck with one hand, he told her to open her mouth; with the other hand he scrubbed the girl's mouth with sand. To his joy he found that beneath the coating of black shone forth a set of beautiful teeth, and, filled with happiness, he brought his wife to his father's kraal. The other two brothers on seeing the girl, rushed to their father saying, 'Come father, come and see your mad son, he has brought this girl home, although she is even now singing her song about her teeth.' The father came, but said nothing, and the youngest brother called one of his sisters and told her to take his newly-acquired wife to his mother's hut. The girls of the village who had heard about this strange girl gathered about her and began to make jokes, so that when the newcomer laughed they might see if the story about her teeth were true. To their surprise they found that the girl had very good teeth. Meanwhile the youngest son told his father that he had brought the girl home as his wife. The father was disappointed. 'Yes, my son,' he said, 'That's all very well, but you have lost all my cattle. What can we do with this girl? I hear she has no teeth, and therefore she cannot eat.' The son did not reply, for at that moment his sister came in and told her father that the newcomer had teeth, for she had seen them. The father said, 'Are you sure?' and being convinced that it was so, he went to his son and said, 'Very well, my son, we shall see your wife to-morrow.' The next day the father entered the hut where the girl was and said, 'I want you to open your mouth. I will give you a sheep for this favour.' The girl did as she was bid and the man saw for himself that she had teeth. The woman in whose hut the girl rested then trilled with her lips, and all three then went out to the main yard, where the father called the elder sons and said, 'What stupid boys you are. Look, this girl has fine teeth, and it has fallen to your youngest brother to find this out and to take her to wife.' The two eldest brothers became very ashamed and would not look at the girl. A few days later large pots of beer were made and all the friends and neighbours came to pay their respects to the new arrival. All spoke of her beauty and her excellent teeth, but the two brothers never saw for themselves, their shame being too great. The story is finished.

5. *The Magic Knobkerrie.*

A man was married to a girl in another village and had paid the lobola.

One day he went to the girl's father and said, 'I want my wife now, as my mother is very old and can no longer cook my food.'

342   FOLK-LORE

The man was a hunter and carried his knobkerrie with him. The following day he went out hunting and, while he was away, the girl's mother put some medicine in his porridge. On his return he waited outside the village and asked his knobkerrie how things were going in the village; the knobkerrie answered, 'You must be careful and only eat meat to-day, there is medicine in the porridge.' He then went on to the village, and when he entered the hut the girl brought him water to wash and his porridge and meat, and then left him. He did not eat the porridge, and when the girl came back she asked him why he had eaten meat only; he replied that he did not want to eat porridge that day. The girl took the porridge and showed it to her mother, and the mother took it and threw it away.

The next day he went hunting again, and on his return he again consulted his knobkerrie, which replied, 'You may eat anything to-day, but do not go inside the hut, as there is a great big hole dug there.' So when he got to the hut he sat down outside. The girl asked him why he would not go in, and he said that it was too hot inside and asked her to bring all his food outside, saying that he would sleep outside too. The girl's mother went to the other old women and told them to ask the *mukwasha* why he would not go inside and to tell him that he had no right to sleep outside the hut and must go inside. The man replied that he felt hot and ill and would not go inside, so he slept outside. Early next morning he went out hunting as before. This time the girl's father and mother put medicine on her body. When the hunter returned and questioned his knobkerrie, it replied, 'You may go inside the hut to-day; the hole is filled up, but you must sleep alone and not go near the girl and her blanket, as they have put medicine on her body to-day.' He went into the hut, sat down and took his food, but when he was going to lie down he asked the girl for a separate blanket, as he was very sick and wished to sleep alone. The girl went out and told her parents. The father went in and questioned him, saying, 'What do you mean by refusing to sleep with my daughter? Do you think she is sick?' The young man replied that he was very sick and wanted to sleep alone. The father was very angry and said that he would pay back the cattle if the young man was not satisfied with his daughter. The young man said, 'Just wait a minute. I want to speak to my doctor. You may hear what he says.' The young man then asked his knobkerrie to tell the father all. The knobkerrie then said to the father, 'On the first night you put medicine in the porridge, the next day you made a big hole in the hut, and on the

FOLK-LORE

343

third day you put medicine on your daughter.' The young man went home and asked his father to come and take his cattle back. That is all.

6. *The Baby and the Rock Rabbit.*

One day a rock rabbit, observing a woman in her garden, came down to her and said, 'Good day, lady, how can you work with your baby on your back ?' 'I am afraid I can't help it,' replied the woman, 'for you see I have no daughter to look after him for me when I am working.' 'Never mind,' said the rock rabbit sympathetically, 'Won't you let me play with him for you ? I will take him a little distance so that he won't cry for you, and we will have fun together.' The woman agreed and the rock rabbit promised to bring back the baby whenever the woman called him. At the end of the day's work the woman cried loudly, 'Rock rabbit, rock rabbit, bring back my baby as I want to go home.' Soon the rock rabbit appeared and gave the child back to its mother. On the following day the woman again went to her garden, and this time she took some dainty food for the rock rabbit who had been so kind to her. She welcomed the rock rabbit on her arrival and, as before, handed over the food and the child to him for safe-keeping. In this way the rock rabbit cared for the child for three days, each evening delivering the child safely to its mother. On the fourth day, however, when the rock rabbit took the child up the mountain as usual, it silently killed it and ate it up, all except a leg, which it put in a small calabash with some gravy, and delivered to the woman that night when she called for her child. 'But where is my child ?' asked the mother in alarm. 'I left it on the mountain, enjoying some freshly killed meat,' replied the wicked rock rabbit. The woman then began to eat the dainty dish which the rock rabbit had brought for her. 'This is very nice meat,' she said, 'I have never tasted such nice rabbit, but its leg is very large, is it not ?' 'Oh yes,' replied the rock rabbit, 'but the rabbits on this mountain are all very large.' Suddenly the rock rabbit rose and, taking his departure, said, 'Oh, I must go. I fear your child will burn itself in the pot of meat I have left cooking.' 'Very well,' said the woman, 'please hurry back with the baby as the sun has set and I must be going.' The rock rabbit did not return, however, and the woman shouted long and anxiously. She was wondering what to do when he at last appeared on the edge of a rock near by, and, making a sign with his finger across his throat, he shouted, 'Why do you cry, lady ? You have eaten the leg of your baby and you remarked on the very nice gravy.' In vain did the mother plead with the rock

FOLK-LORE

rabbit; he only told her that it was useless, for they had both eaten the child. So, filled with fear as to what her husband would do, the woman picked a calabash from the garden and, covering it with a goat's skin, she placed it on her back, as she did with the baby, and after dark went into her hut. She prepared her husband's meal, and while so doing he asked her, 'What is wrong with the baby to-day? Why have you not put it down?' 'Because,' she replied, 'it is still sleeping.' Soon afterwards the husband and wife retired to bed. While the woman was asleep the husband, feeling suspicious because the baby had not cried since its arrival, put his hand across and felt the calabash, which had been filled with water and stuffed up with grass. He pulled out the grass and the water ran all over. Quickly he roused his wife; 'What is this?' he asked in alarm. The wife did not reply, and then her husband, knowing that she had lost the child, drove her from the hut. 'Go,' he said; 'Go and bring back my child.' The husband followed his wife to the garden and again demanded the whereabouts of his child. 'The rock rabbit stole it,' she said weeping. Hearing this the rock rabbit came out on the stone ledge and spoke. 'She lies;' he said. 'We ate the baby together, and she remarked on the niceness of the meat and gravy. I gave her the leg.' The husband was very angry with his wife and, driving her away, he said, 'Go, you must return to your father, you cannot live here any longer.' The next day the man went to his wife's father and demanded all his cattle back, and they were given to him. The story is finished.

7. *The Frog, his Bride, and the Snake.*

A frog once married a beautiful lady. The frog was a player on the *mbila*. Every evening when he came home from work he would amuse himself by playing on his instrument.

One day when the frog was away from home there came the *luvhidi* (a thin, white, harmless snake) and said to the lady: 'Good day, Mrs. Nobody.' The lady replied: 'I am not Mrs. Nobody, I am Mrs. Frog.' 'Thank you, Mrs. Frog, I did not know that. Where is Mr. Frog now?' 'He is out at work now, here is his *mbila* which he plays on when he comes home,' said the lady. 'Will you allow me to play just one tune?' said the snake. And the lady said 'Yes'. The snake began to play as follows:

'Some men have spots,
Some men have lumps.
I know not whether ladies
Have eyes to see;

FOLK-LORE

345

> If they have, why not give me
> A hand in marriage.
> I am so fine and smooth.'

The lady was greatly touched by the song of the snake. She cooked him nice food and he ate it up and went away. She then boiled some coarse meal and put it on the shelf for her husband, the frog. She wrapped herself in a blanket and pretended to be ill when her husband came home. The snake came again soon, and this went on for some time, until at last the frog found it out. Then he prepared a bow and arrow to shoot the snake. When the snake came again, when the frog was away, and began playing on the *mbila*, the frog came back and shot him dead. The story is finished.

8. *The Monkey and the Cattle.*

There was once a monkey who had a number of cattle to tend. It was rumoured that any one who was able to get the cattle from the monkey could keep them for his own. A party of young men went out together, hoping to drive the cattle off and divide them among them. But the monkey had a bow and arrows, and when the young men came he shot them all.

Next day another party of young men went, and they were shot too. Then the people were afraid to go after the cattle any more. Then one day a party of little boys said, 'We can drive the cattle home by ourselves.' The men of the kraal answered scornfully, 'You cannot do what your elders have failed to do.' But the little boys went out without sticks, or bows and arrows, or spears; they took only a small hoe. They dug up sweet potatoes with the hoe and threw them one by one to the monkey, and, while he was busy eating the sweet potatoes, they drove the cattle home. The story is finished.

9. *The Chief with the Half-moon on his Chest.*

A certain chief was born with a half-moon across his chest, and he possessed two wives. The elder of these wives had two sons, but neither of them inherited the half-moon on his chest; but the chief liked the elder wife more than the younger because she had sons, whereas the younger had, at the time, no children. Shortly after, however, the younger wife became pregnant, and on the day of her delivery she called in the elder woman to assist her. The child was born and was a son, and to the surprise and jealousy of the elder woman he had the half-moon imprinted across his chest. Mad with jealousy

FOLK-LORE

the elder woman, observing that the younger was unconscious and unaware of her child, went with it to the cattle kraal, where a bitch had just given birth to some pups a few days previously. Placing the newly-born son in a large beer-pot within the hut, the older woman laid one of the pups beside the mother and, rousing her, pointed to the dog. 'Look,' she cried, 'look what you have given birth to.' On observing her offspring the mother was greatly ashamed and sad, for she did not know what had happened. Later the woman went to the pot to take the child and destroy it, but a rat who had seen everything had secretly taken the child to its hole. The woman being surprised at the disappearance of the child went to her husband and said, 'Your youngest wife has given birth to a dog.' The chief was angry. 'Go,' he said; 'I have no desire to see such a thing. Go and destroy the animal at once.' The woman therefore returned the pup to the cattle kraal. From now on the chief treated his younger wife with cruelty and harsh words, telling her that she had given birth to a monstrosity. Consequently he gave her no presents and told her she must ask her own father for what she wanted in future. The little rat, however, was in the habit of bringing the child to its mother secretly at night for its food, and this comforted the poor woman a great deal.

One day, when no one was about, the elder woman went inside the younger woman's hut and there saw the rat playing with the child, and, being alarmed, she thought of a plan. When the chief returned she pretended to be seriously ill, and to her husband's questions she replied, 'I called in the doctor to-day and he divined with his bones that, if you desire me to recover again, you must burn down the hut of your younger wife.' The chief, loving his elder wife, agreed, and next morning the younger wife's hut was burnt to the ground. The rat, however, had overheard what was about to happen and had quickly taken the child to the cattle kraal for safety. Later the elder wife, while passing the cattle kraal, again saw the rat playing with the child, and she again pretended to be ill, telling her husband that the doctor had divined that unless the cattle kraal was destroyed she must surely die. The chief gave word to have the kraal burnt, but the rat again overheard and secretly fled with his little friend to a neighbouring chief's village; there he placed the child in the visitors' hut, where it grew up. Years later two visitors came to stay in the hut, and they saw the child, now grown up, with the half-moon across his chest. 'Where did you come from?' they asked in astonishment. The boy, who had learnt his life-story from the rat, told the men his father's

FOLK-LORE

name. 'And what are you doing here?' inquired the men. The boy told them his story from the day of his birth. Filled with surprise the two men promised that on the morrow they would inform the boy's father of his whereabouts. Fearing lest the chief's eldest wife should seek to kill him, the boy made the two men promise not to tell her of his hiding place, but only his father.

On hearing the news the old chief was greatly astonished. 'Are you sure he is my son?' he asked. 'Quite,' answered the men, 'for he has the same half-moon across his chest that you have.' The chief immediately summoned his eldest wife and ordered her to have a large quantity of beer prepared. This was done, and on the following night the old chief went to the village where his son was hiding, and seeing the half-moon he was satisfied and listened in silence to the story his son had to relate. 'Stay here to-night,' said the father, 'I shall send for you to-morrow.' On arriving back home the old chief summoned two messengers. One he sent with a lion's skin to fetch his son, and the other he sent to the most important petty chief, telling him to collect all his people and bring them to the main village on the following day. The son on his arrival was secretly placed in a hut, and when all the people had arrived the chief ordered the beer to be brought out. While all were drinking and wondering what was about to happen, the chief brought out his son who was concealed in the lion's skin. Seating his son before the assembly the chief sat near by, and after a short while he rose and, taking the lion's skin from his son, he revealed to all the half-moon across his chest, and the people were greatly surprised. Calling his eldest wife the chief addressed her, 'Where did this son come from?' he asked, but the woman making no reply, only lowered her eyes to the ground. Seeing her guilt the chief said, 'Go, you miserable woman, take your sons and belongings and depart for ever from this village.' Then the old chief addressed his people and said, 'Here is your chief. From to-day I am no longer chief, but my son here will take my place and you must honour him as you have honoured me.' Great rejoicing followed. Many cattle were killed and everybody ate and drank and did honour to the new chief. The story is finished.

A similar story is told among the BaSutho, and it is possible that the BaVenda have obtained it from them. Dornan[1] found that there is a remarkable resemblance between this tale, which is very unusual

[1] Dornan, S. S., *N.A.D.A.*, 1927, pp. 32–4.

FOLK-LORE

among the Bantu, and a tale in Day's *Folk Tales of Bengal*, entitled
'The Child with the Moon on its Forehead and Stars on the Palms
of the Hands.'

10. *Leave these, better things are ahead.*

A certain young man went searching for honey and came across a
village without any people; he noticed there was a kraal full of goats,
and as he went to open it and take the goats out he heard a bird call
out, 'Leave these, better things are ahead.' Further on his way he
came across a sheep kraal, but the bird cried out again, 'Leave these,
better things are ahead.' So he went on, and got to a cattle-kraal,
but again he heard the same cry from the bird. Further on he got to a
hut and the bird kept quiet. He opened the door and an old woman
with four teeth came out and shouted, 'I am going to kill you;' he ran
and got up a tree; he shouted and whistled for his dogs. Meanwhile
the old woman was trying to cut the tree down with her teeth. The
dogs were coming fast; amongst them was a lame dog which was left
far behind the others. When the dogs arrived the old woman killed
them one by one, pulling off their skins. Now, when the lame dog
arrived, he jumped on her back and got hold of her neck and killed
her. The young man went back taking out of the kraal everything he
saw. The story is finished.

11. *How all the Animals got their Colour.*

The colour of all the animals is said to have been painted on by the
meercat. The meercat said to the animals, 'If any one will kill a buck
and bring me the meat I will paint colour on him.'

The hyena heard him, so he went and killed a buck; he ate all the
meat himself and took the bones to the meercat. The meercat said,
'Lie down.' The hyena knelt down, and the meercat painted ugly
marks on him, saying, 'If any one cheats me, I do the same to him.' The
leopard went out hunting and killed a buck and brought it to the
meercat unskinned. The meercat told him to kneel down and painted
him a beautiful colour, saying, 'If any one keeps his word with me I
will do the same to him.' The story is finished.

12. *The Egg that grew bigger while the Man was singing.*

A certain man had eleven sons, and the youngest one was the son of
his second wife. Before the man died he gave to each of the ten elder
sons three head of cattle, but to the youngest he gave a small egg and
told him to keep it outside, far from the kraal, and to sing to it. The

FOLK-LORE

349

father died, and the youngest son used to go and sing to the egg, and the egg swelled and went on swelling until it was very big, bigger than a house. After a time the youngest son was afraid of it and climbed up a tree when he was singing to it. At last, one day when he was singing, the egg burst, and animals of every kraal came out, oxen, sheep, goats, in numbers. He then built his own kraal and lived happily. That is all.

13. *How Animals got their Tails.*

It is said that animals were created without tails by their maker. The maker one day called them to come and select what tails would suit them. The first group of animals appeared and selected the long and best tails. The second group came and received good tails. The last group were the hares, who are very lazy, and they told the other animals to pick out tails for them. The other animals, having taken the best tails for themselves, brought the short and ugly tails for the hares. If you want a thing well done, do it yourself. The story is finished.

14. *The Story of the Dove, the Vulture, and the Hawk.*

The dove, the vulture and the hawk lived together in peace and friendship. All had their mothers. One day the dove's mother became ill and died soon after. The dove told the vulture and the hawk, and they felt pity and sympathy; they spent a few days mourning at the dove's home. A few days later the vulture's mother died, and he told the dove and the hawk and they came and mourned with him. Soon after this the hawk likewise sent a message that his mother, who was a very old lady, was dead. As his friends came to him he said, 'My mother is no more.' The vulture replied, 'Was she a queen?' and the dove said, 'Are we to mourn for such a miserable old thing?' The hawk was very angry with them for not mourning with him too, and in a rage he killed the dove and the vulture. From that day the hawk kills and devours the dove and the vulture. That is all.

15. *Nyamalide.*

A certain girl called Nyamalide went out to play with the other girls, but she forgot her doll and left it by the river. Returning to fetch it she found an old woman there, who said to her, 'Lick me with your tongue.' She did this, and the woman then said, 'Draw water for me.' When Nyamalide went to draw the water she found that the cup was a man's hand and the gourd was a skull. When she had filled it with water she carried it on her head, and the coil to carry it on was a large

350 FOLK-LORE

snake, and the reeds to cover the water were small snakes. They went together to the old woman's village, which was a big one; but the old woman lived all alone. When night came on they cooked their supper, and while the porridge was cooking the old woman told Nyamalide to grind some monkey-nuts to put in the *tshisevho*, and while she was doing this a frog asked her to give him some. She gave him some and he said, 'Give me some more and I will tell you a secret.' She gave him more and he said, 'If you are asked who it is you are eating with, say that you are eating with your grandmother; and if you are asked who it is you are sleeping with, say that it is your grandmother. And whenever you are sent anywhere to do anything, say " 'I have been working for my grandmother'." Afterwards, when the old woman said to Nyamalide, 'Who have you been eating with?' she answered, 'With my grandmother;' then they ate together. The old woman then asked her, 'Who have you been sleeping with?' and she replied, 'With my grandmother;' then they slept together. At night the girl heard the old woman talking to something, and she asked her, 'What is the smell?' The old woman said, 'There is nothing.' It was, however, hyenas returning from the hunt with meat which they threw into another hut.

In the morning the old woman said, 'Grind mealies, for you will go home to-day.' Nyamalide took them from the store-hut, saying, 'It is to help my grandmother.' The old woman helped her and they ground the mealies.'

When the porridge was ready the old woman said to Nyamalide, 'You shall go home to-day.' The old woman opened a small hut which was full of sheeps' skins, and she gave the girl a skirt and apron of skins and pretty beads and other things. Then they went to a mealie hut and the old woman opened it and took out a girl baby, which she gave to Nyamalide. Then they opened another hut full of cows; the old woman told the girl to choose one, and she chose a white cow with its calf. The old woman also gave her the four skins of a cockroach, a bug, a weevil and an ant, saying, 'If the hyenas follow you, crush the skins one at a time.' She also gave the girl a horn and taught her how to blow it, and she sent a bird to go with her and help her.

The girl started off, driving the cow and carrying the baby. The hyenas soon began to follow her and the bird set up a cry. Then Nyamalide threw down the insects' skins, one at a time, and the hyenas stopped to eat them; so she crossed a river and escaped from them. Coming to a kraal some young men saw her pretty cow and

FOLK-LORE

351

tried to take it from her, but she blew her horn and they all fell asleep and she passed on. This happened again at another village.

Nyamalide reached her home at night and entered unseen, as all her people were asleep. Her younger sister brought in a light to put away some dishes, but Nyamalide blew it out; then her mother made a light again to see who had put it out and she found her daughter Nyamalide. There was great rejoicing and all the people of the village were called to admire the cow by the light in the kraal; Nyamalide told them all that had happened to her. Her younger sister thought that she would go to the old woman too, but at the river she refused to do all she was told to do, and she would not give any food to the frog, so she was eaten up by the hyenas. That is all.

SANKHAMBI TALES

16. *The Square House with Four Doors.*

In a year of great scarcity, an old man and his wife were one day wandering in the bush, looking for food, when they suddenly came upon a large square hut having four doors. Viewing it awhile the old lady said, 'What shall we do, husband?' The husband replied, 'I think we ought to try and see what lies within; our spirits will surely help us if the doors won't open under our own strength.' So the old lady began to sing to her spirits; 'As we went walking through the bush we came across this house with four doors, please open it.' To their surprise a door opened, and together they walked in. Inside lay a heap of meat and food of every kind, and beer was there in plenty, so that their hearts were gladdened. And within a short time they had satisfied their great thirst and hunger, and then they lay down to rest. When the time came to return home, both the old people filled their bags and baskets with the good food so that their children at home might all share in the good fortune; then turning to the door which had closed behind them when they entered the hut, the old lady began to sing again: 'While wandering through the bush we found a hut with four doors, please open it.' And the door straightway opened and they passed out and returned home. On their arrival the old man called his brother and told him of the good news, and invited him and his wife to accompany them on the morrow to the mysterious house in the wood. Early next morning, before any one in the village had risen, the party set off, and, arriving at the house in the wood, the old lady sang as she had done before and the door opened. They entered

352   FOLK-LORE

quickly and the door banged behind them, but this did not trouble
them as they felt confident that their spirits would help them when
the time came to open it again. So they feasted and drank and were
happy at their good fortune. When they had had their fill the men
filled their bags and the women their baskets with the good things; then,
turning to the door as before, the old woman began to sing her song,
but to the surprise of them all it refused to open. They became alarmed,
and the husband, pushing his wife aside, himself sang loudly: 'While wandering through the bush we found a house with four doors, please open
it.' But his words had no effect, and the door remained tightly closed.

Suddenly they heard the noise of a hyena just outside the door and
there followed the noise of dumped meat as all the various animals of
the bush came from their day's outing and placed their meat at the
door. The four people were dreadfully afraid. The old man leaped in
terror on to one of the overhanging rafters, whilst his brother and the
wives each jumped into one of the large beer-pots. Meanwhile all
the animals had gathered about their chief, the elephant, outside,
ready for a beer-drink after the hard day's work. 'Open the door,'
said the elephant to one of his followers, and when this was done he
called to the duiker. 'Go,' he said, 'fetch us a large pot of beer that
we may quench our thirst.' The duiker went inside the hut, but soon
returned; 'My chief, the pot is too heavy and I cannot lift it up.'
The elephant called Sankhambi; 'Go you, Sankhambi, and see if you
can bring out the beer.' Sankhambi entered the hut and slipped his
hand in one of the beer-pots. He noticed at once that it contained
something more than beer, but he said nothing and brought it before
the chief. 'Pour it out for us, Sankhambi,' said the elephant, and this
was done, each of the animals receiving a small cup of beer. When all
had drunk, Sankhambi removed the pot to a distance, and there,
unknown to the others, he ate up its contents, which happened to be
the man who had taken refuge in this pot. 'What are you eating,
Sankhambi?' asked some of the animals; but they were assured that it
was nothing and they said no more. The thirst of the animals, however,
remained unquenched. 'Bring out another pot of beer,' said the
elephant, and Sankhambi brought out a second pot. Again the beer
was poured out and again Sankhambi went apart some distance and
ate up the contents, which happened to be one of the wives. The
second pot of beer satisfied their thirst, and the elephant now suggested
that they should go to bed; so all the animals took up their sleeping positions outside, while a few accompanied the elephant and Sankhambi to

FOLK-LORE

353

except a few important ones who accompanied the elephant and Sankhambi to the hut where they always slept. Suddenly a trickle of water came down from the ceiling. 'What is that ?' asked the elephant. Sankhambi pushed his hand through the pieces of meat hanging from the rafters, but did not say what he felt. 'It is only the meat,' he replied, and they settled down again to sleep. Again the water fell upon them, and this time the elephant was angry. 'What is that ?' he inquired roughly. 'I don't know,' replied Sankhambi, and the elephant then roused himself, and putting his trunk upwards, caught hold of the unfortunate old man who had been hiding above. Throwing the old man to all the animals there, the elephant cried, 'There you are, my friends, there is some meat for you. This is what was making that bad smell in our hut which we could not understand.' The old man was immediately eaten up, and after all was finished the animals again settled down to sleep.

Early next morning the animals departed for the bush, but, before going, the elephant ordered Sankhambi to bring out the third pot of beer so that they might quench their thirst before starting out. Sankhambi poured it out as before, and noticing, that it contained something else besides beer, he took it back to the hut, where he was unseen, and feasted on the second unfortunate woman. The elephant told Sankhambi to come, as he was keeping the party waiting, but Sankhambi delayed them until every bit of the meat was finished. The story is finished.

17. *Sankhambi made the Monkeys support the Cave.*

When Sankhambi saw that he was hated by the monkeys, he said, 'What shall I do ?' So one day he said to the monkeys, 'Come, let me show you where there is a lot of honey.' He took them to a cave where the honey was supposed to be. And when the monkeys were inside, Sankhambi began to make a noise and call out, 'The cave is falling in, support it, support it !' The monkeys then used all their strength to hold it up. Sankhambi said, 'All of you help to hold it up, while I go to fetch some sticks.' Then he ran away leaving the monkeys still supporting the cave. And the reason why monkeys have thin hips is because they were starved on the day when Sankhambi made them support the cave. The story is finished.

18. *Sankhambi and the Crocodile.*

Once upon a time Sankhambi was wandering down the river bank with a pair of duiker horns, which he was blowing like a trumpet. The

A 3

354   FOLK-LORE

crocodile heard this and came out of the river and said, 'What are you doing, Sankhambi?' Sankhambi replied, 'Oh! I am playing with my duiker horns.' 'Will you please let me try to blow them?' said the crocodile, and Sankhambi handed the horns to the crocodile. The crocodile blew, and, liking the sound, he wished to keep them, so he darted suddenly back into the water, taking them with him. Sankhambi was filled with grief and thought out for a plan to pay the crocodile back for this trick. A few days later he returned to the same place with another pair of duiker horns and some bird-lime. He blew the horns, and the crocodile appeared carrying the horns which he had stolen. 'I see,' said the crocodile, 'you have got some more horns, Sankhambi.' 'Yes,' replied Sankhambi, 'and now that you have a pair as well, let us both go a little way up the bank and play together.' They both blew the horns for a little while, and then Sankhambi suggested that they should play with the bird-lime. The crocodile agreed, and Sankhambi rubbed the bird-lime all over his own face and told the crocodile to do the same. The crocodile did as he was bid, but did not notice that Sankhambi had first rubbed his face with fat, so that the bird-lime would not stick. Sankhambi, whose eyes were closed, now asked the crocodile, 'Are you ready?' and the crocodile said that he was, and that he had smeared his face all over with the bird-lime. Sankhambi now quickly scraped the bird-lime off his face, and it came off easily because he had covered his face with fat first, and then he took a big stick and began to beat the crocodile. The crocodile wondered what had happened and tried in vain to open his eyes which were stuck fast with the bird-lime. Sankhambi now picked up the horns which the crocodile had stolen, and, after giving him a few more blows, went away, saying, 'I am going away now. You can stay here and burn in the hot sun, and perhaps you will learn not to be a thief in future!'

19. *Sankhambi and the Duiker.*

Sankhambi, feeling hungry, was strolling about wondering what he would do, when he saw a duiker.

'Hullo,' said Sankhambi, 'Can you play with me for a while?' 'Yes,' said the duiker, 'I have nothing to do at the moment.'

Sankhambi proposed that they should play with a fire, and the duiker agreeing, he made a large fire. 'Put me in,' said Sankhambi. 'No,' said the duiker, 'the fire will burn you. If you want to go in, then jump in yourself.' Sankhambi did so, and took care to jump near the edge and out of reach of the flames, but the duiker did not notice

FOLK-LORE

355

this. 'Oh, I am burning, I am burning,' cried Sankhambi, 'pull me out quickly;' the duiker ran and found a bent stick and pulled his friend out. 'It is your turn now to jump into the fire,' said Sankhambi, 'and, when it burns, I will hook you out too.' The duiker leaped into the middle of the flames, and then shouted at once, 'I am burning, Sankhambi, I am burning, come quickly and pull me out.' Sankhambi only laughed. 'You are not cooked yet,' he said. Again the duiker begged to be taken out, but Sankhambi only said, 'You are not cooked yet.' At last the duiker was roasted, and Sankhambi pulled the meat out of the fire and enjoyed a good meal. The story is finished.

20. *Sankhambi and the Baboons.*

Sankhambi found the lion with its cubs, and said, 'Let me take care of them.' The lion agreed, saying, 'Give the pieces of meat to the cubs, and you can have the bones.' Sankhambi ate the meat and gave the bones to the cubs, saying, 'The bones will make their teeth strong.' Sankhambi then ate one of the cubs. When he counted them for the lion in the morning, he counted one twice over. Sankhambi did this every evening, and the lion was deceived until all the cubs were eaten up. When the last one was eaten, Sankhambi bruised himself with sticks and rolled himself in the ashes and sat there looking sad. When the lion returned and said, 'Where are the children ?' Sankhambi said in a small crying voice, 'Sir, the children have been eaten by the baboons. Do you not see how I, too, have been hurt and almost killed ?' The lion said, 'I will find the baboons.' Sankhambi said, 'Let me find them for you.' So he went out and found the baboons playing the game of stones (*mefuvha*), sitting on their tails. Sankhambi said, 'How are you playing ?' and the baboons answered, 'Our tribe holds on tight to the branch of the tree for fear of falling.' Sankhambi taught them to say, 'We have eaten the lion's cubs; what will become of us now ?' The baboons listened to Sankhambi and said this instead, until they got quite used to saying it. Then Sankhambi said to the baboons, 'I will go and dig sweet potatoes for you and will come back carrying them in the grass.' Sankhambi went and tied the lion up in grass, and put the sweet potatoes outside, and came back to the baboons, carrying this. He said to them, 'Let us play the game of stones first, and then we will eat the sweet potatoes.'

Sankhambi said, 'Our tribe holds on tight to the branch for fear of falling.' The baboons replied, 'We have eaten the lion's cubs, what will become of us now ?' as Sankhambi had taught them.

356 FOLK-LORE

A little baboon was sitting near the grass, as he was in a hurry to eat the sweet potatoes, and he saw the grass shake and said, 'The bundle of grass is breathing.' The others said, 'Be quiet.' The little baboon said again, 'There is something in the grass,' for it had seen the lion's eye.

Sankhambi said, 'Come, let us eat the sweet potatoes,' and when the baboons had gathered together, he came up and cut the strings around the bundle of grass. The lion jumped out and killed the baboons, thinking that he had caught the thieves who had eaten his children. Sankhambi was behind the lion and he cut off the tails of the baboons; the lion could not get one to show the other lions at home. Sankhambi did not like the meat of baboons, so the trees remained full of meat. The story is finished.

21. *Sankhambi and the Fruit Tree.*

While Sankhambi was sleeping under a tree he felt the fruit falling on him; he did not know the name of the fruit, so he went and found the hare and asked him to tell him its name; but the hare did not know. They then went and found the duiker and other small buck, but they could not tell them the name of the fruit. So they decided to ask the larger animals of the bush, and sent off the duiker as he is very speedy. The duiker found the buck and he told him the name, but he returned so speedily that he tripped and broke his leg, and by the time that he got back to the hare and Sankhambi he had forgotten the name. The hare was now sent off, but he, too, went so quickly that he tripped and broke his leg, and by the time he returned he had forgotten the name. The tortoise was now sent, and he plodded on slowly, and after a long time he returned without having been delayed by a broken limb, and he told all of them the name of the fruit. More haste, less speed. Slow but sure wins the race.

(The story continues and shows the cleverness of Sankhambi.)

Having now got the name of the fruit, all the animals began to eat. Sankhambi, seeing some fruit at the top of the tree much nicer than the rest, made them all promise they they would not touch it, as it belonged to the elephant, who was considered to be the chief of the animals. That night, when the animals were going to sleep, Sankhambi told them that he slept in a niche among the rocks, and asked the buck to close up the entrance of the hole in which he had settled himself for the night. He found other small holes which the others did not see, but when they had closed up one entrance he said it was all right and they all went to sleep. During the night Sa-

FOLK-LORE

357

nkhambi got up, picked his way out, climbed up the tree, and ate all the elephant's fruit. He then took the skins, went to the sleeping elephant and put them up his rectum. In the morning, to the amazement of all, the fruit was discovered to be missing, and there was great fear, for nobody knew who had stolen it. Sankhambi crept out of his hole and said, 'Let's jump over this big fence and see what happens.' He led, and one by one the animals leaped over the fence; the elephant came last, and when he jumped all the skins fell out. The animals became very angry and accused the elephant of trying to kill them for theft, when he himself had eaten the fruit. In their anger they killed the elephant. Sankhambi now claimed a leg as his share of the dead elephant, and while he was taking it away he began to sing, 'I ate the fruit and blamed the elephant so that he could be killed.' One of the buck overheard this and said, 'What are you saying?' To which Sankhambi replied, 'I am just saying "This leg is too heavy and I want the liver."' He was then given the liver, and after he had dragged it some way he began to sing the same thing. This time another buck heard him. Immediately they all chased him, but he was now close to the river and he leaped into it. The buck felt about for him, but each time they picked him up he said he was a stone and they let him go. Soon he made his way to the opposite bank, and then the river came down in flood and the buck could not get to him. The buck, however, had a beer-drink, and Sankhambi was unable to resist the temptation of going, so in order to disguise himself he got some honeycomb, put in on his head, and stuck a pair of horns in it. He then planted a stick in the ground and got a long piece of string. This he fastened to the stick, and by bending the stick and releasing the string he was shot to the other side. He joined the party and had a good drink, keeping in the shade as much as possible, but the sun got to him, melted the honeycomb, and the horns dropped off. The buck immediately sprang at him, saying, 'Now we have you, you rogue.' But Sankhambi quickly pulled the string which he had kept in his hand and bent the stick back on the opposite side of the river, so that, when he slackened the string suddenly, he was dragged across and once again escaped the anger of his enemies. The story is finished.

22. *Sankhambi and the Elephant.*

One day all the animals decided to live together, so an enormous kraal was built and they all went in, and every one was comfortable, because the dung was spread about and kept them all warm.

358 FOLK-LORE

They found, however, that the dung was being eaten, so they set the monkey to watch. The monkey saw Sankhambi come and eat the dung. He chased him, but the cunning Sankhambi ran and got his bow and arrows and shot the monkey through the leg. The duiker was then told to watch, but he refused as he was too weak. So the hyena was set to catch Sankhambi, but when he chased him Sankhambi shot him, too, through the leg and escaped again.

Next day the elephant watched, but Sankhambi did not come out as early as usual, and the elephant fell asleep, and when he awoke he saw Sankhambi scampering off after having had a good meal. He chased Sankhambi, but Sankhambi ran down a hole, frightening a hare which was there. The hare ran off and the elephant chased him and caught him, but he explained that he was not the culprit; so the elephant returned to the hole, but Sankhambi had squeezed himself into a crevice and the elephant ran past him, so Sankhambi escaped. The elephant saw his little enemy and gave chase. Sankhambi rushed to the river and jumped in, but the elephant, not to be outwitted, began to search the river bed with his trunk. Every time he caught him, Sankhambi would cry out, 'No, no, you have got a root.' The elephant would let go and search again, and when he did get hold of a root the cunning Sankhambi cried out, 'Let me go, let me go.' The elephant then tugged, and tugged, and pulled out only a root. Each time the elephant caught Sankhambi he cried out that it was a root he had caught, and each time the elephant had a root Sankhambi called out, 'Let me go.' So the elephant worked hard and got hot pulling out roots. This went on for a long time, until the elephant was weary and went home, leaving Sankhambi smiling at his enemy's foolishness.

23. *Sankhambi and the Old Woman.*

All the animals of the bush lived in one large kraal, and they were constantly worried by an old woman who stole the dung each day. 'We must do something about this,' said the elephant, and seeing the duiker he said, 'You, duiker, you shall stay at home to-day and see if you can catch this thief.' After the animals had all gone to the bush the old woman appeared and began filling her basket. 'Hey,' said the duiker, 'What are you doing?' 'Go away at once.' The old woman looked angry. 'I will cut off your hind leg,' she said; and, before the duiker could do anything, she cut off his leg, and, placing it in the basket, went away.

The duiker cried all the time until the other animals returned.

FOLK-LORE

'What is this ; ' said the elephant. 'Where is your leg ? Why have you only three ?' The duiker told him what had happened, and all the animals were very angry. Calling on Sankhambi, the elephant said, 'You, Sankhambi, are clever, see what you can do to-morrow.' The next day, after the animals had gone to the bush, the old woman again appeared and began to steal the dung. Sankhambi approached her. 'May I help you fill your basket, grandmother ?' he said pleasantly. The woman was surprised and liked him. 'Yes,' she said, and together they filled her basket. When this was done Sankhambi suggested a game, and the old woman agreed. Producing a piece of string, Sankhambi invited the old woman to tie it around his neck, and when the old woman began to pull the other end he cried out, 'Stop, stop, you are killing me.' The woman stopped, and Sankhambi suggested that she put the string around her neck. This the old woman did, but when she called on her friend to stop pulling the other end he only laughed and pulled it tighter. Dragging her to a tree he tied her up and strangled her. The animals returned and, not seeing anything, the elephant was very angry and shouted at Sankhambi, 'So you have failed, too. I thought you were clever, Sankhambi.' Sankhambi said nothing, but only smiled, and after the elephant had scolded him he produced the basket and gave it to the elephant. The animals were now very pleased, for they knew that Sankhambi had succeeded in killing the old lady, and they all applauded him for his cunning. That is the end of the story.

Riddles, Thai.

Riddle.	*Answer.*
1. A chief presided and the people surrounded him.	The moon and the stars.
2. Red like a snuff gourd from Luonde mountain.	Sunrise, or the moon when it is just coming up.
3. An old lady whose body is formed only of ribs.	A basket.
4. Red in front and black behind.	A veldt fire. (First the red flames, and, as they pass on, the blackened earth is left behind.)
5. My father's spears pierce right through the roof.	Fire is made inside the hut and smoke is seen coming through the roof.
6. An old man whose grey hair is inside his belly.	The grey fibres inside a pumpkin.

FOLK-LORE

360

Riddle.	*Answer.*
7. A tree is dry at the top and from the lower part water can be obtained.	A milking cow.
8. I met a bride and she knelt.	A tortoise coiling up in its shell.
9. I met a chief and he quickly rolled up the skin-bag containing his snuff.	A millepede quickly rolls itself up when touched.
10. Birds fly far, far away, leaving tail feathers behind.	Eyes. (eyes can see a long distance while the person to whom they belong remains behind).
11. What accompanies me wherever I go and then back home?	My shadow.
12. That which does honour to no chief.	A slippery place after rainfall. It makes every one balance and respects no chief.
13. The wives of Raluvhimba clad in cotton wool.	The white strings which come out of mealie cobs.
14. Shut the door so that we can have a dance.	Shut the pot after the first stirring so that it may boil up again.
15. I found Sikwibulu perching by the roadside and I greeted him but he made no answer.	An ant-hill by the roadside. (It speaks to nobody.)

Proverbs.

1. If anything is blown into your eye you cannot see with the other one to get it out.
2. It is always far to go where there are no friends at the end of the journey.
3. Fat must be eaten inside the hut.
4. The fins of a fish are its children.
5. The heart of one man is not a servant of any other man.
6. The dog would hunt, if its owner could talk to it.
7. An old man never stops slanderous talk.
8. The dog that eats another one never gets fat.
9. A dog that is given away has not got a master.
10. A man's elder brother is his heart.
11. A person's mouth can outdo a drum in making a noise.
12. One finger cannot pick up stamped mealies.
13. A person is a person; only a piece of wood has not got ears.
14. A snake that is seen will not bite anybody.
15. The child of a mouse never forgets its path.
16. Things a long way off are always first seen by a coward.
17. Share your sorrows.

FOLK-LORE

18. The work of a medicine-man may cross over, but a chief's son must not cross over; (i. e. a medicine-man may practise in a foreign country, but a chief's son may not make himself chief there).
19. The pot which is poured into (i. e. the beer-pot) is better than that which is cooked.
20. Two vicious snakes do not stay in the same hole; (i. e. two angry people should not live in the same village).
21. When the sun has set throw down your axe; at night there are things abroad that will eat you; (i. e. do not go into the bush at night).
22. To cook for the murderer is to cause those at home to sleep in hunger.
23. The medicine-man cannot heal himself.
24. The mouth is a sore that does not heal.
25. He who casts out his hard-working wife does not laugh; he who has a contented wife laughs.
26. The wife of a basket-maker carries her things in an old worn-out basket.
27. A wise person does not eat at all times; a fool is always eating.
28. He who guides you by night may be trusted by day.
29. A dirty person does not see himself.
30. To be full of beer is to have the belly of a watermelon; (i. e. you will again be hungry).
31. I am wicked myself so that I laugh at wicked ones.
32. A child forbidden an axe leaves a knife of its own accord.
33. Do not laugh at lameness while a child, for lameness comes in old age.
34. If you whisper of that which happens to others, to-morrow it will happen to you.
35. If you do not hear when you are told you will hear in your sleep.
36. Rich things seek each other.
37. He who refused to be told wanted to see (with his own eyes).
38. The poison (on the arrow-head) has eaten the man who put it on.
39. In the village of a coward the sound of war is not heard.
40. To be too smart will lead to trouble.
41. Spears eat those that make them.
42. He who scatters the fire will be burnt.

XXV

MISCELLANEOUS BELIEFS AND SUPERSTITIONS

The Origin of Death.

LIKE so many of the Bantu, the BaVenda associate the origin of death with the chameleon. According to the Venda tradition the creator sent a millepede to go quickly to tell the people of the world that they would never die. On the way to deliver its message it saw a *tutulwa* tree and, feeling hungry, it wasted time eating the fruit. Meanwhile the slow hesitating chameleon was sent to tell the people that he was the messenger of death. The chameleon arrived first and delivered his bad news, and when the millepede finally arrived it was too late.

So to-day the chameleon is feared and disliked by every MuVenda, who kills it by forcing open its mouth with a stick and filling it with snuff. Chameleons are always killed if they are caught, as they were the instrument which caused death and so much sorrow in the world.

Dreams.

Dreams are omens portending good or evil to the dreamer and his family. After dreaming of anything unusual a MuVenda generally asks a *nganga* to interpret it for him, so that by sacrifice or magic he may avert the threatened calamity. He does this also if he dreams of an ancestor, who only appears in this way desiring propitiation. To have frequent dreams of ordinary things and people is dangerous, as if they come true the dreamer is considered to be a source of danger to the community in which he lives; so a man rarely discusses such dreams with his neighbours. Dreams connected with water, rain, rivers, floods, waterholes, &c., are good omens. A dream of beer portends trouble and is nearly always the forerunner of the death of the dreamer or one of his lineage. Dreams of baboons, lions, and mealies, especially those connected with the pouring of the grain into the mealie pits, are also bad omens and the forerunners of death. A dream of blood foretells a severe outbreak of fire in the village, and a dream of fire is followed by enemy raids and war.

Omens.

1. A small two-horned beetle foreshadows the coming of cattle, so that a man seeing one of these little creatures coming towards him is delighted, as he knows that he will have good luck with his cattle.

MISCELLANEOUS BELIEFS AND SUPERSTITIONS 363

2. A python coiled up with its head resting on top of the coil is symbolic of a cattle kraal and a lucky omen.

3. Two snakes on the road are signs that the traveller will hear good news at the place he is visiting. A python moving along in front of him has the same meaning.

4. A snake once struck must always be followed up and killed, as, if it happens to be in the act of shedding its skin, when it makes its escape, the skin of the person who first struck it will fall off.

5. It is lucky to find an ostrich's nest and eggs complete.

6. The discovery of a manis is very lucky; it must be taken to the chief's village, where its flesh will be cooked up with a sheep and the potage divided among all the men of the village to bring them good luck.

7. If snuff falls on the ground it must not be picked up, as it is a sign that the spirits have asked for it and it must be left for them.

8. If the food that is offered to a stranger falls down he must not eat it, as he believes that his spirits have in this way warned him against eating the food which would have killed him.

9. A man setting off on a visit, and hearing a *makuri* bird (finch) singing overhead, goes on his way happy in the knowledge that his host will be ready to receive him and will give him a hearty welcome.

10. If a man is going on a journey and sees a secretary bird on his road he will turn back, as the bird is warning him of danger ahead.

11. An owl sitting on a hut is really a dangerous *muloi* in disguise.

12. The appearance of a species of earthworm on the path is a warning to the beholder that one of his relatives is dead.

13. It is tabu for a man to kill a cat, as if he does the spirit of the dead cat will prevent the spirit of the man who killed it from escaping from his body when he dies. This is why the little children kill all the cats.

14. If a frog is found in a beer-pot all the beer must be thrown away, as any one that drinks the polluted liquid will die.

15. If a MuVenda helps another to salt he must always pinch him, or the two will soon fight.

16. If a man is working out of doors and feels a drop fall on him he thinks that one of his spirits is spitting at him, and himself spits on the ground to quiet it.

APPENDIX I

MEFUVHA

This game is played by men only, on a solid wooden board made from the trunk of a tree, in which four rows of square holes are cut out. At either end there may be two larger hollowed recesses which are used as receptacles for the counters. There are an equal even number of holes in each of the four rows, but there may be any number of holes from six to twenty-eight in a row, the usual number being between sixteen and twenty. Sometimes, instead of on a board, the game is played in little holes scooped out in the ground. There are two players, each man commanding two rows. Each starts by putting two stones or pips into each hole in his own two rows, except the left-hand hole of the front row, which is left empty, and the adjoining hole into which he only puts one. The game represents a cattle raid and the stones are the cattle. The player who first removes all his opponent's stones is the winner. Some of the ejaculations, used to describe moves and positions, appear to be archaic words, and could not be explained by the players.

Method of Play.

1. The moves are made anti-clockwise, and there is a regular opening move which is always followed.

2. Stones are picked up from one hole and placed one in each following hole. If, however, the last stone does not fall in a vacant hole, the pile is picked up and the stones again dropped, one at a time, in the following holes. This is repeated until eventually one stone ends in a vacant hole. A single move may entail many movements of stones around the two rows before a vacant hole is obtained.

3. When the counter finally comes to rest in a vacant hole in the front row the player shouts '*Thuku!*' a hit (onomatopoeic, implying that the shot has hit the mark). After achieving a *thuku*, the player removes all the stones in the hole immediately opposite and the hole behind it on his opponent's side; if there are no counters in the hole immediately opposite, he may not remove those behind and no hit is scored.

4. After scoring a *thuku*, the player is entitled to a forfeit, the *thuro*. He may take the contents of any hole on the opponent's side as his *thuro*. This ends the move, and the next player has a turn.

5. As long as any hole contains two or more counters no single stones may be removed.

Khandami. Any two or more stones which, when moved according to the rules, end in a vacant hole, are called *khandami* (meaning unknown).

PLATE XLVIII

MEFUVHA

NDODE

APPENDIX I 365

Khosi or mboho (chief or bull). Two or more stones which command a favourable position, and are capable of playing a protracted move, are called *khosi* or *mboho*.

There may be several *khandami* or *makhosi* on the board, the component counters and positions of which are changing continually.

'*Nde!*' Tramp! (onomatopoeic, expressing the sound of the tramp of marching feet). When single stones are moved from one hole to another without making a hit, the player, as he makes the move, exclaims '*Nde!*' '*Wa-a-a!*' When two counters are simply moved forward and split into singles without any further move, the player says '*Wa-a-a!*'

Tabus. It is tabu to play this game after sunset, for fear that, by playing at cattle raiding after dark, a real raid might be provoked. During the rainy season it is tabu to use fruit pips as counters for fear that hail will fall instead of rain.

Explanatory Game, with 6 holes in each row

A	o^{12}	o^{11}	o^{10}	o9	o^8	o7
	o^6	o5	o4	o3	o^2	o^1
B	o^1	o^2	o3	o4	o5	o^6
	o7	o^8	o9	o^{10}	o^{11}	o^{12}

Opening Move. B. No. 3, two stones taken, one to No. 2, one to No. 1. *Thuku!* (I hit).
Remove stones from No. 6 A and No. 12 A.
Thuro. Take stones from No. 10 A.

Second Move. A. Does same opening move, placing one stone in No. 2 and one stone in No. 1. *Thuku!*
Remove stones from No. 6 B and No. 12 B.
Thuro. Stones from No. 11 B.

Third Move. B. Take stones from No. 8. Put one in No. 9, one in No. 10. Pick up all No. 10. Put one in No. 11, one in No. 12, and one in No. 6. *Thuku!*
Remove No. 1 A and No. 7 A.
Thuro. Stone from No. 9 A.

Fourth Move. A. Take two stones from No. 5, and put one in No. 4 and one in No. 3. *Thuku!* Pick up No. 3 B.
Thuro. Stone from No. 2 B.

Fifth Move. B. Take three stones from No. 9. Put one in No. 10, and one in No. 11, and one in No. 12.
Pick up two stones in No. 12. Put one in No. 1 and one in No. 2.
Pick up three stones from No. 2. Put one in No. 3, one in No. 4, one in No. 5. *Nde!* (hit blank).

366 APPENDIX I

Sixth Move. *A.* Take two stones from No. 8. Put one in No. 9, one in No. 10. He says '*Wa-a-a!*' (because he has split up the two stones and cannot carry on any more).

Seventh Move. *B.* Take stone from No. 6. *Mboho* (Bull). Put one in No. 5 and one in No. 4. Pick up No. 4, put one in No. 3 and one in No. 2. Pick up stones in No. 2, put one in No. 1 and one in No. 7.

Pick up three from No. 7. Put one in No. 8, one in No. 9, one in No. 10. Pick up from No. 10. Put one in No. 11, one in No. 12. *Nde!*

Eighth Move. *A.* Take two from No. 11 (*Khandami*). Put one in No. 12, one in No. 6. *Thuku!*

Pick up No. 1 B.

Thuro. Stone from No. 8 B.

Ninth Move. *B.* Take two stones from No. 3 (*Khandami*). Put one in No. 2 and one in No. 1. *Thuku!*

Pick up No. 6 A and No. 12 A.

Thuro. Stone from No. 2 A.

Tenth Move. *A.* Take three stones from No. 4. Put one in No. 3, one in No. 2, and one in No. 1. *Nde!*

Eleventh Move. *B.* Take three stones from No. 11. Put one in No. 12, one in No. 6, and one in No. 5.

Take stones from No. 5. Put one in No. 4 and one in No. 3. *Nde!*

Twelfth Move. *A.* Take two stones from No. 3. Put one in No. 2 and one in No. 1.

Take stones from No. 1. Put one in No. 7 and one in No. 8. *Nde!*

Thirteenth Move. *B.* Take from No. 12. Put one in No. 6 and one in No. 5. *Thuku!*

Pick up No. 2 A and No. 8 A.

Thuro. Stone from No. 7 A.

Fourteenth Move. *A.* Take one stone from No. 10 and put it in No. 11. *Nde!*

Fifteenth Move. *B.* Take two stones from No. 6. Put one in No. 5 and one in No. 4.

Take two stones from No. 4. Put one in No. 3 and one in No. 2.

Take two stones from No. 2. Put one in No. 1 and one in No. 7. *Nde!*

Sixteenth Move. *A.* Take stone from No. 11 and put it in No. 12. *Nde!*

Seventeenth Move. *B.* Take two from No. 1. Put one in No. 7 and one in No. 8. *Nde!*

Eighteenth Move. *A.* Take stone from No. 12 and put it into No. 6. *Nde!*

Nineteenth Move. *B.* Take two stones from No. 3, put one in No. 2 and one in No. 1. *Thuku!*

Pick up No. 6 A.

Thuro. Stone from No. 9 A.

B. wins.

APPENDIX I

367

NDODE

Women never play *mefuvha*. Instead, they play a variation of 'five stones'. Two players sit opposite to each other and mark out a small circle, about 8 inches in diameter, on the ground between them. They put 8 to 12 small pieces of potsherd inside this ring. The player has a small stone or potsherd in her hand, and the game consists of throwing up the stone and, while it is in the air, scraping three or more pieces out of the circle, catching the stone again and throwing it up, and, while it is in the air, returning two of the three pieces (or one less than were removed), catching the stone again, throwing it up again, and scraping out three more pieces. The player continues until she lets her stone drop or makes a mistake, when the other player has a turn.

The player who succeeds in emptying the circle, without missing the thrown-up stone, wins.

APPENDIX II

TABLE OF HEIGHT AND HEAD MEASUREMENTS

Height is given in centimetres; length and breadth in millimetres.

Men.	Height.	Cranial.			Nasal.		
		Length.	Breadth.	Index.	Length.	Breadth.	Index.
1	164·0	195	146	74·9	54	44	81·5
2	172·0	200	142	71·0	48	50	104·2
3	177·9	194	150	77·3	48	43	89·6
4	168·8	195	152	77·9	45	46	102·2
5	167·0	195	142	72·8	47	38	80·8
6	167·6	195	150	76·9	43	44	102·3
7	165·7	192	146	76·0	39	40	102·6
8	162·6	182	144	79·1	45	39	86·7
9	169·1	197	150	76·1	51	47	92·2
10	164·3	191	144	75·4	50	43	86·0
11	177·1	203	149	73·5	50	45	90·0
12	171·8	210	160	76·2	44	49	111·2
13	167·7	191	150	78·5	45	43	95·5
14	158·5	194	145	74·7	50	42	84·0
15	164·0	185	139	75·1	47	42	89·4
16	180·5	189	141	74·6	53	44	83·0
17	174·6	204	144	70·6	34	40	117·6
18	163·0	185	147	79·4	45	39	86·7
19	178·0	201	144	71·7	52	52	100·0
20	166·2	192	145	75·5	47	47	100·0
21	168·3	195	150	76·9	49	41	83·7
22	172·6	192	139	72·3	50	39	78·0
23	170·2	190	147	77·3	50	44	88·0
24	173·2	203	148	72·8	53	46	86·8
25	174·5	200	150	75·0	52	53	102·0
26	170·1	186	148	79·6	53	48	90·6
27	167·7	201	149	74·0	42	44	104·7
28	154·2	195	145	74·3	51	43	84·3
29	170·2	205	143	69·8	44	43	97·7
30	161·0	190	138	68·3	40	44	110·0
31	171·0	195	146	74·8	44	43	97·7
32	161·2	187	146	78·0	52	44	84·7
33	184·2	199	145	72·9	55	52	94·6
34	170·5	205	142	69·2	49	50	102·0
35	162·7	200	144	72·0	48	44	91·7
36	175·8	187	142	76·0	52	42	80·8
37	170·4	200	147	73·5	50	46	92·0
38	178·0	198	145	73·2	51	51	100·0
39	173·1	189	144	76·1	50	47	94·0

APPENDIX II

Men.	Height.	Cranial.			Nasal.		
		Length.	Breadth.	Index.	Length.	Breadth.	Index.
40	178·5	204	154	75·4	51	49	96·1
41	162·8	180	137	76·2	55	42	76·4
42	167·7	199	154	77·3	44	44	100·0
43	160·4	190	155	81·5	54	47	87·1
44	170·0	199	150	75·3	45	40	88·9
45	177·0	195	147	75·3	47	45	95·8
46	165·0	194	149	76·9	54	58	107·4
47	159·0	198	145	73·2	47	46	97·9
48	176·5	195	149	76·4	54	41	76·0
49	153·5	200	149	74·5	45	45	100·0
50	161·1	194	143	73·7	59	45	76·3
51	166·0	200	152	76·0	54	46	85·2
52	165·0	193	144	74·5	46	44	95·7
53	168·7	195	142	72·9	44	42	95·5
54	170·0	192	144	72·9	47	47	100·0
55	159·0	190	154	81·0	44	40	90·9
56	163·5	197	159	80·6	44	45	102·3
7	165·0	200	151	75·5	47	50	106·3
58	164·4	199	150	75·4	47	42	89·4
59	170·0	196	151	77·0	43	44	102·3
60	169·6	196	144	73·4	47	46	97·9
61	176·2	204	141	69·0	50	47	94·0
62	170·0	193	141	73·0	52	47	90·4
63	177·0	197	146	74·0	57	56	98·2
64	172·0	187	152	81·2	45	47	104·4
65	166·0	195	152	77·9	44	43	97·7
66	168·2	201	158	78·6	51	42	82·4
67	165·6	191	143	74·9	49	46	93·9
68	169·7	199	144	72·3	47	51	108·5
69	169·0	197	145	73·5	46	44	95·6
70	164·4	190	139	73·0	50	47	94·0
71	177·9	197	143	72·5	47	46	97·9
72	160·3	190	145	76·2	47	49	104·2
73	157·4	191	148	77·4	46	47	102·1
74	168·4	202	145	71·8	46	45	97·8
75	163·0	194	145	74·8	44	44	100·0
76	160·4	186	145	78·0	46	40	86·9
77	175·2	186	148	79·5	47	46	97·9
78	159·0	181	144	79·6	46	42	91·3
79	167·7	193	147	76·2	47	45	95·8
80	169·0	180	142	78·9	42	44	104·8
81	157·0	194	146	75·3	42	47	111·9
82	169·0	197	150	76·1	47	43	91·5
83	186·0	195	140	71·8	50	40	80·0

APPENDIX II

Table of Height aud Head Measurements (cont.)—

Men.	Height.	Cranial.			Nasal.		
		Length.	Breadth.	Index.	Length.	Breadth.	Index
84	164·6	205	137	66·9	47	50	106·3
85	164·5	199	149	74·9	50	43	86·0
86	170·2	193	144	74·7	47	47	100·0
87	171·5	193	142	73·6	47	48	102·1
88	161·2	193	151	78·2	47	49	104·2
89	171·2	197	154	78·1	50	49	98·0
90	170·0	196	147	75·0	49	47	95·9
91	176·8	200	144	72·0	50	59	118·0
92	158·4	196	145	74·0	50	47	94·0
93	167·0	199	156	78·3	47	49	104·2
94	170·3	202	150	74·2	50	51	102·0
95	177·3	195	145	74·4	49	43	87·8
96	164·5	193	147	76·2	49	47	95·9
97	175·4	204	147	72·0	53	46	86·8
98	173·5	206	152	73·8	48	43	89·6
99	162·6	203	142	69·9	52	41	78·9
100	174·3	202	149	73·6	54	42	77·8
101	165·3	197	143	72·5	45	42	93·3
102	167·5	199	145	72·9	46	43	93·5
103	166·3	198	147	74·2	47	47	100·0
104	169·4	194	147	75·8	47	50	106·3
105	163·4	185	152	82·1	51	49	96·1
106	168·0	194	147	75·7	50	51	102·0
107	163·4	195	151	77·4	53	46	86·3
108	165·4	199	144	72·4	47	46	97·9
109	170·0	203	150	73·8	52	45	86·6
110	172·0	203	149	73·2	52	45	86·6
111	163·0	201	150	74·6	50	43	86·0
112	173·4	204	159	77·9	54	49	90·7
113	163·0	200	146	73·0	47	47	100·0
114	161·0	193	145	75·1	41	44	107·3
115	163·8	206	160	77·7	48	44	91·7
116	169·7	196	158	80·6	53	52	98·2
117	178·4	198	147	74·3	47	43	91·5
118	165·3	199	144	72·4	49	42	85·7
119	164·6	193	146	75·7	51	48	94·2
120	166·0	188	142	75·5	54	44	81·5
121	165·4	201	155	77·2	49	44	88·8
122	161·0	190	145	76·3	47	46	97·9
123	167·2	209	148	70·8	50	40	80·0
124	165·5	194	152	78·4	51	48	94·2
125	162·0	183	145	79·2	54	44	81·5
126	169·8	196	151	77·1	45	42	93·3

APPENDIX II

371

Men.	Height.	Cranial.			Nasal.		
		Length.	Breadth.	Index.	Length.	Breadth.	Index.
127	175·3	200	154	77·0	53	45	84·9
128	167·3	196	160	81·7	49	47	95·9
129	165·7	199	145	72·9	54	48	88·9
130	162·0	195	150	76·9	46	44	95·7
131	167·0	201	144	72·0	45	45	100·0
132	167·0	192	147	76·6	51	41	80·4
133	173·3	201	150	74·7	49	43	87·1
134	174·0	202	154	76·3	46	50	108·7
135	160·0	192	151	78·7	48	47	97·9
136	160·3	183	140	76·5	46	46	100·0
137	176·0	188	142	75·5	44	45	102·2
138	155·3	193	148	76·7	44	46	104·5
139	158·6	195	144	73·9	49	47	95·9
140	173·4	202	148	73·3	53	40	75·5
141	164·1	205	142	69·2	50	48	96·0
142	168·3	204	155	76·0	47	47	100·0
143	163·3	199	146	73·4	50	42	84·0
144	154·0	189	143	75·7	46	42	91·3
145	169·0	199	147	73·9	48	51	106·2
146	165·7	211	152	72·1	60	50	83·3
147	167·1	194	148	76·3	53	41	77·4
148	171·0	201	146	72·6	47	47	100·0
149	162·0	187	148	79·2	47	45	95·8
150	165·0	203	154	75·9	46	48	104·3
151	166·0	187	145	77·5	48	44	91·7
152	175·6	203	150	73·9	46	44	95·7
153	164·0	196	147	75·0	53	42	79·3
154	172·4	188	143	76·1	43	39	90·7
155	162·6	199	139	69·9	48	48	100·0
156	170·3	201	151	75·1	51	45	88·3
157	171·1	196	145	74·0	46	47	102·1
158	168·1	192	151	78·6	47	46	97·9
159	169·1	194	147	75·8	46	42	91·3
160	162·4	207	154	74·4	50	44	88·0
161	164·3	208	152	73·1	50	45	90·0
162	170·2	197	145	73·6	53	42	79·3
163	169·2	202	143	70·8	47	50	106·3
164	161·0	182	145	79·7	45	44	97·8
165	158·4	185	145	78·4	45	41	91·2
166	164·2	194	145	74·8	45	44	97·8
167	162·2	204	147	72·1	47	48	102·1
168	164·4	197	145	73·6	48	46	95·9

B b 2

372 APPENDIX II

Table of Height and Head Measurements (cont.)—

Women.	Height.	Cranial.			Nasal.		
		Length.	Breadth.	Index.	Length.	Breadth.	Index.
1	163·0	180	140	77·8	49	40	81·7
2	157·5	190	146	76·9	47	42	89·4
3	150·0	189	137	72·4	42	38	90·5
4	159·0	191	147	77·0	47	43	91·6
5	159·0	189	145	76·7	45	40	88·9
6	140·0	178	134	75·2	45	44	97·8
7	157·0	197	142	67·0	44	35	79·6
8	159·4	193	142	73·6	47	39	83·0
9	155·0	186	145	77·9	47	41	87·3
10	158·4	188	147	78·1	48	39	81·3
11	147·0	182	133	73·0	45	39	86·7
12	156·5	186	144	77·3	51	46	90·3
13	154·4	184	156	84·7	39	38	97·5
14	153·0	188	140	74·4	47	39	83·0
15	148·0	187	150	80·2	48	40	83·4
16	144·0	180	144	80·0	46	36	78·3
17	168·2	197	142	72·1	50	38·5	77·0
18	159·3	191	137	71·7	51	43	84·4
19	144·0	181	145	80·1	47	37	78·8
20	153·2	198	148	74·7	43	39	90·7
21	148·5	188	142	75·5	46	33	71·8
22	149·2	192	137	71·3	45	41	91·2
23	151·0	185	133	71·9	37	45	121·7
24	150·0	192	143	74·5	45	42	93·4
25	161·0	184	134	72·8	44	35	79·6
26	165·3	188	145	77·2	50	47	94·0
27	149·3	185	145	78·4	46	41	89·2
28	154·3	182	136	74·7	50	36	72·0
29	152·2	177	137	77·8	43	40	93·0
30	154·2	184	134	72·8	45	38	84·5
31	150·0	185	142	76·8	45	38	84·5
32	153·0	190	146	76·8	45	44	97·8
33	146·1	197	149	75·7	39	40	102·5
34	154·7	199	151	75·9	46	40	87·0
35	145·2	177	145	81·9	39	37	94·8
36	160·4	195	148	75·9	45	39	86·7
37	150·0	188	137	72·9	40	40	100·0
38	142·3	185	143	77·3	39	37	94·8
39	155·0	190	144	75·8	40	34	85·0
40	152·0	192	140	72·9	47	37	78·8
41	151·0	181	136	75·1	39	41	105·1
42	159·3	186	146	78·5	47	34	72·4
43	155·4	186	142	76·3	43	40	93·0

APPENDIX II

373

Women.	Height.	Cranial.			Nasal.		
		Length.	Breadth.	Index.	Length.	Breadth.	Index.
44	157·4	198	142	71·7	47	39	83·0
45	144·0	182	140	76·9	41	39	95·1
46	159·0	199	139	69·9	49	37	75·6
47	162·2	183	146	79·8	46	38	82·6
48	151·0	185	145	78·4	47	41	87·3
49	162·4	185	143	77·3	46	38	82·6
50	162·2	188	142	75·5	45	40	88·9
51	157·6	185	140	75·7	46	44	95·7
52	151·2	185	136	73·5	40	41	102·5
53	157·0	185	137	74·1	42	41	97·6
54	151·0	190	141	74·2	41	37	90·3
55	153·2	193	140	72·5	42	42	100·0
56	158·1	178	140	78·6	41	36	87·8

APPENDIX III

LIST OF TREES AND SHRUBS MENTIONED IN THE TEXT
(with their identification in some cases).

Plant.	Meaning of Name.	Identification.
bopa vhafu	to tie death	
bwere	soft watery porridge	
dzhesi-khondo	the rush that cries (from *dzhesi*, rush, and *u hondwa*, to cry)	
dundu	the name of the large *tshirundu* basket; the bulb, *thulwi*, used in the spearing game, is like this basket in appearance	
khatakhathane (or *pha-thane*)	from *u phata*, to build; it is used to hold the fence together	
luangalala	from *u angalala*, to rise up	*Cassytha filiformis*
luthanga	reed	*Phragmites communis*
mpesu	from *u pesula*, to flick, i.e. the tail of the bush buck	
mpeta	from *u peta*, to fold up or dissolve	*Royena pallens*
mphimbi	from *u phimbila*, to be sour	*Garcinia Livingstonei*
mubadali (or *u kona nguluvhe*)	from *u omba dali*, to stay the fever (or to beat the pig)	*Capparis corymbifera*
mudedede	from *u dededza*, to lead a child	*Heteropyxis natalensis*
mudzidzi	from *u dzidzi*, to beat the drum, or the throb of the head in a headache	*Artabotrys monteiroae*
mudziwa	from *u dziwa*, to be despised	
muembe		wild custard apple
mufula	from *u fula*, to pick fruit	
muhwidzi	from *u hwida*, to pluck—i.e. that which causes you to pluck	
mukundandou	from *u kunda*, to overcome, and *ndou*, elephant—i.e. so tough that the elephant cannot break it	
mukundulela	the way of force	*Niebuhria triphylla*
mulanga	from *u langa*, to discuss	*Dombeya rotundifolia*
munengeledzi	from *u nengeledza*, to make to disappear in a certain direction	*Salix Wilmsii* Seem
muramba	from *u ramba*, to call together	a type of wild orange
murombe (or *muri vha u omba*)	from *u omba*, to peg	
murombuli	from *u rumbula*, to make a hole right through, to impregnate	
musese	from *lisese*, buttocks	*Peltophorum africanum*
museto	from *u seta*, to rub off by friction	*Pretrea zanguebarica*

APPENDIX III

375

Plant.	Meaning of Name.	Identification.
musununu	from *sunununu*, a thin stream shooting out	Bamboo of a species found only in one wood near Tshaula
musudzunwane		
mutate	from *u tata*, to drive out	
mutanzwa	from *u tanzwa*, to clean	*Ximenia caffra*
mutata-vhana	from *u tate*, to be afraid, and *vhana*, children	*Dodonaea viscosa*
mutunu		
mutshetshete	from *u tsheta*, to quiet	*Zizyphus mucronata*,
muvhungu		a species of creeping rubber
muvhuyu	thick-set	*Adansonia digitata*, baobab
muvuvhu	from *mvuvhu*, hippopotamus	*Combretum erythrophyllum*
muzwilu	from *u zwila*, to take all power away, to hypnotize	
muzenzhe		*Cussonia spicata*
ndalumuwafhi	where am I bitten?	
ndilela	to long for me, from *u lela*, to cry	*Conyza* sp., possibly *C. ivaefolia*
phaladzane	generic term for grass	
tshidzimba vhalisa	*tshidzimba* is the cake of mealies and monkey-nuts taken for food on a journey *vhalisa*, shepherds	*Lantana salvifolia*
tshidzungudza	from *u dzungudza*, to shake to and fro (i. e. of the head)	
tshimammbe	smell	
tshiphandwa	from *u phandwa*, to crush (the second stamping of the mealies after the bran has been taken out)	*Gymnosporia senegalensis*
tshirungulo or *thungulu*	from *u rungulula*, to pierce again	*Loranthus daefolia*, a species of ilex
tshinyanyu	from *nyanyu*, dazed (onomatopoeic)	

ARCHAEOLOGICAL NOTE

SINCE writing the section on archaeology I have again visited Vendaland, where I obtained from reliable informants the following facts of archaeological interest, which may be of use to a future investigator.

1. In Kwakani district, in Mphephu's location, engravings on rock of human footprints and animals' spoor.

2. In petty chief Mumahoi's district, in Mphephu's location, knee-marks and handprints of a man smoking a pipe. The site of this impression is called Bianana (from *mbia*, pipe). The actual pipe has recently been removed by a medicine-man.

3. In Mabeani district, in Mphephu's location, on the Lutshele river, a deep engraving of a human foot, without toes.

4. In Tshalamulumgi district (under petty chief Murila), in Rambuda's location, engravings of human hands and feet, and animals' spoor. There are rock-paintings, presumably Bushman, near this site.

5. In Fondwe district (under petty chief Ratogwa), of Tshivhase's location, holes engraved in rock for playing *mefuvha*.

None of these sites have ever been investigated with the exception of No. 1, which was visited by Colonel Lyle, Sub-Native Commissioner at Louis Trichardt.

BIBLIOGRAPHY

BARTELS, M. (i) Die Koma- und Boscha-Gebräuche der Bawenda in Nord-Transvaal (quotes Beuster). Berlin, Verh. Ges. Anthrop., 1896. 35–6.

(ii) Zwei Zauber-Hölzer der Bavenda in Transvaal. Berlin, Verh. Ges. Anthrop., 1896, 109–10, 2 figs.

(iii) See under WESSMAN, R. (i).

(iv) See under BEUSTER, C. L. (iii).

BENT, J. T. The Ruined Cities of Mashonaland. London, 1896, 8vo, 377 pp. illustr., maps.

BEUSTER, C. L. (i) Das Volk der Vawenda. Berlin, Zeits. Ges. Erdk., 14, 1879, 236–40.

(ii) See under BARTELS, M. (i).

(iii) and BARTELS, M. Schienen-Verbände für Knochenbrüche bei den Bawenda. Berlin, Verh. Ges. Anthrop., 1896, 365–6, fig.

BLEEK, D. F. The Naron. A Bushman Tribe of the Central Kalahari. Cambridge, 1928, 4to, 67 pp.

BULLOCK, CHARLES. (i) Notes on the Ba-Venda. Salisbury, Native Affairs Department Annual, 4, 1926, 62–6.

(ii) The Mashona. Capetown, 1928.

(iii) Religion of the Mashona. South African Journal of Science, 1927. xxiv. 525–9.

CATON-THOMPSON, G. The Zimbabwe Culture: Ruins and Reactions. Oxford, 1931. 320 pp. 100 illustr.

DICKE, B. H. A Bavenda Sacred Object. Johannesburg, Rep. S.A. Assn. Adv. Sci., 23, 1926, 935–6, pl. xx.

DORNAN, S. S. Moon Lore amongst the Bantu. Native Affairs Department Annual. 1927, 29–35.

DUGGIN-CRONIN, A. M. The Bantu Tribes of South Africa. Cambridge and Kimberley, 1928. Reproductions of Photographic Studies. Vol. I, Section 1. Plates I–XX. The BaVenda, and LESTRADE, G. P. An Introductory Article on the BaVenda and Descriptive Notes on the Plates.

GENSICHEN, M. Bilder von unserem Missionsfelde in Süd- und Deutsch-Ost-Afrika, zugleich Fortsetzung der Kratzensteinischen Geschichte der Berliner Mission für die Jahre 1893 bis 1901. Berlin, 1902, 8vo, viii+518 pp., illustr., maps (Bavenda, 403–24).

GOTTSCHLING, E. The Bawenda: A Sketch of their History and Customs. London, J. Roy. Anthrop. Inst., 35, 1905, 365–86, pl. xxvii.

GRANT, WILLIAM. Magato and his Tribe. London, J. Roy. Anthrop. Inst., 35, 1905, 266–70.

GRÜNDLER, W. Geschichte der Bawenda-Mission in Nord-Transvaal. Berlin, 8vo, 102 pp., illustr., map.

378 BIBLIOGRAPHY

HADDON, A. C. Copper Rod Currency from the Transvaal. Man., 1908, No. 65.

HALL, R. N., & NEALE, W. G. The Ancient Ruins of Rhodesia. London, 1904, 8vo, map and illustr., xlviii, 404 pp.

HARRIES, C. L. The Sacred Baboons of Lomondo. Johannesburg, 1929.

HOFMEYR, S. Twintig jaren in Zoutpansberg. Kaapstad, 1890, 8vo, viii+ 322 pp.

JUNOD, HENRI A. (i) The Life of a South African Tribe. London, 1927, 2 vols., 8vo, 1219 pp. illustr.
(ii) Some Features of the Religion of the Ba-Venda. Johannesburg, Rep. S.A. Assn. Adv. Sci., 17, 1920, 207–20.
(iii) Le Totémisme ches les Thongas, les Pédis et les Vendas. Genève, Le Globe (Organe de la Soc. Géogr. de Genève), 63, 1924, Mém. 1–22.
(iv) Customs connected with Smallpox among the Baronga. Rep. S.A. Assn. Adv. Sci., 1919, pp. 694–702.

LESTRADE, G. P. (i) Some Notes on the Ethnic History of the Bavenda and their Rhodesian Affinities. Johannesburg, Rep. S.A. Assn. Adv. Sci., 24, 1927, 486–95.
(ii) Some Notes on the Political Organization of the Venda-Speaking Tribes. Africa, Vol. iii, No. 3, July 1930, pp. 306–22.
(iii) The *mala* System of the Venda-Speaking Tribes. Bantu Studies, 1930, Vol. iv, pp. 193–204.
(iv) See under Duggin-Cronin, A. M.

Native Custom and Marriage Laws, Report from the Select Committee on. (Pretoria), fo., xi+97 pp.

Native Tribes of the Transvaal, Short History of the. Pretoria, Transvaal Native Affairs Department, 1905, fo., 67 pp. (Bavenda, 62–4, 67).

POSSELT, F. Some Notes on the Religious Ideas of the Natives of Southern Rhodesia. South African Journal of Science, 1927. xxiv. 530–6.

ROBERTS, NOEL. A Few Notes on Tokolo, a System of Divination practised by the superior natives of Malaboch's Tribe in the Northern Transvaal. South African Journal of Science, 1914–15, xi. 368–70.

SCHOFIELD, J. P. The Ancient Workings of South-East Africa. Salisbury Native Affairs Department Annual, No. 3, 1925, 6–12.

SELIGMAN, C. G. and B. Z. The Bari. J. Roy. Anthrop. Inst., lxii. 1928, 400–79.

STOW, GEORGE W. The Native Races of South Africa. London, 1905, 8vo, xvi, map, illustr., 618 pp.

STUBBS, E. The History of the BaVenda. Grahamstown, 1912 [pamphlet, o.p.].

VOLSCHENK, A. J. C. Donker Zoutpansberg. Kaapstad, 1923, 8vo, 77 pp.

THEAL, GEORGE M'CALL. History and Ethnography of Africa south of the Zambezi, A.D. 1505–1795.

BIBLIOGRAPHY

WESSMANN, R. (i) and BARTELS, M. Reife-Unsitten bei den Bawenda in Nord-Transvaal. Berlin, Verh. Ges. Anthrop., 1896, 363–5.

(ii) The Bawenda of the Spelonken. London, 1908, 8vo, 154 pp., illustr., map.

WHEELWRIGHT, C. A. Native Circumcision Lodges in the Zoutpansberg District. London, J. Roy. Anthrop. Inst., 55, 1905, 251–5.

WILMOT, A. Monomotapa (Rhodesia). London, 1896, 8vo, xxiv, 259 pp., maps and illustr.

Language.

MEINHOF, CARL. Das Tsi-venda. Linguistische Studie. Leipzig. Zs. D. Morg. Ges. 55, 1901, 607–82.

SCHWELLNUS, TH. and P. (i) Die Verba des Tsivenda. Berlin, Mitt. Sem. Or. Spr., 7, Abt. 3, 1904, 12–31.

(ii) Wörterverzeichnis der Venda-Sprache. Hamburg, 1919. Beiheft Jahrb. Hamb. Wiss. Anst., 36 (1918), 51–78.

GLOSSARY OF SOME OF THE TSHIVENDA WORDS USED IN THE TEXT

All relationship terms are translated on pages 181–4.

deza (pl. *madeza*), BaLemba xylophone.
dzembe (pl. *malembe*), hoe.
—, sacred iron or copper ring.
dzumo, ritual meal.

halwa, beer.

kholomo, cow.
khomba, dangerous (used as alternative name for girls' initiation).
khoro, public court-yard.
khwali (pl. *dzikhwali*), leader of age-set in war.

lidabe (pl. *midabe*), young instructor in initiation ceremonies.
lidikana (pl. *madikana*), initiate in circumcision lodge (Sesutho word).
lidzinga (pl. *madzinga*), initiate in circumcision lodge.
u losha, to greet.
ludedi, belt.
ludo, stick carried by old women.
ludodo, secret ceremony at joint initiation.
luhome, sacred flower.
lukhata, waist-band.
lumwe, divining dice representing young woman.
luselo, basket-lid used for winnowing.
u luvha, to salute a chief.

mabako, pincers used in wire-drawing.
madambi, black magic.
madi, water.
magoka, iron sheet with holes, used in wire-drawing.
magota, chief's council.
mafhefhe, a circumcised man.
mafhoro, entrance gate.
mahundwani, children's game of 'villages'.
maine, medico-magician.
maine vha mushongo, 'finder' by medicine.
— *mvula*, 'finder' by rain.
— *tshele*, 'finder' by the rattle.
— *vhambeu*, 'finder' by seeds.
makhadi, intermediary in marriage ceremonies.
mala, main part of lobola.

malembe (sing. *dzembe*), hoes.
—, sacred iron or copper rings.
malugwani, instructor in tribal dances.
maphuga, chief's bodyguard.
maphungo, waist-band of ostrich egg-shell.
marimba, small drum.
masila, cloth woven by BaVenda.
mathanngwa, a tribal dance.
mbila, xylophone.
mboho, bull.
mbudzi, goat.
mefuvha, stone game.
mesina, copper.
mme a domba, mother of the *domba* (master of the ceremonies).
molombo, possession cult and dance.
mudavhu, lover.
mudinda (pl. *vhadinda*), messenger.
mudzimu (pl. *medzimu*), spirit.
mudzivho, ceremony to obtain rain.
mufari mbudzi, carrier of the goat (officer in circumcision lodge).
mufari ndau, carrier of the lion (officer in circumcision lodge).
mufharo, type of basket.
mufhoho, eleusine.
mukhoma, headman; chief's right-hand man.
mukhombo, umbilicus.
mule (pl. *vhale*), initiate in *musevetho*.
muloi (pl. *vhaloi*), witch or wizard.
muluvhe, girl assistant in *musevetho*.
mungoma (pl. *mingoma*), diviner:
munna (pl. *vhanna*), man.
murole, age-set.
murundu, circumcision school.
musadzi (pl. *vhasadzi*), woman; wife.
musadzi muhulwane, great wife.
musanda (pl. *vhamusanda*), chief.
musevetho, girls' 'circumcision' school.
musuku, copper.
—, special copper ingot.
musumu, chief's portion (of anything).
muta, small yard outside huts.
mutavha, set of players in tribal dances.
muthannga (pl. *vhathannga*), young man.
mutei (pl. *vhatei*), initiate.
mutobvu, lead.

GLOSSARY

381

mutupo, sib.

muvhire (pl. *vhavhire*), boy assistant in *musevetho*.

muvundu (pl. *mivundu*), district of country.

mvubelo, beer-pot.

ndalama, shell or ivory ornament.

ndau or *dau*, lion.

ndilo, platter; bowl.

ndou, elephant.

ndzadzi, part of lobola.

negota, important official; petty chief.

nemungoza, master of ceremonies at *domba*.

nganga (pl. *dzinganga*), medicine-man.

ngoma, drum.

—, head-band.

—, scene in *domba*.

nhundi, studs on copper ingot.

nko, big beer-pot.

nngwe, leopard.

nonyana, spirit of the *musevetho*.

nyalumati, special chief's messenger.

nyamita, official in charge of women in chief's village.

nyamutei, mistress of the initiates in *domba*.

pamba, medicine for protection against *muloi*.

u pembela, to dance.

phala-fhala, horn of sable antelope usually blown on ceremonial occasions.

u phasa madi, to spit out water (name given to usual act of propitiation).

pfene, baboon.

ratshihotola (pl. *vhoratshihotola*), old man in circumcision school.

sali, charcoal (name given to a symbolic object used in *domba*).

shedu, small apron worn by all girls.

singo, elephant's trunk.

u tevula, to pour out (at harvest festival).

thahu, ritual object worn after *vhusha*.

thakhata, possessions inherited from father.

—, aching bones.

thondo, boys' initiation school.

tshiala, tuft of hair for attachment of war-badge.

tshidhadyani (pl. *zwidhadyani*), spirit monstrosity.

tshidongo, flat pot.

tshife, priest or priestess.

tshikodo, praise-name.

tshilombo, spirit of the *molombo*.

tshilume, divining dice representing young man.

tshipata, instrument of torture in initiation schools.

tshirengwarengwane, sacred piece of ground for agricultural ritual.

tshirivha, skin garment worn by all married women.

tshirovha, sacred war-axe.

tshirundu, type of basket.

tshisevho, savoury eaten with porridge.

tshisi (pl. *zwisi*), division of country.

tshitungula (pl. *zwitungula*), sacred object.

tshivhambo, public meeting hut.

tsindi, skin garment worn by all men.

tuda, important Venda constellation.

tungu, calabash shaped like cottage-loaf.

turi, species of stoat.

twalima, divining dice representing old woman.

vhazhe, officer in circumcision school.

vhumala, main part of lobola.

vhami, divining dice representing old man.

vhusha, girl's initiation.

vhutamba vhutuka, washing away of boyhood (boy's initiation).

INDEX

Abortion, 38, 90, 120; of cows, 39.
Adultery, 152; abortion after, 90; punishment for, 221–2; of chief, 204.
Age-sets (*murole*), 71, 193–4.
Agriculture, 34–7.
  lands and gardens, 34, 35, 166.
  crops, 34, 35–6; list of, 36; fertility of, 313–15; maize (mealies), 35, 36, 37, 49; eleusine (*mufhoho*), 35, 36, 49, 253, 254; sugar-cane (*impye*), 36, 254.
  agricultural work, distribution, 32, 35; tilling, 35, 89, 313; ploughing, 35, 40, 153, 227, 228; sowing, 252–3, 313; reaping, 36, 48, 253–8; threshing, 36; winnowing, 46, 57.
  granaries, 30, 31, 36–7.
Ancestor-spirits, *see* Religion.
Archaeology, 5–8, 376.
Arrows, 69–70, 78; in folk-lore, 345, 358, 361.
Ashes, in initiation (*domba*), 108; in medical treatment, 28, 40.
Astronomy, 226–7; sun, 226; moon, 90, 226, 228, 316; stars, 226, 227; shooting stars, 226–7, 230; *tuda* constellation, 227, 228, 229, 309.
Avoidances, 151–2, 172.
Axe, description of, 61–2; battle-axe, 70; theft of, 222; sacred, 72, 248, 249; on bowl, 293, 298.

Baboons, as ancestor-spirits, 190–1, 240, 257; dreams about, 362; skull in treatment of new-born baby, 87; bones used for divination, 266; on bowl, 296; in folklore, 355–6.
Ba-Ila, 26, 253; divining dice, 290.
BaKaranga *or* Mashona, position, 1; connexion with Dzata, 6; language, 9, 26, 302, 304, 307; connexion with Venda history, 12, 14, 15, 71; twins, 93; absence of circumcision, 126; hunting-net, 79; beads, 27; giving name to wind, 226; Mwari their supreme deity, 230; bull-cult, 243; stonecult, 245, 256; possession, 302–3; divining dice, 266, 284, 285, 290; divining bowl, 299–300.
BaLemba, position among BaVenda, 18; traders of beads, 27; potters,

52; iron-workers, 59–61; copper workers, 58, 62–8; musical instrument of, 320; tribute to chief in lieu of service, 217; introduced fowl, 44; tabus on meat, 41; in circumcision lodge, 126, 136.
Bamboo for flutes, 317.
BaNgona, history, 10–12; spirits, 238; harvest rites, 258–9; symbol on bowl, 294.
BaPedi, raids against BaVenda, 18; in circumcision lodge, 126, 136; divining dice, 286, 290.
Bari, unusual terminology, 178.
BaRozwi *or* BaLozwi, connexion with Venda history, 15.
Basketry, 56–8.
BaSutho, position, 1; baskets, 57; in circumcision lodge, 126, 136; songs, 136–8; Venda chiefs of Sutho origin, 17; Venda sibs of Sutho origin, 188, 189; influence on dialect, 192; giving name to wind, 226; connexion with Majaji, 312; musical instruments, 317, 318, 319; in folk-lore, 347.
Bat, in initiation ceremonies, *vhusha*, 108, *domba*, 114; tabu to eat, 47; in magic, 278.
BaThonga, position, 1; raids, 19; baskets, 57; stamper, 55; trade in hoes, 61, 75–6; in circumcision lodge, 126, 136; sibs of Thonga origin, 188, 189; influence on Venda language, 9, 192; meteorology, 225; counting, 229; medico-magician, 284; treatment of small-pox, 272; divination bones, 266; possession, 303; folklore, 330.
Beads, description, 26; connexion with Zimbabwe, 26; possible origin, 27.
Beer, kinds and preparation of, 35, 48–50; beer-drink, 253, 258, 316, 324; in exchange for work, 35, 154; in payment of *nganga*, 32, 268; of chief, 203, 204, 209, 210; as offering to ancestor-spirits, 254, 255, 256, 257; songs about, 327, 328; beer hut, 30, 31; beer pots, 52; beer strainer, 58; in folk-lore, 336, 337, 352, 353, 357, 361, 362.
Bellows, 60.

384 INDEX

Birth, normal, 85–90; abnormal, 90–3; of chief, 208; of chief in folk-lore, 345–6.

Bow (weapon), 69, 78, 80; in folk-lore, 345, 358.

Bow (musical), 319.

Bowl, see Medicine and Magic (divination).

Bracelets, see Ornaments.

Brass, 58, 65.

Buis, 1–2, 205.

Bull, see Cattle, Religion (ancestor spirits).

Burial,
 ceremonies, 162–3; purification after, 164–5; of pregnant women, suicides, lepers, strangers, 163; of consumptives, 163, 310; of children born abnormally, 91, 310; of sheep's head, 163.
 of chief, 206, 236; of Phaphuli chiefs, 210–12; of Tshivhase chiefs, 207; of Lwamondo chiefs, 212; of Vhatavhatsinde chiefs, 212; of Netshitongani petty chiefs, 212–13.

Bushmen or Barwa, 226; paintings, 8, 376; divining dice, 290, 291.

Calabash or gourds, 36, 53; rite, 147, 148.

Cattle, 37–44.
 history of, 37–8; types, 38, 39; care of, 39, 40, 95; East Coast fever, 37, 42, 44, 79, 232; other diseases, 40; dipping, 42–4; theft of,222; killing of, 40–1; as tribute, 41, 210, 248; as gift to visitors, 39; as fine, 87, 152, 221, 222, 223, 279; as payment, 281, 285; as ritual meal, 164, 207; as offering to deity, 232, 233, 310; twin-calves, 39, 92–3, 218; omens about, 362–3; on bowl, 294, 295, 296, 297; in folk-lore, 345, 350, 360.
 lobola, see Marriage.
 sacred cattle, 242–5; propitiation of, 254, 255.
 milk, 47, 275; milking, 39, 95.
 cattle kraal, 30; miniature, 87.
 skin, dressing of, 59; used for clothing, 24; to wrap corpse, 161, 162, 206, 210.
 cow-dung for softening skin, 23; for smearing and plastering, 30, 37; as medicine, 40.
 keeper of chief's cattle, 199–200.

Chameleon, in hunting, 80; march in murundu, 135; as messenger of death, 362.

Charcoal, in personal decoration, 27; in decoration of huts and yards, 31, 34.

Charms, against witchcraft, 249, 277, 278–9; in marriage, 147; in travelling, 74, 262; in war, 72.

Chief, 195–213.
 position and daily life, 201–5; localities tabu to, 205; etiquette towards, 158; death and burial, 205–8, 236; installation, 208–10; variant forms of burial and installation, 210–13; connexion with deity, 230, 231, 232, 233; in ancestor cult, 243, 253–6; in thondo, 103, 104; village, 29; revenue, 217, 218; drums, 205, 316, 317; planning death of, 224; in folk-lore, 345–7.
 nature of chieftainship, 195–8.
 chief's relations, 196–8; sister (ma-khadzi), 196–7, 198, 206, 207, 208, 209, 255, 322; brother (khotsimunene), 195, 196, 197, 198, 206, 207, 208, 209, 211, 216, 219; khadzi, 195, 196, 198, 206, 209, 210, 211; ndumi, 195, 196, 198, 204, 206, 209, 210, 211, 250; other relations, 198, 216.
 chief's wives, 24, 26, 110, 201, 208, 209.
 chief's officials, 198–201.
 mukhoma, duties of, 199, 201, 204, 219; in government, 214, 215, 216, 217; in installation of chief, 209; in initiation (vhutamba vhutuka), 105.
 negota, duties of 199; in government, 214, 216; in initiation (thondo), 104.
 nyalumati, 201, 280, 282.
 other officials, 198–201.

Chiefs, BaVenda (1929).
 Khaku, history, 16.
 Khuthama, history, 16.
 Lwamondo, history, 17; animal ancestors, 190–1, 257; village, 30, 190.
 Mbulahene Mphephu or Mphephu, history, 16; marriage, 208; places tabu to, 205; in initiation ceremonies (murundu), 125, 137, 193; connexion with ancestor spirits, 243; with deity, 232, 233; with Dzata, 6, 311; horses of, 45; musuku of, 66; wooden models of, 55–6; village of, 29–30; location, 10, 236, 292, 294.
 Phaphuli, history, 16, 17; in connexion with dipping, 43.

INDEX

Chiefs—*cont.*

Rambuda, history, 16; sacred bull of, 243; village of, 30.

Senthumule, history, 16, 17; village of, 29.

Thengwe or Nethengwe, history, 10; as member of Tshivhase's council, 216; village of, 30.

Tshivhase, history, 16, 17; description of, 203; in initiation ceremonies (*murundu*), 127, 134, 137; wives of, 201; son of, 314; council of, 216; sacred bull of, 243.

Chiefs, past BaVenda.

Makhado, history, 16, 19, 71, 208; influence on circumcision rites, 125; connexion with age-sets, 193, 194; with place tabus, 205; burial, 236; drum of, 316.

Mphephu (old), history, 16, 19; marriage, 208; burial, 236; places tabu to, 205; in initiation ceremonies (*murundu*), 126, 127; connexion with ancestors' spirits, 243; with deity, 232, 233; with Vhapfumbe sib, 190; horses of, 45.

Tshiendeulu or Netshiendeulu (old), history, 10, 12, 13.

Ramapulana or Ramabulana, history, 16, 19; connexion with copper workings, 63, 64; connexion with age-sets, 193; burial, 236; name of Mphephu's bull, 243.

Thoho-ya-Ndou, history, 12, 13, 15, 16, 214, 231; connexion with Dzata, 6, 7; with crocodile, 81; drum, 316.

Tshivhase (old), description, 202–3; burial, 212; daughter of, 215; sacred cattle, 243.

Chiefs, petty, part in government, 201, 214, 215, 216, 217.

Madzivhandila, 17.

Manenzhe, 10, 317.

Netshiavho, history, 10; connexion with Lake Fundudzi, 237–8; with Nyakhalavha, 215.

Netshitongani, 212–13.

Netshitumbe, history, 11; in harvest rites, 258–9; beads of, 26.

Paswane, history, 17.

Ratomba, 205.

Takalani, 93, 216, 219.

Chiefs, women petty, Nyakhalavha or Khalavha, 215; Nyadenga or Denga, 215.

Child life, 95–100, 159.

Circumcision, *see* Initiations.

Clay, 34, 50, 53, 130; models in initiation (*domba*), 120; models made by children, 96, 97.

Climate, 5.

Clothing, 22–5.

Colour, in decoration, 34, 56; significance of red, white, black, and yellow in initiation, 117, 118, 120, 122; white clay in *murundu*, 130, 135; ceremonial use of red ochre, 109, 112, 123, 135, 141, 148; red sap to protect tobacco, 314; theory about red and white, 261; black oxen and goats, 162, 232, 233, 243, 245; coloured cloth in *molombo* 304–5; yellow coloured copper, 65; in folk-lore, 348.

Copper, 62–8.

ancient working (J. M. Calderwood's notes), 6, 62–4; mines, 8; smelting, 64, 65; wire-drawing, 65, 66; wire-work, 25, 58; bracelets, 25; *musuku*, 66–8; sacred rings, 247; 248, 249; as symbol in marriage, 261.

Councils, 215–17.

Counting, 229.

Crime, *see* Law and Justice.

Crocodile, veneration and fear of, 81–2; miscellaneous beliefs about, 241, 278; connexion with *muloi*, 274, 275, 276, 307; tabu to eat, 47; chief's stuffed, 204; pebbles from stomach of, 211; in treatment of diseases, 270; on bowls, 293, 295, 297, 298, 299; in folk-lore, 354.

Crops, *see* Agriculture.

Dances, 316, 320–5.

tshikona, 320–3; in initiation schools, 102, 114; in honour of chief, 205; at installation and death of chief, 207, 209, 210; in harvest rites, 254, 256; in rain ceremonies, 231, 310, 311; in folk-lore, 337.

mathanngwa, 105, 320–1, 323.

in initiation ceremonies: *thondo*, 104; *vhutamba vhutuka*, 105; *vhusha*, 107, 108, 109; *domba* (python dance), 112, 115–16, 122, 309, 328; *murundu*, 133, 134; *musevetho*, 139, 140.

at Chief Phaphuli's accession (*u pembela*), 211; in possession (*molombo*), 302–8, 329.

Death, 161; origin of, 362; of infants, 84, 91; of chief, 205–8; divination after, 280–3, 291–2.

Defloration, 108, 111, 113, 123.

C C

386 INDEX

Diseases, *see* Medicine and Magic.
Divining Bowls and Dice, *see* Medicine and Magic (divination).
Divorce, 152.
Dogs, for hunting, 45, 77, 78; tabu to eat, 47; in *mahundwani*, 99; girls in *domba* disguised as, 119; dangerous to travellers, 74; protected from crocodile, 278; in history of Thoho-ya-Ndou, 12; on bowl, 297; in folk-lore, 346, 348, 360.
Domestic animals, 44–5. *See also* Cattle, Goats, Dogs.
Dreams, 241, 362.
Drought, 230, 233, 309, 310; in folk-lore, 336.
Drums, 53–4, 316–17; description of *ngoma*, 53, 54; description of *marimba*, 54; methods of playing, 316; in *tshikona* and *mathanngwa* dances, 320, 322; in initiation ceremonies (*vhusha*), 107, 108, 109 (*domba*), 114, 115, 116; in *molombo*, 303; special beat for war, 71, 316; of chief, 316, 317; beaten by chief, 205; of Thoho-ya-Ndou, 13, 316.
Dzata, history, 6, 12, 14; description of, 6–7; dead chief's head pointed towards, 206; rain-making ceremony at, 311.

East coast fever, 37, 42, 44, 79, 232.
Earth, Venda ideas of, 225–6.
Elephant (*ndou*), hunting, 76–7; tabus, 77; connexions with chiefs, 159, 188, 204, 206; tooth as charm, 88, 204, 206; name for sib, 187; symbol in initiations (*domba*), 114, 122, 123, (*murundu*) 128, 129, 131, 132; on bowl, 294, 297, 298; in folk-lore, 352–3, 356, 357–8, 359.
Eleusine (*mufhoho*), 35, 36, 49, 253, 254.
Etiquette, 157–60.
in modes of address, 159–60; in connexion with chief, 202, 204; with chief's relations and officials, 197–201; in drinking beer, 48, 49.
European contacts, trading, 22, 25, 76, 77; cloth, 23, 24; chief's houses, 31; fire-arms, 74, 78; effect on social system, 194.
Exogamy, 175, 185, 186.

Family, *see* Kinship (family life).
Fat, in hair dressing, 27; preparations and uses, 48, 101; use after initiations, 109, 141; use before marriage, 147; in folk-lore, 360.
Father, *see* Kinship.
Father's sister, *see* Kinship.
Father's brother, *see* Kinship (*khotsimunene*).
Father's father, *see* Kinship (*makhulu*).
Fertility, means of obtaining, 83, 84, 314–15; in connexion with initiation ceremonies (*domba*), 123, 124, 309; of animals, 309, 310; of crops, 310, 313–15.
Fines, 218, 221–4.
Fire.
domestic, 33, 154, 159; in initiation ceremonies (*thondo*), 102, (*vhutamba*) 106, (*vhusha*) 107, 108, (*domba*), 114, 123, (*murundu*) 128, 129, 131, 134, 135; of chief, 207, 311; for purification, 164; caused by lightning, 225; cremation, 212; in rain-making, 311, 312; in dreams, 362; in folk-lore, 354, 355, 359, 361.
fire-stick, 102, 114, 207; fire-arms, 74, 78.
Fish, 47, 237; fishing, 80, 81.
Flutes, 316, 317, 321–3.
Folk-lore, 330–61; Sankhambi, 330, 351–9; riddles, 359–60; proverbs, 360–1.
Food, 46–8; division of meat, 41; preparation of grain, 46; meals, 154–5; ritual meals, 164–5, 207, 221.
Fundudzi, Lake, position of, 3; connexion with Vhatavhatsinde sib and Netshiavho, 10, 212, 237, 257; as secret name in *domba*, 114, 123; tabu to Makhwinde chiefs, 205; in folk-lore, 336, 337.

Games, boys', 95–6; girls', 97; children's mixed, 97–9; *mahundwani*, 99–100, 124; *mefuvha*, 154, 310, 355, 364–6; *ndode*, 367.
Goats (*mbudzi*), 44.
care of, 95; as medium of barter, 76; theft of, 104, 222; as fines, 221, 222, 223; as payment, 32, 110, 123, 200, 268, 281; in treatment of disease, 270; in marriage, 144, 146–7, 150; as present to wife's relations, 148, 150, 151, 324; in purification rites, 164, 165.
ancestor spirits, 245–6; in rite of goat with clothes, 251–2; in killing ancestor spirit, 252.

INDEX

387

Goats—*cont.*
as model in *domba*, 121–2.
as totem of Makhwinde sib, 186;
method of killing, 187.
skins for clothing, 22, 23, 24, 71;
for bellows, 60.
milk, 47.
kraal, 30, 31.
Government, 215–18.
chieftainship in, 195–8, 214; officials, 198–201, 214; district
council, 215; private council,
215–16; great council, 216–17;
revenue and taxation, 217–18.
Granaries, 30, 31, 36–7.

Hail, 225, 227.
Hair, kinds of, 20; methods of dressing, 27, 71; after illness, 268–
9; in mourning, 165, 207–8, 282;
in punishment of *muloi*, 284; in
propitiating spirits, 238.
Harvest, 253–9; time decided by
stars, 227.
Head and height measurements, 20;
table of, 368–73.
Heirs, 166, 167–71; to female 'fathers', 170–1; birth of chief's,
208, 209.
History of BaVenda, 9–19.
Hoes, manufacture, 60–1; as lobola,
38; as taxation, 217; sacred,
247, 248; in *murundu* song, 132;
rite of hoe handle, 242.
Hunting, 76–80; by big boys, 96;
net, 79; traps, 77, 78.
Huts, 30, 31–4; *thondo*, 101, 102;
tshivhambo, 107, 108, 112, 113,
114, 115, 116.
Husband, *see* Kinship.
Hyena, tabu to eat, 47; agent of
muloi, 274; on bowl, 293; in folk-
lore, 348, 350, 352; tail of, 72,
310.

Incest, 224.
Industries, 52–68.
Initiations, 102–41.
boys' school (*thondo*), 101–5; building, 101, 102; opening, 102;
where held, 103; description,
103–5; members as Chief's body-
guard, 72; summary, 124–5.
boys' initiation (*vhutamba vhutuka*),
105–6; description, 105–6; summary, 124–5.
girls' initiation (*vhusha*), 106–10;
description, 106–9; *thahu* worn
after, 25, 109–10; summary,
124–5.

joint initiation (*domba*), 111–24;
where held, 111; members, 112;
managers, 112; opening, 112–14;
law, 114–15; python dance, 112,
115–16, 122, 309, 328; symbolic
representations, 116–22; concluding ceremonies, 122–3; wooden
models used at, 55, 120, 121;
summary, 123–4, 124–5.
boys' circumcision (*murundu*), 125–
38; history, 101, 125–7; building
of school, 127–8; managers, 128;
members, 128, 129; ritual fire,
128, 129, 131, 132; operation,
129–30; life, 130–4; concluding
ceremonies, 134–5; formulae,
132–3; songs, 136–8; age-sets,
135, 193–4; summary, 135–6.
girls' 'circumcision' (*musevetho*),
description,138–41;formulae,140.
Inheritance, 166–71; of cattle, 167.
Iron, 59–62; smelting, 59, 60, 61;
manufactures, 61–2; sacred rings,
247–8; bracelets, 25, 58.
Ivory, 19, 25, 59, 76, 77.

Justice, *see* Law and Justice.

Khadzi, see Chief's relations.
Khalavha, woman petty chief, 215.
Khaku, 16.
Khotsimunene, see Kinship.
Khuswane, 236.
Khuthama, 16.
Kinship, system and general behaviour patterns, 172–81; terminology, 181–4; lineages, 185;
in sibs, 185–6.
family life, 153–7.
home, 30–1; polygyny, 142–3;
children, 84, 93–4, 95–100; in
marriage, 149–50; man's work,
35, 153; woman's work, 35,
153–4; position of father, 155;
uterine brothers and sisters,
155–6; importance of age, 156;
etiquette, 157–60; meals, 154–
5; division of meat, 41; sleeping accommodation, 155. *See also*
Marriage.
mother (*mme*), 173, 181.
carrying baby, 24–5; in children's
domestic training, 100, 154; in
domba, 114, 123; in *murundu*,
131–2, 135; in *musevetho*, 139;
reserve of children towards, 106–
7; in marriage of youngest son,
167; lineage, 185; ancestor-
spirits, 245–6, 247–8, 259–61.
See also Birth, Marriage.

388 INDEX

Kinship—*cont.*
father (*khotsi*), 172, 181.
at birth of child, 86, 87–8; reserve of children towards, 106–7; position in family, 155. *See also* Property, succession and inheritance.
wife, great (*musadzi muhulwane*), 149, 167, 173, 175.
garment of, 23–4; bracelets, 25; home, 30, 31, 154–5; work, 35, 153–4; property, 166–7; in inheritance, 167–9; of other women, 143–4, 170–1; model in *domba*, 120–1. *See also* Birth, Marriage.
husband, makes *tshirivha* and bracelets for wife, 24, 25; at wife's pregnancy, 84; at birth of child, 86, 87–8; at wife's abortion; 90; after wife's twins, 92, model in *domba*, 120–1. *See also* Marriage.
khotsimunene, in kinship system, 172, 173, 180, 182; in naming child, 88; of chief, 195, 196, 197, 198, 208, 209, 211, 216, 219.
father's sister (*makhadzi*) in kinship system, 174, 182; arranges succession, 167, 168, 170, 171; gives name to child, 88; in ancestor worship, 242, 249–50, 253, 255, 258; as name for moon, 90, 226. of chief, 196–7, 198, 206, 207, 208, 209, 255, 322.
makhulu, in kinship system, 172, 176, 177, 181; as mother-in-law, 151, 324, 325; as term of address, 157, 158; name of pole in *murundu*, 134; name of spirit in *musevetho*, 140; name for deity, 230, 232; name for ancestor spirit, 243, 244, 245, 254.
malume, in kinship system, 174, 175, 177, 178, 182; in marriage, 143; in ancestor worship, 246, 251.
muduhulu, in kinship system, 177, 178, 179, 184; in ancestor worship, 246, 255.

Language, 9; dialects, 192; Tshikaranga, 9, 26, 302, 304, 307; Sesutho, 132–3, 136–8; symbolic, 114–15, 202.
Law and justice, concepts of, 218–19; officials, 197, 198, 199, 219; trials, 219–21; crimes and punishments, 221–4.
Lead, 65; as symbol in marriage, 261.

Leopards, hunting of, 77; tabu to eat, 47; as ancestor spirits, 239, 240; as name of age-set, 193; wooden models, 55–6, 121; skin as tribute to chief, 15, 77; as emblem in war, 71.
Lightning, 225, 230, 277; lightning-bird, 225, 269, 277; on bowl, 296.
Lineage, patrilineal, 185; matrilineal, 185; sister of head of, 167–8, 249–50. *See also* Kinship.
Lions (*ndau*), hunting, 77; tabu to eat, 47; as honorific title, 157, 158, 203, 220; in initiation ceremonies (*thondo*), 103; as name for fire-brand in *murundu*, 131; as ancestor spirits, 212–13, 239; in dreams, 362; on bowl, 297; in folk-lore, 355–6.
Lobola, *see* Marriage.
Lwamondo, *see* Chiefs, BaVenda, 1929.

Magic, *see* Medicine and Magic.
Maize and mealies, *see* Agriculture, Food.
Majaji, 232, 311, 312–13.
Makhado, *see* Chiefs, Past BaVenda.
Makhadzi, see Kinship (father's sister).
Makhulu, see Kinship.
Makhwinde, *see* Sibs.
Malume, see Kinship.
Manenzhe, petty chief, 10, 13.
Marriage, 142–52.
arrangements, 144–7; ceremonies, 147–8; position of bride in her new home, 148–50.
lobola, 38, 39, 143–4, 146, 176, 177; hoes substituted for cattle, 37; copper as, 67; compounded by money, 43.
cross-cousin marriage, 175–9; elopement, 150–1; pre-marital unions, 110, 111; other irregularities, 152; death before marriage, 242, 259.
Mashona, *see* BaKaranga.
Matabele, 18, 290.
Mbulahene Mphephu, *see* Chiefs, BaVenda, 1929.
Measurements, 20, 368–73.
Medicine and magic, 262–308.
medico-magicians, list of specialists, 263–4; how to become, 264–5; effect on society, 300–2; equipment, 265–7.
medicine-man or *nganga*, description, 263; kinds of, 263–4; of chief, 206, 211, 310; Mushapa's equipment, 266–7; associated with *mungoma*, 280, 282, 283,

INDEX

389

Medicine and magic—*cont.*
284, 301; with *muloi*, 274, 275, 276, 277, 278, 279; with possession, 302, 303; in treatment of disease, 267–73; in ancestor worship, 249; in building, 31–2, 101–2; in fire-lighting ritual, 114, 207, 311; in fertility rites, 314; in rain-making, 312; in mortuary rites, 162, 163, 164, 165; in folklore, 330–5, 361.

diviner or *mungoma*, description, 263, 264, 266; in connexion with *muloi*, 279–84, 291–2; with possession (*maine vha tshele*), 303–7; in ancestor worship, 246, 247, 248; in rain-making, 311, 312; in law-suits, 220.

divination, 279–302.

divining dice and bones, 284–91; description and interpretation, 265–6, 267, 284–90; learning use, 264–5; in ancestor worship, 249; in treatment of disease, 268; to discover a *muloi*, 279–82; in law-suits, 220; connexion with bowls, 291, 293, 294, 295, 296, 297, 299; among other Bantu, 290–1.

divining bowls, 291–300; Tshiobi's bowl interpreted, 293–6; Mukharu's bowl interpreted, 296–9; connexions with Zimbabwe, 291, 299–300.

witchcraft, 223, 273–9.

muloi, 264, 267, 273–84, 301; as ancestor spirit, 252; in possession, 305, 307; preventing rain, 310; discovered by divining bowl, 291–2; on bowl, 293, 294, 295, 297.

medicines and magical preparations.

in disease, 267–73; in connexion with child-birth, 83, 84, 85, 86, 87; for purification of widows, 164, 165; against the *muloi*, 274, 276, 277, 278, 279; in war, 72; for producing rain, 310; love-potions, 110–11; on bowl, 294, 295, 297; in folk-lore, 342.

diseases, 267–73.

abdominal trouble, 270; bleeding from nose and mouth, 269; blood diseases, 260, 261; bone diseases, 260, 261, 270–1; consumption, 271; convulsions, 272; ear trouble, 271; fractures, 273; headache, 271; leprosy, 272; madness, 272; malaria, 5, 269; pneumonia, 269–70; rheu-

matism, 269; septic wounds, 273; snake-bite, 272; sprains and stiffness, 272–3; toothache, 273.

diseases of cattle, *see* Cattle.

Menstruation, 38, 106, 118, 260, 261, 314.

Metallurgy, 59–68.

Meteorology, 225–6.

Milaboni, 7, 30.

Monoliths, 7–8, 30.

Monomatapa, 15, 27.

Months, 228.

Moon, 90, 226, 228, 316; in folk-lore, 345–8; 359.

Mother, *see* Kinship.

Molombo, 302–8.

Mother-in-law, *see* Kinship (*makhulu*).

Mother's brother, *see* Kinship (*malume*).

Mourning, 165; for chief, 207–8.

Mphaphuli, *see* Chiefs, BaVenda, 1929.

Mphephu, *see* Chiefs, Bavenda.

Muduhulu, 177, 178, 179, 184; in ancestor worship, 246.

Mukharu, bowl of, *see* Medicine and Magic (divining bowls).

Muloi, *see* Medicine and Magic (witchcraft).

Murder, punishment for, 223; to aid fertility, 314–15; to hasten death, 161; of babies, 91, 93.

Mushapa, 266, 267, 286.

Music, 316–38

Musical instruments, 316–20.

bows, 319; flutes, 316, 317, 321, 322, 323; horns: *phala-fhala*, 104, 200, 210, 227, 231, 255, 259, 312, 317, 323, *khwata*, 317; *lugube*, 318; pipes, 316; rattles, 307, 319–20; *tshijolo* and bow, 318–19; xylophone: *mbila*, 316, 320; in folklore, 338–9, 344, 345; *deza*, 53, 320. *See also* Drums.

Mwari, *see* Religion (Deity).

Naming ceremony, 88–9.

Ndumi, *see* Chief's relations.

Negota or *Gota*, see Chief's officials.

Netshiavho, *see* Chiefs, Petty.

Netshiendeulu, *see* Chiefs, past BaVenda.

Netshitongani, petty chief, 212–13.

Netshitumbe, *see* Chiefs, Petty.

Nganga, *see* Medicine and Magic (medicine-man).

Ngoma, as name for headband, 26; in initiation ceremonies (*domba*), 116–22. *See also* Drums.

Numbers, 229.

INDEX

390

Ochre, 30–31, 34, 109, 112, 123, 135, 141, 148, 261, 277.
Ordeal by poison, 282.
Ornaments, 25–7.
  beads, 25, 26–7.
  bracelets and anklets, 25, 58; in lieu of service, 217; in marriage, 145, 146, 147; ritual use, 87, 147, 162, 238, 268; as payment, 269, 311; core, 43, 79.
  headbands, 26.
  shells, *ndalama*, 25–6; ostrich egg shell, 25, 26; cowries, 26, 291.
  thahu, 25, 56, 109–10.
  waistband, 25.
Owl, agent of *mulôi*, 274, 278; tabu to eat, 47.

Phafuli, BaThonga diviner, 284.
Phaphuli, chief, BaVenda, 16, 17, 43, 210–12.
Phasa madi, 250, 251, 252, 253, 265, 305, 310.
Phiphidi Falls, 3, 238, 257.
Physical characteristics of BaVenda, 20–2.
Pipe, 50–1, 376.
Poison, 282; for arrows, 69.
Political organization, *see* Government.
Population, 1.
Possession or *Molombo*, 302–8.
Pottery, 52–3; in lieu of service, 217; ritual use, 162, 238.
Pregnancy, 84–5, 152.
Priest of Mwari, 234, 236; BaNgona priest, 11, 258, 259.
Priestess, 250; in harvest rite, 255.
Property, 166–7; in family, 155–6.
Puberty, *see* Initiations.
Punishments, 221–4.
Purification, after child-birth, 87–8; after birth of twins, 92; after abortion, 90; after disease, 268–9; in connexion with consumption, 271; after crime, 221; after burial, 164, 165.
Python, tabu to kill, 309, 310; in connexion with possession, 303; in treatment of disease, 161, 267, 270; to aid fertility, 83, 309, 310; as good omen, 363; in folk-lore, 330–6.
  python dance, 112, 115, 116, 122, 309, 328.

Rain, description, 225; rainfall, 5; rain-making, 231, 232, 233, 234; 309–13; in dreams, 362.
Raluvhimba, *see* Religion (Deity).

Ramapulana or Ramabulana, *see* Chiefs, past BaVenda.
Rambuda, 16, 30, 243.
Ranwasha, sacred stones of, 244, 245.
Ratomba, 205.
Religion, 230–61.
  Deity, 230–6.
    Raluvhimba, identified with Mwari, 230; conceptions of, 225, 226, 230, 231, 232, 236, 240, 310; propitiation of, 43, 232–3; appearance at Luvhimbi, 231; in folk-lore, 360.
    Mwari, identified with Raluvhimba, 230; cult of, among Ba-Karanga, 233–6; propitiation of, 310; in fertility rites, 313; visited by chief's messenger, 201.
  ancestor-spirits, 240–61.
    types of, 245–6; rites connected with, 241–59; review of ancestor cult, 259–61.
    embodied in: sacred cattle, 242–3, 244, 245, 246, 249, 255, 260; sacred goat, 245–6, 249, 260; other sacred animals, 212–13, 257; sacred stones, 243–5, 255, 256; other sacred objects, 88, 246–9, 252, 253.
Revenue, 217–18.
Ritual:
  agricultural, hoeing, 89, 313; sowing, 252–3, 313; harvest, 253–8; rain-making, 309–13.
  in daily life, at marriage, 147–150; to ensure pregnancy, 83, 84; at child-birth, 85–8; in disease, 267–9; after death, 161–5; in connexion with sibs, 187–91; at chief's death, 206–8; in war, 72, 73–4; for travellers, 74–5; with divining dice, 264–5, 268, 281–2; with divining bowl, 291–2; meals, 164, 207, 221.
  miscellaneous rites, *u bwisa mwana*, 89; child shown to moon, 89–90; calabash in marriage ceremony, 147, 148; final marriage rite, 149; 'goat with clothes', 251–2, hoe-handle, 242; *mudzivho*, 311; *u phasa madi*, 250–1; sexual intercourse, 118, 122; to end family disputes, 156; *u pembela*, 210–12.

Salt, 40, 47–8, 189, 363.
Sandals, 23, 132.
Scarification, 28.
Schoemansdal, 19, 59, 64, 76.
Seasons, 228–9.

INDEX

391

Senthumule, *see* Chiefs, BaVenda 1929.

Shadow, 241; in folk-lore, 360.

Sibs, 185–92.
found in Vendaland to-day, 187–90; *tshikodo* of, 186, 187, 188, 189; identified by divination, 281, 282; on bowls, 293, 294, 295, 296, 297, 298.
Makhwinde sib, history, 6, 7, 9 11–17, 18; description, 187–8; tabus, 13, 187, 205, 237; in connexion with rain-making, 311; burial, 212; chief's drums, 316; on bowl, 297.
Vhatavhatsinde sib, (singular: *muta-vhatsinde*), history, 7, 9, 10, 11, 13, 14, 18, 231; description, 187; connexion with initiation ceremonies (*thondo*), 101; with Lake Fundudzi, 237; burial, 212; as praise-name, 188, 220.

Slaves, 74.

Smellers-out, 264, 279.

Snakes, tabu to eat, 47; as animal ancestors, 240, 257; belief about child-birth, 83, 116, 123; superstitions, 363; on bowl, 297; in folk-lore, 344–5, 350, 360; treatment of snake-bite, 272.

Snuff, 50; as offering, 233, 251; etiquette in taking, 159; songs about, 325–6; box or pot, 50, 53; superstition about, 363.

Songs, 323–4, 325–9; in initiation ceremonies, (*domba*), 328; (*murundu*), 136–8; singing as accompaniment to ordinary action, 324; *molombo*, 329.

Soul, 191, 239, 241.

Spears, 70, 222; sacred, 211, 246, 247, 256; on bowls, 296, 298.

Spirits, *see* Religion (ancestor spirits); Possession.

Stamping, 46, 55; stamping blocks, 31, 33, 46, 55; stampers, 46, 55, 225.

Stars, *see* Astronomy.

Sterility, of women, 83, 84; of cattle, 38.

Stoat (*turi*), in magic, 274, 275, 278; on bowl, 295, 299; skin in medicine, 267.

Stones, phallic, 7–8, 30; cooking, 33; sacred, 243–5, 255, 256; from crocodile's stomach, 211.

Stone ruins, 6–7.

String, 58.

Suicides, 163.

Swazis, 17, 71, 191.

Tabus.
in fertility rites, 309, 310; in pregnancy, 85; in child-birth, 86; connected with clothing, 23, 24; with sibs, 189, 190; with chief's movements, 205; about cattle, 38, 40, 41; about game, 80; about elephant's trunk, 77; about food, 47; of BaLemba, 41; miscellaneous, 362–3.

Taxation, 217–18; for dipping, 42; for initiation, 105, 110, 139.

Teeth, first, 93–4; in disease, 273; in folk-lore, 339–41.

Territorial divisions, 214–15.

Thatching, 32–3; grass, 4, 43.

Thengwe or Nethengwe, 10, 30, 216.

Thoho-ya-Ndou, *see* Chiefs, past BaVenda.

Thondo, see Initiations.

Thovela, 236; god of pregnant women, 85; story about, 112, 113.

Thunder, 225, 230, 309.

Time, 229.

Tobacco, 36, 50, 314.

Totemism, 185–92.

Trading, 75–6.

Travelling, 74–5; of chief, 204; charms in, 74, 262; omens, 363.

Trees, list of, 374–5.

Tshiendeulu, 10, 12, 13.

Tshikobakoba, 55, 205.

Tshiobi, bowl of, *see* Medicine and Magic (divining bowls).

Tshishongo, 112, 113, 236.

Tshivhase, *see* Chiefs, BaVenda.

Twins, 91–3, 310; twin calves, 39, 92–3, 218.

Uterine nephew (*muduhulu*), in kinship, 177, 178, 184; in ancestor worship, 246, 255.

Venda, meaning of word, 12.

Vhatavhatsinde, *see* Sibs.

Vhusha, see Initiations.

Vhutamba vhutuka, see Initiations.

Village, 7, 29–31.

War, 70–4; prisoners, 73, 74; war feast, 73–4; discontinuance of, 30; ritual at outset of expedition, 72; human flesh used in war, 73; war feast, 73–4.

Water, of Lake Fundudzi, 237; in ancestor worship, 248, 250, 251, 311; in rite of bringing out child, 89; ritual washing in initiation ceremonies, 108, 109, 123, 124, 135, 141; in marriage ceremonies,

392 INDEX

Water—*cont.*
    146, 147, 148; ritual washing in mourning ceremonies, 164.
Weaning, 94.
Weapons, 69–70.
Weaving, 58–9; *masila* cloth, 24, 58–9, 75, 76, 206, 211, 212.
Widows, purification of, 164–5; inheritance of, 169–70; under chief's protection, 29.
Wife, *see* Kinship.
Winds, 226.
Wine, palm, 50.
Witchcraft, *see* Medicine and Magic.
Woodwork (drums, milk-jugs, platters, cups, spoons, porridge-sticks, stamping-blocks, stampers, doors, bowls, and models), 53–6.
Women:
    clothing, 23–4; ornaments, 25–6; decoration, 27–8; desire for children, 83–4; in the *thondo*, 101–2; after death of, 161, 162; age-sets, 194; work of, 32, 35, 38, 52, 56, 153–4; etiquette, 157, 159, 204; beer-drinking, 48–9; in killing of animals, 41, 44; in preparation for sowing and harvest, 253, 254; property, 38, 166–7; may lobola wives, 143–4; in succession, 167–9; as female 'fathers', 170–1; as petty chiefs, 215; as priests, 249–50, 255; as medico-magicians, 264; in *molombo*, 303–8; as rain-makers, *see* Majaji; as *muloi*, 274; ancestor spirits, 245–6, 247–8, 259–61; on bowl, 298; musical instruments played by, 316, 318, 320.

Xylophone (*mbila* or *deza*), *see* Musical Instruments.

Zimbabwe, 6, 7, 26, 27, 30, 81, 291, 299–300.
Zulu, 18; as compared with BaVenda, 21; harvest rites of, 253.

PRINTED IN GREAT BRITAIN AT THE UNIVERSITY PRESS, OXFORD
BY JOHN JOHNSON, PRINTER TO THE UNIVERSITY